BERNARD SHAW

Agitations

Letters to the Press 1875–1950

correspondence columns—the supreme test of British tolerance and respect for political balance and nonconformity—had become a hallowed tradition, notably in *The Times,* which accorded the hospitality of its column to every conceivable variety of eccentric from cuckoo watchers to advocates of left-handed kippers.

Shaw's entrée to the press in the eighties and early nineties was at first confined to a handful of newly established radical papers and journals like the *Workman's Times* and the Social Democratic Federation's *Justice,* and to a few Liberal papers like the *Pall Mall Gazette,* the *Daily Chronicle,* and *The Star* (in which Shaw's "Corno di Bassetto" music criticism appeared), which reached for profit both to the lower middle and the working class. And even here Shaw thought it advisable at times to veil his presence by resort to pseudonyms, some two dozen of them. Gradually, however, as a growing audience of readers came to recognize and react to the colorful and challenging personae in which Shaw had clothed himself in his idiosyncratic music and drama criticism, the more conservative papers bowed to Shaw's originality and admitted him, even if only as privileged fool, into their correspondence columns. They would, however, tolerate his opinions nowhere else in their pages, to the exclusion even of reports of his lectures, and the letters would habitually be sanitized by derisive editorial rebuttal and aspersions set in close proximity to them.

On occasions when an editor rejected one of his "outrageous" utterances Shaw blithely passed it along to an editor of rival political persuasion or greater liberality to publish as "a rejected letter," to the disparagement of the offending paper. Eventually only the imperturbable editor of *The Times* held out against this cunning stratagem. Elsewhere the now aged Shaw was being solicited as "good copy," worthy of advertisement on the hoardings for guaranteed sales, whatever the utterance might be.

Britons (especially in the days before the introduction of the wireless) perused their newspapers and journals avidly and thoroughly, and Shaw saw to it that they had a generous helping of GBS to digest with their breakfast or dinner. He was himself a voracious devourer of newspapers, meticulously marking off with slanted strokes, circles, exclamation marks, and interrogation points, in blue crayon, the materials that were to become ammunition for his counterattack both from the lecture platform and in an unending flow of correspondence, public and personal.

Through a subscription to Durrant's Press Cuttings service, Shaw kept abreast of the criticisms of himself in the provincial

Introduction

OF THE MANIFOLD occupations in which Bernard Shaw was involved during his ninety-four years of life none was more felicitous than that of professional debater. Swiftly mastering the dialectics of debate, after a nervous initial confrontation of an audience from a podium at the age of twenty-five, by deliberately picking quarrels "in order to teach myself by practice to fight for my ideas" and "by doggedly making a damn fool of myself until I got used to it," Shaw metamorphosed into one of the most brilliant rhetoricians and spellbinding orators of his generation. With a keen eye for detecting illogicality and irrationality, with an outsider's objectivity, and with an Irish gift for energetic articulateness and metaphor, the transplanted youthful Dubliner became a past master of thrust and riposte. Before the end of the century Shaw had, by his own reckoning, addressed more than a thousand audiences, besting his challengers and harassers on practically every occasion.

As his reputation as speaker and journalist grew, so did his audiences. No lecture hall in London, however, was large enough to satisfy Shaw, nor were his auditors, mostly radicals predisposed to reform, sufficiently satisfying targets for his polemical utterances. It was the vast British public and its Establishment that he was hellbent on reaching, and reach them he did when, providentially, a new avenue to this larger audience was opened by the introduction in 1888 of the halfpenny evening newspaper and the ensuing rapid proliferation of the British press. By the early nineteen-hundreds London had more than two dozen daily newspapers, several Sunday papers, a horde of weekly political and social journals, and, for good measure, an invasion by the provincial, Scottish, and Irish press.

Enormous in size (well over two feet in height and a foot and a half wide), with at least seven columns of small print to a page, and a greater ratio of text to advertisement than in our time, Britain's newspapers had vast acreages of space to fill and editors could afford to be indulgent to readers who wished to communicate their thoughts and opinions to their fellows. Moreover, the

Contents

In memory of

WILLIAM ARCHER

"... *when he went he took a piece of me with him.*"

Printed in the United States of America
Design by Jeremiah B. Lighter

Library of Congress Cataloging in Publication Data

Shaw, Bernard, 1856–1950.
Agitations: letters to the press 1875–1950.
Includes index.
1. Shaw, Bernard, 1856–1950—Correspondence.
2. Dramatists, Irish—20th century—Correspondence.
3. Shaw, Bernard, 1856–1950—Political and social views.
4. Newspapers—Sections, columns, etc.—Letters to the editor. I. Laurence, Dan H. II. Rambeau, James.
III. Title.
PR5366.A4 1985 822′.912 [B] 82-40256
ISBN 0-8044-2493-4

BERNARD SHAW

Agitations

Letters to the Press 1875–1950

Edited by
Dan H. Laurence
and
James Rambeau

FREDERICK UNGAR PUBLISHING CO.
New York

and foreign press, cramming his coat pocket with brown paper envelopes full of cuttings for perusal in spare moments on train journeys and on holidays. His responses to these criticisms traveled to virtually every civilized community in the world, emerging in print in Dumfries and Cork, St. Louis and Saskatoon, and, translated, in Tokyo, Zwickau, Moscow, and Belgrade.

Although Shaw calculated that he had lost at least four years of his life writing "superfluous letters," during which time he could as easily have written three good plays, he manifestly derived enormous enjoyment from epistolary debate. Not infrequently he participated in two or three of them concurrently, for weeks at a time, in different journals, locking horns with opponents as varied and gifted as G. K. Chesterton, Hilaire Belloc, H. G. Wells, Arnold Bennett, Frank Harris, Ernest Newman, and Julian Huxley, almost invariably, with characteristic generosity, allowing his opponent to have the final word. Before submitting his letters to London editors, however, Shaw would frugally revise and expand many of them into full-scale articles, peddling these to foreign news agencies in Fleet Street for extra (and profitable) mileage through American or Continental syndication.

The correspondence that flowed from Shaw's Bar-Lock typewriter in the early days and, later, from his hardworked Biro pen came spontaneously: there was no outlining, no drafting, and no more revision than that necessitated to correct his secretary's misreading of his shorthand draft. Notwithstanding Jacques Barzun's recent assertion (in an essay on William James as author) that "there is nothing more inimical to writing than talking," with "one mode of communication disabl[ing] the mind for the other," Shaw's written word and his spoken one were remarkably akin in their unique clarity and conviction. The phraseology in both instances was vernacular, yet "rare and dynamic," in the words of H. M. Tomlinson, "straight as a ray of light, such as we get once or twice in a few centuries, as the result of passionate morality that happens to be gifted with the complete control of full expression." A born improver of occasions, Shaw cut in on correspondence debates to proclaim his heterodoxies with the "blasts and benedictions" that, in Sean O'Casey's phrase, "[fell] over the land like the thistledown from a blown-out dandelion." It mattered not which side of a debate Shaw elected to join. Like the legendary Talmudist who allegedly challenged God to put any assertion to him and he'd prove the opposite, Shaw found his sustenance in the joy of argument.

It was the far-off *New York Times,* of all the world's principal newspapers, which appears to have been the first to define Shaw's methodology and to take his full measure when, on 27 May 1894, it informed its readers that "[Shaw's] knowledge of his subject is thorough, but he is fond of being at war with his fellow-men, especially those among them who are attached to traditions and conventions. He likes to shock his public. But his oddity is not mere affectation. Mr. Shaw has an extremely original mind, but it is a strong mind, too. His view of things may be as queer as Claude Monet's, to whom the grass is pink and the sky is purple, but like the great impressionist, he has that force of character which makes the thinking man, who believes in green grass and blue sky, pause and wonder if he has been wrong all his life."

The correspondence column became Shaw's pulpit, from which he spiritedly broadcast his clearsighted ideals. Carlylean to the core, he worshiped duty and destiny (he called these the Life Force) as related vitally to the mysterious universe we inhabit, and this highmindedness served to keep his criticisms banteringly goodhumored and dispassionate. "I spent fifteen years of my life," he informed T. E. Lawrence, "writing criticisms of sensitive living people, and thereby acquired a very cultivated sense of what I might say and what I might not say." The playwright Benn Levy, in a memorial address in 1951, affirmed this when he remarked of Shaw, "No man ever hit so hard and scored so often and hurt so little. For there was no malice behind his mighty blows." Shaw's own favorite phrase was *sans rancune.*

The more than 155 hitherto uncollected Shaw letters that make up this volume—the astonishingly broad range of subjects including theology, economics, political science, drama, social theory, war, language, and mathematics—were written between three and nine decades ago. Though they deal for the most part with events and situations long buried and forgotten, they retain an astonishing immediacy, for the arguments they contain are elevated by an extraordinary mind to a higher plane, coalescing into a principle that transcends the topical, leavened by a wit that can make the most complex and abstruse subject palatable.

DAN H. LAURENCE
JAMES RAMBEAU

June 1984

Editors' Note

SHAW'S TYPOGRAPHICAL STYLE, like his ideas and attitudes, distressed most editors of newspapers and journals, who imposed house style on his writings. Some, however, accepted his unconventional dicta, which stripped the text of its superfluities; a few compromised. The texts of Shaw's letters to the press are, as a consequence, stylistically consistent only in their inconsistency, and we have preferred in this edition to leave them that way rather than to aim for an unnatural tidiness. We have, however, silently corrected obvious typographical errors and occasional inconsistencies in style or spelling within an individual letter where an editor—or Shaw's secretary in transliterating his shorthand—has nodded; we have done away with the capitalized run-on subheads favored by some of the popular press in Shaw's lifetime; titles of publications have been regularized by italic setting; salutations and valedictions have been given uniformity. Archaic spellings of foreign names and places have been retained, with substitution of present-day variants in headnote and footnote references. Faulty sentence structure and omitted words have been dealt with by insertions in square brackets. For the sake of cohesion we have occasionally departed from an otherwise chronological arrangement of texts by juxtaposing letters dealing with a single subject, and we have not scrupled to shorten, amend, or substitute captions of letters for greater clarity or to avoid repetition, a precedent for which was established by Shaw when he prepared his Collected Edition in 1930–32.

The texts are hitherto uncollected, some of them effectively complementing correspondence published in the Collected Edition in *What I Really Wrote about the War* and in *Doctors' Delusions, Crude Criminology, and Sham Education*. Place of publication, except as otherwise indicated, is London. Standard abbreviations used in annotations are *DNB* (*Dictionary of National Biography*) and BL (British Library). English style of dating, with the day preceding the month, has been employed to conform with Shaw's standard usage. Shaw's age, provided in running heads, is advanced only after 26 July of each year, his birthdate.

We have aimed to be bounteously helpful in our annotations, but ask the reader to recognize that it would have been impossible within the permissible space of this volume to provide all of the pertinent background some of the letters demand, for which standard political, economic, and social histories must be consulted.

For permission to publish texts of letters by Shaw's contemporaries, we wish to thank Nicolas Barker, Michael Hornby, and executors of the estates of G.K. Chesterton and H.G. Wells. For the text of Shaw's hitherto unpublished letter on "General Maxwell's Alleged Breach of Discipline" we are indebted to Mrs. Virginia Ackert, and for that of "Insanity and the Law" to the Archivist of *The Times,* London.

We also acknowledge, with gratitude, invaluable research assistance from Leonard N. Beck (Subject Collections Specialist, Library of Congress), Kenneth Craven (Humanities Research Center), Aparna Dharwadker, Ellen Dunlap (Director, Rosenbach Museum and Library), George Goossens (British Library Newspaper Library), Sir Rupert Hart-Davis, Norman MacKenzie, Mander and Mitchenson Theatre Collection, William Matheson (Chief, Rare Books, Library of Congress), Peta Sievwright, J. Percy Smith, Graham Storey, Felix F. Strauss, Kathleen Tillotson, Stanley Weintraub, and Samuel A. Weiss. Equally helpful were the Local History Department of the Kensington High Street (London) Library, the staffs of the Pattee Library of Pennsylvania State University and the San Antonio Public Library, and the following Penn State students who generously provided help with transcriptions and proofreading: Michelle Amick, Mary Patricia Callahan, and Brennan and Angela Alaimo O'Donnell.

To Philip Winsor, whose faith in this book and good judgment have guided and sustained us in our efforts, we acknowledge an enormous debt and tender our warmest thanks.

D.H.L.
J.R.

DUBLIN EVANGELISM

[Shaw's first published letter, signed "S.," appeared in *Public Opinion* on 3 April 1875; it concerned a revival meeting in Dublin conducted by the American evangelists Dwight Lyman Moody and Ira D. Sankey.]

Sir,—In reply to your correspondent, "J. R. D.," as to the effect of the "wave of Evangelism," I beg to offer the following observations on the late "revival" in Dublin, of which I was a witness.

As the enormous audiences drawn to the Evangelistic services have been referred to as a proof of their efficacy, I will enumerate some of the motives which induced many persons to go. It will be seen that these were not of a religious, but of a secular, not to say profane, character. Predominant was the curiosity excited by the great reputation of the Evangelists, and the stories, widely circulated, of the summary annihilation, by epilepsy and otherwise, of sceptics who had openly proclaimed their doubts of Mr. Moody's divine mission. Another motive exhibits a peculiar side of human nature. The services took place in the Exhibition Building, the entry to which was connected in the public mind with the expenditure of a certain sum of money. But Messrs. Moody and Sankey opened the building "for nothing," and the novelty combined with the curiosity made the attraction irresistible. I mention these influences particularly, as I believe they have hitherto been almost ignored. The audiences were, as a rule, respectable; and as Mr. Moody's orations were characterized by an excess of vehement assertion, and a total absence of logic, respectable audiences were precisely those which were least likely to derive any benefit from them. It is to the rough, to the outcast of the streets, that such "awakenings" should be addressed; and those members of the aristocracy, who by their presence tend to raise the meetings above the sphere of such outcasts, are merely diverting the Evangelistic wave into channels where it is not wanted, its place being already supplied. And as, in the dull routine of hard work, novelty has a special attraction for the poor, I think it would be well for clergymen, who are nothing if not conspicuous, to render themselves so in this instance by their absence. The unreasoning mind of the people is too apt to connect a white tie with a dreary Church service, capped by a sermon of platitudes; and is more likely to appreciate "the gift of the gab,"—the possession of which by Mr.

Moody nobody will deny,—than that of the Apostolic succession, which he lacks.

Respecting the effect of the revival on individuals, I may mention that it has a tendency to make them highly objectionable members of society, and induces their unconverted friends to desire a speedy reaction, which either soon takes place, or the revived one relapses slowly into his previous benighted condition, as the effect fades. And, although many young men have been snatched from careers of dissipation by Mr. Moody's exhortations, it remains doubtful whether the change is not merely in the nature of the excitement rather than in the moral nature of the individual. Hoping that these remarks may elucidate further opinions on the subject,

I remain, Sir, yours, &c.,
S.

QUACK REMEDIES FOR DYNAMITE

[In 1883 and 1884, dynamite explosions in public places, probably the work of Irish agitators, began to occur in England; authorities tried in various ways to control the manufacture and movement of dynamite. Shaw's contribution to the public discussion appeared in the socialist journal *Justice* on 21 June 1884; his pseudonymous signature is a variant of a pseudonym, "G. B. S. Larking," used in the same journal on 15 March.]

Sir,—As a result of the steps recently taken by the Government to prevent the importation of dynamite, two more explosions have been successfully prepared and executed. Their immediate results, serious as they were to the unfortunate persons who were injured, were happily trifling in comparison with those which might have been produced without greater risk or expenditure if the blow had been aimed at an artery or vital organ of the great body of London. That the blow was not so aimed may be due to the forbearance of the Dynamitards. It may also be due to their stupidity and impatience. Assuming the latter and more probable conjecture to be the true one, the safety of London is hanging on the chance that not one of the thousands of clever and sensitive men who have suffered by the operation of our industrial system will bear sufficient ill-will towards those who have profited by it to lend their brains and their bitter patience to the work of destruction. It is true that the thoughtful sufferers generally become Socialists and detest the Dynamitards. But every such generalisation has its exceptions. One exception in this case may wreck London; cut off its supplies; and turn the chronic famine of the east into acute famine of the entire metropolis, with riot, pillage, and a carnival of rascaldom as the sequel. The privileged classes, by their accredited mouthpieces of the press, seem partly conscious of this danger. They denounce the explosions as "dastardly outrages," an expression which conveys a gratifying assurance of the public spirit and correct principles of the person using it, but one which has hitherto failed, in spite of sedulous reiteration, to convert Dynamitards into good citizens. Persons bringing black bags into the country are to be stopped at all ports and searched. This measure—to treat it as seriously as it deserves—is objectionable from the point of view of Free Trade. Any junior member of the Cobden Club can expose the false economy of insisting on being blown up by home-made dynamite by restricting the competition of foreign manufacturers who produce an equally effective and possibly cheaper article. If we adopt protection in the interest of our native anarchists, we can hardly refuse to extend it to our farmers. Dynamite, let it be remembered, can be made without difficulty from materials of which the sale cannot be restrained, as they are in common use for various social purposes. Full instructions are to be found in dictionaries of the arts on the shelves of our public libraries; and equally reliable rules of thumb may be obtained for a trifling present from miners on strike or out of work. Another suggestion relates to increased public watchfulness. Persons who "carry out with them bags of considerable weight and size, and return, if they do return, with loads very much lightened," are to be denounced to the police. This, if carried out, would lead to the wholesale denunciation of postmen, who unquestionably do carry out with them bags of considerable weight, and size, and return with loads very much lightened; but whether the public would be compensated for the inconvenience by any addition to their security against dynamite is not clear. The final cry of the newspapers is for more detectives. Now, apart from the ugly suspicion that to create a force for the discovery of explosives is practically to create a demand for explosions which that force will supply for itself if no one else will, it is a public humiliation for a society to come under the protection of the meanest of its own servants. Espionage may annoy honest folk: its only effect on the enemies of society will be to make them more malignant. If society wishes to be free from enemies, let it do as its units have to do—not make any! So long as the introduction of every labour-saving machine, and the recoil after every indecent scramble for wealth, throws men destitute and desperate upon the streets, with their wives and children vainly asking them for bread, so long will there be a virus of class hatred spreading, which no method of vaccination by virtuous indignation, by Custom House vigilance, by surrendering our liberty to the police, or even by a public spirited regard on the part of each individual to lodgers who carry bags of considerable weight and size, can in the very least prevail against. Let our Government, and other Governments, try, instead, the effect of an eight hours bill (to begin with). It would give employment to some of those idle heads for whom Satan finds mischief still to do, and will give to all a sufficient interest in and friendly feeling towards society to induce any man to think twice before attempting to blow it up.

Yours, &c.,
G. B. L.

EVICTIONS IN GLENBEIGH AND IN LONDON

[Glenbeigh was a district in the extreme south of Kerry consisting of about fifteen thousand acres of reclaimed and unclaimed bog and mountain land unfit for cultivation. Its inhabitants depended on work as day laborers and servants, but as unemployment was high and no jobs were available, they fell badly into arrears on their rents. On 12 January 1887, the managers of the estate of an absentee landlord, the Hon. Rowland Winn, commenced on his orders to evict his Irish tenants by firing or demolishing their miserable dwellings. An outcry in the *Pall Mall Gazette* led to a subscription "for the relief of the sufferers" and to a pseudonymously signed letter from Shaw published on 23 February 1887.]

Honored Sir and Governor,—As a humble subscriber to your paper I make so bold as to differ from you when you says that evictions in Glenbeigh is unjust, and chuckings-out in London is just, and that there's why popular feeling is agen one and not agen the other. I say that chuckings-out here is as bad in regard of onfairness and worse in regard of unhumanity, because the British working man is no more able to pay and no more in fault nor what the Irishman is, and there arnt no London hedges and ditches for him to build a shanty in when the eviction is over. Honored

Sir, comfortable coves what is well paid for writing in the newspapers does not know the rights and wrongs of these things. If you look at it right, it is like this. The Irish agriculturer goes to market and finds that he cannot get the high prices he formerly did for his produce, therefore it is impossible that he should pay what he formerly did to his landlord. This is owing to the state of trade and foreign competition, which is not his fault. Now, Sir, I say it is just the same with the British worker. The produce that he brings to market is his labour; but when trade is bad and foreign competition brisk he cannot get the same wages for it as before, and often cannot sell it at all at any price. This is no fault of his; and therefore I say that it is as impossible for him to pay the rent he used when in full work at full wages as it is for the Irishman. Yet he is to be flung into the streets, and them as flings him is to be told by clever ones such as you that it serves him right, and that it is very different from Lord Clanricarde.[1] Sir, I say it is not different, and that it is enough to make us workers go to the Socialists, who, if they do nothing for us, have at least the feeling heart to tell us that we are not considered as we ought. Sir, if you supress this letter to please persons in high stations, you are not the man I take you for.

Jesse Dodd

EAST-END CLUBS

[With the rise of socialism in Britain, promulgated by the newly founded Social Democratic Federation (1881) and, three years later, by the Fabian Society and William Morris's Socialist League, a vast number of workingmen's associations and clubs (more than two hundred in London alone) came into being, combining labor, liberal, radical, anarchist, socialist, or progressive politics and social conviviality, with the latter tending not infrequently to overwhelm the former. Shaw's pseudonymous letter was published in *The Star* on 13 June 1888.]

Sir,—Not long ago somebody (probably a gentleman) said that workmen's clubs were "drinking dens." The statement was indignantly contradicted, with a praiseworthy view to taking the conceit out of its author; but now that he has been duly shut up and sat upon, there can be no harm in suggesting that a very suit-

[1]Lord Clanricarde was famous for his devotion to the cause of the Irish landlord, and his refusal to accept any limitations of the landlord's power.

able form for this particular sort of contradiction may be found in Dickens's "Barnaby Rudge." In that work, a master locksmith accuses his journeyman of having just been drinking. The journeyman replies:—"As a general principle, and in the most offensive sense of the word, sir, I consider you a liar. But in that last observation you have unintentionally—unintentionally, sir—hit upon the truth." "Drinking den" is far from being a bad description of many a club that professes to be political and claims to represent the organised Radicalism of its district.

It is not worth while quarrelling with the word "den," since it is merely a West-end expression to describe a resort of the working-classes, and by no means an inappropriate one, as working men cannot afford much luxury in the way of decoration, handsome furniture, and plenty of room. Indeed, if any gentleman chooses to describe a workman's house as an eating den, a sleeping den, and on one dreaded day in the week a washing den, all rolled into one squalid dwelling den, he will not be very wide of the facts, whatever may be the value of his genteel opinion about them. But the very discomfort of a working man's home throws him more and more on the comfort of his club. He gets shelter, company, and cheap refreshment there, out of the way of the children, the washing, and the worry of his mockery of a home. He finds recreation of another sort there too—concerts, entertainments, nigger minstrels, and the like.

The only drawback is that sometimes the hall or theatre of the club is wanted by an obscure but troublesome body called "the political committee" for a lecture or a meeting about Home Rule, or the School Board election, or something uninteresting of that sort. However, it is easy to stay away on such occasions, particularly as abstention leads to the lecturers and M.P.'s staying away for the future. Now, a club managed on these lines may be a very good social institution; but it has nothing to do with politics, and therefore it has no right to call itself—as it invariably does—the "Tooley-street Liberal Club," or the "Rosherville Radical Club and Institute." Where does the Radicalism come into bagatelle and nigger minstrelsy? I have in mind a so-called Radical Club in the north-east of London with more than a thousand members. If you, Mr. Editor, will favor them with a political address next week you will be lucky if the secretary succeeds in coaxing and driving 60 of them into their big hall to hear you; and out of that 60, 40 will crowd near the door so as to be able to slip out for refreshment after ten minutes or so of the severe mental application of listening to someone else talking about their neglected public duties. Yet at any conference or federal meeting of London Radicals the delegates of that club will claim to represent a political force equal to the full membership, whereas everybody who is behind the scenes knows very well that there are other clubs, much younger and smaller, yet ten times as politically interested and active.

Now this state of things is not going to get better; it is going to get worse. The political committees need not think that the social development of the clubs can be checked or forced back to make way for anything else. Look at the West-end clubs, for example! They have so completely lost their place in politics that the ordinary man no longer knows or cares which side the Carlton, the Raglan, or the Reform belong to, and doubts whether the Eighty and the Cobden are clubs at all in the ordinary sense. Just so the East-end clubs will lose their places by the social activity of the club gradually edging out the political, one effect of this being that as more and more members join for the comfort of the club without thinking of its politics, they will object more and more to the subject being dragged in afterwards; and so "talking politics" will come to be regarded among the members as what West-enders call "bad form." The political committee may remain, practically electing themselves because nobody cares enough about it to oppose them; but they will not really represent the club at all. And when it comes to this, what will the Metropolitan Radical Federation represent? The shadow of a shadow will be substantial in comparison.

It seems to me that the time is coming for political organisation outside the clubs, which must be abandoned to their social function since experience proves it to be their natural one. But it would be premature to offer any precise suggestion until the East-end clubmen have said their say. Perhaps you will think it worth while to open the correspondence column of *The Star* to the subject for a few days.

Yours, &c.,

Orion

THE FABIAN SOCIETY

[Shaw, who had joined the Fabian Society in September 1884, was for nearly thirty years its principal draughtsman of tracts and manifestos and its spokesman in the press. The letter, pseudonymously signed, was published in *The Echo* on 13 August 1888.]

Sir,—In your "Touch-and-Go Paper" at the 11th instant, "Anglo-Saxon," with the strong common sense of a downright heart of oak, asks some six dozen questions about Socialism. Now, an Anglo-Saxon of the blunter sort can ask more questions in an hour than a Fabian can answer in a year; but a few replies by way of sample may not be amiss. "What do the Fabian Socialists aim at?" Answer: Exactly what they profess to aim at in their prospectus, a copy of which I enclose. "Is it intelligible, is it reachable, is it practical, is it suitable to members of society now?" Yes. "Will it butter parsnips?" No. "Can we see it in the blowing clover or the ripening corn?" No. "Will it staunch tears now falling and mitigate suffering now endured?" Yes. "Will it give industry a new field of action, and open the way for additional moral victories over folly and sin?" Yes. "Is it graspable?" That depends on the capacity of the grasper. "What have Socialist lecturers and teachers actually done?" Given their time, their labour, their fortunes, and their lives to the people; been the first to foresee and struggle for every measure that has permanently benefited the workers; educated the men who won the freedom of the Press, and fought for the People's Charter; justified the Factory Acts against the political economists, and the Education Acts against the individualists; foretold the failure of Free Trade and Sheffield Trade Unionism to settle the labour question; convicted the wage system of economically leading to worse conditions for the labourer than even chattel slavery; appealed as economists, philosophers, and historians, to the intellect of the working man, when Parliamentary candidates were gulling and bribing him with catchwords and election pledges; attacked international hatreds and misunderstandings so successfully that French workmen, for the first time in history, shared the bread of English comrades in their hour of need; taught those who would listen to them the uselessness of mere angry insurrection; forced the Liberal party, the Press, and even the Church to face the fact that the social question is the question of questions; insisted on the right of the people organised as a true State to own the sources of production;

showed that this never could be effected until the consummation of democracy made such a State possible, and that until it was effected the people must compete with one another in selling their labour at the lowest price to the class which now monopolises those sources of production; taught all the young Radicals their political creed from its root in the land question to its completion in the Social Democratic state of the future; and to-day, having gained the confidence of the politically active workers of London, in spite of starvation, ostracism, ridicule, calumny, and personal violence, are able to point to the undeniable fact that every step of progress during the century has been effected by an instalment of Socialism in the shape of a transfer of rent and interest from the proprietary class of the people, either by taxation or shortening of the working day, and to show, with perfect precision, the steps by which the balance is to be transferred. I pause to allow "Anglo-Saxon" an opportunity of breathing, and am, Sir, your obedient servant,

A Fabian

IN PRAISE OF "THE SILLY SEASON"

[Pseudonymously signed; *Pall Mall Gazette,* 31 August 1888.]

Sir,—Can you tell me why it is that the newspapers are always so interesting at this season of the year? I have often noticed that in August and September the articles begin to grow fresher and more varied; the hackneyed political subjects are dropped; anecdotes, descriptions of new scientific inventions, pretty accounts of the country, and deep thoughts about life take the place of the ordinary routine matter which no one ever reads. Is it because the gentlemen who write go away for autumn? Because, if it is, I am sure we should be quite content if they stayed away altogether, though no doubt they are thought very clever in their own set. I never enjoy the papers so much as in August; and I am sure there are plenty of people who think just the same. I hope you won't mind my saying so; but I feel certain that a great deal of money is wasted by newspaper proprietors on literary refinements and cleverness that only bore commonplace people like yours truly,

Amelia Mackintosh

BLOOD MONEY TO WHITECHAPEL

[*The Star*, 24 September 1888.]

Sir,—Will you allow me to make a comment on the success of the Whitechapel murderer in calling attention for a moment to the social question? Less than a year ago the West-end press, headed by the *St. James's Gazette*, the *Times*, and the *Saturday Review*, were literally clamoring for the blood of the people—hounding on Sir Charles Warren[1] to thrash and muzzle the scum who dared to complain that they were starving—heaping insult and reckless calumny on those who interceded for the victims—applauding to the skies the open class bias of those magistrates and judges who zealously did their very worst in the criminal proceedings which followed—behaving, in short, as the proprietary class always does behave when the workers throw it into a frenzy of terror by venturing to show their teeth. Quite lost on these journals and their patrons were indignant remonstrances, arguments, speeches, and sacrifices, appeals to history, philosophy, biology, economics, and statistics; references to the reports of inspectors, registrar generals, city missionaries, Parliamentary commissions, and newspapers; collections of evidence by the five senses at every turn; and house-to-house investigations into the condition of the unemployed, all unanswered and unanswerable, and all pointing the same way. The *Saturday Review* was still frankly for hanging the appellants; and the *Times* denounced them as "pests of society." This was still the tone of the class Press as lately as the strike of the Bryant and May[2] girls. Now all is changed. Private enterprise has succeeded where Socialism failed. Whilst we conventional Social Democrats were wasting our time on education, agitation, and organisation, some independent genius has taken the matter in hand, and by simply murdering and disembowelling four women, converted the proprietary press to an inept sort of communism. The moral is a pretty one, and the Insurrectionists, the Dynamitards, the Invincibles, and the extreme left of the Anarchist party will not be slow to draw it. "Humanity, political sci-

[1]During the Whitechapel murders by "Jack the Ripper" in 1888–89, General Sir Charles Warren was commissioner of the Metropolitan Police.

[2]Match manufacturers, the object of reform proposals concerning their working conditions.

ence, economics, and religion," they will say, "are all rot; the one argument that touches your lady and gentleman is the knife." That is so pleasant for the party of Hope and Perseverance in their toughening struggle with the party of Desperation and Death!

However, these things have to be faced. If the line to be taken is that suggested by the converted West-end papers—if the people are still to yield up their wealth to the Clanricarde class, and get what they can back as charity through Lady Bountiful, then the policy for the people is plainly a policy of terror. Every gaol blown up, every window broken, every shop looted, every corpse found disembowelled, means another ten pound note for "ransom." The riots of 1886 brought in £78,000 and a People's Palace:[3] it remains to be seen how much these murders may prove worth to the East-end in *panem et circenses.* Indeed, if the habits of duchesses only admitted of their being decoyed into Whitechapel backyards, a single experiment in slaughter-house anatomy on an aristocratic victim might fetch in a round half million and save the necessity of sacrificing four women of the people. Such is the stark-naked reality of these abominable bastard Utopias of genteel charity, in which the poor are first to be robbed and then pauperised by way of compensation, in order that the rich man may combine the idle luxury of the protected thief with the unctuous self-satisfaction of the pious philanthropist.

The proper way to recover the rents of London for the people of London is not by charity, which is one of the worst curses of poverty, but by the municipal rate collector, who will no doubt make it sufficiently clear to the monopolists of ground value that he is not merely taking round the hat, and that the State is ready to enforce his demand, if need be. And the money thus obtained must be used by the municipality as the capital of productive industries for the better employment of the poor. I submit that this is at least a less disgusting and immoral method of relieving the East-end than the gush of bazaars and blood money which has suggested itself from the West-end point of view.

Yours, &c.,
G. Bernard Shaw

[3]An educational and recreational institution in the Mile End Road created for working people. Although uncompleted, it had been operating since 1887.

THE VIZETELLY PROSECUTION

[Henry Vizetelly, a publisher who specialized in translations from the Russian and French, was prosecuted in 1888 for "publishing an obscene libel"—Emile Zola's *The Soil* (*La Terre,* 1876). Sir Edward Clarke, the solicitor-general, helped prosecute the case. The jury, according to the *DNB,* refused "to listen patiently to the recital of twenty-one passages selected by the solicitor-general to establish the case." Vizetelly, following his lawyer's advice, pleaded guilty and paid a fine of £100. Shaw's letter appeared pseudonymously in *The Star,* 2 November 1888.]

Sir,—I wish that *The Star,* as a Radical paper, would try to educate jurymen in the principles of liberty of speech and of the Press, instead of discussing whether M. Zola has "the charm, the humor, the style which redeem the works of Rabelais, Chaucer, and Boccaccio." I grant you it is absurd to defend what is called M. Zola's obscenity on the ground that Rabelais was obscene. A dramatist charged with drunkenness might just as reasonably plead in excuse the occasional inebriety of Shakspere. The question at issue in Mr. Vizetelly's case was not whether M. Zola may or may not do everything that can be proved to have been done by the classic French writers whose example in literature he has expressly condemned and repudiated, but whether a writer may or may not expose to society its own wickedness. Nobody has ventured to pretend that what M. Zola describes does not exist. But, its existence being admitted, two views of M. Zola's duty concerning it are put forward. First, the British Pharisee's view, which is that it is M. Zola's duty to hide the evil and pretend that there is no such thing. Second, M. Zola's own view that it is his duty to drag it into the light and have it seen to. I agree with M. Zola; and (with all due respect) I defy *The Star* to declare publicly that it disagrees with me; I defy the jury who found Mr. Vizetelly guilty on a false issue to justify their verdict on the true issue; and I defy Mr. Vizetelly to deny that he richly deserves the fine inflicted on him for striking his colours at the reading, in the manner of Mr. Pecksniff,[1] of a series of inelegant extracts. In future, I presume, we must obey the precepts of Dickens's Mrs. General,[2] and study to appear ignorant of everything that is not perfectly proper, placid, and pleasant, being kept in order by the knowledge that Sir Edward Clarke is repeating "papa, potatoes, poultry, prunes, and

[1]In Dickens's *Martin Chuzzlewit.*
[2]In Dickens's *Little Dorrit.*

prism,"[3] to himself, in order to get the proper expression of countenance for an effective prosecution speech if we transgress. Whilst the poor man rots, our published descriptions of him must, according to law, be scrupulously plagiarised from Longfellow's "Village Blacksmith," and whilst that most venomous of all social pests, the rich man's son, sows his wild oats, we are not to tell on him on pain of fine and confiscation. One can only wonder at the state of mind of the persons who believe that such conditions as these will purify and elevate literature.

Let me conclude with a piece of practical advice. If you, sir, ever find yourself on a jury to try a prisoner on an indictment for seditious libel, blasphemous libel, or obscene libel, just shut your ears tightly, and do not utter a word until, in answer to the clerk of the court, you declare the prisoner—no matter who he is, or what he has done—not guilty.

Yours, &c.,

A Novelist

We largely agree with our correspondent. We stated that it was not the business of the law to interfere in such cases. [Ed., *Star.*]

THE ABOLITION OF CHRISTMAS

[Pseudonymously signed; *Pall Mall Gazette,* 27 December 1888.]

Sir,—I confess I am a little disappointed that *The Star* has allowed its first December to pass without a word in favor of the movement for the abolition of Christmas. Costly, disagreeable, and brutalising as this festival always is, it is seldom so inopportune as on this occasion. I offer you my personal experience as an example, without further preface than the remark that the average Englishman, when he has to enjoy himself to order on a set occasion, either eats and drinks too much, or else goes for a fatiguing walk on a wet day. Frequently he begins with the latter expedient and ends with the former. On this Christmas Eve I happened to travel by a morning train occupied by persons bound for a day in the country. When they were tired of watching the drops chasing one another down the windowpanes, a man next me, who had a

[3]These are "all very good words for the lips: especially prunes and prism." Dickens, *Little Dorrit,* Book II, chap. 5.

copy of the *Standard*, exclaimed, "I don't know what people are coming to. Four more murders this morning." Instantly the moody holiday-makers roused themselves. "Whitechapel?" was the question that came from them all with a common impulse. "No," said the *Standard*-bearer, "all in the country except the one at Limehouse." Everybody turned away disappointed. "Lime'us!" said one man disparagingly; "that's the same old 'un." Our informant felt that he had raised our hopes unwarrantably, but he insisted on the fact that the murders were very horrible, and that the victim in one case was a very old man. But nobody vouchsafed further attention to his provincial horrors until I helped him out by politely asking—with reference to the old man—"How?" "Sledge-hammer over the face" was the reply. "Sledgin' her over the face," said the Lime'us man, with a flash of interest, "What's that?" "Sledge-hammer, sir, sledge-hammer. Knocked the unfortunate old man's face in." "Oh," said the other, deeply disillusioned, as he relapsed into listless silence. I quitted this festive company at the next station, and went about my business, anxiously calculating how little I could, without meanness, give to the people who expect Christmas-boxes from one, from the troublesome and haughty flunkey, who considers that the largesse of a true gentleman should always be in gold, to the useful and hard-working person who is overjoyed at the sight of a shilling. I have no doubt that such people are as anxious and unsettled about what they may get as I am about what I should give, and that for the time they cannot help hating me as much as I cannot help hating them. Probably they expect more than they get, and spend more than they expect on the strength of it.

Pursuing my way through the streets I am reminded by the decorations for sale in the stationers' shops that "there were shepherds abiding in the field, keeping watch over their flocks by night." Presently a butcher's establishment, its sawdust reeking with blood, and its sharp hooks impaling a ghastly grove of carcasses, convinces me that the cows, instead of abiding in the field, have been preparing for a merry Christmas in the slaughter-house. I turn to the stationers' again—for at least there is no blood there—and look for a moment at the heaps of Christmas cards. They interest me, because I have read with interest about the Eastern worshippers who pray by machinery, one revolution of a wheel being the mechanical equivalent of offering up a prayer. Here we discharge the offices of friendship in the same fashion. Drop a penny into the stationer's till, and out comes an envelope and a card with a robin and some bad verses on it. Drop another penny into the postmaster's till, and out comes a stamp. Write "with love and good wishes" on the card, enclose it in the envelope, address it to the bore or the poor relation whom you really cannot be bothered with personally, stick on the stamp, shoot the whole into the scarlet temple at the next street corner; and there you are. The poor relation cannot complain of being neglected after that, any more than the oriental god can when the wheel has been turned at him. I hurry on among the gutter children who are starving, shivering, and going to the devil because the labor that might have fed, clothed, and taught them has been, by a remarkable stroke of national economy, devoted to the production of Christmas cards. I perceive that the public-houses are already doing a stirring trade; and here and there I notice a woman apparently playing the spy on a postman or policeman, enjoying her Christmas in an agony of anxiety lest her husband should be encouraged by the season and its effusive hospitalities to get drunk on duty and sacrifice place, pay, and pension to the inner light which shows him that it is a poor heart that never rejoices. From these reflections I am rescued by the cheery cry of the boy with the evening paper. I purchase, and learn that the Queen has addressed to her Parliament a speech, which I, as a loyal subject, hasten to read, though I soon perceive that a retired life has left her Majesty rather out of it as to what is actually going on in the world. If, for instance, her gracious relations with all foreign Powers really continue to be friendly, then those relations must be of a strictly private character. The machine gun massacre of the Soudanese,[1] and the mountain battery cannonade of the unfortunate Thibetans,[2] are indulgently passed over as, respectively, "a brilliant military operation" and "a disturbance, terminated without difficulty"—quite a Christmassy way of looking at them. Further on it appears that her Majesty is under the impression that her Indian dominions "have enjoyed general tranquillity and prosperity during the past year." It is sincerely to be hoped that this royal and rosy view of the situation will not lead our sovereign to send one of her grandchildren to test the tranquillity and prosperity of the little

[1]In a battle in the Suakin district on 20 December, the Anglo-Egyptian army used machine guns against the "Dervishes"; the results were an estimated 400 dead.

[2]An event reported in *The Times,* 24 December; an unidentified number of Gurkhas were killed as the British sided with China in their territorial claims against Tibet.

ones who are celebrating yuletide in the ginning mills of Bombay in the manner set forth in the latest blue-book of the Factory Commission there. Doubtless the book has not reached the Empress's hands; for though she tells her lords and gentlemen that Zanzibar has been blockaded to prevent the slave trade,[3] there is no allusion to the necessity of blockading Bombay with the same object.

Somehow, the speech on the whole failed to cheer me. I went into the streets again, and found many persons excited and drunk, but none happy. I saw, too, that though the shops were lighted with double rows of burners, and the show of wares very brave and tempting, yet for every dainty thus publicly displayed there were a hundred poor people to stare hungrily at it and go empty and envious away, the whole thing being to the majority a huge torment of Tantalus. Those who bought most freely were persons to whom good cheer was evidently nothing exceptional, and who were probably more troubled by their livers than by their appetites. The great machinery of merriment seemed to catch everybody between its cogs, and transfer their seasonable smiles to the opposite side of their mouths. So I went home to bed, and lay there listening, whilst London, as it got drunker and drunker, trolled its obscenities or shrieked its hysterical passions under my windows. I live in a London square, but as it is unfortunately not Trafalgar-square, the passer-by may awake its echoes just as the spirit moves him. Morley's Hotel is now the only place in London where children and nervous invalids are safe from stentorian performances of the latest music-hall refrain between midnight and half-past two in the morning. As it was Christmas morning on this particular occasion, they kept it up merrily until half-past four, when the waits[4] kindly arrived to support them with orchestral accompaniment.

Mr. *Star* Editor, I ask you, on your honor, are you any the better for Christmas? Or do you know anybody who is? If not, will you help in its abolition? which is now the life-work of—

Yours truly,
William Watkins Smyth
Christmas Day Abolition Society,
Spire View, Canonbury, N.

[3]The British and German navies commenced a blockade of the Zanzibar coast on 29 November.
[4]Street singers of Christmas carols.

RUSSIAN PRISONERS AND ENGLISH POLITICIANS

[British public interest in the Russian use of Siberian exile for dissidents had been roused by the publication of a series of articles by the American George Kennan in the *Century Magazine* between May 1888 and November 1889; the series was later published in book form as *Siberia and the Exile System* (1891). On 16 December 1889, *The Times* reported a massacre of exiles in Yakutsk, which had taken place on 4 April. Further dispatches confirmed that some thirty exiles were fired on by policemen and soldiers, and at least six exiles were killed. In London, the Workmen's Protest Committee organized a Russian Martyrs demonstration held in Hyde Park on 9 March 1890. Shaw's letter appeared in the *St. James's Gazette* on 11 March.]

Sir,—Will you allow me to use your columns to point out the cruel difficulties which the friends of the Russian Constitutional party are encountering in their appeal to England for help? They do not ask much. For advocating reforms which the most timid English Conservative regards as necessities of political life, they are subjected to transportation, penal servitude, solitary confinement, corporal punishment—all administered with a savage slovenliness which adds every sort of indignity and indecency to their sentences. Some years ago they asked us, for pity's sake, to say at least that we were disgusted at the treatment they were suffering. We took no notice. Now that Mr. Kennan's articles have made some stir, and that the *Times* has described how Ostashkin, the Vice-Governor of Yakutsk, last year massacred a deputation of exiles who appealed to him against a murderous change in the transport regulations, it has occurred to a lady to make a final appeal to the world on behalf of her fellow prisoners at the cost of her own life. The matter was simple: it was only a question of giving the Governor a slap in the face and getting flogged to death for it, which was accordingly done.[1] As a protest from the influential classes here would put a stop to these extremities and to the open encouragement of the officials who perpetrate them, the friends of the prisoners not unnaturally now ask whether we are yet roused to make that protest, and, if not, how many more human sacrifices we require to bring us up to that point. If the word goes to Siberia that the English would like to see another woman

[1]Identified in *The Times* as Nahyda Sihida (and in Kennan's book as Hope Sigída), the lady in fact slapped the face of the director of the Kará prison; on 6 November she was flogged and died of the one hundred blows.

flogged to death to make their minds quite easy as to the propriety of passing any remarks on the subject, there will be no difficulty in finding a Russian exile willing to offer herself for that purpose.

Unfortunately, there are party considerations in the way of a united protest from men of all parties to shame the Russian Government. The Unionists are afraid that the platform of protest will be turned to account by Home Rulers to compare Mr. Balfour to Ostashkin and Saghalien to Tullamore.[2] The Gladstonians, being apparently void of political principle, have no guide except the jumping cat; and, until their fugleman adds Russian atrocities to the list of Neapolitan, Bulgarian, and Balfourian, atrocities, they will hold their tongues, with a vague notion that backing Holy Russia is the correct Liberal line. The Radicals and Social Democrats have protested, of course; but what does the Russian Government care for demonstrations by unofficial and uninfluential riff-raff—demonstrations which it regards as no more than so many riots? When I was asked to speak in the Park on Sunday I begged the organizers of the demonstration to get some respectable person instead; knowing well that a post card from Mr. Gladstone, and a few platitudes from Mr. John Morley or Mr. Haldane,[3] would do more good in Siberia than a Ciceronian oration from a Social Democrat. But catch Mr. John Morley on the rail of a wagon between Radicals and Socialists, or Mr. Haldane giving the enemy cause to twit him with succumbing to the Fabian fascinations of Mr. Sidney Webb![4] All Russia might be flogged to death, it seems, before the gentlemen of England would sink perfectly irrelevant differences so far as to profess themselves scandalized. Perhaps they do not realize the weight that such a profession would have. If so, they are too modest. The Classes in England, bad as they are, are morally superior to the bureaucracy of Russia, and so may assume the right to lecture it, with full faith that the lecture will have considerable effect. Will you, Mr. Editor, by urging them to speak out, give the "Friends of Russian Free-

[2]Arthur James Balfour was the Conservatives' chief secretary for Ireland, 1887–91; Sakhalin, an island used as a tsarist place of exile; Tullamore, the notorious Irish prison in which the English incarcerated political prisoners.
[3]Respectively, Liberal MP for Newcastle-on-Tyne, 1883–95 and former editor of the *Pall Mall Gazette* (1880–85); Liberal MP for East Lothian, 1885–1911.
[4]English economist and socialist, for more than sixty years Shaw's principal colleague in the Fabian Society and close personal friend.

dom" that countenance which I am convinced they will seek in vain from the Gladstonian press?

Yours, &c.,
G. Bernard Shaw

IBSEN

I

[Although Shaw was one of Ibsen's strongest and earliest British champions, he had no success in obtaining stage representation of the Norwegian's works from the theatrical establishment. Ibsen's reputation as a purveyor of the sordid was so low in England that actor-managers would not permit members of their companies to be besmirched by appearances in productions of his plays, and none of the principal managers ever produced or sponsored an Ibsen play. The London critical reception of *Ghosts* in March 1891 was so violent and vitriolic that probably the kindest thing said of the play was that it was "a dirty act done openly." Shaw's first letter here, published in the *Pall Mall Gazette* on 9 January 1891, addressed itself to the problem of the reluctance of leading managers (Henry Irving, Johnston Forbes Robertson, John Hare, T. B. Thalberg, Charles Wyndham, and George Alexander) and theater lessors to involve themselves.]

Sir,—I have an appeal of rather an unusual nature to make to you on behalf of the English stage. Have you any experience as an actor? Could you and the members of your talented staff manage to fill up the casts of "The Doll's House" and "Rosmersholm" any time this month that would be most convenient to you? The theatre shall be forthcoming; your wardrobes shall be of the best; all expenses are provided for; and your own critic will probably do every justice to your creation of Rosmer—which is the part you would help us best by doing. If you refuse, there is no more chance of the current generation becoming acquainted with the works of the greatest living dramatic poet than there seems to be of their hearing the later masterpieces of Richard Wagner in an English opera-house. You must not suppose that so unreasonable an application would be made to you had not every other means of putting Ibsen on the stage been tried without success. You will say—and truly—that the production of great plays is neither your business nor mine, but that of Mr. Irving and his fellows and rivals in management. But Mr. Irving is content to have done for Goethe and Sir Walter Scott what the Gaiety management has done for "Carmen": he finds Casimir Delavigne's Louis XI. more to his taste than Bishop Nicholas in "The Pretenders." The other managers follow Mr. Irving's example. But, you will ask, are there not actors to be found both able and willing to play Rosmer, Helmer, and so on, if it be indeed true that the theatre is ready and the money in hand? So there are; but they are all fulfilling engagements with Messrs. Irving and Co., who refuse to allow them to appear at the projected Ibsen matinees. The managers will neither play Ibsen themselves nor allow any one else to play him. In 1889 Mr. [Charles] Charrington and Miss Janet Achurch had to go into management themselves at a heavy risk to put on "The Doll's House." As managers they were able to offer Mr. [Herbert] Waring, for example, a regular engagement as well as the enviable chance of "creating" the part of Helmer. At present we naturally turn to Mr. Waring to "create" the part of Rosmer at an experimental matinee; but the management of the Shaftesbury Theatre vetoes the proposition. Mr. Forbes Robertson, at the Garrick, is suggested; but Mr. Hare will not hear of it. Mr. Thalberg, at the Adelphi, is approached; but the Messrs. [A. and S.] Gatti are inexorable, perhaps mistrusting the reaction of Ibsen on the popular taste for Adelphi melodrama. The result is that the performance of "Rosmersholm" which Miss Florence Farr all but formally announced for the 15th inst. must be postponed unless you, Mr. Editor, will play Rosmer. And Miss Marie Fraser's undertaking to produce "The Doll's House" on the 27th is in jeopardy because Mr. Wyndham has nipped one proposed Dr. Ranke in the bud; and Mr. Alexander has done the like by another; whilst an obvious one at the Shaftesbury is likely to share Mr. Waring's fate. It is useless to look to the Lyceum: Mr. Irving's veto is a foregone conclusion. Mrs. John Wood is equally hardhearted on the subject of matinees. In desperation I have suggested that the part of Rosmer be offered to Mr. Robert Buchanan;[1] but it is very doubtful whether his conscience would permit him to contribute in any way to the diffusion of Ibsenism. Hence my last card, an appeal to you personally. Even if you refuse, something will have been gained if the public know definitely whom they have to thank for the exclusion from the stage of the best of modern dramatic literature. Perhaps, too, the managers may be roused to render a reason for their opposition to an experiment which interests them so di-

[1]Robert Buchanan, popular playwright and novelist, was a particularly virulent anti-Ibsenite.

rectly that they ought to be well pleased at escaping an invitation to contribute funds as well as "kind permissions." Surely artists of their eminence cannot be jealous of the reputations which might grow out of performances of Ibsen's plays. Still, that hypothesis is sufficiently plausible to make it advisable for them either to relent, to explain, or to come forward and play the unfilled rôles themselves. Mr. Irving as Rosmer, Mr. Wyndham as Dr. Ranke, Mr. Hare as Krogstad would be welcomed as warmly by the public as by the Ibsen *entrepreneurs* and by

Yours, &c.,
G. Bernard Shaw

II

[Shaw's "own account" of *Brand* appeared in *The Quintessence of Ibsenism* (1891); his letter to the *Daily Chronicle* was published on 18 November 1891.]

Sir,—Your article on "Brand" places *The Daily Chronicle* in the position of being the one morning paper in London which can be trusted to deal with the highest contemporary literature. It will probably mark a turning point in Ibsen's criticism; and I have so strong a sense of its importance that I am loth to pass by its reference to my own account of "Brand" without a word of explanation. I did not mean that Ibsen wrote this great dramatic poem as a warning against Brand's idealism. I have as little doubt as you that, in spite of the irrepressibly strong common-sense which occasionally finds ironical expression in it, it was written, on the whole, in a fit of enthusiasm for that idealism. But impressive as the poem is, and passionately as many of us must admire the hero's character, the fact remains that his devotion led to nothing, and could lead to nothing but the destruction of himself and all those upon whom he was able fully to impose it. I have simply pointed out that when, having created Brand, Ibsen came to think him over in cold blood, he recognised that he was a sublime nuisance, and that the proper place of the idealist in the drama of modern life is that of the villain of the piece. This is evident from the subsequent dramas, in every one of which the idealist is unmistakeably held up, not as an example, but as a warning.

Yours, &c.,
G. Bernard Shaw

REVOLUTIONARY PROGRESS AT OXFORD

[Shaw had come to Oxford to address the Oxford Reform Club on 21 February 1892. The preceding evening, after dining with one of the university dons, F. York Powell, he dropped by the rooms of Thomas A. V. Best at Magdalen College for a personal visit. "I expected a mere chat on things in general," he noted in his diary, "but when I arrived there were 15 or 16 undergraduates assembled; and I was called on for a lecture. An opposition party outside screwed us up [i.e., locked them in] and wrecked the adjoining room. It threatened to be a very serious business; but I got out at last with a whole skin. Could hardly get any sleep afterwards." The leader of the student rag was Simon Joseph Fraser, later fourteenth Baron Lovat. Shaw's letter about the adventure appeared in the *Pall Mall Gazette,* 22 February 1892.]

Sir,—Will you be so good as to allow me to use your columns to thank the members of Magdalen College, Oxford, for the very enthusiastic reception which they have just accorded to the first Socialist who has ever lectured within their walls? The greatest difficulty with which a public speaker has to struggle is the tendency of the audience to leave before the conclusion of his remarks. I therefore desire especially to thank the thoughtful and self-sacrificing body of undergraduates who voluntarily suffered exclusion from the room in order that they might secure the door on the outside and so retain my audience screwbound to the last syllable of the vote of thanks. I desire to explain, however, that I do not advocate the indiscriminate destruction of property as a first step towards Socialism, and that their action in entirely wrecking the adjoining chamber by a vigorous bombardment of coals, buckets of water, and asafoetida, though well-meant, was not precisely on the lines which I was laying down inside. Nor, though I expressed myself as in favour of a considerable extension of Communism in the future, did I contemplate the immediate throwing of all the portable property in the lobby into a common stock, beginning with my own hat, gloves, and umbrella. Not that I grudge these articles to Magdalen College, but that I wish them to be regarded as an involuntary donation from myself to the present holders rather than as having been scientifically communized.

Speaking as a musical critic, I cannot say that the singing of the National Anthem which accompanied these modest beginnings of revolution was as successful as that of "Ta-ra-ra-boom-de-ay" which one of my friends within the room loudly supported, at the general request, by a pianoforte accompaniment. It is injurious to the voice, I may add, to sing in an atmosphere rendered somewhat pungent by the projection of red pepper on a heated shovel.

I need not dwell on the friendly care which was taken not to unscrew the door until our proceedings were entirely over. I wish to say, however, that we should not have incommoded our friends by crowding the staircase had not the rope formed of two blankets, by which we originally intended to proceed from the apartment directly into the open air, unhappily given way under the strain of being energetically steadied at one end by the outside and at the other by the inside party. There was really no danger of the friction igniting the blankets, so that the pains of the detachment posted at an upper window to keep them drenched with water were unnecessary. The gentleman who rendered me a similar attention from the landing above as I descended the stairs also wasted most of his moisture through infirmity of aim; but his hospitable desire to speed the parting guest was unmistakable.

Although my admirers mustered in such numbers that there were at least three times as many persons outside the door as inside (including a don), I am credibly assured that if I had lectured in Brasenose my reception would have been still more overwhelming; and I quite believe it. I was the more overcome as I visited Magdalen under the impression that I was to pass a quiet hour chatting with a few friends, and had no idea until I arrived that I was expected to address a meeting, or that my advent had aroused so deep an interest.

Yours, &c.,
G. Bernard Shaw

THE SPLIT INFINITIVE

I

[Throughout his career Shaw engaged in numerous skirmishes concerning English usage. In these letters to the *Daily Chronicle*, he attacked especially those who would rule all split infinitives as "bad English." The first letter appeared on 2 September 1892.]

Sir,—If you do not immediately suppress the person who takes it upon himself to lay down the law almost every day in your columns on the subject of literary composition, I will give up taking *The Chronicle*. The man is a pedant, an ignoramus, an idiot, a self-advertising duffer. A little while ago, when somebody pointed out to him a case of the misuse of "and which," the creature, utterly missing the point, rushed about denouncing every sentence containing "and which" until some public-spirited subscriber of yours stopped him by a curt exposure which would have shamed any corrigible human being into humble silence for at least a month. Yet he has already broken out in a fresh place. Mr. Andrew Lang, moved by a personal antipathy to "split infinitives" and to sentences ending with the word "such" (for example, Shakespeare's line, "No glory lives behind the back of such") once made a jocular attempt to bounce the public out of using them by declaring that they were bad English. Of course, all competent literary workmen laughed at Mr. Lang's little trick; but your fatuous specialist, driven out of his "and which" stronghold, is now beginning to rebuke "second-rate newspapers" for using such phrases as "to suddenly go" and "to boldly say." I ask you, Sir, to put this man out. Give the porter orders to use such violence as may be necessary if he attempts to return, without, however, interfering with his perfect freedom of choice between "to suddenly go," "to go suddenly," and "suddenly to go." See that he does not come back; that is the main thing. And allow me, as one who has some little right to speak on the subject, to assure your readers that they may, without the slightest misgiving, turn their adverbed infinitives in any of the three ways given above. All they need consider is which of the three best conveys by its rhythm the feeling they wish to express.

The sentences quoted from a Bishop as examples of bad English are perfectly correct. When the Bishop wrote, "They are a plantigrade animal," he was simply constructing a booby trap; and it would have been kinder on your part to have kept your specimen out of its way. Be advised by me, Mr. Editor; send him adrift and try an intelligent Newfoundland dog in his place.

Yours, &c.,
G. Bernard Shaw

II

[*Daily Chronicle,* 26 February 1898.]

Sir,—We must all, I am sure, feel deeply indebted to Mr. Frederick Breese for explaining that the infinitive must not be split because it is one word, and not two. For example:—

"Tobe or not tobe: that is the question!" How magical the effect of those eight words is under this remarkable illumination! Thank you, Mr. Breese; thank you.

Yours, &c.,
G. Bernard Shaw

THE WORMWOOD SCRUBBS MURDER

I

[E. Belfort Bax, a philosophical writer who was also Shaw's predecessor as music critic of *The Star,* was one of many who protested the sentencing to death of George Samuel Cooke, a police constable, for the murder of Maud Smith, a prostitute with whom he had consorted. Bax, in a letter published in *The Star* on 17 July 1893, argued that Cooke's case "suggests some curious reflections as to what constitutes murder as distinct from justifiable homicide." Shaw's first letter appeared in the same paper on 18 July; his second, in which he replied to some of the other correspondence on the subject, appeared on 25 July, the day Cooke was hanged.]

Sir,—From most windows overlooking London streets, especially unfashionable ones, you can witness, any night you choose to wait for it, the following scene:—First you hear in the distance the voice of a woman, incessant, nerve-racking, hysterical, nag-nag-nagging, occasionally rising to a scream. Then a man comes in sight, head down, hands in pockets, close-reefed, so to speak, as he doggedly trudges before the squall. After him the woman, whose words you can now distinguish, railing, taunting, threatening, cursing, proclaiming his infamy with every conceivable indecency of word and venom of insult, now hurrying up to him defiantly to provoke a blow, presently shrinking back a little in fear of one, but always lashing herself into greater fury, and deliberately and violently thrusting away from her any habit of self-respect that may assert itself during her momentary pauses for breath. Nobody is surprised at this procession of two: it is the usual thing—his wife, or some woman of whom he has grown tired. It passes away into the shadows between the lamps with the nag, nag, nag, still going on. Suddenly the dogged footsteps cease, and the woman screams in earnest. One or two experienced flaneurs, who knew this was coming, and stopped to watch for it, are more or less pleased, according to the vigor and success of the blow. If it has knocked her down, and the man is himself a bit hysterical, he kicks her furiously. But this is the extreme instance: usually it is only a black eye. The police do not interfere unless the procession delays too long in reforming and proceeding on its way, in which case the formula is to the woman, "Come, get on here. Get home," and "Take her home" to the man. If, however, the parties are young and tolerably well dressed, and the man complains of persecution by a strange woman, they are moved on in opposite directions by a judicious mixture of remonstrance, bullying, and a hustle or two.

Now it is idle to discuss whether these assaults are justifiable or not. You might as well discuss whether people are justified in bleeding when they are cut. Unless a man's patience is angelic, or his good-humor impenetrable, or unless he is cowed by his tormentor, a violent nervous crisis on his part is only a question of the duration of the torture. Women know this perfectly well; and the ill-used wife braves it out of a mere frantic impulse to do something desperate; whilst the discarded mistress deliberately provokes it in the hope that there will be reaction of tenderness after the violence, and that she may regain the man's affection in this way at the cost of a blow or two. When the blow comes from a young and inexperienced man, it is perfectly reckless, because he does not strike whilst he has any self-control or remorse left—see, for example, Cooke's striking confession on this point. It is only the habitually brutal and seasoned husband who, when he administers "something to stop her jaw," calculates how far it is safe to go.

Let us suppose that Cooke's "victim," instead of provoking him in this way, had lashed him across the face with a horsewhip. Cooke would in that case be sure of a commutation on the ground of "unwomanly" provocation. But the provocation having been eminently "womanly," as well as ten times harder to bear, the male public regards it with a silly sort of voluptuous indulgence, and Cooke, in spite of Mr. Belfort Bax's protest, and the recommendation of the jury, will probably swing for it. Now it is not good public policy to hang a man for doing what any average citizen would have done under the same circumstances. At the same time it is not good public policy to allow people to kill one another on "provocation," or on any ground but that of urgent defence of their own lives. If we give nagged men carte blanche we shall have Wormwood Scrubbs tragedies by the score. On the other hand, if we allow women unlimited privileges to infuriate, we shall have to continue hanging men on their account who are just as good citizens for all reasonable purposes as Cooke may still be presumed to be.

The fact is that the Wormwood Scrubbs murder is an instance of lynch law produced by anarchy. What were the woman's rights as against Cooke's desertion; and what was his remedy as against her persecution? Absolutely none that she could enforce or he resort to. Public sentiment encouraged her, as a heartbroken woman, to make claims on him which were naturally those of a wife. At the same time it called upon him, as a respectable police officer, to break off a disreputable connection. Result, a frightful mess and the violent death of the woman. Public sentiment, having thus disposed of her, now proposes to hang him, and so get clear of the whole difficulty. But the difficulty will recur to-morrow or the next day with some other pair. We shall never be rid of these butcheries until we make up our minds as to what a woman's claims exactly are upon a man who, having formerly loved her, now wishes to get free from her society. If we find that she has some claims, let us enforce them, and protect the man from any molestation that goes beyond them. If she has no claims, do not let us have men going in fear of being discharged from public employment for acting on that assumption.

There are people who will say that all this is beside the real point, which is, according to them, that if people enter into illicit relations they must take the consequences. The reply is that there is no must in the matter at all. The consequences, ranging from loss of self-respect to loss of life, are so objectionable that no sensible community would tolerate them for a moment unless they deterred people from entering into such relations. They have no such effect, and they never will. But even if we abandon the illicit relations to their fate, what about the same difficulty as it arises between duly married people? One party comes to dislike the other; and the other is jealous and will not consent to a separation. Is the one who persists in trying to force the other to submit to a no longer welcome relation to be encouraged and sympathised with, or to be sternly discountenanced? That is the question we will not face. The subject is a disagreeable one; and we prefer to shuffle along with our "conjugal rights" which we dare not enforce, our "whom God hath joined let no man put asunder" theory, tempered by judicial separation and divorce, and our gallows to settle all awkward cases.

We can of course put a rope round Cooke's neck as easily as

we put into his hand the bludgeon which he put so startlingly to the use for which bludgeons are made. But what a relief it would be if he were to escape and slip out of the country! And that is not the feeling that we ought to have about a man whom we are going to hang.—

Yours, &c.,
G. Bernard Shaw

II

[*The Star,* 25 July 1893.]

Sir,—I am loth to ask you for more space but I cannot resist the desire to ask the public how it feels now that it has hung a man because it has arrived at nothing better in the way of a sexual code than the mass of contradictory sentiment which your lady correspondents have launched at me for protesting against abandoning them to lynch law.

It is quite useless to attempt to draw me into an idle squabble as to which party is in fault when women nag and men beat them. In the Wormwood Scrubbs case both parties conceived themselves to have an intolerable grievance. There being no law on the subject, they fought it out by brute force, and the woman was killed. There is a law on the subject of unofficial killing, and Cooke has been officially killed to-day in consequence. I have raised the question as to whether this is a satisfactory arrangement from the public point of view, and immediately the bystanders, instead of answering the question, began to take sides as between the man and the woman, according to their inconsiderate sympathies in the quarrel.

Let me take a point or two from the lady's letter yesterday. In her opinion the woman was "dreadful, a disgrace, all that was most sordid and horrible." And her conclusion is that the man therefore should have devoted his life to her. The man, she is careful to add, was "a low scoundrel": ergo, nothing could repay the woman for the loss of his affection. Is it conceivable that a lady with intelligence enough to write a letter at all could write like this on any other subject without laughing at herself? It is precisely this sort of unreason that has got the woman killed and the man hanged.

At the bottom of all the unreason, however, will be found the old theory that an act of sexual intercourse gives the parties a life-long claim on one another for better for worse. Formerly this claim was only recognised when the act was sanctioned by legal marriage. Even in this form it proved so intolerable that the "for better for worse" clause had to be modified by divorce and judicial separation. Every sensible man and woman in this country at present desires an extension of divorce, so that people may no longer be legally padlocked to criminals, drunkards, lunatics, viragoes, and domestic bullies as they are at present. Unfortunately, this movement towards greater freedom is getting mixed up with a quite reactionary sentimental demand for the giving of conjugal rights to unmarried persons. Anything more terrifying than this it would be hard to conceive. To be tied for life to the man or woman you have deliberately married is sometimes bad enough, but to be tied to the libertine who seduced you, or the prostitute who once sold herself to you, is a penalty for youthful incontinence which passes human endurance. Yet the theory advanced by your lady correspondents in the Cooke case involves nothing less than this. Cooke was not married to the woman he killed. If he had no right to discontinue her acquaintance (to "cast her off" is a mere question-begging phrase) then no man has a right to discontinue the acquaintance of any prostitute or woman friend with whom he has once had intercourse. And now mark what this involves. You practically cannot give conjugal rights to the unmarried woman without giving them to the unmarried man too. Consequently my critics are bound to this, that if to-morrow we have a case of a young woman who has been seduced by a policeman, and who wishes to be rid of him and to get respectably married, the policeman will have the right to claim a renewal of the intercourse, to dog her footsteps, threaten and abuse her, drive her from her situation, and make her life a misery to her. Suppose this does occur, and the woman in desperation kills her tormentor, will the woman be hung? Not if it can be prevented by the protests of the ladies who are now clamouring at me for trying to get some good out of the miserable case, for which we are all to blame. Their verdict would be that the policeman was a blackguard and that he deserves his fate. And if I were to write to the papers about the poor fellow's broken heart, his "fondness" for her, and the fact that she had "lived on him," such foolish arguments would be scorned except as proofs of my alleged hatred of women.

In my first letter I did not express my opinion as to whether the woman had any solid claim on Cooke or not. I simply asked that we should make up our minds one way or the other, and not leave it to be settled next time by bludgeoning and the gallows. But I do not mind committing myself as far as to say that I cannot for the life of me see what claim the woman had. My opinion of her conduct in persecuting him is exactly what my opinion of him would have been if she had dropped him and he had persecuted her except that I make allowance for the fact that her head was filled with pernicious nonsense about its being his "natural duty" to keep her. I need hardly add that this opinion of mine would not be in the least bit modified if it were proved—as it has not been—that he had lived on the earnings of her prostitution and so brought himself very nearly down to the level of the shareholders in the joint stock companies which pay women wages that can only be brought up to subsistence point by an occasional resort to the streets.

I hope I have made myself quite intelligible this time.

Yours, &c.,
G. Bernard Shaw

THE EMPIRE PROMENADE

[Shaw's notions of social reform often brought him into conflict with other reformers. In a letter published in the *Pall Mall Gazette* on 16 October 1894, he challenged the conclusions of Laura Ormiston Chant, a well-known social critic, about the money earned by prostitutes soliciting in the lounge of the Empire Theatre in Leicester Square, a popular music hall and home of ballet which had earned an unsavory reputation as a gathering place for the demimonde. He also dismissed the stance of Lady Henry (Isabel) Somerset, reformer, writer, and editor, who had written on behalf of the National Vigilance Association to condemn as obscene the "Living Pictures" (a series of tableaux reproducing famous works of art "in the flesh") heading the bill at the Palace Theatre. Shaw's review (and defense) of the performance was published in the *Saturday Review* on 6 April 1895.]

Sir,—In the interview on "The Aim of the Purity Crusaders," this evening, your interviewer reports Mrs. Ormiston Chant verbatim as follows:—"Why, I had a girl here from the Empire lounge—a girl earning her £20 and £30 a week from the lounge habitués." That single utterance of Mrs. Chant's is calculated to make more prostitutes in a week than the "Living Pictures" will in ten years. The impression it produces is that a girl has only to resort to the Empire lounge to make an income of £1,000 a year—exactly what every procuress assures the girls whom she is tempting into prostitution. Mrs. Chant says, "I am not a woman who is easily deceived." Now, I am a man who is very easily deceived; but if I were to invite a prostitute to come and look at my house, as Mrs. Ormiston Chant very kindly did, I should forgive the girl for trying to represent her income to me as between £1,000 and £1,500 a year; but I should not believe her.

Even the London County Council, with its "moral minimum" of twenty-four shillings a week for men, has not dared to propose more than eighteen shillings for women; and a third of that sum will purchase an incredible quantity of daily drudgery done by vigorous young girls, who, in earning it, have to sacrifice their beauty, their youth, their health, and their self-respect far more completely than any woman, however licentious, need do with an income of a thousand a year at her command. Marriage to these girls means living indecently in one room with a man legally licensed to abuse them as no frequenter of the Empire dare abuse a prostitute, and that, too, without her consent, and possibly in the presence of her own children. A woman would not submit to such an existence if she had the alternative of earning a thousand a year under the much decenter and healthier conditions, both moral and material, which an income of £1,000 a year must under any possible circumstances secure. I therefore appeal to Mrs. Ormiston Chant, since her statement may have already decided the fate of a few women hesitating on the brink of prostitution, and since I have not the smallest doubt it will be used to that end by persons whose trade it is to organize and exploit prostitution, to supplement it by letting those who have read it know, if she can, how much an ordinary young woman can earn as a prostitute; how often she earns it; how much she has to pay out of it for lodgings, clothes, and the services of some man to protect her from violent and drunken visitors; what her relations with the police are; what the effect on her health is of the life she has to lead, in short, how far her life is worth living in point of comfort, quite apart from conscientious scruples. We all—or at least those of us who are capable of being rational on the subject—know that our prostitutes do not end by jumping off Waterloo Bridge; but there is no sort of sense in plunging into exaggerations in the opposite direction. If the lot of the casual prostitute plying for hire in the streets and the music-halls includes anything like an income of £20 to £30 a week, all I can say is that her appearance belies her most wofully.

My scepticism as to the fate of the ordinary woman on the streets does not affect the damning fact that if a poor girl, either by chance, or by illegitimate inheritance from a gentleman father, is pretty and ladylike, it is better for her to trust to the protection of some rich and tolerably kind man of the upper classes than to place herself at the disposal of modern capitalism as a barmaid, a whitelead worker, a sempstress, a matchgirl, or half a dozen of the other alternatives offered by us to women as the reward of virtue. It cannot be too clearly understood that it is not the foolishly openhanded young gentlemen of the Empire lounge who cheapen women. It is our pious shareholders who use them up by the thousand, and who make them into most ugly living pictures of premature old age, clad in miserable garments that have an indecency far more disgraceful to us than the rosy nothings worn by the more fortunate living pictures at the music-halls. It is all nonsense for Mrs. Chant, if she will forgive my saying so, to bring a girl from the Empire to her own house by way of showing her how much better it is to be a respectable woman. Society does not offer the girl the alternative of enjoying Mrs. Chant's position. If you wish to be fair with her, you must take her down Drury-lane, and ask her whether she does not think it better to be one of the respectable mothers of families who live in its courts, and enjoy the privilege of having their eyes blackened by real lawful husbands. If she were quite frank she would tell you at once that she was quite sure that it would not; and she would probably ask you how you would like it yourself—a question which you could hardly answer candidly without giving away your whole case against her.

The problem then for Mrs. Chant and those who, with her, wish to abolish prostitution, is to make it better worth an attractive girl's while to be a respectable worker than to be a prostitute. There are two ways in which this can be done. One is by improving the condition of the respectable woman, the other is by making prostitution intolerably dangerous and unpleasant by employing men for twenty-four shillings a week and a blue uniform to so harry the prostitute and drive her from one resort to another that even wage slavery as described by the lady commissioners of the Labour Commission shall become preferable to the streets and the music-hall lounge. Leaving out of the question for the moment the extreme wickedness of choosing the second alternative when the first is available, the second is condemned as a really effective remedy by the fact that it is impracticable. Any attempt to define prostitution so as to get a workable criminal law against it would raise questions which society will not face at present, because they are not ripe for settlement. When George Eliot goes to live with a man who is married to another woman; when a member of a royal family contracts a morganatic marriage; when a young lady marries an old man for money, or a young man marries a millionairess, then you have cases both of illicit intercourse, speaking humanly, and sale of the person with which no police interference would be tolerated. And you may obviously have cases which combine the two features, and with which police interference would be equally impossible. Yet if you are going to penalize prostitution without touching such cases, you will have to draw a line between them; and the question is, Where is that line to be drawn? Mrs. Ormiston Chant and Lady Henry Somerset will reply, as they have so often virtually and virtuously replied, "At impurity." Unhappily nobody knows what impurity means. I see the words purity, impurity, anti-impurity, purity crusade, and so on all over the newspapers; and the more I examine the context in which they are used, the more I am persuaded that the word impurity has no fixed meaning. I find it used to denote severally: (1) the possession of a sexual function; (2) consciousness of the possession of a sexual function; (3) desire to exercise that function; (4) exhibition of the human body; (5) clothing of the human body in particular ways—for example, replacing a skirt by a pair of knickerbockers; (6) exposure of the female body only, without prejudice to the free exhibition of the male figure by our athletes and acrobats; (7) all sexual intercourse; (8) sexual intercourse between persons not married to one another; (9) selling sexual intercourse; (10) purchasing sexual intercourse; (11) attempting to attract any person by an appeal to the sexual instinct; (12) desiring that the licences of the Empire and Palace theatres may be renewed. I break off here for want of space and breath, not for want of additional meanings, or rather ambiguities. I ask Lady Henry Somerset, or Mrs. Ormiston Chant, or any one else who is avowedly working for the establishment of purity, to reduce that ideal to a code of regulations, the observance of which they will recognize as constituting us pure persons living under a pure government. Until that is done conclusive discussion is impossible.

I may add that I have not seen the "living pictures," though I feel rather inclined to repair this omission; and that my attitude towards Lady Henry Somerset is one of entire respect for her activity and conviction as a public worker. It is just on that account that I am anxious to know exactly what she and her friends are driving at.

Yours, &c.,
G. Bernard Shaw

THE CHARGE AGAINST GEORGE ALEXANDER

[The actor-manager George Alexander had been accused by the police at Chelsea of consorting with a prostitute; he had in fact, as he explained in a letter to the *Daily Chronicle,* been appealed to by the prostitute for money. Shaw defended Alexander in a letter published in the same paper on 7 November 1895.]

Sir,—Will you allow me to make a brief protest, in all our interests, against the injustice done to Mr. Alexander by the prudery of the Press? A police officer accuses Mr. Alexander of intercourse with a prostitute in the ordinary pursuit of her trade. For this definite and, under the circumstances, entirely incredible charge, the Press substitutes one of "disgraceful conduct," which may mean anything, credible or incredible. Had the charge against Mr. Alexander been reported exactly as the police officer made it, Mr. Alexander's letter of yesterday's date would have been superfluous.

Perhaps I may be allowed to add that the circumstances as described by Mr. Alexander up to the point of the intervention of the policeman have occurred to me more than once, and I doubt not to many other people as well. It is, therefore, just as well that humane and unsuspicious citizens who feel their own social responsibility for prostitution of the miserable kind that appealed to Mr. Alexander's charity should be warned—first, that a common prostitute dare not contradict a policeman; second, that since—thanks to male legislation—solicitation of a man by a woman is a punishable offence, whereas a man may solicit a woman with impunity, a prostitute can hardly be expected to confess to having taken the initiative in a conversation; third, that begging is also an offence involving an inevitable sentence of imprisonment; and finally, that the more utterly pitiable the woman of the streets is, the more impossible it is to convince either herself or a policeman (not to mention the magistrate) that any man could have an honest motive in speaking to her.

Yours, &c.,
G. Bernard Shaw

THE SATARA SENTENCES

[Press censorship in Imperial India was strict, and sedition trials against Indian editors and publishers was a common occurrence. An editorial in the newspaper *Mahrani* (published in Islampur) in the summer of 1897 comparing Indian moves toward independence unfavorably with those of Canada led to the sentence of "transportation for life" for the editor (Keshalkar), the judge at Satara having overruled the assessors' verdict of not guilty in order to pass this drastic verdict. Shaw's letter was published in the *Daily Chronicle* on 3 September 1897.]

Sir,—May I ask whether India has been seized by Russia? I am taking my holiday at present out of the reach of the latest news; but I am informed that an Indian editor has been sentenced to transportation for life (to Siberia, presumably) for writing an article advocating the independence of India. Such an event is a mere matter of routine in Russia; but under English rule it would indicate that the Government had been precipitated by panic into an extremity of cowardice and folly worthy of Dublin Castle[1] a century ago. Hence my anxiety to know the true state of the case.

The idea of such a sentence is, of course, to "strike terror" into the hearts of malcontents. That effect will be successfully produced on a handful of journalists without talent or character enough to be dangerous, at the cost of making rebels of all the public-spirited men, white or coloured, whose conviction of the superiority of our rule in India to anything that the Indians or the Russians are at present capable of substituting for it is our only justification for being in India at all. This conviction is robust enough to withstand the serious drawbacks to our rule due to military nervousness and to the common Anglo-Indian tendency to regard India partly as a lucrative official preserve, and partly as Tom Tiddler's Ground[2] pure and simple. It will not withstand

[1]Headquarters of the representative of the British government, the lord lieutenant of Ireland.

[2]A phrase from a children's game song referring to a place where one may easily acquire a fortune or make a place for oneself in the world.

sentences of transportation for life on editors who desire to see India placed on the same footing as Canada, and who have the courage and the ability to say so.

I do not know enough about India to be able to judge whether the Indian Press can safely be allowed the license which the English Press systematically abuses. But I am certainly not prepared to waste five minutes' attention on the advocates of terrorism. We are none of us nowadays exactly Whigs; but the lessons which the Whigs gained their eminence in history by learning and teaching—and freedom of speech and of the Press was the most valuable of them—can hardly be so utterly forgotten in England as they are by the judges of Keshalkar. The true remedy for the dissemination of dangerous opinions and false information is the counter-dissemination of salutary opinions and correct information. In this country the newspapers occasionally tell the truth, and the Government denies it from the Treasury Bench, knowing that its denial will be reported equally with the newspaper's contradiction of it. There is no reason why this custom should not be made compulsory in India—or here, if compulsion were necessary. To suppress news, and at the same time to commit acts of avowed tyranny, is to set in motion something far more dangerous than the most unscrupulous newspaper: to wit, the imagination of a superstitious and supersubtle race. The right thing to do is to insist that every editor, in the newspaper in which he is free to proclaim such views and tell such stories as he pleases, shall reserve space for official reports, which should be prepared, as part of the routine of the Government of a subject race, by a department of skilled journalists. The editor should be absolutely free to contradict and denounce the department, or to implore his readers not to read the Government column. The latter course would be especially valuable in securing it an eager perusal. Half a column of competently told authentic news, and the other half of effective comment, would paralyse twenty columns of Baboo balderdash, instead of making a hundred million rebels at one stroke, as a sentence of imprisonment for life does.

I am aware, of course, that rulers whose proceedings will bear publication and will put to shame the accusations of malcontents do not rush into panic-stricken cruelties at the first shock to their frontier from unarmed tribesmen. It is clear that whether Keshalkar has been sent to Siberia by the Russians, or to the Andamans by the English, his judges must have been most desperately afraid of him. The first thing a weak and cowardly ruler does is to "put his foot down" on something weaker than himself, and then look round anxiously to see whether the world is trembling with the terror of his exploit. Therefore my suggestion will probably not be adopted just now. But I throw it out for consideration later on, when events will have proved the contemptible futility of attempting to restore public confidence by gagging the Press.

Yours, &c.,
G. Bernard Shaw

THE STAGE AS A PROFESSION

[Under the heading "The Stage as a Profession," an unidentified correspondent in the *Morning Post* on 24 November 1897 took the position that, as the stage was now a recognized profession, which "sets up a claim to respectability, and demands respect," it could no longer "be regarded as a harbour of refuge for those whose lives have spelt failure." Accordingly, to remedy most of the present evils, including elimination of the actor-manager "star" system, he called for the establishment of a School of Histrionic Art (or "Conservatoire"), which would perceptibly raise the standard of excellence in the theatre, so that "the stage would cease to be overcrowded by the mediocre and the indifferent."

In an interview published the next day the actor-manager Herbert Beerbohm Tree reminded readers that, though he had already proposed such a scheme (he was, in fact, to found an acting school at His Majesty's Theatre in 1904 that eventually became the Royal Academy of Dramatic Art), "Acting is not a precise science, and though there is an infinity to be learned in acting there is infinitely little that can be taught. The best training an actor can receive nowadays is in such companies as [those which] play the Classical Drama and the old comedies throughout the Provinces." Another actor-manager, William Terriss (fated to be murdered at the private entrance to his Adelphi Theatre just three weeks later), warned on 26 November that the stage was at best a precarious profession, entrance to which should not be encouraged. "How easy to attempt: how difficult to succeed," he lamented. "The prizes are few—very few . . . Far better any other calling than that of the average actor or actress in the ranks. . . . I would say to any man or woman who proposes to adopt the Stage as a profession, pause ere you take the plunge. The road is long and weary . . ."

Shaw's contribution to the discussion was published on 29 November.]

Sir,—Your Correspondent is right as to the technical incompetence of English actors. In fact, he understates the case, because he judges our actors by what he sees them do on the stage; and that, as you will readily see must be the case, consists mainly of what they can do, and not of what they cannot. Unless a play is carefully contrived to conceal the deficiencies of our existing stage resources it has no chance of being produced, unless the author is in a position to force it on the manager—in which case it generally fails. Properly speaking, the players do not act the author's parts: it is his parts that act the players. In the case of actors of unquestionable and eminent vocation, this process, far from being dispensed with, is carried to its extreme. What happens is that an actor or actress catches the public fancy in a particular sort of part, and so gains a position on the London stage. It then becomes the business of the fashionable author to introduce that particular sort of part into all his plays, and to retain that particular performer to play it, until at last we have every gifted actor checked in his development and condemned to waste his prime in caricaturing his first success; whilst every play that is produced becomes a mere device for exhibiting these stalking-horses. Thus Miss Fanny Brough is doomed perpetually to play Miss Fanny Brough; Mr. Cyril Maude (until he escaped under his own management into "The Little Minister") to play Mr. Cyril Maude; and Mr. Weedon Grossmith to play Mr. Weedon Grossmith. I purposely select cases of actors of proved versatility and width of range to illustrate the evil. Add to the parts that are cut to the measure of the hits made by our born actors those cut to the measure of the untrained incompetence of their less gifted colleagues, and you get a drama in which half the performers are having their mannerisms stereotyped and the other half their deficiencies concealed. The result is the same both ways: there is no exhibition of ineptitude; and yet ineptitude is the secret of the staleness and artificiality of the whole entertainment. The moment our dramatists allow their genius to work according to its own nature, without regard to the practical need for parts either wholly "actor-proof," or else stock actor-fitted parts under new names, the risk of failure is enormously multiplied. The system at last leads to so complete a substitution of the art of exploiting actors for that of dramatic composition that it is more profitable to compile an absurdly bad farce for a popular performer than to trust a serious drama to our best actors. Compare, for example, the fate of "Magda" with that of "Oh, Susannah!"[1]

[1]*Magda,* a translation by Louis N. Parker of Hermann Sudermann's *Heimat,* with Johnston Forbes-Robertson and Mrs. Patrick Campbell, opened at the Lyceum

It must be observed that this is nobody's fault. M. Tout le Monde is at the bottom of it all; and M. Tout le Monde must be educated. But it is the actor who must educate him; and who is to educate the actor? Your Correspondent suggests a Conservatoire. But what does he mean by a Conservatoire? Is it to be an officially recognised "dramatic studio," where English actors, sorrowfully confessing that they do not know their business, are to undertake to teach it to others? Or is it to be an institution like the French Conservatoire, where, in addition to the old-fashioned calisthenics and elocution, actors are to be taught that there is one "right" way (all others "wrong") of taking a chair and sitting down on it, of kneeling at a lady's feet, of picking up a handkerchief, of howling an alexandrine, of shaking hands (right hand with right and left with left), and so forth? Are the passions to be catalogued there, and each one assigned its "right" grimace and gesture? For this is what "teaching dramatic art" means, and always necessarily must mean, in spite of the plausible disclaimers of its professors. True, it has its uses. For instance, the French teachers can take a housemaid and train her to go through the part of the Queen in "Ruy Blas"[2] without committing a single solecism; whereas an English manager must look for a lady of sufficient natural and socially acquired qualifications to pass muster with a London audience in the part, solecisms or no solecisms. One result of the English plan is that the *Morning Post* is calmly discussing the Stage as a profession for ladies and gentlemen; whilst in France it is not so long since the late Alexandre Dumas[3] wrote to a young lady of means and position who wished to go on the Stage, in terms which in England would have seemed overstrained if she had proposed to become a ragpicker. Thus our system—or rather no-system—undoubtedly does put a premium on talent and social training, by relieving them from the competition of the French machine-made acting. But it fails to provide certain qualifications which are incidental to the French system.

The exact state of the case is that the French actor, though a trained artist, is a bad actor because he has been taught to act, and

Theatre on 3 June 1896 and expired after fifteen performances. *Oh! Susannah,* a farcical comedy by Mark Ambient, Alban Attwood, and Russell Vaun, had been playing at the Royalty since 5 October 1897. It eventually attained a run of 161 performances.

[2]Poetic drama by Victor Hugo (1838).

[3]Dumas *fils,* who died in 1895.

the English actor is a bad actor because he is not a trained artist. Acting, as Mr. Beerbohm Tree has pointed out, cannot be taught. An actor is, by definition, a person born with the faculty of acting. But that faculty is limited by the power of the actor to execute his conceptions. Coquelin[4] was born able to understand Mascarille,[5] but not to catch Anselme's[6] purse with his heels and throw it to the back of the stage, or to launch forty alexandrines at Lélie[7] in less time than it takes an English ghost in "Hamlet" to get through four lines of blank verse. The actor should be a first-rate athlete, by which I do not mean that he should break records in feats of strength—your "muscle-bound" strong man is useless on the stage—but that he should have a skilled command of his nerves and muscles, for relaxation and inertion as well as stimulation and exertion; that his organs of speech should be trained like a pianist's fingers, until he can strike a consonant as Paderewski strikes a note; and that he should have a specially complete control of the muscles of his face. He should have an expert's ear for phonetics, and be able with promptitude and certainty to pronounce some 12 or 20 pure vowels, and combine them into diphthongs, practising them with the alphabet every day as Madame Patti practices her scales, and so acquiring the power to analyse dialects and foreign sounds, and reproduce them scientifically instead of merely mimicking their most salient traits. These are the true qualifications required by the actor: his mere accomplishments, such as fencing, dancing, the conventions of Italian pantomime, and so on, he can learn at present as easily as he can learn French, by simply going to the people who teach them. Elocution he should carefully avoid; and its professors should be capitally punished.

Now, the first thing that will strike any intelligent surveyor of the course of instruction I have sketched is that its application is by no means limited to the requirements of the actor. The barrister, the clergyman, the platform, parliamentary, or municipal politician: in short, the whole army of public men and public speakers, reinforced by the still larger battalions whose livelihood

[4]French actor long associated with the Comédie-Française, and the first performer of Cyrano de Bergerac in Rostand's play of that name (1897).

[5]The kind of shrewd and impudent servant who appears in several of Molière's comedies.

[6]Shipwrecked nobleman in Molière's *L'Avare* [*The Miser*] (1668).

[7]Young man in Molière's *Sganarelle* [*The Imaginary Cuckold*] (1660).

depends on their personal address (for example, physicians in general practice, and Bond-street shop assistants of both sexes), all want just such an academy as the actor wants. Its more advanced classes might go beyond the requirements of the unambitious gentleman; but as a school of grace, good manners, and refinement of speech it would attract thousands of non-theatrical students, whose presence would effectually prevent it from becoming a mere hotbed of cabotinage. We should thus have a university of the arts of life; and the specialisation of those arts for the theatre could be acquired by its graduates in the only way in which it ever is acquired: that is, by actual practice on the stage. Such a university could be endowed without offence to those who regard the theatre as a pernicious institution. The main difficulty would be to find trustworthy teachers. In our public schools of music the teaching of instruments by people who have succeeded as players is satisfactory. The teaching of singing by people who have failed as singers is destructive and ruinous. I am not proposing a fresh opening for the sort of gentleman who plays the Soothsayer for 50s. a week on the stage, and is ready off it to teach anybody how to play Brutus and Antony for half a guinea a lesson. But the difficulties in this respect are not greater than those which attach to all educational schemes.

I hope, by the way, that Mr. [William] Terriss's hint will not be lost on those of your younger readers who may be a little stage-struck. The Stage is a profession in which people may succeed in spite of a license in personal conduct which would ruin them in more prosaic walks of life. But for all that there is no profession in which the competition of character is keener—certainly none which is more demoralising to those who succumb in that competition. If this correspondence suggests that the Stage is an eligible profession for ladies and gentlemen in search of a light and elegant occupation, it will do shocking harm. Acting is an eligible profession for persons of great energy of character, indomitable industry, and unconquerable vocation. It is also a desperate resource for the residuum of middle-class families on the down grade. But it is not yet any better than that. Women may be excused for flocking to it because of their unfair exclusion from other professions. For men, in the absence of the rare qualifications I have mentioned, there is no excuse at all.—

Yours, &c.,
G. Bernard Shaw

THE APOSTROPHE

[*Glasgow Herald,* 26 April 1898]

Sir,—In the very able and interesting review with which you have honoured my *Plays Pleasant and Unpleasant,*[1] your reviewer asks the following question. "Why does Mr. Shaw so object to the use of the apostrophe as to disfigure his pages with theyd and youd?"

The answer is that I did so to avoid disfiguring the pages. It is admitted on all hands that the Scotch printers who have turned out the book (Messrs Clark, of Edinburgh)[2] have done their work admirably; but no human printer could make a page of type look well if it were peppered in all directions with apostrophes and the ugly little gaps beneath the apostrophes. I am sorry to say that literary men never seem to think of the immense difference these details make in the appearance of a block of letterpress, in spite of the lessons of that great author and printer, William Morris, who thought nothing of rewriting a line solely to make it "justify" prettily in print. If your reviewer will try the simple experiment of placing an open Bible, in which there are neither apostrophes nor inverted commas, besides his own review of my plays, which necessarily bristle with quotation marks, I think he will admit at once that my plan of never using an apostrophe when it can be avoided without ambiguity transfigures the pages instead of disfiguring them. He will, I feel confident, never again complain of youd because a customary ugliness has been wiped out of it. I have used the apostrophe in every case where its omission could even momentarily mislead the reader; for example, I have written she'd and I'll to distinguish them from shed and ill. But I have made no provision for the people who cannot understand dont unless it is printed don't. If a man is as stupid as that, he should give up reading altogether.

Yours, &c.,
G. Bernard Shaw

[1]Published on 18 and 19 April 1898.
[2]The firm of R. & R. Clark, Ltd., chosen by Shaw because it was a union house, served as his printer for more than half a century, until Shaw's death in 1950.

BRÜNNHILDE'S "DECEIT"

I

[Dr. William Ashton Ellis, a physician as well as the first translator of Wagner's prose works into English, objected to a review of *Die Götterdämmerung* by the *Daily Telegraph*'s music critic, Lionel Monckton, which appeared on 13 and 15 June 1898. Monckton argued that Brünnhilde was "swearing to a lie" in the second act of the opera when she accused Siegfried of deception. When, on 23 June, the *Daily Telegraph* had not yet published his rebuttal, Ellis wrote to the *Daily Chronicle,* which published it the next day. Rather than "swearing to a lie," Ellis argued, Brünnhilde "is absolutely and literally bewildered by the 'tangle' in which she finds everything involved. . . . In a state of utter collapse must she have passed that night, cowering in the farthest corner of her cave to avoid all sense of the intruder's presence. There is not a line to suggest that she knew it was Siegfried, disguised, who shared the cavern with her; rightly therefore does she call it a 'lie' when Siegfried speaks of the sword's dividing them. . . . Let anyone hear this glorious woman's dying speech, and then accuse her of deceit!" Shaw entered the controversy with a letter published in the *Daily Chronicle* on 28 June 1898.]

Sir,—My friend Mr. Ashton Ellis will not suspect me of any complicity with the poor little pleas our older critics still put forward from time to time to extenuate the giant blunder they made years ago in explaining to the British public that Wagner was a cacophonous charlatan, and "Der Ring" a long drivel of recitative without arias. But Mr. Ellis must not too hastily conclude that everything the *Daily Telegraph* says about Wagner is necessarily wrong. In this instance it is right, and Mr. Ashton Ellis's heroic attempt at a counter theory utterly hopeless.

The truth of the matter is that the Brünnhilde of the second act of "Die Götterdämmerung" cannot be identified for a moment with the Valkyrie of "Die Walküre" and "Siegfried." "Die Götterdämmerung" is not a later work than the three music dramas which precede it in order of performance; and if we attempt to manufacture a case for it as the glorious climax, fruition, culmination, summit, and crown of a mighty masterwork, we shall land ourselves in desperate confusion. "Die Götterdämmerung" is, in conception, the immediate successor of "Lohengrin," and, like "Lohengrin," is not a music drama, but an opera—and a very operatic opera at that, with trios, quartets, grand scenas for the prima donna with the chorus lining the stage and taking not the slightest notice of her, grandiose oaths and conjurations (including an oath of vengeance for three conspirators, conceived for theatrical effect, exactly like the oath of Renato, Samuel, and Tom in the third act of Verdi's "Un Ballo," or the oath of Othello and Iago in the second act of the same composer's "Otello"); a thundering chorus which Spontini would have written if he could, and all those splendid artificialities of grand opera which not only do not occur in the true music dramas which occupy the first three evenings of "The Ring," but cannot even be conceived as intruding upon them. Let me remind Mr. Ellis of the history of "The Ring." Wagner at first proposed nothing further than a single work, entitled "Siegfried's Death," founded on the Nibelungen legend. In it Brünnhilde is simply a "strong part," like Lady Macbeth; in fact, she is practically identical with Hiordis, Ibsen's Brünnhilde in "The Vikings," a fierce woman whose love has been turned to deadly jealousy and revenge. This Brünnhilde, remember, unlike Wagner's Valkyrie, is an old acquaintance of Gutrune. Further, she is an expert in magic. Let anyone now read the second act of "Die Götterdämmerung" in the light cast by these facts. Brünnhilde's unaccountable recognition of Gutrune the moment she sees her, her black rage at her own betrayal, her divination of the Tarnhelm trick when Gunther breaks down under cross-examination about the ring, her false accusation of Siegfried, and her villainous plot with Hagen to stab him in the back at the hunt—all belong to the original heroine of "Siegfried's Tod." That very title still remains in the text, led up to as an emphatic stage point. Siegfried himself, far from being the novice who has met only one glorious woman and learnt fear from her, talks slightingly of women like an old hand, and says that "their tantrums are soon over." Hagen, with his fine solo, is a frankly operatic basso cantante villain. The fact that out of all this operatic stuff there grew the original and vivid characters of the three music dramas proper of "The Ring," instead of those dramas degenerating into mere opera in the middle of the third act of "Siegfried," as they must seem to do to any intelligent spectator who takes them in their ostensible order, cannot be too jealously insisted on by all true Wagnerians. I have not space here to trace the process which evolved "Das Rheingold" from "Siegfried's Tod," but I may say that it is quite lucidly traceable, and that the clue to it is in the necessity for providing Siegfried, the moment Wagner began to see in him not merely an operatic hero, but the type of a world-force, with an adequate antagonist instead of the mere stage villain Hagen. That antagonist is the counter world-force typified by Wotan, the true hero of the music dramas.

It must be carefully noted that "Die Götterdämmerung" is not only not the end of "The Ring"; it is not even the beginning, although it led to the beginning. It is no part of it at all, except musically. A few threads are mechanically tied up in it; for instance, it makes a formal end of the gods; but these were really disposed of when Siegfried laughed at Wotan, shivered his spear, braved the fires of hell only to find that they were an illusion and a lie, and found the truth in the very place that Godhead and Cunning had forbidden to man. After that there was nothing left for Wagner to do but drop the finished world-allegory and weave the still unexhausted musical material into a magnificently sensational opera. The music of "The Ring" was composed in the order in which the four works now stand; so that though the libretto of "Die Götterdämmerung," comes before the poem of "Das Rheingold," its score is of later date and greater technical mastery. As against that we may set the straightforward sincerity and simplicity of the music drama as compared to the monstrous grandiosity and outrageous and impenitent false pathos of the opera. That last scene is gorgeous enough as a sound-tissue to excuse Mr. Ellis's adoration of it; but it is senseless; one always feels that the only possible comment for Siegfried to make is:—

> "Perhaps you did well to dissemble your love;
> But why did you kick me downstairs?"[1]

In the original text there is an attempt to give some sort of philosophical air to the orgie of sentimentality by a few lines about love being the final solution of the social problem (an announcement made nearly half a century before in Shelley's youthful attempt at a "Ring"—"Prometheus Unbound"); but Wagner had not the heart to set it to music when it came to the point; and it has nothing whatever to do with the true theme of "The Ring"—the conflict between Wotan and Humanity.

[1]A slightly modified quotation ("Perhaps it was right to dissemble your love;/ But why did you kick me downstairs?") from John Philip Kemble's play *The Panel* (1788).

I am fully conscious of the shock with which many fire-new converts to the Bayreuth faith will receive this invitation to despoil "Die Götterdämmerung" of the chief honors of the tetralogy, especially as probably the more operatic it is the better they like it; but I can assure the true adepts that if we attempt to stand the pyramid on the apex from which it was originally built downwards, it will topple and crush us.

Yours, &c.,
G. Bernard Shaw

II

[The controversy was joined by Edward A. Baughan, drama and music critic of the *Daily News,* in a letter published in the *Daily Chronicle* on 2 July 1898.]

Sir,—Possibly Mr. Ashton Ellis has already knocked down Mr. Bernard Shaw's ingenious card-castle with a few facts. In case he has not I supply them here. In a letter to Liszt, dated May 29, 1852, Wagner says, "My Nibelung tetralogy is completely designed, and in a few months the verse also will be finished." In a subsequent letter, the composer says, "My new poems for the two Siegfrieds I finished last week, but I have still to write the two earlier dramas, 'Young Siegfried' and 'Siegfried's Death,' as very considerable alterations have become necessary. I shall not have finished entirely before the end of the year." The poem of the "Ring" was privately published at the beginning of 1853, and publicly in 1863. Mr. Shaw is quite right in his history of the conception of the Tetralogy, the order of which was:—"Siegfried's Death," "Young Siegfried," "Die Walküre," and "Das Rheingold," but he has made a mistake in blandly supposing that Wagner did not rewrite the whole as soon as his conception was complete.

What Mr. Shaw calls the operatic character of "Die Götterdämmerung," is, in my opinion, due to a modification of Wagner's views. After the second act of "Siegfried," there was a long gap in the composition of the "Ring." That interval was employed by Wagner in composing "Tristan und Isolde" and "Die Meistersinger." In "Tristan" there is not much that can be called operatic; but I would point to the famous love-duet as a considerable modification of the severely Wagnerian methods of "Die Walküre," and the first two acts of "Siegfried." Then in "Die Meistersinger" we have duets, trios, quintets, and several choruses. True, it is supposed to be a comic opera, and anything is allowable, they say, in a comic opera. Let us leave it out of the question. Then we come to the love-duet in "Siegfried," which Mr. Shaw calls operatic. It *is* operatic in the sense that musical beauty when appropriate is not cut out to square the theories of a doctrinaire, as it is in "Die Walküre" and "Siegfried." After this act came "Die Götterdämmerung," with its trios, quartet, and chorus. After "Die Götterdämmerung" came "Parsifal," with its trios and choruses. And more important than these formal characteristics of opera is the modification in Wagner's vocal style. In "Das Rheingold," "Die Walküre," and the first two acts of "Siegfried," Wagner wilfully sacrifices vocal beauty to a theory of declamation. Often he goes out of his way to make the voice descend in the scale when, according to all musical and dramatic logic, it should ascend; he shirks natural vocal climaxes because they seemed to him then to be operatic; he patches the voice with the orchestra, so that the whole makes a vocal and orchestral symphony, and the voice no longer leads. After composing "Tristan" he found that dramatic and musical beauty were not incompatible, and henceforth he entered his last and finest vocal style. If this style, so full of melody and dramatic expression, be operatic, why, then, so much the better for opera. But Mr. Shaw does not really object to the operatic Wagner; he is only poking fun at the ultra-Wagnerians, who worship their master's tentative weaknesses. Some six years ago I had the honor of giving a lecture on the development of opera before the Musical Association, and in that lecture I severely denounced all concerted music (as was becoming in a young Wagnerian). Mr. Shaw was one of my audience, and in a speech he gave he paternally chided me for being a Wagnerite. I turn to the verbatim report in the "proceedings" of the association, and I find Mr. Shaw was more or less on the side of musical beauty in opera. Indeed, he delivered himself of the following opinion: "The Italian quartets, &c., so often to be found in Donizetti and Verdi, to my mind show how much superior opera is to the spoken drama."[2] I know it is not fair to quote a man's opinions of six years ago; but per-

[2]Remarks in a discussion following Baughan's lecture "The Development of Opera," 9 February 1892. Published in the *Proceedings of the Musical Association 1891–92;* collected in *Shaw's Music,* 1981.

haps after a long course of dramatic criticism, and after having written many plays, Mr. Shaw may look with some indulgence on his youthful utterance.

As to Brünnhilde's deceit, can there really be two opinions? All through Wagner's prose works he speaks of Brünnhilde's vengeance on Siegfried for his falseness; Brünnhilde herself cries aloud for vengeance. One would imagine from the annoyance of the Wagnerians that a woman never wishes to be revenged on a man unless she can encompass her ends by fair means.

Yours, &c.,
Edward Baughan

III

[Shaw's response to Baughan appeared in the *Daily Chronicle* on 5 July 1898.]

Sir,—I am much indebted to Mr. Baughan for supplying in detail the facts upon which my former letter was founded. His dates and quotations precisely confirm my view. The fact that he begins his letter by proposing to use those data "to knock down my ingenious card castle" only shows how very few musicians are fit to be trusted with facts.

I have not "blandly supposed that Wagner did not rewrite the whole as soon as his conception was complete." I have simply pointed out that the second act of "Die Götterdämmerung" is hopelessly inconsistent with the other three dramas, and perfectly consistent with the original conception of "Siegfried's Tod." "Die Götterdämmerung" could not have been re-written as a sequel to the Wotan tragedy, because it has nothing to do with that tragedy. No possible re-writing could harmonise the revengeful murderess, who tells Hagen how to stab Siegfried, with the daughter of Wotan. Mr. Baughan's innocent observation hereupon that "one would imagine that a woman never wishes to be revenged on a man unless she can encompass her ends by fair means" is one which I trust he may yet live down. There was only one possible way for Wagner to preserve the homogeneity of "The Ring," and that was by omitting "Die Götterdämmerung" altogether. Naturally he did not care to sacrifice a powerful tragic opera in this way. Probably he retraced his original path from "Siegfried's Tod" to "Das Rheingold" without anything like the clear consciousness of the transition which a critic may without arrogance profess twenty-five years later. Creative genius always works ahead of intellectual consciousness. No man knows the meaning of what he has done until he has done it; and most of the creative geniuses of the world have shared a good deal of the conservatism and prejudices of their day as against the ultimate goal of the impulse their works have given to human thought.

As to Mr. Baughan's notion about the sacrifice of vocal beauty and the shirking of vocal climax in the first three music dramas, I should like him to cite a few illustrative passages. Any person who has studied the vocal style of these works by actually singing them, will, I think, be simply puzzled by Mr. Baughan's remark. Especially is that point about vocal climax a staggering one. With ordinary bad German singing the music dramas are generally made to sound like nothing but volleys of vocal climaxes from end to end. Even the deliberately ugly music of Alberich is so artistically ugly that a good singer can enjoy singing it and make the audience share his satisfaction. Besides, Wagner explicitly tells us that he did not compose "on principle" in this sense.

Yours, &c.,
G. Bernard Shaw

THE MAHDI'S SKULL

[When the Anglo-Egyptian army under Lord Kitchener defeated the Mahdists at Omdurman in 1898, thus establishing the British control of the Sudan, the tomb of the Mahdi (Mohammed Ahmed), Moslem leader and hero of the capture of Khartoum in 1885, was destroyed by the Sirdar (British commander of the Egyptian army). Shaw's letter appeared in the *Morning Leader*, 6 October 1898.]

Sir,—There are one or two considerations apparently overlooked by the secretary to the Royal College of Surgeons, if I may judge by the report of a conversation with him in your issue of 30 Sept. He declares that if the Mahdi's skull is sent to the college he will accept it. To realise the probable consequences it is necessary to go back a little.

A little time ago I was informed by a member of my family who happened to be reading the newspaper that the body of the Mahdi had been dug up by the Sirdar and mutilated, the trunk being cast into the Nile and the head forwarded to Cairo. I, of course, pointed out at once that the story was an old one dished up for the sake of sensation, its original being the history of the body of Oliver Cromwell, which, at the Restoration, was dug up from its grave in Westminster Abbey, mutilated, and exposed at Tyburn and Temple Bar. This piece of history has hitherto been used to mark the Tartar-like savagery of English society 200 years ago. Macaulay's comment on it is well known.[1]

Judge of my astonishment when, on mentioning the canard (as I unhesitatingly took it to be) to some apparently civilised contemporaries of my own, I found that they not only believed the story, but entirely approved of the alleged action of the Sirdar. They said that there was a good reason for it—that if the Mahdi's body were left in its tomb, Mahdists from all parts of the Soudan would make pilgrimages thither to worship at it. I confess I did not catch the point; it seemed to me that St. Thomas à Becket might be dug up and Canterbury Cathedral demolished on precisely similar grounds.

The case was then shifted a little. It was said that the pilgrims would bring disease to Khartoum; that they would fight with one another (like Christians); that they would slay the English garrison (poor defenceless lambs!); and, finally (supposing all these contentions to fall to the ground), that on discovering the Mahdi's tomb in ruins, and learning that the English had thrown his body to the crocodiles and carried off his head to London, they would lose all their reverence for their prophet, and be so struck to the soul with the refinement, humanity, advanced civilisation, and deep religious sentiment of the British nation, that they would instantly embrace the form of Christianity professed by the Sirdar, and settle down for the rest of their lives as peaceful and loyal subjects of the Anglo-Egyptian Empire.

It is hardly conceivable that the story should turn out to be true; but it is none the less rather serious that so many of the people who believe it seem to have no sense of its savagery and its idiocy. "You must remember," they say, "that these Dervishes are superstitious brutes, and that you must deal with them accordingly," by which they mean that we should behave superstitiously

[1]*History of England*, vol. 1 (1848), chap. 2: "Cromwell was no more; and those who had fled before him were forced to content themselves with the miserable satisfaction of digging up, hanging, quartering, and burning the remains of the greatest prince that has ever ruled England."

and brutally ourselves. I presume that if the next expedition of the Sirdar is undertaken against cannibals, public opinion of this sort will demand that he shall eat every chief whom he conquers, as otherwise the native population will not be persuaded that he is really stronger than they.

However, I am forgetting the secretary of the College of Surgeons, and the warning to him which is the purport of this letter. Suppose it should turn out that some vampire has really stolen the head of the Mahdi and sent it to the Royal College! The inevitable result is only too obvious. Englishmen know by their own religion that when a prophet's disciples visit his tomb and find it empty, they at once conclude that it has been miraculously taken up to heaven. Englishmen know also that any story that they may hear of the sufferings of that body, or of insult and mutilation, will only give a deep pathos to their faith, and kindle in them a piously implacable hatred of the enemies of God who have done these outrages. Clearly, then, the apprehended pilgrimages of mere devotees to Khartoum would at once be replaced by pilgrimages of fierce fanatics to the College of Surgeons, each of whom would consider Paradise cheaply purchased by the trouble of leaving his knife in the heart of the High Priest of that Temple, as the Dervishes would certainly suppose our craniological secretary to be.

He will, I hope, excuse this reduction to absurdity of a piece of folly which is none the less ghastly because we are bound to assume that it is the revolting invention of some unusually reckless war correspondent, thirsting for revenge on the Sirdar for his unhandsome treatment of the Press.

Yours, &c.,
G. Bernard Shaw

THE TRAFALGAR CELEBRATION AND THE TSAR

[In the fall of 1898 Tsar Nicholas proposed, as *The Times* reported on 6 October, "a pause in the development of European armaments," to be discussed at a peace conference. Shaw, in a letter published in the *Daily Chronicle* on 13 October, used the tsar's proposal as a springboard for an attack on British chauvinism.]

Sir,—Are we to understand from the letter of Mr. William Caius Crutchley, secretary to the Navy League, that our first response to the Tsar's pacification proposal is to be a Trafalgar celebration? No doubt the celebration and testimonialisation of remarkable events and eminent men will always be cherished in England as a means of procuring notoriety for noisy nobodies. But since peace hath her victories no less than war, I suggest that if the Press is in the least in earnest in its compliments to the Tsar it should refuse to give gratuitous advertisements to those specially obnoxious nobodies who can find nothing better to celebrate than battles. A celebration of Trafalgar is a celebration of a French defeat, no less than of an English victory. Suppose the French, after letting sleeping dogs lie for nearly a century, were suddenly and without any provocation, to begin to celebrate all the victories they won at that period, and that all the other nations were to follow suit! That would produce a nice, pacific state of public feeling, would it not? I sincerely hope that "the lord mayors and mayors of the various towns in Great Britain" may emphatically refuse Mr. Crutchley and his league the "co-operation and assistance" he has demanded for an enterprise which is either a piece of wanton mischief or a public demonstration in favor of an increase in our naval armament.

The worst of it is that our silly bellomaniacs are missing a magnificent opportunity for a really great demonstration. Can we not go to Trafalgar-square on the anniversary of the battle and pull down the column which commemorates it? The Prince of Wales could dislodge the first stone. Can we not do the same by all our other battle mementos? They only serve to keep open sores that might long ago have been healed and forgotten without them. The Vendôme column has been pulled down once in Paris in the name of peace. The French put it up again, strangely enough, as part of their policy of carefully obliterating all traces of that sanguinary fight for the idea of human solidarity, which was the only part of the war of 1870–71 not wholly shameful to our species. The sooner that column comes down again the better; and if the Emperor of Germany could be persuaded to demolish every one of these pestilential Sieges Thurms[1] and the like which still enable the horror and infamy of that monstrous outburst of homicide to haunt Europe in the worn-out disguise of "glory," Germany would be a pleasanter land to travel in for all of us as well as for Frenchmen.

May I add that I do not myself believe in disarmament? Iron-

[1]Presumably Shaw's error for Siegestürmer (victory towers).

clads and Maxims do not fight: men do. Men fought long before weapons were invented, and if every weapon in Europe were destroyed to-morrow, we could have a battle the next day if we wanted to, and a battle much more horrible, brutal, and violent than the scientific massacre which has just happily rid the Soudan of its chivalry and heroism. War will come to an end when three or four of the Great Powers have become humane enough to determine to have no more of it, and to police the world to that effect. Events are hastening that consummation. A very genuine disposition towards peace is being produced by the extreme terror inspired by the magazine rifle and the machine gun, even in the hands of men who are such ridiculously bad shots that a whole army of them, firing as hard as they can at a dense mass of Dervishes for twenty minutes, only succeed in killing as many as one single machine gun would have done in that time if every bullet had found its billet. It is useless for Englishmen, or any other sort of men, to pretend that their native bravery is such that modern magazine fire is as invigorating to them as a shower bath. The risks of battle, hitherto much less than (for example) the risks of childbed or medical practice, are now becoming for the first time in history really serious; and if any considerable attempt were made to teach soldiers to shoot, they would become intolerable. This is the real meaning of the Tsar's Rescript, and its hopeful reception.

What we have to aim at, then, is not disarmament, but a combination of America and the Western Powers to suppress civilised war by internationalised force of arms, and to dispassionately extirpate barbarous races, whose heroism, chivalry, patriotism, and religion forbid them to live and let live. Unfortunately, these romantic characteristics, especially as displayed in war, lend themselves to literary and dramatic display; and that is why the Press, being necessarily literary, will not give them up, and seeks to combine the most eloquent aspirations towards universal peace with a demand for local bombardment (in Crete),[2] and the apotheosis of the chivalrous Emirs, "to Iran and to vengeance true,"[3]

[2]After the Cretan insurrection of 1896–97 had led to war between Greece and Turkey, in which the Greeks were decisively defeated, the Great Powers in 1898 forced Turkey to evacuate from Crete.

[3]These words, in the third tale of Thomas Moore's *Lalla Rookh* (1817), are from a passionate speech by Hafad, leader of the Persian fire-worshippers in a brave but doomed struggle against their Arab masters.

with the moral rectitude of the Britons who mowed them down by machinery.

I plead for a little clear thinking, and—as an inevitable consequence—the decisive snubbing of the Navy League and its steeplejacks.

Yours, &c.,
G. Bernard Shaw

DEAD BODY DIET

[During 1898, Shaw underwent an operation on his left foot, suffered a broken left arm, married Charlotte Payne-Townshend, completed *The Perfect Wagnerite* and *Caesar and Cleopatra,* and began *Captain Brassbound's Conversion.* He also found time to correct, in a letter published on 26 December 1898 in the *Freeman's Journal,* Dublin, the account of his injuries and recuperation offered by the London correspondent of that paper.]

Sir,—Your London correspondent has been good enough to furnish you with a harrowing account of my broken leg, and the refusal of the ruptured tendons to unite in consequence of my persistence in vegetarianism. I feel that London correspondents must not be permitted to plunge my native town into gloom at Christmas time in this manner. There is no broken leg; there are no ruptured tendons; the condition of the patient far from showing "no substantial improvement," is most disappointing to the believers in dead body diet; and those of my friends and admirers who were lately consoling me with assurances that I was dying for want of meat have now either dropped the subject or are considering whether they will not themselves abandon the butcher.

It is true that I am invalided at present by a necrosed bone, the sequel to an abscess caused by an injury to my left foot, and that in spite of my vegetarianism my recovery is the usual slow process familiar to meat-eating victims of that very troublesome disease. It is also true that I have aggravated my condition by falling down stairs, breaking my arm, and rupturing the tendons of my wrist, not to mention other mishaps which befell me. But the arm and wrist are perfectly sound again without the slaughter of a single ox on my account. Considering that during the seven months into which all these misfortunes (involving two operations) have been crowded, I have produced a book and a five-act play, and got married in my spare time, I think I may safely assure your correspondent that if he succeeds in getting anything better out of his Christmas turkey and sausages than I shall out of my stirabout, we shall all be glad to have full particulars from him.

You will, I hope, excuse my troubling you at this length about my private and personal condition; but really when I think of the horrors of the butchers' shops at this season I cannot allow your correspondent to invest me with imaginary broken legs in order to terrify naturally humane people into submitting to the tyranny of the slaughterman.

Yours, &c.,
G. Bernard Shaw

THE BEST COTTAGE LIBRARY

[*Surrey Times*, Guildford, 18 February 1899.]

Sir,—Very few books are suited to a cottagers' library, and these few very good ones. The reason for this is that only the greatest writers can see life from the general human standpoint as well as from the standpoint of their class in society. A book written from the point of view of the middle or propertied classes is neither interesting, useful or even intelligible to a cottager. He cannot read Thackeray and Mr. Henry James, Mesdames Sarah Grand and Humphrey [*sic*] Ward, Mr. Swinburne and Omar Khayyam, in order that he may understand the essays of Messrs. Andrew Lang and Augustine Birrell, and ape the fashionable literary tastes of the day. No literature that is in any sense class literature, and no literary merit that is in any sense academic, will really appeal to him; and it should be plainly understood that this is one of the advantages of his honourable status as a worker, and not one of the disadvantages of his poverty.

First, then, I take strong exception to the assumption that the Bible and Shakespeare are indispensable to begin with. I well remember the exclamation of a very earnest clergyman that if only the Bible could be got rid of for a hundred years, religion would have some chance at last in England. This remark, startling as it will seem to those who most need to have it made to them, will be well understood by all clergymen who know the extent to which the Bible has become to the Englishman what the prayer-wheel is to the Thibetan. He reads a chapter in it daily or weekly, and believes that he has thereby laid up treasure in heaven for himself, assuming that he believes and understands what he reads merely because he has not allowed himself to think about it. Until this way of approaching the Bible is so far forgotten that a cottager can bring a perfectly free and simple mind to the study of it, just as he would to any other literature (for the Bible is not a book, but a literature) he will be better without it than with it.

As to Shakespeare, it must not be supposed that he will make the same impression on a cottager as on the Athenaeum Club. Literary men think Hamlet the hero of heroes, because he typifies all their own faults and futilities. No cottager would, without prompting, feel much respect for him. The chief objection to Shakespeare is the glamour which his genius casts over the vilest style in English literature—the Elizabethan blank verse style, strenuously and artificially showy and theatrical; deliberately and impenitently nonsensical. I would not on this account deprive a cottager of 'The Merchant of Venice' and 'A Winter's Tale'; but I should very vehemently protest against his being infected with the sort of collector's mania for 'Marlowe's mighty line,'[1] which attacked Charles Lamb and has been inherited by Mr. Swinburne, or with the infatuation in which Mr. Sidney Lee claims for Shakespeare the divine attributes of omniscience, infallibility, and perfection.

The chief book in the library of an English cottager should be John Bunyan's 'Pilgrim's Progress.' It was written by an English cottager, and is by far the greatest book within a cottager's reach—immeasurably superior, both as literature and drama, to anything and everything of Shakespeare's. Like all the greatest story books, it should be read by children; indeed, it is for the cottager's child—that is, for the cottager of the next generation—that the library should be selected. With 'The Pilgrim's Progress' and 'The Holy War' should be 'Don Quixote,' 'Reynard the Fox,' 'Aesop's Fables,' 'Gulliver's Travels,' 'Robinson Crusoe,' 'The Vicar of Wakefield,' 'John Gilpin,' and 'The Ancient Mariner.' All these should be read by children, and re-read later in life, when they have outgrown their adolescent taste for the rhetorical-theatrical-sublime style, of which they will find plenty in Shakespeare and Byron to impress them in their teens. Scott's 'Ivanhoe,' Dumas' 'Musketeers,' and Dickens' 'Great Expectations,' are the most suitable novels. Ibsen's 'Peer Gynt' is indispensable. A cot-

[1]Ben Jonson, "To the Memory of Shakespeare" (1623), line 30.

tager with a turn for thinking should have a shelf stored with Boswell's 'Johnson,' Cobbett's and Kropotkin's 'Advice to Young Men,'[2] Shelley's 'Queen Mab,' with the notes, Ruskin's 'Unto this Last,' Morris's 'Dream of John Ball,' Tolstoi's "Essay on Art,' and Darwin's 'Expression of the Emotions in Man and the Lower Animals.' £2 will not go much farther than this, if so far; so I close the list here with the warning that it is only one list out of many that might be made.

Finally, no studious cottager should be content with a £2 shelf of books. He should use his vote to compel the Parish, Rural District, and County Councils to establish public rate-supported reading-rooms in all our villages, in which each cottager could find plenty of books which he could never afford to purchase for himself. Any society of working-men desiring to study social, political, and historical questions, can send to the Fabian Society, 276, Strand, London, W. C., for the loan of a box of the newest and best books about them, at a cost of half-a-crown and the carriage of the book box. A hundred of these boxes are at present in active circulation. No doubt, other societies do the same thing. The £2 shelf, therefore, need not be encumbered by expensive theological and political works which can be obtained from propagandist societies.

Yours, &c.,
G. Bernard Shaw

AS YOU DON'T LIKE IT

[*Farnham, Haslemere & Hindhead Herald,* 15 July 1899.]

Sir,—May I, as a dramatic critic of some experience, be allowed to volunteer a pronouncement on the late open-air performance of "As you like it" in Sir Frederick Pollock's woods on Hindhead?[1] I need not add any compliments to those which have already been paid to the merits of that achievement. Often as I have seen the play performed by the most accomplished profes-

[2]William Cobbett's 1829 work was entitled *Advice to Young Men.* Peter Kropotkin's political tract was called *An Appeal to the Young* (first published c. 1881 as *Aux jeunes gens*).
[1]An amateur performance of the forest scenes of *As You Like It* had been presented on 5 July.

sional comedians of England and America, I have never before heard such rapturous and unanimous praise lavished by an apparently delighted audience on everybody concerned. I foresee two possible results of this. One is that the performers will at once abandon their present profession and ruin themselves by going on the stage. I have known that happen on less provocation. The other, and the only one I propose to take into account now, is that they will repeat the effort. My dread lest they should do so under the very erroneous impression that their last attempt cannot be improved upon nerves me to venture on a word of criticism.

I feel I must disappoint them at the outset by saying nothing about the acting, except that I have seen all the parts worse done at one time or another by professional actors at first-rate London theatres. Let that suffice for such flattery as can be extracted from it in view of the present condition of the English stage. But I must add that I have never seen a more exasperatingly amateurish presentation of the play. What is an amateur actor? In the proper sense of the word he (or she) is an actor who plays for love instead of for money. But in the sense which has been fastened on it by the misdeeds of the amateurs themselves, it means an actor who is not merely a bad actor (plenty of professional actors are that), but one who is bad with the special and unbearable badness produced by imitating the theatre instead of imitating life. The able professional in all the arts tries to conceal the artificiality of the technical processes he is forced to employ. The author tries to avoid being "literary;" the actor dreads being "theatrical." The amateur does exactly the reverse. The more he can denaturalize himself the more literary he is, the more painty he is, the more theatrical he is, the nearer he feels to success. On the stage he will not speak with his own voice, will not behave with his own manners, will not wear clothes that fit him, will persist in trying to identify himself with the unreal character in the play, instead of giving the poor phantom life by identifying it with his own real self. He is, therefore, often better when he is deliberately imitating his favourite professional actor than when he is trying to disembody himself into what he calls his "conception" of his part. In short, he believes that an actor is one who successfully pretends to be somebody else, like a criminal evading a policeman by means of a disguise. An actor is really one who has cultivated and intensified *himself* to such a degree that he can persuade audiences to pretend that they see other people embodied in him. Thus acting, in the amateur sense, is the one thing that the skilled actor avoids above all things. And acting, in the skilled actor's sense, is a thing that the amateur would regard as the abnegation of acting.

Whoever grasps this distinction will understand why it is that no fairly presentable performer ever fails as Hamlet or Rosalind. Every man believes himself to be a Hamlet; every woman a Rosalind. Consequently, in playing the parts, they do not "act" in the amateur sense; they try to be their best selves, and generally succeed, whereas in Othello and Lady Macbeth they generally make themselves ridiculous. "As you like it" was carefully written by an experienced dramatist to make the most of this natural law; consequently a version of "As you like it," with all the seriously unflattering characters left out, as they were on Hindhead, could not but "act itself," even with amateurs. "Thank you for nothing" is not a polite speech: but it is not the business of a critic to be polite. Good manners in him consist in sincerity, not in smooth speech.

But why do I call the representation amateurish when I admit that the play, as cut, carried the actors safely over that pitfall? I will explain. Weary of the theatre and its conventions, its unreal scenes, and false lights, and stuffy air, I went to the Hindhead performance full of pleasant anticipations. "Here," I said to myself, "Rosalind" will tread, not on nailed boards, but on real mossy sod. Here there will be no footlights and battens, but a real sunlight—"no enemy but winter and rough weather." Here the banished duke will really sit under the shade of melancholy boughs, and breathe scented airs high above the sea level. Birds will sing; crickets will chirp; Sir Frederick's woods, not being amateurs, will not pretend to be anything but what they are, and I, consequently, will be able to pretend that they are the forest of Arden. Full of these joyous hopes, I hastened to the place of performance, and behold—a cottage piano! My heart sank; I knew that people who would put a piano in the forest of Arden would do anything. I turned with a pang of dread to look for footlights; and there, sure enough, was an imitation "float," ridiculously made of bracken leaves, and white soup plates full of cut roses. Then I knew what I was in for; and the event fulfilled my worst apprehensions. Amiens sang "Blow, blow" to the piano, the setting being ultra-19th century, in the style of Blumenthal.[2] Orlan-

[2]Jacob Blumenthal, pianist to Queen Victoria, was a popular songwriter.

do's sonnets were represented by sheets of the smartest Bond Street notepaper, with the address and the nearest railway station neatly printed at the top, the page being otherwise virgin. Some of the men's costumes were too absurd for even an opera chorus. Silvius, a personable gentleman who spoke his lines excellently, struggled in vain against the comic effect of a tunic made for a much shorter man. The indigent Corin, who might quite fitly have worn the gaiters and smock which are still to be seen on old agricultural labourers in England, wore a thin Cheapside tunic with two rows of velvet, and, of course, tights. Everybody wore tights. It is impossible to persuade an amateur that he is acting unless he has tights on. It may be obvious to any gamekeeper that no man could possibly face the wear and weather of a forest life and keep his voice, or for the matter of that his life, without good boots, breeches, and buckskin. But the amateur, because he has seen this ignored in some silly or impecunious theatre, ignores it in Sir Frederick Pollock's woods, and stands there, like a ghastly travesty of a mediaeval tailor on strike, making sensible men long for a hearty shower of rain to wash away his folly. Need I add that the foresters' weapons were of the most aggressively theatrical absurdity. The man who killed the deer had providently borrowed an assegai; but all the rest had the familiar tin-headed impostures which pass muster poorly enough by gas light, but which, under the sun of heaven, simply insult the spectator's understanding. The village carpenter and blacksmith would have been glad to turn out a few credible pikes for the sum charged by the costumier for the hire of his stagey arsenal; but no, that would not have looked like the real—theatre! Is it to be wondered at that men thus made ridiculous could not walk the woods like real foresters, and could only stand staring in fascinated desperation at the very persons it was their chief duty to ignore; to wit, the audience?

After all this, it did not need the wanton mutilation of the text to put one out of temper. Even the late Mr. Augustin Daly had more respect for Shakespear than to cut out the best dialogues of Touchstone, and many of Rosalind's most quaintly pretty lines. It will not bear remembering, this version of the play; I find that even after a week it still makes me splenetic. I went to it in the most amiable disposition towards everybody concerned; at the end no prudent person would have trusted me with a thunderbolt.

Do me the justice, Mr. Editor, to remark that I am complaining of nothing that can be excused on the ground that the wrongdoers were amateurs. The acting was as good, and in several instances more than as good, as I expected or had any right to expect. If Shakespear had been present to superintend the rehearsals, and the amateurs could have been persuaded to do what he told them, he could have produced a quite adequate performance with the talent at his disposal. But this is no excuse for faults due to a wilful disregard of sincerity and good sense. Our Hindhead and Haslemere population makes an almost oppressive parade of its devotion to art. Go where I will in the neighbourhood, I cannot escape from Bedford Park architecture, photographs from the early Italian masters, Morris or pseudo-Morris wall papers, and clangorous grand pianos ready for Schumann and Brahms at a moment's notice. My opinion of a good deal of this ready-made art I shall keep to myself until I return to town. But I cannot help asking what is the use of staring at photographs of the figures of Benozzo Gozzoli,[3] if, when it comes to dressing a Shakespear play, you cannot see that your shabby tunic is several inches too short for you, and your spear as foolish as the baton of an undertaker's mute?[4] What does your knowledge of music come to if you cannot sing in the forest of Arden without a piano banging a modern drawingroom accompaniment on the grass? What is the current fashionable chatter about poetry and Shakespear worth, when gentlemen who would rather die than walk down Bond Street in my hat, will wear any second-hand misfit in one of Shakespear's plays? What sort of devotion to Nature is that which tries to make a real wood look like a real stage?

It is time to pause for a reply, Mr. Editor. The best form the reply can possibly take is a repetition of the performance with its follies left out.

Yours truly,
G. Bernard Shaw

[3]Fifteenth-century Florentine painter and goldsmith; notable as a pictorial narrator.

[4]A mortician's assistant posing as a mourner, silent from grief.

"THE GUILTY PARTIES IN CHINA"

[All during the summer of 1900 rumors of a popular rising in China—later to be called the Boxer Rebellion—circulated in England. On 16 July the *Daily Mail* published a telegram purporting to be an account of the slaughter of members of the foreign legations in Peking. The *Saturday Review* in an unsigned leading article on 21 July urged "acts of retribution," including the possibility that "Peking should be . . . effaced." The article called for "the defeat of the Government," for "it will not be till the flags of the Allies float over the gates and palaces of Peking that the lesson will have been driven finally home." Shaw's attack on this leader was published in the *Saturday Review* on 28 July.]

Sir,—In the article with the above title in your issue of 21 July, which is not signed, and might therefore be taken as expressing the policy of the *Saturday Review* if the sentiments expressed in it were less monstrous, the writer observes in passing, with a calm worthy of Mr. Gilbert's Mikado, that "the decapitation of Prince Tuan and Tung Fuh-siang[1] on the scene of their crime will be among the first and most obvious acts of retribution." He goes on to suggest that Peking should be "effaced, and a tablet should be erected to record that here once stood the accursed city in which the rites of hospitality due to the stranger from afar were violated by the murder of men, women and children of a status which nations in all ages have regarded as privileged and inviolable."

May I ask why, if we accept the "obviousness" of retaliation and terrorism as a necessary part of English policy, we are to let Tuan and Tung off with mere decapitation in a country where an offender is not held to be really severely punished unless he is cut into a thousand pieces? What has become of the humour and invention of the *Saturday Review*, that it makes so tame a proposal? Why not inoculate the two foreign devils with cancer or hydrophobia, or sew up glass tubes of croton oil in them and then break the tubes, or rack them with electric currents, or drag them to pieces with motor cars, or otherwise prove to the Chinese how far our civilisation excels theirs in the intensity of its torments and the

[1]Prince Tuan, the violently antiforeign president of the Tsungli Yamen (Foreign Affairs Board) and court favorite of the empress dowager, was supreme commander of the Boxer hordes. General Tung Fu-hsiang, an ex-bandit who also stood high in the empress's favor, was leader of the Kansu Mohammedan army.

modernity of its methods? And when we undertake the "effacement" of "accursed cities," is it wise to indulge in sentimental inscriptions about women and children in view of the fact that cities of a million inhabitants cannot be effaced without inflicting considerable inconvenience, amounting in many cases to death, on the women and children who inhabit the city? I put it to you, Mr. Editor, that a writer should be as careful not to mix his religions and moral systems as not to mix his metaphors. If we are going back to the methods of Peter the Blackguard and Timour the Tartar, let us face the fact that we cannot take the humanitarian sympathies and indignations of Lord Shaftesbury[2] back with us. Indeed, I do not see why we should desire to be troubled with them, since they must needs seem the most snivelling weakness to a stalwart whose great revenge has stomach for effaced cities and chopped-off heads. Why, Imperial Peter put pregnant women on the rack, and hung to the window bars of his sisters' prison cells the decomposing corpses of their accomplices. He had the courage and logic of your contributor's passions.

There is, however, one of Lord Shaftesbury's points of view which deserves a little more consideration from the *Saturday;* and that is the high Tory point of view. If our foreign policy—or for the matter of that our domestic policy—is to be a mere matter of retaliation, terrorism and bad blood, then it is clear that the most violent criminal at present in our prisons is more fit to be our Foreign Minister than Lord Salisbury,[3] who is probably more or less weakened by humanitarian superstitions. For all we know to the contrary, Lord Salisbury may be of opinion that the object of civilized government, and the reason for its being aristocratic, is that without it the world would be abandoned to the passionate delusions and rancours of the fighting, flogging, duelling, torturing, foreigner-hating, retaliating, human-sacrificing, sentimentalising plebeians who, if they were allowed, would spend their lives savagely punishing with one hand the atrocities which they are savagely committing with the other. An English gentleman may hold that opinion without being a Christian, or anything eccentric

[2]Presumably Anthony Ashley Cooper (d. 1885), seventh Earl of Shaftesbury, a social reformer who worked in the middle of the nineteenth century to ease the miseries of the working classes in the face of the Industrial Revolution.

[3]Robert Arthur Talbot Gascoyne-Cecil, third Marquis of Salisbury, had been prime minister and was at this moment the foreign secretary.

or impracticable of that sort. The Socialists are very emphatic on the subject: in these days of democracy it is only the Socialists, from Karl Marx forward, who are still Tory enough to impartially denounce the "lumpen-proletariat" and "canaille" as no less politically immoral than the bourgeoisie. Events have now ripened sufficiently to force all men of any character to ask themselves whether modern democracy means that all the ability and nobility in the nation is to be employed in holding a candle to its mediocrity and its mob, instead of in genuine leadership. If the English nation is going to treat the Chinese nation as a drunken English navvy would treat a drunken Chinese one who had injured him, then in the name of common sense give the navvy Lord Salisbury's portfolio, and leave Lord Salisbury free to study in his laboratory. But don't call that Toryism or Conservatism. It is nothing but the most horrible, most cowardly mobocracy that can be imagined; and the mob itself will be the first to despise it.

The war in China is part of a series of inevitable wars for the establishment of an international level of civilization. If the Western level of civilization gets reduced by the passions which war excites to the level of the refractory civilizations which it attacks, the world-force which is flinging the West on the East will vanish; and the victory will be to the hardiest and skilfullest slayer—a distinction which we hope belongs to the Chinaman rather than to the Englishman. We are already handicapped by the fact that we have disgraced ourselves by frightful relapses from the little eminence we have struggled to. We blew men from the cannon's mouth in the ecstasy of our terror and vindictive rage during the Indian Mutiny. We dug up the Mahdi's corpse the other day and mutilated it: an offence against civilization which no Chinaman could underbid. During the South African war we have listened with far too much tolerance to the delirious rancours and terrors of writers who have wrought themselves to the pitch of believing that the world consists of a fox called the British Empire and a pack of hounds called the Powers, who will tear it to pieces unless it buys a dozen more sets of false teeth. All these relapses are symptoms of cowardice, a complaint with which we are greatly afflicted nowadays in consequence of the nervous modern ways of living, which have made an end of our old stolidity. And the more nervous we grow, the more we asseverate our indomitable courage, and throw Victoria Crosses about until they become the reward, not of valour, but of the unexpected and reassuring absence of positive pusillanimity. We are belying the ground on which all our wars must now be fought: to wit, the superiority of British civilization to the civilizations that come into conflict with it. That ground is cut from under our feet by every act and impulse of ours that is a *common* act and impulse instead of being a noble one. War being in itself a degradation to civilization, it is when war begins that the standard of civilized instinct must be most jealously upheld. The customary terms of morality: namely, that the Englishman will behave quite humanely as long as nobody provokes him to be a savage, will not do for a nation under arms; for there is a martial law of morals which is far more important than the martial law of discipline. Revenge, under any extremity of provocation, must be absolutely barred; for there is no end to it but the destruction of the whole human race. Unless a nation can keep its head and its heart when its men are being shot from beneath white flags, when its women are being ravished and its children slaughtered by foreigners drunk with its blood, then that nation has not the moral grit nor the intellectual self-control that will win in the long run; and its reliance on its pluck, or whatever other schoolboy name it may give to its rage, will save it no more than Dervish pluck saved the Khalifa.[4]

I am sorry to sermonise in this fashion, Mr. Editor; but I am convinced that you have many readers who do not want to decapitate their enemies and efface foreign towns, and who are growing more and more alarmed at the license now accorded to the expression of passions which in the eighteenth century would, in *Saturday Review* society, have stamped their propagandists as buccaneers. Please remember that only the other day we actually executed an elephant in London for murder;[5] and that from executing animals to burning witches, torturing witnesses, and sacking towns, is a much shorter step than any that lay between the British Empire and barbarism twenty years ago.

Yours, &c.,
G. Bernard Shaw

[4]Abdullah el Taaisha ("The Khalifa"), Arab leader of the dervishes in the Sudan, succeeded Mohammed Ahmed as Mahdi in 1885; he was defeated at Omdurman by Kitchener in 1898 and killed by British forces a year later.
[5]On 18 February 1900 an elephant, "Charlie," escaped from a menagerie at the Crystal Palace and trampled an attendant to death; a London firm of gunmakers was brought in by the police and used five guns to dispatch him.

THE HOUSING CONFERENCE

[On 30 and 31 July 1900, Shaw attended a conference on working-class housing sponsored by the Sanitary Institute; his letter on housing problems appeared in the *Daily Express* on 3 August.]

Sir,—There is much truth in your observation that poor men cannot afford to live in London, and that rich men can. For example, the man with twenty-five shillings a week and four children, whose wife very kindly showed me on Monday the three-room flat which is let to them by the London County Council at Millbank for ten shillings a week, is very clearly a man who cannot afford to live in London.

And the Mayor of Richmond, who entertained the conference so hospitably yesterday afternoon in the beautiful grounds of his riverside house, is equally clearly a rich man who can afford to live in London. But in perverse defiance of the economic harmonies, this obstinate pair of men will not change houses. The poor man persists in living in London, where he cannot afford to live, because his work is in London, and its hours do not leave any margin for travelling. The rich man, who can afford to live in London, lives at Richmond because he likes it better.

How do you propose to deal with this situation? Let me remind you that the perversity is aggravated by the fact that the poor man pays a higher rent, calculated either per foot of cubic space occupied or as a proportion of his income, than the rich man.

The people who both can and will go out of London if houses, guaranteed sanitary and soundly built, are provided for them belong to the middle class, great numbers of whom are poorer than the artisan class. They would leave behind them streets of houses which could easily be made more habitable than these monstrous and horrible block dwellings can ever be. If ever you have to live in a slum, Mr. Editor, take my advice: live in a horizontal, not a perpendicular, one.

Yours, &c.,
G. Bernard Shaw

CIVIC PURITY

[*St. Pancras Guardian,* 18 April 1902.]

Sir,—The report in your last issue of a so-called investiture by the Mayor of the members of the St. Pancras Borough Council with "badges of office" presented by Mr Alderman Regnart,[1] and your comment on my appearance at the Council without a badge, makes it necessary for me to explain my position in your columns. Both the report and the comment are founded on a misapprehension of what has taken place. There is no such thing as a badge of office for St. Pancras Borough Councillors. The official insignia of the Council are the mace, the robes of the Aldermen and the mayoral robe and chain. No other insignia have been adopted by the Council; and the fact that at the last Council meeting several Councillors wore an ornament presented to them by Mr Alderman Regnart no more constitutes that ornament a badge of office than if it had taken the form of a watch or a scarf pin. My own reason for refusing to accept this private and unofficial decoration is that I do not see why there should be one rule for a sanitary inspector and another for a Borough Councillor. If a sanitary inspector took five pounds worth of gold from Mr Alderman Regnart, I should move his immediate dismissal; and no eloquent tributes to the disinterestedness of Mr Regnart's generosity, much less the production of a written undertaking by the inspector to return the five pounds whenever called upon, would weigh with me for a moment. Mr Regnart represents a firm which contemplates extensive building operations in the ward I represent; and it is in the power of the Borough Council, by slackness in the enforcement of its sanitary by-laws, by taking a lenient view of street obstruction by vans, and, above all, by showing favour in the matter of assessment to rates, to make it worth any large firm's while to give the Council not only gold, but diamonds. It is to no purpose to say that Mr Regnart never dreamt of such considerations; that he desires only to heighten the imposing effect of the Council's sittings; and that Messrs Maple's complaints of our assessments prove that we do not under-assess them. What would be thought of a judge who took presents from litigants and justified

[1]Horace G. Regnart, an alderman of the Borough of St. Pancras and one of its leading merchants, was president of Maple & Co. He was knighted in 1907.

them by saying that they were entirely disinterested and that he always charged against the litigant who made the present? The Borough Council is no less bound to be above suspicion than the Lord Chief Justice. It is the successor of a Vestry in which presents were openly accepted by committee chairmen from contractors; and I do not see that such presentations were a whit more scandalous than the spectacle of our Assessment Committee going to Tottenham Court-road to assess Messrs Maple with £5 worth of Messrs Maple's gold hanging round their necks.

Until last week I was under the impression that I had convinced my colleagues by these arguments that our indebtedness to Mr Regnart must stop at the mace, which is a public and not a personal ornament. The matter had been brought before the Parliamentary Committee; and the members were so impressed by the view of the case for which I acted as spokesman, that the subject was dropped without even the technically obligatory report to the Council. Some months had elapsed when I suddenly received, in a holiday week which I usually spend on the Continent, three days' notice of the unofficial meeting reported in your columns. As I happened to be in England, I was able to send a formal protest to the Town Clerk; but it is unfortunate that the time for the presentation should have been so chosen as to give the scoffers at municipal prestige an excuse for calling it not merely unofficial but almost clandestine.

I, of course, quite understand that the feelings which actuated the Mayor, the Town Clerk, and the Aldermen were entirely amiable. The badges have been in their hands for many months past; and the question was what to do with them. It seemed ungracious to throw them back on Mr Regnart's hands. There was reason to believe that a majority of the Councillors frankly wanted them and could see no harm in accepting them. The simple thing would have been to bring forward a resolution formally adopting them as official insignia, and thanking Mr Regnart for his munificence. But it was known that in that case the motion would be opposed, and that one speech at least (my own) would spoil the harmony of the proceedings. Accordingly, it was decided to make the presentation unofficially, by holding a technically private reception of the Councillors by the Mayor, in the Town Hall, at a moment when there was every probability of the dissentients being out of reach. To such a reception the dissentients could in any case come only as guests of the Mayor and Mr Regnart. This good-natured evasion of the difficulty ends, as might have been foreseen, in forcing me to beg the wider circulation of your columns for what would otherwise, probably, have dropped still-born in an unreported speech.

My fellow Councillors will, I hope, understand that I am not accusing them of corruption in accepting the badge. But I am sometimes driven to wonder whether the intelligent corruption of Tammany[2] can really be as mischievous as the political childishness and inconsequence, the thoughtless insensibility to public opinion, and the easy going satisfaction with a gentlemanly good fellowship as the highest virtue demanded by public life, which the Vestry has bequeathed to us. At all events here have we in St. Pancras shewn a way by which every Aldermanship in London may be openly sold to whoever bids highest in solid gold for the honour. I hope the example will not be followed. I venture to say that there is not a ratepayer in St. Pancras who believes that the impartiality of the Council as between himself and Mr Regnart's firm will be unaffected by this "distribution" (I quote the word from the letter of invitation to the presentation) of gold ornaments to the Councillors; and I believe that the Councillors who refuse the badge will suffer neither in the confidence of their constituents nor in the cordiality of their personal relations with Mr Regnart, whose ability and experience they value as highly as their more compliant colleagues value his generosity.

Yours, &c.,
G. Bernard Shaw

LOST FAITHS

[In a lecture on 25 January 1903, Shaw had given his audience a sample of the views on the superman and eugenics expounded in his as yet unpublished *Man and Superman*. Brief accounts of the lecture, a standard feature of the London newspapers of the time, apparently led various correspondents to write rebuttals to the newspapers. Shaw's reply to two of them appeared in the *Daily News* on 2 February.]

Sir,—I am always deeply touched by the anxiety of the public to claim my personal authority for their own opinions and habits. The eagerness with which our cannibal newspaper correspondents

[2]Tammany Hall in New York was still a byword for dishonest machine politics.

announce from time to time that I have given up vegetarianism (or, at least, that Tolstoy is dying of it, and that I ought to give it up) shows the value that is attached to my example. It is now claimed that I have given up Socialism. I am sorry to disappoint the Unsocialists; but, as a matter of fact, the lecture which has provoked this correspondence was founded on my conviction that no tolerable social life—that is to say, no improvement on the present abominable condition of civilized mankind—is possible without Socialism. And by Socialism I mean not only municipal gas and water, but the complete acceptance of Equality as the condition of human association, and Communism as the condition of human industry. This conviction, far from having been weakened by the practical, political, and social experience I have gained since the days when, as a young man, I preached it as a matter of abstract economic theory, has grown with my growth, and become strong enough to keep me rigidly to its point whilst the general Socialist movement has been swaying and wavering and wobbling and splitting in all directions before the transient gusts of pro-Boerism, anti-Anglican School Boardism, and the rest of the accidents of party politics.

The general proposition of my lecture was that the human species has not evolved perceptibly within historic time, and that it is therefore idle to believe that we who are now living will or can do otherwise than the men of the oldest civilizations of which we have any record. The point is of particular importance at the present moment, because we have just reached that point in civilization at which Empires have always broken down. I mean the point at which our social organization, partly by growth, partly by the conquests which that growth enables it to achieve, has become so vast and complex that its management overtaxes the political capacity of its human units, requiring from them a magnanimity both of character and intellect which the average man not only does not possess himself, but which he will not tolerate in his statesmen. And this, please observe, is not because he does not approve of magnanimity as he understands it, but because a magnanimity that transcends his own seems to him not to be magnanimity at all, but simply a bewildering and monstrous moral perversity.

As a melancholy proof that men's conduct remains the same in spite of the warnings of even the most special personal experiences and the most disinterested personal character, I need only cite the fact that Mr. G. J. Holyoake and Mr. Herbert Burrows[1] are to-day writing to the newspapers about a lecture of an hour's duration, which they have not heard, on the strength of a report only a few lines long. That is to say, they are acting precisely as any Primrose League[2] secretary of 21 might be expected to act. They cannot help it. I should do the same myself. But now that they have come into the field, what is their opinion on the main point I have raised? They have been all their lives lecturing, agitating, organizing, preaching in season and out of season a more excellent way than the beaten track in which the human race has trudged as far back as we can trace it. Can they point to the slightest sign of their more excellent way being taken? Have they been able to take it themselves? Would a foreign observer, unable to understand the language spoken by Mr. Holyoake, Mr. Burrows, and myself, and therefore unacquainted with our views and aspirations, gather from our mode of life that we differed in any respect whatever from our next-door neighbours? Dare we say that if any of the Federations and Societies and Leagues and Churches that we have known or helped to organize were substituted for the House of Commons, or any other public body, it would be free from any one of the failings that such bodies present at present, or that it could go to the full length of its social theories in the teeth of public opinion any more than, for instance, Cromwell could?

I am aware, by the way, that changes do occur; that grievances do get remedied as the under dog becomes the upper dog in the political strife; and that discoveries of the physical properties of things accumulate and enable us to fight with high explosives and to gamble through the telephone. But I must not repeat my whole lecture here; nor, indeed, do I feel disposed to anticipate objections which assume that I am a fool and an ignoramus, and that I have left out of account all the optimistic commonplaces of Macaulay's history. I defined very carefully on the platform the limits within which improvements are possible without any further evolution in human capacity or character; and my conclu-

[1]Holyoake was the inventor of the word "secularism" in 1854 and a longtime radical propagandist and publisher. Burrows was a member of the Social Democratic Federation and one of Shaw's most frequent critics. His lecture "Man and the Superman: Bernard Shaw on Himself and the Universe," on 11 October 1903, led to correspondence by Shaw and Burrows in *Justice* on 21 November.
[2]A conservative association founded in memory of Benjamin Disraeli.

sions were stated with the very fullest discount for the possibilities of mere reforms.

The remedy I proposed was obvious enough. What is required is a new sort of man. We have produced new sorts of horses, new sorts of apples, new sorts of flowers. We have always been trying to produce a new sort of man by the imposture which we call education. Imagine trying to educate a mediaeval warhorse into a modern racehorse, or a crab-apple into a Ribston Pippin! Who, pray, is to educate the educators? We must breed our new sort of man; and until we do that Mr. Holyoake and Mr. Burrows may preach themselves black in the face; the dog will still return to his vomit and the sow that was washed to her wallowing in the mire.

Yours, &c.,
G. Bernard Shaw

FLOGGING IN THE NAVY

[Flogging, a traditional form of punishment in the British navy, came under periodic attack. By 1904, the Humanitarian League was campaigning against it and asking for a parliamentary investigation. Shaw, in a letter in *The Times* on 2 September, alluded to a recent naval punishment of two dozen strokes of the birch and dismissal from the service of a boy who had stolen two postal orders. On succeeding days various correspondents to *The Times,* notably Vice-Admiral C. C. Penrose Fitzgerald, debated with Shaw about the merits of flogging. Shaw's rebuttal, summarizing these disparate arguments in the first paragraph, was published in *The Times* of 11 October.]

Sir,—This correspondence has been so fertile in quick changes that even my professionally-trained dramatic powers make it difficult for me to follow it. We have had all the familiar stage conventions of the Navy—the breezy, choleric, landlubber-despising, rope's-ending old salt; the pious, simple seaman with his Bible open in his hand at the Proverbs of Solomon and his thick-rimmed spectacles on the binnacle; and the rough seadog who bites on a bullet and takes his two dozen as a civilian takes a cold bath, scorning alike the "morbidly hysterical and sensitive" lads who do not revel in a flogging and the feeble-minded civilian cranks who have always supposed that the whole point of flogging lay in the floggee's objection to it. And now we have the

Cornish fisherman whose lads would scorn an unflogged Navy, and who regard the difference between a village loafer and a smart seaman as due solely to the difference in poignancy between the parental strap or boot toe and the ship's corporal's cane.

I submit to your correspondents, without the smallest respect, that all this is claptrap, good enough, perhaps, for a nautical melodrama in an inland booth, but out of place in a serious discussion in the columns of *The Times*. Let me try to formulate a few propositions which are, at least, worth arguing.

The radical objection to flogging is not its cruelty, but the fact that it can never be cleared from the suspicion that it is a vicious sport disguised as reformatory justice. Imprisonment is much crueller—so atrociously cruel, in fact, that it is endlessly amazing to any humane person that it should not only be tolerated, but dealt out wholesale in periods of years at a time without shocking any one. But, cruel as it is, it is at least free from the taint of corrupt passion. It does not gratify even the vilest of us to look at Pentonville Prison. When the police raid a disorderly house they never find there the convict cell and the tin of skilly. They always find the implements of the ship's corporal.

In ordinary civil life it is possible to be too particular on this point. But on board ship, and in prison, the moral conditions are morbid, especially in modern navies, which are physically unhealthy, our battleships being incipient consumption hospitals. When a Cornish lad is cuffed by his mother, or when he provokes his father to give him a trouncing which no ship's corporal could improve on, there may be no great harm done; and there is certainly no question of the transaction being a disguised debauch. But any one who will argue from this that it is wise or decent to take a ship's crew, consisting of adolescent lads and men who are cooped up for long periods together without the society of women, and parade them to witness the operation which has already been sufficiently described in your columns, must be a person either utterly ignorant of the real difficulties of the situation, or else so coarsened and hardened by the results of disregarding them as to care very little what a sailor is, provided he has been thrashed into technical efficiency and prompt obedience.

The Chinese, inveterately democratic and logical, flog their admirals as well as their humbler heroes. And certainly, if flogging is all that our admirals say it is, the quarter deck should be strenuously kept up to the mark by the cat and the birch; for an admiral can send a battleship to the bottom when a boy can only hurt his own digestion by a clandestine cigarette. But does the public realize that we actually do allow the captain of a ship to be condemned, without any misconduct on his part, to the cruellest of all tortures—solitary confinement? So absurd and inhuman are the superstitious rites which we call discipline, that the attainment of command practically makes the captain a solitary prisoner in his cabin, and forbids any man in the ship to treat him as a fellow-creature. I submit quite seriously that this is the simple explanation of the fact that whereas men who command railways, who direct great engineering works, who lead political parties, who edit newspapers, who organize industrial combinations, show in their conduct and utterances all the mental superiority which their functions involve, naval officers who have passed through the ordeal of command write and talk like short-tempered nurses or common sailors. This is not often brought into public notice; but we do not forget the appalling catastrophe of the sinking of the Victoria by the Camperdown.[1] Such milder lights as have twinkled occasionally since then on the quarter-deck intellect from letters to the Press are not reassuring.

It must be remembered that it is in time of peace that all this so-called discipline produces its worst effects. In time of war discipline keeps itself; and the stupidest officer is nerved to extraordinary efforts by the tremendous stress of battle. But in time of peace and fine weather, when there is nothing to do but housemaid your ship, scrubbing clean boards, polishing speckless metal, and driving sulky and bored officers and men through factitious struggles with sham emergencies, the strain on every one's temper is very great; and it is then that the flogging system does its worst.

Unfortunately flogging can always depend on the support of timid people who pass their lives in terror of children, of servants, of soldiers, of sailors, of tramps, of labourers, of dogs, of anybody or anything that can strike or bite or rebel. These people call themselves lovers of discipline, and clamour for whips and muzzles and complete systems of intimidation. I am sorry for them. The bravest of us are only brave relatively; and none of us can afford to despise a coward. But the cowards would be the first to suffer from the reign of terror they are always clamouring for.

[1]In June 1893, while the British fleet was in the Mediterranean, engaged in tactical exercises, the flagship *Victoria* was rammed by the *Camperdown,* with a subsequent loss of three hundred sixty-four officers and men.

They had better continue to be terrified by shadows than get something real to fear.

There are only two possible methods of keeping order in a ship or anywhere else. One is to give everybody a *status*, with a certain responsibility and respect attached to the *status*, as well as fair pay and honourable conditions. Under such circumstances 99 out of 100 men and lads will keep themselves in reasonable order without further pressure than that of public opinion and their own self-respect. The hundredth, who will not, can be discharged, and, in the last social extremity, killed. The other system is intimidation. Under it half your forces are wasted in coercing the other half; and the loss through friction and bad blood is enormous, without counting the horrible unhappiness of it. It is also politically impossible to carry it out with any thoroughness nowadays. But perhaps the main objection to it from the point of view of the subordination is that any fool can keep order (of a sort) with a whip in his hand, whilst under the other system the officer must govern by character, or rather make his men govern themselves by character, so that the officers become a highly selected class. The flogging system would never have flourished but for the old practice of giving commands to men of family, officers neither born nor made, who could not, like Paul Jones, do without the cat, because they were not Paul Joneses, and should never have been placed in command of anybody. The case against flogging is thus seen to be exactly parallel with the case against industrial sweating. It is true that some officers cannot command without flogging, just as some employers cannot make profits without sweating. The effect of the abolition of flogging or the passing of a Factory Act is to force these officers and employers into retirement or into subordinate positions to make room for those who are able to succeed under the raised conditions. That is how the national standard of character and conduct goes up from time to time. The opposition of many officers and employers to the process is natural enough. When they tell us that they cannot succeed without the cane, the birch, and the "Song of the Shirt,"[2] there is no reason to disbelieve them. Abler men can and will—that is enough for us.

[2]Thomas Hood's 1843 poem, the lament of a widowed mother laboring over piecework shirtmaking, had been inspired by a report in *The Times* on 26 October of that year which drew attention to working-class conditions in London. The poem was instantly famous.

Finally, let us not suppose that what is called "perfect discipline" is possible under any system. The officers in a ship cannot have things all their own way. Sailors die inconveniently; captains go melancholy mad inconveniently; men give way to momentary flashes of temper; scurvy, smallpox, fogs, typhoons, and other unlooked-for things upset the routine of a ship and interfere with the plans of her commanders. It is of no use to say that we will not stand these things—we have to stand them; and even if among them must be included so unnerving and cataclysmic an upheaval of all order as "a young monkey cocking a snook" at an undignified admiral, the admiral had better pretend not to see it, and the nation had better replace him with a dignified admiral as soon as possible.

Yours, &c.,
G. Bernard Shaw

G.B.S. AND NIHILISM

[*The Star,* 4 February 1905.]

Sir,—Some person, presumably a Russian police-agent, has entrapped two London newspapers into stating that I "introduced myself as a Nihilist" at the meeting in Queen's Hall on the 1st instant. As your paper is one of the victims, will you be so good as to give publicity to my flat contradiction of this most impudent report?

Nihilism, with its interesting personalities, its literary turn, its long roll of martyrs and self-sacrifices, and its occasional picturesquely explosive murders, no doubt appeals strongly to the romantic imagination of the English middle-classes. I have no sympathy whatever with it. Any fool can be a martyr; any enthusiastic girl student can be driven to self-sacrifice by the apparent hopelessness of sensible and effective action. It is a crime to encourage such wanton suicide by admiring and applauding it. If the people of Russia want self-sacrifice, the existing order seems to me to afford them all the opportunities they can reasonably desire; and a revolution is (in that case) uncalled for. My own political philosophy is that of the Tsar and the Grand Dukes, though I happen to differ with them as to the most desirable form of government. I quite agree with them that it is their business to sacrifice, not themselves, but their opponents. I agree with them that to deliver over their country without a struggle to Nihilism would be a crime, and to trust to a mob unintelligent enough to attempt to vanquish troops by waving icons at them a folly.

The revolution in Russia has clearly to fight the Tsar; and the Tsar, as a gentleman and an autocrat, has to fight the revolution, whether he likes it or not. The sooner the revolution faces that fact, and gives up the study of Turgenieff's novels, and the really dastardly notion that it is heroic to get college lasses and lads into ruinous trouble as romantic conspirators, the sooner Russia will get a more liberal constitution.

It is clearly England's business to show her sympathy with the revolution, unless, indeed, we are on the side of autocracy against our own system, in which case we had better change it. It is just as proper for an Englishman to send money to the revolutionists to buy cartridges as it was to send it to Count Tolstoy to buy loaves in the days of the Russian famine. And, if it were tactically expedient, it would be just as proper for the Government to make war on the Tsar in the interests of the disfranchised of St. Petersburg as it was to make war on President Kruger in the interests of the disfranchised of Johannesburg.

Yours, &c.,
G. Bernard Shaw

BERNARD SHAW ABASHED

[*Daily News,* 17 April 1905]

Sir,—I am unspeakably abashed to find that I have written you a reproachful letter calling you to account for a blunder made, not by the *Daily News,* but by the *Daily Chronicle.*[1] I make no attempt to extenuate my carelessness. As the American Vigilance Committee said to the widow, when they had lynched her husband for a horse stolen by somebody else, the laugh is with you. I am very sorry, and beg you to excuse an error committed when I was blinded by an intolerable sense of wrong.

I am too much out of countenance now to pursue the quarrel with the *Daily Chronicle,* but that is no reason why I should not pick a fresh one with Mr. Chesterton. In your issue of Saturday Mr. Chesterton[2] occupies three-quarters of a column, under

[1]Shaw's earlier letter, published on 15 April, had accused the *Daily News* of misrepresenting his views on Shakespeare given in an address on 12 April.

[2]Gilbert Keith Chesterton was a regular contributor to the *Daily News,* as "G. K. C."

the heading "The Great Shawkspear Mystery," with a condensed report of my lecture last week on Shakespeare at the Kensington Town Hall, at which, to his disgrace, he was not present. And then, if you please, he has the—I really do not wish to be too popular in my language, but I think I must just this once be allowed to say the cheek—to explain that my congenital insensibility to the contents of my own lecture accounts for my dislike of Shakespeare (whom I do not dislike). There is a most horrible ingratitude in this, because when I was challenged on that occasion to mention some modern writers who could compare with our monstrously overrated Elizabethans in literary power or surpass them in insight, one of the names I gave was that of Gilbert Chesterton. I now withdraw that nomination. I apologise for Mr. Chesterton. I blush for him. The Elizabethans were mostly shallow literary persons, drunk with words, and seeking in crude stories of lust and crime an excuse for that wildest of all excitements, the excitement of imaginative self-expression by words; but I do not believe the worst of them—not even Chapman or Webster—would have stayed away from a lecture of mine and then re-invented the most obvious part of it and offered it to the public as a specimen of what my fallen nature is incapable of perceiving in the spacious times of great Elizabeth.

I will now, with your permission, give a very brief summary of what I actually did maintain in an address which, fully reported, would have occupied an entire page of the *Daily News,* and which was honoured by the London Press, which well knows that the vast majority of its readers never read Shakespeare, or anything concerning him, by a couple of dozen lines compiled by gentlemen of the Press who were so fascinated by my eloquence that they forgot to do their work, and had, when the spell ceased, to extemporise a few sentences of the kind that their editors expect from them when I am their theme.

1. That the idolatry of Shakespeare which prevails now existed in his own time, and got on the nerves of Ben Jonson.

2. That Shakespeare was not an illiterate poaching labourer who came up to London to be a horseboy, but a gentleman with all the social pretensions of our higher bourgeoisie.

3. That Shakespeare, when he became an actor, was not a rogue and a vagabond, but a member and part proprietor of a regular company, using, by permission, a nobleman's name as its patron, and holding itself as exclusively above the casual barn-

stormer as a Harley-street consultant holds himself above a man with a sarsaparilla stall.

4. That Shakespeare's aim in business was to make money enough to acquire land in Stratford, and to retire as a country gentleman with a coat of arms and a good standing in the county; and that this was not the ambition of a parvenu, but the natural course for a member of the highly respectable, though temporarily impecunious, family of the Shakespeares.

5. That Shakespeare found that the only thing that paid in the theatre was romantic nonsense, and that when he was forced by this to produce one of the most effective samples of romantic nonsense in existence—a feat which he performed easily and well—he publicly disclaimed any responsibility for its pleasant and cheap falsehood by borrowing the story and throwing it in the face of the public with the phrase, "As You Like It."

6. That when Shakespeare used that phrase he meant exactly what he said, and that the phrase "What You Will," which he applied to "Twelfth Night," meaning "Call it what you please" is not, in Shakespearean or any other English, the equivalent of the perfectly unambiguous and penetratingly simple phrase, "As You Like It."

7. That Shakespeare tried to make the public accept real studies of life and character in—for instance—"Measure for Measure" and "All's Well that Ends Well"; and that the public would not have them, and remains of the same mind still, preferring a fantastic sugar doll like Rosalind to such serious and dignified studies of women as Isabella and Helena.

8. That the people who spoil paper and waste ink by describing Rosalind as a perfect type of womanhood are the descendants of the same blockheads whom Shakespeare, with the coat of arms and the lands in Warwickshire in view, had to please when he wrote plays as they liked them.

9. Not, as has been erroneously stated, that I could write a better play than "As You Like It," but that I actually have written much better ones, and, in fact, never wrote anything, and never intend to write anything, half so bad in matter. (In manner and art nobody can write better than Shakespeare because, carelessness apart, he did the thing as well as it can be done within the limits of human faculty.)

10. That to anyone with the requisite ear and command of words, blank verse, written under the amazingly loose conditions

which Shakespeare claimed, with full liberty to use all sorts of words, colloquial, technical, rhetorical, and even obscurely technical, to indulge in the most far-fetched ellipses and to impress ignorant people with every possible extremity of fantasy and affectation, is the easiest of all known modes of literary expression, and that this is why whole oceans of dull bombast and drivel have been emptied on the head of England since Shakespeare's time in this form by people who could not have written "Box and Cox"[3] to save their lives. Also (this on being challenged) that I can write blank verse myself more swiftly than prose, and that, too, of full Elizabethan quality plus the Shakespearean sense of the absurdity of it as expressed in the lines of Antient Pistol. What is more, that I have done it, published it, and had it performed on the stage with huge applause.[4]

11. That Shakespeare's power lies in his enormous command of word-music, which gives fascination to his most blackguardly repartees and sublimity to his hollowest platitudes, besides raising to the highest force all his gifts as an observer, an imitator of personal mannerisms and characteristics, a humorist, and a story-teller.

12. That Shakespeare's weakness lies in his complete deficiency in that highest sphere of thought, in which poetry embraces religion, philosophy, morality, and the bearing of these on communities, which is sociology. That his characters have no religion, no politics, no conscience, no hope, no convictions of any sort. That there are, as Ruskin pointed out, no heroes in Shakespeare. That his test of the worth of life is the vulgar hedonic test, and that since life cannot be justified by this or any other external test, Shakespeare comes out of his reflective period a vulgar pessimist, oppressed with a logical demonstration that life is not worth living, and only surpassing Thackeray in respect of being fertile enough, instead of repeating "Vanitas vanitatum" at secondhand, to word the futile doctrine differently and better in such passages as "Out, out, brief candle." Finally, that this does not mean that Shakespeare lacked the enormous fund of joyousness which is the secret of genius, but simply that, like most middle-class English-

[3]A farce (1847) by J. Maddison Morton, later adapted as a one-act comic opera, "Cox and Box," by Arthur Sullivan and J. C. Burnand (1866).

[4]*The Admirable Bashville* (1901), adapted by Shaw from his novel *Cashel Byron's Profession,* is written in Elizabethan-style blank verse. It was performed in London by the Stage Society on 7 June 1903, under Shaw's own direction.

men bred in private houses, he was a very incompetent thinker, and took it for granted that all inquiry into life began and ended with the question, "Does it Pay?" Which, as I could have told him, and as Mr. Gilbert Chesterton could have told him, is not the point. Having worked out his balance-sheet and gravely concluded that life's but a poor player, etc., and thereby deeply impressed a public which, after a due consumption of beer and spirits, is ready to believe that everything maudlin is tragic, and everything senseless sublime, Shakespeare found himself laughing and writing plays and getting drunk at the Mermaid much as usual, with Ben Jonson finding it necessary to reprove him for a too exuberant sense of humour.

This is a very hasty sketch of my views on Shakespeare; but it is at least an improvement on the silly travesties of my lecture which have been disabling the minds of my critics for the past few years.

Yours, &c.,
G. Bernard Shaw

THE QUEEN'S COUP D'ÉTAT

[On 13 November 1905 Queen Alexandra issued an appeal to the charitably disposed to "assist her in alleviating the sufferings of the poor starving unemployed during this winter." Relief, under the Unemployed Workmen Act, was dependent on voluntary contributions from the public. The Queen contributed £2000; eventually subscriptions of over £150,000 were made. Shaw's letter was published in *The Times* on 14 November.]

Sir,—Like everybody else in London with a spark of social compunction, I am boundlessly delighted with the very womanly dash made by the Queen to do something for the unemployed. She has waited for Parliament to deal with the question, and Parliament has done nothing—has, indeed, with great difficulty been prevented from doing less. She has waited for the Prime Minister to advise, and the Prime Minister avows his utter helplessness. The resources of the Constitution being thus exhausted, she has boldly thrown the Constitution to the winds and taken the matter in hand herself. She has said, in effect, to our wise men:—"Well, if you cannot get my people work, I will give them bread. Who will come and help me?"

In doing this the Queen has precipitated a crisis that was

bound to come sooner or later. The situation is not new. In cities like ancient Rome or modern London competitive commerce always finally creates a proletariat too numerous to be effectually coerced and too clever to be duped by spurious political economy and pious platitudes about the sacredness of law and order. In 1886, when the windows of the clubs in Pall-mall were broken, the classes represented by those clubs immediately paid £49,000 ransom to the Mansion-house fund, most of which went into the hands of the anything-but-hardworking.[1] Trade revived and staved off the emergency for a time; but it is upon us again, and now the question is, Are we to accept *Panem et Circenses* as a regular part of our metropolitan organization? We must, if the alternative is to leave the unemployed to choose between starvation and plunder. The Queen will not allow us to starve her people. She has forced our hand, and is going to organize Panem (the circuses will come later) with her own hands, unless we find work and wages for the unemployed, who, by the way, will very soon acquire a taste, like their social superiors, for incomes without work.

It is a critical situation, and one that may become dangerous if those who understand it are too courtly or too cowardly to speak out. The Queen's charity is the last resource of a bankrupt civilization. If we can do nothing better we must adopt it, and she is right to force the alternative on us. But can we do nothing better?

For my part I see no difficulty in finding work for the unemployed. Take the places they live in, for instance. There is the urgently necessary work of knocking those places down, burning their putrid *débris,* and replacing them with decent dwellings in airy and handsome streets. The spots to begin with are already marked by Mr. Charles Booth on the map of London in black.[2] If instead of directing the attention of the unemployed as in 1886 to the possibility of extorting a demoralizing ransom by destroying the houses of other people, we could set them to the eminently

[1]On 8 February 1886, two rival meetings, led by socialists and protectionists, met in Trafalgar Square to protest unemployment, and then rioted. Mansion House funds were also raised by appeal to the charitable public to meet the needs of the poor during emergencies.

[2]Booth's *Life and Labour of the People in London* was published in seventeen volumes, the last of which appeared in 1903.

desirable and honourable work of destroying their own and building better ones to replace them, the Queen would not need to empty her private purse with the heartbreaking knowledge that her money would save her people's lives at the expense of their characters.

It is true that there is no commercial demand for a new and decent city; but pray for what great social work is there any commercial demand? How long more will it take us to see that great nations work for national profits, and keep the little souls who can understand nothing but commercial profits out of the national councils?

I wish I could persuade the Queen that there is no lack of money, no lack of work, no lack of charity. It is character and statesmanship that we want, and these, alas! cannot be created by cheques and subscription lists.

Yours, &c.,
G. Bernard Shaw

WOMAN SUFFRAGE

[On 23 October 1906, ten women were arrested at the House of Commons and charged with "using threatening and abusive words and behaviour with intent to provoke a breach of the peace or whereby a breach of the peace might have been occasioned," according to the police report in *The Times* of 25 October. Anne Cobden-Sanderson, a daughter of the noted economic negotiator Richard Cobden, was one of the ten women ejected and arrested; her husband, in a letter to *The Times* published on 30 October, described her treatment in prison as including solitary confinement for "23 of 24 hours" a day and refusal of her request for pen and paper. Shaw's letter appeared in *The Times* on 31 October.]

Sir,—This is a terrible moment in our national life. We are not often thoroughly frightened. When England trembles the world knows that a great peril overshadows our island. It is not the first time that we have faced dangers that have made even our gayest and bravest clench their teeth and hold their breath. We watched the Armada creeping slowly up the Channel. We wiped our brow when chance revealed the treason of Guy Fawkes. We are listening even now for the bugle of the German invader, and scanning the waves we rule for the periscope of the French submarine. But until now we have faced our fate like men, with our

Parliament unshaken in our midst, grandly calm as the Roman senators who sat like statues when Brennus and his barbarians charged bloodstained into their hall. When Charles Bradlaugh,[1] the most muscular man in England, dashed into the House of Commons to claim a seat in that august Assembly the police carried him, titanically struggling, down the stairs, deposited him in the yard with a shattered fountain pen, and disdainfully set him free to do his worst. It was but the other day that a desperado arose in the Strangers' Gallery of the House of Commons and burst into disorderly eloquence. Without a moment's hesitation the dauntless attendants hurled themselves upon him, and extruded him from our Legislature. He was not haled before the magistrate; he was not imprisoned; no man deigned to ask securities for his good behaviour; the British lion scorned protection against so puny an antagonist.

But the strongest nerves give way at last. The warriors of Philip were, when all is said, only men. German soldiers, French bluejackets, Guy Fawkes, Bradlaugh, and the stranger in the gallery, bold and dangerous as they were, were no females. The peril to-day wears a darker, deadlier aspect. Ten women—ten petticoated, long-stockinged, corseted females have hurled themselves on the British Houses of Parliament. Desperate measures are necessary. I have a right to speak in this matter, because it was in my play *Man and Superman* that my sex were first warned of woman's terrible strength and man's miserable weakness.

It is a striking confirmation of the correctness of my views that the measures which have always been deemed sufficient to protect the House of Commons against men are not to be trusted against women. Take, for example, the daughters of Richard Cobden, long known to everybody worth knowing in London as among the most charming and interesting women of our day. One of them—one only—and she the slightest and rosiest of the family—did what the herculean Charles Bradlaugh did. To the immortal glory of our Metropolitan Police they did not blench. They carried the lady out even as they carried Bradlaugh. But they did

[1]English freethinker and radical, elected to Parliament in 1880, who was denied his seat because his widely known atheism was held to invalidate the parliamentary oath. In August 1881 the reelected Bradlaugh attempted to force an entry into the House of Commons but was ejected by the police. Not until 1886 was he permitted to take the oath.

not dare to leave her at large as they left him. They held on to her like grim death until they had her safe under bolt and bar, until they had stripped her to see that she had no weapons concealed, until a temperate diet of bread and cocoa should have abated her perilous forces. She—and the rest of the terrible ten.

For the moment we have time to breathe. But has the Government considered the fact that owing to the imperfections of our law these ladies will be at large again before many weeks are passed? I ask, in the name of the public, whether proper precautions have been taken. It is not enough for Mr. Herbert Gladstone, Mr. Haldane, Mr. Asquith, and Sir Henry Campbell-Bannerman to sit there pale and determined, with drawn lips and folded arms, helplessly awaiting a renewal of the assault—an assault the consequences of which no man can foresee. It is their duty without a moment's delay to quadruple the police staff inside the Houses of Parliament. Westminster and Vauxhall bridges should be strongly held by the Guards. If necessary, special constables should be enrolled. I am no coward; but I do not want to see a repetition of the folly that found us unprepared in 1899.[2]

I submit, however, that if these precautions are taken we might, perhaps, venture to let Mrs. Cobden-Sanderson and her friends out. As a taxpayer, I object to having to pay for her bread and cocoa when her husband is, not only ready, but apparently even anxious to provide a more generous diet at home. After all, if Mr. Cobden-Sanderson is not afraid, surely, the rest of us may pluck up a little. We owe something to Mr. Cobden-Sanderson, both as one of our most distinguished artist craftsmen and as a most munificent contributor in crises where public interests have been at stake. If Mrs. Cobden-Sanderson must remain a prisoner whilst the Home Secretary is too paralysed with terror to make that stroke of the pen for which every sensible person in the three kingdoms is looking to him, why on earth cannot she be imprisoned in her own house? We should still look ridiculous, but at least the lady would not be a martyr. I suppose nobody in the world really wishes to see one of the nicest women in England suffering from the coarsest indignity and the most injurious form of ill-treatment that the law could inflict on a pickpocket. It gives

[2]Probably a reference to the meeting in London in the summer of 1899 of the International Conference of Women.

us an air of having lost our tempers and made fools of ourselves, and of being incapable of acting generously now that we have had time to come to our senses. Surely, there can be no two opinions among sane people as to what we ought to do.

Will not the Home Secretary rescue us from a ridiculous, an intolerable, and incidentally a revoltingly spiteful and unmanly situation?

Yours, &c.,
G. Bernard Shaw

A LECTURE ON "THE NEW THEOLOGY"

[On 16 May 1907, Shaw delivered a lecture on "The New Theology." Among those whom it offended was Agnes Lady Grove, whose letter to *The Academy* appeared on 22 June. Shaw's response was published one week later.]

Sir,—I hope Lady Grove does not suspect me of being ignorant of her religion or indifferent to it. I know it only too well. At this very lecture of which she speaks I had hardly left the platform when a lady who I think must have been the Devil, beautiful as a goddess and nobly arrayed, came to me and taunted me with this religion, scorned me for not having preached it, and turned her back on me as on the Man with the Muckrake or other creature walking in darkness.

But what am I to do? Polytheism is all very well for polytheists: you have a goddess of love (or a god of love, according to your sex) and you have a god of cancer and epilepsy. You adore the one and either propitiate the other or try to forget him. You may even ignore him, like a child who pulls the raisins out of a cake and leaves the dough on the plate. But people will not stand this from me. They are monotheists: they will not nowadays tolerate as much as two gods waging eternal war on one another from heaven and hell, much less a whole pantheon. They will not accept even life and death as two things: they have learnt from Weismann[1] that death is only a device evolved by natural selection to economise life. The old conceptions of maliciously destructive fundamental energies at work no longer hold them: they reject

[1]German biologist whose essay on the "Origin of Death" was widely known at the time.

them as not only depressing and terrifying, but incredible to people of any serious vitality. Yet cancer and epilepsy are facts, with plague, pestilence and famine and all the evils from which we pray to be delivered; and the intellectual problem is to find a tenable conception of a force which, though it has produced cancer and epilepsy, tetanus and diptheria, curved spine and hare lips and the impulses of poisoners and torturers as well as love and beauty and divine ecstasy, is nevertheless a force with honourable intentions. My theology supplies such a conception, and Lady Grove's does not: that is why I satisfy the monotheists, and why she satisfies only the polytheists, who like to have love and cancer in what Mr. Andrew Lang[2] would perhaps call deitight compartments.

I know that my "ignorant and inexperienced god" disgusts people who are accustomed to the best of everything. The old-fashioned gentleman who felt that God would not lightly damn a man of his quality has given place to the lady who declines to be saved by a deity who is not absolutely first-class in every particular. Sir Isaac Newton's confession of ignorance and inexperience seems to her to mark a lower grade of character and intelligence than the assurance of Mr. Stiggins,[3] who knows everything and can move mountains with hi[s] faith. I know this high-class deity very well. When I hire a furnished house for my holidays, as I often do, I find his portrait in the best bedroom. It is the portrait of a perfect gentleman, not older than thirty-eight, with nice hair, a nice beard, nice draperies, a nice pet lamb under his arm or somewhere about, and an expression which combines the tone of the best society with the fascination of Wilson Barrett[4] as Hamlet. The ladies who worship him are themselves worshipped by innumerable poor Joblings in shabby lodgings who pin up the Galaxy Gallery of British Beauty on their walls. Far be it from me to mock at this worship: if you dare not or cannot look the universe in the face you will at least be the better for adoring that spark of the divine beauty and the eternal force that glimmers through the weaknesses and inadequacies of a pretty man or a handsome woman; but please, dear sect of sweethearts, do not mock at me

[2]Scottish man of letters—poet, translator, and anthropologist—whose second edition of *Myth, Ritual, and Religion* was published in 1899.

[3]The Reverend Mr. Stiggins, "the red-nosed man," was a religious hypocrite who sponged off women in Dickens's *Pickwick Papers*.

[4]A popular English actor and manager.

either. You have your nicely buttered little problem and are content with its nicely buttered little solution. I have to face a larger problem and find a larger solution; and since on my scale the butter runs short, I must serve the bread of life dry.

Yours, &c.,
G. Bernard Shaw

DOMESTIC EXPENDITURE

[*Liverpool Daily Post & Mercury,* 15 August 1907.]

Sir,—Since my domestic expenditure has become the subject of a strenuous correspondence in your columns under the curiously irrelevant heading of Socialism and Liberalism, and since matters have gone so far that one gentleman, on demanding to be given the lie, has been given it, and that, too, by a correspondent in holy orders, I had better step in and explain matters.

It is unfortunately true that I am paying less than £21 a week for the house I occupy at Llanbedr.[1] I can only plead, in extenuation, that it was the most expensive house I could get. It is a very delightful place; and the low rent is due to the moderation of my landlord, and not to any economy on my part. However, the overstatement is not excessive, and when £30 a week is added for the hire of the excellent F.I.A.T.[2] motor-car in which I have been visiting the district, it will be admitted that I am spending as much as can be reasonably expected from a man of my busy life and simple habits.

As to the computation of my domestic staff at six persons only, I can easily dispose of that. The actual number is seven.

May I take this opportunity of informing the large number of undeservedly unfortunate persons who daily write to me for pecuniary assistance, that I am a Socialist. This means that I spend money, but do not give it. I detest charity, and, far from desiring to ransom the existing social system, am doing my best to overthrow it.

My main objection to it is that it makes a really costly life impossible. My ideal is a society in which everybody shall spend at least £50,000 a year on himself alone, and, of course, earn it. At

[1]Shaw was holidaying on the Welsh seacoast at Llanbedr, near Harlech.
[2]Fabrica Italiana Automobili Torino, the "Fiat."

present I find it impossible to spend more than a few paltry thousands, and these I have to steal, producing poverty and anxiety for others without really escaping it myself. I am forced to be cheap and dishonest in a country where cheapness, contentment in squalid poverty, "the simple life," and all the cognate abominations are set up as virtues. It cannot be too thoroughly understood that Socialism gives no quarter to such moral perversions, and that poverty, charity, and cheapness will no more be tolerated in a Socialist State than such comparatively innocent activities as burglary, incendiarism, and rapine.

Yours, &c.,
G. Bernard Shaw

KULIN POLYGAMY

[Three articles on the subject of unrest in India in *The Times* of 23 September 1907 stirred a controversy. Among the first correspondents to question the articles was Sir Henry Cotton, a longtime civil servant in Bengal, chief secretary of the government 1891–96, and since 1906 the Liberal MP for Nottingham. Cotton's point was that the articles were unfair to the Bengalis; he claimed it was false to suggest that Kulin polygamy was a prevalent practice. (The Kulin was an aristocratic Brahmin sub-caste in Bengal.) Cotton was in turn refuted by Sir George Birdwood, an Anglo-Indian official in the Statistics and Commerce Department of the India Office, who claimed that Kulin polygamy was a widespread practice. Shaw entered the dispute with a letter published in *The Times* on 5 October.]

Sir,—Will you allow me, as a subject of the British Empire, to join Sir George Birdwood in his protest against the gross insularity with which the subject of Kulin polygamy has been discussed in your columns since Sir Henry Cotton, by putting his denial of its existence in the form of a defence of Indian morality, assumed that the test of morality is simply conformity to English custom? In this all your correspondents except Sir George have followed him, the only difference being that his intentions were civil, and theirs openly offensive. To an Indian that can hardly weigh as a difference at all. If (to illustrate) an Indian paper were to publish a controversy between two Bengalis, one holding up the Archbishop of Canterbury to the execration of all pious Hindus as a Christian, and the other defending him as a man of far too high character to be tainted with the Christian superstition, the Archbishop would hardly feel much more obliged to his defender than to his assailant.

If the Empire is to be held together by anything better than armed force—and we have neither energy nor money enough to spare from our own affairs for that—we shall have to make up our minds to bring the institutions and social experiments of our fellow-subjects to a very much higher test than their conformity to the customs of Clapham.[1] It is true that mere toleration for its own sake is out of the question: we are not going to tolerate suttee or human sacrifice on any terms from anybody, if we can help it. We are far too tolerant as it is, if not of other people's abominations and superstitions, at all events of our own, which are numerous and detestable enough in all conscience. But before we begin to hurl such epithets as "revolting" and "abhorrent" at any customs of our Indian fellow-subjects, we had better consider carefully why we are shocked by them. Very few of us are trained to distinguish between the shock of unfamiliarity and genuine ethical shock. Kulin polygamy is unfamiliar: therefore it shocks us, and causes gentlemen of ordinary good breeding to use abusive and intemperate language in your columns. Under these circumstances, I, having ascertained that my opinion in this matter is representative enough to be of some importance, am emboldened to say that the institution of Kulin polygamy, as described by your correspondents, does not seem to me on the face of it an unreasonable one. Let me compare it with our own marriage customs. We are told first that the Bengalis do not marry out of their caste. To them, therefore, the promiscuity which we profess must be "revolting" and "abhorrent"; but we have the ready and obvious defence that our promiscuity is only professed and not real, as our Deputy-Lieutenant class and our commercial traveller class, for instance, do not intermarry. Further, the Bengalis hold that it is part of the general purpose of things that women should bear children, and that childlessness is a misfortune and even a disgrace. It will not be disputed, I think, that this, under the surface, is as much an occidental as an oriental view. Again, the Bengalis attach great importance to their children being well-bred. So do we. On all these points the only difference between India and England is that England holds her beliefs more loosely, less religiously, less thoughtfully, and is less disposed to let them stand in the way of pecuniary gain and social position.

[1]A working-class community in the south of London.

How then do the parents of an English family, of the class corresponding to the Indian Brahman class, secure well-bred grandchildren for themselves and also for their nation? They use their social opportunities to put their daughters promiscuously in the way of young men of their own caste, in the hope that a marriage with some one or other will be the result. Frequently it is not the result: the daughter becomes an old maid, one of the wasted mothers of a nation, which, as Mr. Sidney Webb and Professor Karl Pearson[2] have warned us, is perishing for want of well-bred children. Even when chance is favourable, and the daughter finds a husband, she often refuses to become a mother because her religious and social training has taught her to regard motherhood as a department of original sin, and to glory, not in the possession of children, but of a husband; so that the childless woman with a husband despises the mother who has no husband.

What does the Bengali father do under the same circumstances according to Sir Henry Prinsep?[3] He selects a picked man—a Brahman representing the highest degree of culture and character in his class; and he pays him £700 to enable his daughter to become the mother of a well-bred child.

Now this may strike the parochial Englishman as unusual or, as he would put it, "revolting," "abhorrent," and so forth; but it is certainly not unreasonable and not inhuman. Far from being obviously calculated to degrade the race, it is, on the face of it, aimed at improving it. Sir George Birdwood has just told us in your columns that the Kulin "happen, for the most part, to be of fine physique." Sir George has no doubt also noticed that the products of our system happen, for the most part, not to be of fine physique. Is it quite clear that this is mere happening? Is it not rather what one would expect under the circumstances? And is the practice of taking deliberate steps to produce and reproduce men of fine physique really revolting and abhorrent to our British conscience as distinguished from our British prejudice?

Let us, however, do justice to our system, indefensible as it is in many respects. It secures what most men want: that is, a shar-

[2]Of University College, London: successively a professor of applied mathematics, geometry, and, beginning in 1911, the first Galton professor of eugenics. He was the author of various collections of essays and lectures, the most widely read of which was *The Grammar of Science* (1892).

[3]Sir Henry Prinsep was in the Bengal civil service, a judge of the high court (Calcutta), 1878–1904.

ing out of the women among the men so that every Jack shall have his Jill, and the able men and attractive women shall not accumulate partners and leave mediocrity unprovided. If this were the end of public policy in the matter, and if the race might safely take its chance of degeneracy provided monogamy, even on the hardest conditions, were maintained, there would be nothing more to be said. But as the whole Imperial problem before us is fundamentally nothing else than to produce more capable political units than our present system breeds—in short, to breed the Superman—this is not a time to rail at experiments made by people who are not under the harrow of our prejudices, or to persist in calling the customs founded on those prejudices by question-begging names such as purity, chastity, propriety, and so forth, and to speak of a Brahman who is the father of a hundred children as a libertine with a hundred wives. Any man of thirty may have a hundred children without having a wife at all and still be positively ascetic in his temperance compared with an average respectable and faithful British husband of the same age. And if the hundred children "happen, for the most part, to be of fine physique," the nation will be more powerful and prosperous in the next generation than if these hundred children were replaced by a hundred others of indifferent physique, each having a different father, promiscuously picked up in a Clapham drawing-room.

A system which limits the fertility of its men of fine physique to the child-bearing capacity of one woman, and wastes the lives of thousands of first-rate maiden ladies in barrenness because they like to own their own houses and manage their own affairs without being saddled with a second-rate or tenth-rate man, must not take its own merits for granted. It may be the right system; it may be bound up with all that is best in our national life and fortunate in our national history; it may be all that our stupidest people unanimously claim for it. But then again it may not. The evidence on the other side is weighty; and the population question is pressing hard on us. The case must be argued, not assumed; and the final verdict will be that of history and not of our modern suburban villas with no nurseries.

Yours, &c.,
G. Bernard Shaw

DRAMATIC CENSORSHIP

[The refusal by the Lord Chamberlain, on the recommendation of his reader George Alexander Redford in 1898, to license Shaw's play *Mrs Warren's Profession,* made of Shaw an inexorable adversary of governmental censorship. Enraged by the circumstance that an earnest playwright had perforce to submit to the whim of an irresponsible bureaucrat from whose decision there was no possible appeal, Shaw fought implacably for a freedom for the theater comparable to the freedom accorded the press.]

I

[*The Nation,* 16 November 1907.]

Sir,—In view of the deputation of playwrights which the Prime Minister is to receive next week,[1] it is perhaps as well to say a word on the practical working of the censorship. Nothing that can be said on the subject of the political principle involved is likely to be new to Sir Henry Campbell-Bannerman. He does not need to be told that the popular theory of leaving the drama in the hands of some man of the world who is also a gentleman of tact and good sense, is just about as reasonable and as creditable to the political competence of those who are satisfied with it as a proposal to leave the whole country in the hands of the King, because he also is a man of the world, with a European reputation for tact and good sense. I have no doubt that many loyal people would think such a suggestion admirable; for nothing is more alarming nowadays than the oblivion into which the political axioms which Liberalism established by three hundred years of struggle have fallen. You cannot look down the correspondence column of a newspaper without finding some unashamed proposal from an ordinar[il]y sane gentleman to deal with whatever social evil happens to be the topic of the day, by giving some perfect gentleman autocratic powers to set it right. Such people are too lazy to emigrate to Russia, where their political notions are constitutionally recognized and acted upon very thoroughly (with all the results that might be expected); so they clamour for the Russianising of

[1]Because of the illness of the prime minister, Sir Henry Campbell-Bannerman, the delegation (from which Shaw tactfully absented himself) was received by his deputy, Herbert Gladstone.

our English Constitution, and see nothing in the hesitation of the Government to gratify them but flat Anarchism—wherein they find themselves at one with that perfect gentleman the Czar.

At all events, I shall take the obnoxiousness of the censorship to Liberal principles for granted, and explain how the institution actually works, for the better technical instruction of Ministers, and the disillusion of the visionaries who imagine that Mr Redford is a kindly, wise, tactful, earthly Providence taking a common-sense view of the wholesomeness of every play presented to him, and arriving at a rough-and-ready, but in the main sound, conclusion as to whether it should be performed or not.

It sounds very simple. Most hopelessly foolish solutions of social difficulties do sound simple. To begin with, you want a man who will undertake to know, better than Tolstoy or Ibsen or George Meredith or Dickens or Carlyle or Ruskin or Shakespeare or Shelley, what moral truths the world needs to be reminded of—how far the pity and horror of tragedy dare be carried—on what institutions the antiseptic derision of comedy may be allowed to play without destroying anything really vital in them.

Now it is clear without argument that no man who was not a born fool would pretend for the moment to be capable of such a task; and the reason that some censors have talked as if they were capable of it is that some censors have been born fools. The Prime Minister would be as much horrified at having such godlike powers attributed to him as Paul and Barnabas were at Lystra when the people sacrificed to them. I am far from sure that Mr Redford, if we offered him a sacrifice occasionally, would not accept it with complacency; but I may be doing him an injustice. There is, of course, a strong *primâ facie* case against him. When a young gentleman, on such a superhuman task as the above being proposed, springs from his desk in a bank, and says blithely: "Oh, there is no difficulty. Hand Tolstoy and the rest over to me: and I will censor them all right enough for two guineas a play, and a few hundred a year as a stand-by in case I extinguish the drama altogether." This is, in effect, Mr Redford's attitude; and, so stated, it certainly seems to reach the limit of flippant folly and conceit. But, of course, this is not how the situation presented itself to him. He was simply given a post in his Majesty's household, and was naturally very glad to get it. As to the work, it had been done before somehow by an ordinary mortal, and therefore could presumably be done again by another ordinary mortal. That is to say, there must be rules; and when there are rules an official has nothing to do but administer them, just as a judge need not be a Solon: his business is not to make laws, but to see that the laws are obeyed.

Now it is hard on Mr Redford that we place so much more responsibility on him than on a judge, though we give him a much smaller salary. We ask him not only to administer the law, but to make the law in his private wisdom as he goes along. For he is not bound always by his office rules. Sometimes they become too glaringly old-fashioned for even a Lord Chamberlain to persist in. Sometimes new emergencies arise for which there are no rules; and then Mr Redford has to legislate for the drama of this unhappy realm out of his own head, which was never made to bear such a strain. On the whole, he is happiest when he has office rules or traditions to fall back on.

What are these rules? First and most intolerable, the infamous rule that dramatic art is too unclean a thing to be allowed to be religious. It may be lewd, and it may be silly; but it must not dare touch anything sacred. The Bible is to be a closed book to it. It may send the blackguard to the drinking-bar between every act, and to a worse place at the end of the play; but it must not send him to church or to prayer, or even into the street to do good works.

What would the art of painting be if it had been under this execrable ban since its invention? If no painter had ever been allowed to paint Christ or the Apostles or the Saints or the Virgin; if the great spiritual dynasty of Italian painters, from Cimabue and Giotto to Tintoretto, had been forbidden to paint anything but Venuses for licentious noblemen, and told if they complained that the restriction did not prevent Jan Steen from being a great artist, where would painting be nowadays? Where would Christianity be? Suppose the art of music had been in the same chains, and Handel had been tethered to Italian opera and forbidden to compose *The Messiah!* The ignorant and dissolute may imagine that we should still have the operas of Offenbach and the waltzes of Waldteufel. They err to the very depths. Offenbach and Waldteufel made their confectionery of the crumbs they picked up from the bread of life the great Masters made when they were expressing their religion in music. There is no fact on earth better established than that it is only in the effort to express those great waves of the human spirit that pass over the world from time to time that art becomes great, and discovers new enchantments to arrest our attention and change our souls. Had Mr Redford exercised his functions in Athens, there would have been no Aeschylus, no Sophocles, no Aristophanes, no Euripides. Had he exercised it in Elizabethan England, there would have been no Shakespeare except the Shakespeare of *Venus and Adonis*. How any author, actor, or manager with a grain of self-respect, can dumbly suffer this abominable excommunication; how he can actually pay Mr Redford compliments and defend his detestable office against the righteous wrath and revolt of its victims, would be amazing if one did not know that the worst effect of making men helots is that they soon learn how lucrative are the arts of slavery, and lose their desire to be free.

Of the remaining taboos (for the whole system is one of taboo) three are of vital consequence, because they explain why it is that Mr Redford licenses vicious plays, and refuses to license serious and exemplary ones. In the case of a play which came before the Courts in the course of a civil action, the judge expressed his astonishment that the King's Reader of Plays should have certified that it did not "in its general tendency contain anything immoral or otherwise improper for the stage."

But the judge did not understand the situation. The play contained nothing that is taboo at the Lord Chamberlain's office. Had the author introduced a scene in which the prophet Daniel appeared and rebuked its worst passages, Mr Redford would at once have refused to license the play. Daniel is taboo. To get him licensed you must change him to Jack Sheppard, or Jane Shore,[2] who are both perfectly in order.

Here are the three great taboos on the question of sex:

1. You must never mention an illegal obstetric operation.
2. You must never mention incest.
3. You must never mention venereal disease.

"And," Mr Redford will explain, "would any gentleman desire to mention them on the public stage?" The reply, which will shock Mr Redford, is, Yes. If gentlemen do not deal energetically with these subjects in public, they will be dealt with by blackguards in private.

"But, surely," our noodles will begin, "the theatre is not the

[2]Sheppard was a notorious early eighteenth-century highwayman, hanged at Tyburn at the age of twenty-two. Shore, the sixteenth-century mistress of Edward IV, later was accused of sorcery by Richard III.

proper place—!" Why not? If the theatre is the proper place for the representation of the passions that lead to these things; if the dramatist is actually thrust back on such subjects whenever he attempts to deal with holier matters; if he must exhibit vice without its real consequences (as distinguished from those sham consequences of remorse and forgiveness, or despair and suicide, which not one of the spectators believes to be inevitable or even probable) how is he to avoid corrupting the morals of the nation? The innocent people who write letters to *The Nation* in support of the censorship think, no doubt, that the rule against mentioning these things is only part of a general rule prohibiting all allusion to vice. They mistake. The playwright may wallow in the representation of every sort of vice that dare be mentioned at all without intolerable shame; and Mr Redford will give him a two-guinea certificate of its propriety, provided only that he does not represent it as leading to an illegal operation, or to venereal disease, or to an insoluble doubt as to possible consanguinity between the children of those who practise it: that is to say, to the only retribution that has any deterrent reality for the spectators.

For instance, take the play called *Waste*, by Mr Granville Barker, Mr Redford's latest victim.[3] Consider the position into which the refusal of a licence for that play has put Mr Barker! The public knows that Mr Redford has licensed plays so abominable that I myself, when trying to bring the question of the censorship before the public through the Press, have failed to induce editors to allow me to describe them in their papers. There is also the well-known protest from the judicial bench cited above. The inevitable conclusion drawn from the man in the street is that if Mr Barker has gone beyond the tolerance that licensed these indescribable and unmentionable plays, he must have produced something quite hideously filthy. But I can tell the story of *Waste* here without the smallest offence, and, with Mr Barker's permission, I will.

Waste is a play about the disestablishment of the Church.

[3]Harley Granville Barker was an actor, playwright, and associate of Shaw in this struggle and others. *Waste*, written in 1907, had been scheduled for performance on 19 November until the censor's refusal of a license unless the play was "amended" to a degree intolerable to its author caused its cancellation. On 24 November, a private performance was given under the auspices of the Stage Society. The censoring of *Waste* was directly responsible for the 1909 parliamentary inquiry into the working of the stage censorship.

The hero is an able Parliamentary leader who has crossed the floor of the House from the Radical side to the Conservative, because he has induced the Conservatives to dish the Liberals by dealing with the Church themselves. One can quite conceive Mr Sidney Webb getting round Mr Balfour in this way (after all, the Irish Local Government Act passed by the Unionists was not less likely on the face of it) if Mr Balfour would give Mr Webb the revenues of the Church for some of his Collectivist projects—which, by the way, is just what the Conservative leader in *Waste* proposes to do. Mr Barker has dramatized this amusing and suggestive political situation with real political insight and first-hand knowledge of our political personnel. But the scheme fails in the play through a private indiscretion of the sort that has ruined two political careers and crippled another in our own time. The protagonist becomes the father of the unborn child of a married lady. The lady avoids the birth by an illegal operation which kills her. The scandal makes the hero politically impossible, just as the O'Shea divorce made Parnell politically impossible. The great scheme for disestablishing the Church is wasted. The political services of the man who devised it are wasted. Hence the title *Waste.*

Mr Redford does not object to the indiscretion. He does not object to the adultery, or to the illegitimate child. The plays he has licensed are full of such incidents. It is the illegal operation that is taboo. Take *Waste,* and degrade its fastidiously fine style into the basest bar-loafer's slang; smudge out its high intellectual interest into the most sickening lascivious sentimentality; introduce incidents which could not be described in these columns; but suppress the illegal operation. Mr Redford will then license it like a lamb. That is how taboo works.

I have myself had a play prohibited by Mr Redford. People imagine that he refused to license it because the heroine is a prostitute and a procuress. They are indeed wide of the mark. The licensed drama positively teems with prostitutes and procuresses. One of the most popular melodramas of our time is called *The Worst Woman in London.*[4] In Mr Hall Caine's excellent play, *The Christian,*[5] you may on any night you please see the prostitute, the procuress, and the *souteneur,* on the stage at the Lyceum Theatre; and you will be none the worse for it. You can also see in

[4]A play by Walter Melville first presented in 1899 and revived in 1903.
[5]A revival of Caine's play, first produced in 1899, had been running at the Lyceum Theatre since August 1907.

many a humble melodrama a brothel on the stage, with its procuress in league with the villain and the bold bad girl whom he has ruined, all set forth as attractively as possible under the protection of the Lord Chamberlain's certificate.

But in my play the consequences of promiscuity are not shirked. I provide the feast (an acridly medicinal one); but I also present the reckoning. The daughter of my heroine meets the son of one of her mother's clients, who falls in love with her. And the two have to face the question, Is he her half-brother? only to find it unanswerable. That is one of the inevitable dilemmas produced by "group marriage." To suppress it is to pack the cards in favour of such arrangements. My refusal to pack them brought me into conflict with the taboo against incest. That is why *Mrs Warren's Profession* is forbidden, whilst dozens of plays which present Mrs Warren as well-dressed, charming, luxuriating in "guilty splendour," and suffering nothing but some fictitious retribution at the end in which nobody believes, because everybody knows it need not happen in real life, teach their cynical lesson to the poor girl in the gallery, and send the young man in the pit into the arms of the best imitation the streets can offer him of the guiltily splendid young lady he has been admiring inside.

One more example of the censored play. There is a much more powerful deterrent to prostitution than the doubts as to consanguinity set up between the children of the parties to it. That deterrent is the disease which the libertine transmits to his legitimate offspring and through it at the moment of birth to his wife. Now that it is idle to threaten people with hell, it is as well that they should know what does really threaten them. Sarah Grand took up this grim question and struck a doughty stroke at the National conscience in her most famous novel, *The Heavenly Twins*. Had she attempted to do the same thing in a play, Mr Redford would have suppressed it, and left her under the suspicion of having penetrated some enormity too dark even for the tolerance of the censor who licensed *The Giddy Goat*.[6] Brieux, the sternest of living dramatic moralists, has dealt with the same theme in his *Les Avariés* [*Damaged Goods*], in the most uncomfortable clean-handed, direct, truthful fashion. On the stage the hero's doctor tells him the truth about the state of his health with all a doctor's frankness, and forbids him to get married just then. He marries,

[6]An adaptation by Augustus Moore of Léon Gandillot's farce *Ferdinand le noceur,* produced in London in 1901.

nevertheless; and his child pays the penalty. Mr Redford will not license that play. If Brieux had confined himself to representing the scenes in which the man got the disease and made them as attractive as possible, without any hint of the unpleasant consequences, Mr Redford would have licensed it without turning a hair. But to mention the penalty! no; that is too disgusting. Besides, the people who make their living by the trade in disease would raise a clamour against such an exposure in the name of outraged decency.

Ibsen, in his *Ghosts,* has dealt with the same subject and come under the double taboo; for he not only represents the son as inheriting his father's disease but points out another by no means improbable result. His father's illegitimate daughter has been taken into the house as a servant, by way of making some sort of reparatory provision for her. As she is a pretty girl, the son falls in love with her. Here the possible complication of incest is added to the actual complication of disease. "Horrible," says the Lord Chamberlain. Ibsen, if alive, would probably ask whether the Lord Chamberlain wished him to make it agreeable. And the Lord Chamberlain would certainly reply that if he could not make it agreeable, he had better not touch it at all.

And there you have the effect of the censorship in a nutshell. It does not forbid vice; it only insists that it shall be made attractive. It does not forbid you to put the brothel on the stage; it only compels you to advertise its charms and suppress its penalties. Now it is futile to plead that the stage is not the proper place for the representation and discussion of illegal operations, incest and venereal disease. If the stage is the proper place for the exhibition and discussion of seduction, adultery, promiscuity and prostitution, it must be thrown open to all the consequences of these things, or it will demoralize the nation. Either prohibit both, or allow both. The censorship admits that it cannot prohibit both. To do that would be to wipe the theatre out of existence, and to reduce the adult population to the status of children in the nursery. To allow both would be to allow everything that public opinion will allow: that is, to confess that the censorship is of no use, and the salaries of its officials a waste of money. Sooner than do this, it buys off the licentious playwrights and managers by licensing their agreeable plays, and suppresses the stern, public-spirited and intellectually honest writers who insist on drawing the moral. The natural and inevitable result is that the British drama has become an impudent and shallow-hearted propaganda of gaiety in the policeman's sense of that word. And the censorship, having committed this crime against public morals, points to the lewdness of the plays it has itself not only licensed, but practically dictated, to prove that theatrical managers and dramatic authors are such filthy wretches that they cannot be trusted with the rights and responsibilities which all other artists enjoy.

The *Saturday Review* suggests that Mr Redford should be removed, and I put in his place. It is just as if the testing of watches at Kew had been complained of, and it were suggested that the Astronomer Royal or Lord Kelvin should be given the job. I am too busy as an author to spend my life reading other people's manuscripts; and the market value of my time is probably ten times that of the King's reader of plays. Yet there are people who are suggesting a whole tribunal of eminent men of letters to carry on the censorship. When they have found the men and found the salaries, it will be time enough to discuss the proposition.

The sensible course is obvious. Abolish the censorship of plays altogether, root and branch. Continue to license theatres from year to year as much as you like, just as you license public-houses or music-halls. License me from year to year as a dramatist if you will, just as you would license me as a motor-car driver. License the managers to manage; and by all means license Mr Redford to express his opinion of their productions in the *London Gazette,* if you value it. But let the play be born and take its chance with the consciences of men just as it came from the conscience of the author. If he shocks you, respect his courage and inspiration, even whilst you stone him. If he shocks you basely and lewdly, or, worse still, pleases you that way, at least do not give yourself a two-guinea certificate of propriety under cover of giving it to him.

Yours, &c.,
G. Bernard Shaw

II

[*The Nation,* 8 February 1908.]

Sir,—In your issue of the 16th of November you were good enough to insert a letter from me on the Censorship of Plays, dealing with the refusal of the Censor to license Mr. Granville Barker's play Waste. In that I committed myself to the assertion that the Censor's objection, instead of being founded, as his supporters imagine, on general ethical principles, or—to put it in another way—on any pretension on the part of the King's Reader of Plays to have any higher sources of ethical inspiration than Mr. Granville Barker, was a matter solely of the observance of an absurd rule forbidding dramatists to mention the subject of obstetric surgery.

Whenever an obviously well-founded statement is made in England by a person specially well acquainted with the facts, that unlucky person is instantly and frantically contradicted by all the people who obviously know nothing about it. This was what happened to me. I was not only contradicted on the point of fact, on which, as I am now going to prove, I was exactly right; but I also had against me that utter lack of political principle which divides us at present, not into supporters and opponents of the freedom of the stage, but into persons who liked Mr. Granville Barker's play, and therefore think that Mr. Redford should be utterly abolished for daring to refuse it a license, and persons who, not liking the play, hold that Mr. Redford's refusal to license it is a satisfactory and final proof of the desirability of the Censorship. It will be remembered that when Mr. Redford refused to license M. Maeterlinck's Monna Vanna,[7] all the critics denounced the Censorship furiously because they were delighted with the incident of the condottiero and the lady in the tent. But when Mr. Granville Barker substituted for these allurements a long discussion on the disestablishment of the Church, a subject in which the critics take no interest, they forgot all about Monna Vanna, and declared one after another that the Censorship is an excellent institution, and that the Lord Chamberlain deserved well of his country for driving Mr. Barker off the stage. And to save their faces, they implied that what Mr. Redford had objected to was the adultery, the illegitimate child, and the seduction scene.

Now mark how plain a tale shall put these gentlemen down. In order to secure his legal rights in countries not ruled by Mr. Redford, Mr. Granville Barker has been compelled to accept momentarily all the alterations of his play demanded by the Censor, so as to be able to obtain a license and give one technically public performance of it in the United Kingdom. Accordingly, last Tuesday week, at the Savoy Theatre, the play, in a form duly guaranteed by the Lord Chamberlain as not containing "in its general

[7]Alfred Sutro's 1902 adaptation of the Maeterlinck play was not licensed for performance until 1914.

tendency anything immoral or otherwise improper for the stage," was performed before a select audience by perhaps the most remarkable cast—judging by the celebrity of its members in literature—that has ever appeared on the stage in London.[8] With the exception of the one eminent dramatic critic who opposed the Censorship on principle, and who is disabled on this occasion from criticism by the fact that he undertook one of the principal parts in the play, the Press was not represented; and I was therefore deprived of the pleasure of challenging our critics personally to put their finger on one single noticeable alteration in the play except the substitution of a conventional and incredible suicide by poison for the death under illegal operation of the unlicensed version. The seduction scene was there, word for word as it originally stood—that scene which so many critics cited as an instance of the horrors from which the Censorship protects us. The adultery was there; the illegitimate child was there; everything was there that was supposed to be the forbidden fruit of the Lord Chamberlain's garden. I am infinitely obliged to Mr. Redford for so precisely confirming my description of the real operation of the Censorship, and routing in shame and confusion his own credulous and inconsiderate supporters.

Let us consider the effect of the alteration by which Mr. Redford considers that he has purified the English stage. The question at issue between Mr. Redford and Mr. Barker was not as to whether the persons in the play should act immorally or not. Mr. Redford had no objection to the immorality: he has given it the Royal sanction. The difference between them was as to the retributive consequences of that immorality. Mr. Barker presented an entirely credible, probable, and highly deterrent result of the immorality. Mr. Redford has insisted on an entirely incredible one. As the law stands at present a man may commit adultery with another man's wife with absolute legal impunity, provided the husband has himself been unfaithful. This was the position in Mr. Barker's play. If the lady had not resorted to an illegal operation, and had not unluckily died under that operation, the career of her

[8]The cast of readers for the copyright performance on 28 January 1908 included Gilbert Murray, Mr. and Mrs. H. G. Wells, William Archer (the "eminent dramatic critic" alluded to in the next line of Shaw's letter), Laurence Housman, Lillah McCarthy, St. John Hankin, and Charlotte and Bernard Shaw (the latter billed as "Late of the Theatre Royal, Dublin").

accomplice would not have been wrecked. That was the real risk that Mr. Barker's protagonist ran; and that was what ruined him. Now it would be absurd of me to say that Mr. Redford is anxious that public men should not be discouraged from adultery by reminding them of consequences that are natural and reasonably probable. It would be equally absurd to say that Mr. Redford must be anxious to conceal from the public the fact that it is perfectly well known in the medical profession that illegal operations are undertaken by qualified practitioners of much higher standing than the obscure and needy doctors who are imprisoned from time to time on this charge. But it is not at all absurd to say—and I accordingly take the liberty of saying it—that if Mr. Redford really had so desired, his action in Mr. Barker's case would have exactly carried out his wishes. Has any man ever been deterred from committing adultery by the possibility of his accomplice committing suicide by poison? I once knew a man who refused to insure his life because he was absolutely certain that the Judgment Day was fixed for Easter Sunday in the year 1889. I have heard of a man who refused to take an otherwise eligible house at the foot of a Welsh mountain which he suspected of volcanic tendencies. But I cannot believe that even these two would have denied themselves the smallest gratification for fear of somebody committing suicide—especially stage suicide. What Mr. Redford has done is to license the crime and virtually suppress the retribution. That is a very characteristic example of the way in which the Censorship, with the best intentions, always contrives to do exactly the opposite of what it is supposed to do, what it is meant to do, and what I have no doubt Mr. Redford honestly intends to do.

A few minor alterations, which have been demanded as a matter of taste, raise the question: Whose taste? In certain classes in this country it is considered good taste to discuss delicate subjects by innuendo. There is a solid reason for this in the fact that in the classes in question, the vocabulary applicable to sch subjects is coarse, and is used freely for the exchange of insults as well as for the exchange of ideas. In other classes, at the more cultivated end of the social scale, the system of conversing by innuendo, by blanks and dashes, and by the initial letters which help the blushing police constable to spare the delicacy of the bashful magistrate, is an unendurable vulgarity. You can be simple and outspoken, or you can hold your tongue; but you must not embarrass yourself or the company by self-consciousness or half measures.

The stage, unfortunately, is not yet as much at its ease in reproducing the manners of the cultivated classes as in imitating the tricks and fashions of newly enriched weekenders. When there is anything delicate to be discussed, it has to take refuge in innuendo; and the Lord Chamberlain's department, corrupted by endless reading of plays, has become as sensitive in the wrong place and in the wrong way as an eighteenth century stage duenna. Accordingly, in the licensed version of Waste, one notices a few passages where the decent directness and unconsciousness of the original version have been replaced by blanks left to be filled in by the imagination of the spectators, without any guarantee that their imagination will be in any way superior to Mr. Barker's, and with even a considerable probability that they will fill in a great deal more than Mr. Redford has cut out. Fortunately, there is very little of this; but what there is is all to the bad.

In short, the Censorship has not only made a stupid and mischievous scandal by suggesting to the public that one of the finest products of our modern dramatic literature is a deplorable indecency; it has actually first had the play altered for the worse, and then guaranteed it as being altered for the better. Which, I repeat, is just precisely what I said it would do. I claim no merit for the prophecy. Everybody who has seriously studied the action of the Censorship could have predicted the event with equal exactness.

By the way, I notice in your paper, over the unfamiliar signature M.,[9] a series of dramatic criticisms of which I should speak in high terms if I could pretend to be indifferent to the fineness of hand with which M. has manipulated my own plays. But since we are on the subject of the Censor's notion of the proper way to treat adultery on the stage, may I ask whether M. has seen Dear Old Charlie,[10] and if so, what he thinks of it from that point of view?

Yours, &c.,
G. Bernard Shaw

[9]Henry William Massingham, editor of *The Nation*.
[10]A cheap and somewhat lascivious comedy from the French by Charles Brookfield, who, ironically, would succeed Redford in 1912 as Joint-Examiner of Plays with Ernest Bendall.

MARRIAGE AND ITS CRITICS

I

[Caleb Williams Saleeby, a young M.D. from Edinburgh and author of the recently published *Evolution: The Master-Key* (London, 1906), was apparently invited by the *Pall Mall Gazette* in November 1907 to reflect on the nature of marriage, probably because his book had included a short chapter on "Evolution and Marriage" in which he rather stunningly concluded that "evolution surveys the whole history of animal reproduction, and its verdict is that monogamy is not merely the ideal state, as all admit, but is demonstrably the state towards which animal life has long directed itself as towards a goal" (p. 239). In his article published in the *Pall Mall Gazette* on 28 November 1907, Saleeby marshals evidence (mostly from the work of Edward Westermarck on marriage and Ebenezer Howard on community planning) for an attack on "the present literary movement against marriage," begun by "a curious medley of persons, including a playwright [Shaw] and a writer of more or less scientific fiction [H. G. Wells]," which "may fairly be taken as indicative, in part, of a desire to explain, or explain away, or justify, their own experience." Saleeby's argument depends entirely on citing the authority of Herbert Spencer and other early sociologists and concludes that "it is the fate of the children . . . that has determined the historical predominance of monogamy at all ages in human history." Shaw's first letter was published in the *Pall Mall Gazette* on 2 December.]

Sir,—When Dr. Saleeby begins that treatise on Marriage which he says he hopes to undertake some day, he will, I hope, be quite independent of his scientific reputation. For the book will certainly destroy it, if any of it is left by that time, unless his form improves very considerably.

Let me, for the amusement of your readers, stand Dr. Saleeby on his head, just to show how easily it can be done by any one who has given ten minutes' serious thought to his subject.

Almost every sentence of his article depends for its coherence on the assumption that marriage and monogamy are the same thing. For instance, I say that the institution of British marriage, which the other day condemned a woman with infant children to remain the wife of a convicted murderer, who will be let loose on her and her unfortunate children just at the moment when these latter are beginning life for themselves, is abominable and inhuman. Dr. Saleeby does not conclude that I am an opponent of British marriage as it exists at present: he concludes that I am an opponent of monogamy. He then makes a second jump to the assumption that an opponent of monogamy—one of the apostles, for instance—is necessarily a polygamist. His third jump is to the conclusion that a defender of polygamy—Martin Luther, for example—cannot be an honest man, and is moved by "a desire to explain, or explain away, or justify, his own experience."

Again, I have said [in "Don Juan in Hell"], and I now repeat, that Marriage, as practised in our country, is the most licentious of human institutions. I also object to it that its promiscuity is a public danger. By human promiscuity, I mean, as all scientific writers mean, the abstention of the community from any interference in sexual selection. Such non-interference is of course not complete: we have a few restrictions as to close consanguinity; but we carry individual license to such an appalling length that a person afflicted with a communicable disease of the most dreaded and disastrous kind can marry and communicate that disease with absolute impunity as far as the law is concerned, although the same persons can be punished for giving one another a slap in the face. This promiscuity co-exists with monogamy, and actually claims to share its moral sanction. On the other hand, the defence offered for the polygamist systems is that they are less promiscuous—that is to say, that they involve higher selection—than monogamist ones. Kulin polygamy, like Salt Lake City polygamy, is defended on the ground that it is better for the race to breed from its picked men only than to breed on the One Man One Woman principle. The plea may be valid or it may not: my point here is that when Dr. Saleeby puts "monogamy on the one hand and promiscuity on the other," he shews that he has not got so far as to analyze his material and define his terms, much less master his subject. He adds to the confusion by identifying promiscuity with Free Love, which he further defines as Free Lust. Here we cannot follow his mental processes, because we none of us know what Free Love means. It cannot mean the love that can be purchased in the streets of every civilised city under our existing system every night, because that love is not free: on the contrary it costs so much that we have young workmen and clerks openly advocating and contracting marriage on the ground that it is economical. The nearest thing to Free Love that we have—and it is certainly near enough in all conscience—is our system of paying the man for the woman's services to the State as wife and mother, and then refusing to give her any legal remedy for his theft if he spends her money at the public-house or with the bookmaker.

The emphasis that Dr. Saleeby lays on the way in which Westermarck turned the tables on Herbert Spencer[1] shews that he does not see that he shares Spencer's fate. The generalization that monogamy is the characteristic marriage form during the savage stages of evolution, and that polygamy appears only in the higher stages of civilisation, may be a sound one; but in the present state of mental confusion about marriage it is hardly wise to push it into vogue as one of these pseudo-scientific commonplaces which are so easily turned to account by the privateers of the social fleet. After our experience of a Manchester school of political economy, we do not want a Piccadilly Circus school of social science, especially as there is nothing in Westermarck to prove that polygamy is not one of the vices and perils of the capitalistic phase of civilisation instead of an upward step in social evolution. Dr. Saleeby thinks that he has made the generalization innocuous by pointing out that the numbers of the sexes are normally equal, and by remarking that "history has not been made by any really polygamous races." But this opportunist argument is not conclusive; and the statement of historic fact is glaringly questionable. I may dispose of it, before dealing with the opportunist argument, by asking Dr. Saleeby how he proposes to make the English people believe it in the face of the Old Testament and the history of Islam?

Now for the opportunist argument. I call it opportunist because it commits Dr. Saleeby to allowing every man to have four wives in case a war cuts off three-quarters of our male population, just as much as it commits him to monogamy with the numbers as they stand at present. Its practical acceptance to-day is a matter of economic necessity for the enormous majority of us. Many of us cannot afford one wife, much less two. Most of us are so poor that when we marry we cannot afford the common decency of a separate bedroom: even our municipal housing schemes take that gross national indelicacy for granted. Monogamy enforces itself under such circumstances. But what does monogamy mean exactly?

Henry VIII. was a strict monogamist. He never married another wife until her predecessor was either divorced or had died (with or without the existence *[sic]* of his executioner). Nelson was a polygamist and a polyandrist combined. He was a party to

[1]In his *History of Human Marriage* (1891).

a "group marriage" consisting of Sir William Hamilton, Lady Hamilton, and himself (the two men being affectionate friends) at the time when his lawful wife was alive and undivorced. Milton married three different women. Charles II. married only one. A later monarch [George II], when his dying wife advised him to marry again, burst into tears and swore that he would be faithful to her memory for ever, adding "J'aurai des maîtresses." Milton, Charles, and the Royal George were all monogamists. Mahomet was a polygamist, like Abraham, Isaac, and Jacob. Dr. Saleeby can now amuse himself by sorting them out, first technically, and then morally. If he can reconcile the resultant categories, any newspaper will give him space for the demonstration. If he cannot, let him climb modestly down from the moral high horse he has ridden at me, and tackle his subject without Pecksniffing.

If Dr. Saleeby had not had his scientific faculties lamed by a medical training he would see at a glance that the equal numbers of the sexes only leads to monogamy when you limit the meaning of monogamy to one wife at a time. In this sense, if we all exchanged wives every Christmas at a national game of general post, we should still be monogamists, rock-founded on Dr. Saleeby's science. But what would the Church say to such monogamy?

Dr. Saleeby will now protest that I am shirking his baby argument. Of polygamy he says: "The babies are a nuisance: they die like flies, and, like flies, unregretted. The form of marriage which does not permit the babies to survive, *they* [the babies] *do not permit to survive*. There is the beginning and end of the whole matter in a nutshell." If it is, so much the worse for Dr. Saleeby's argument; for as it happens, and as everybody who has investigated our social conditions knows, it is in our own monogamous country that the babies die like flies, not only unregretted, but insured. It is in monogamous France and England, and not in polygamous Turkey or Arabia that the scare about the dwindling of the population has made the State endowment of parentage a pressing question. Dr. Saleeby turns up his nose at the State. "Anything less like a mother than the State I find it hard to imagine." He may well say so. When the State left the children to the mothers, they got no schooling; they were sent out to work under inhuman conditions underground and overground for atrociously long hours as soon as they were able to walk; they died of typhus fever in heaps; they grew up to be as wicked to their own children as their parents had been to them. State Socialism rescued them from the worst of that, and means to rescue them from all of it. I now publicly challenge Dr. Saleeby to propose, if he dares, to withdraw the hand of the State and abandon the children to their mothers as before. At present mothers cannot afford to take care of their children; and the State can.

Towards the end of his letter Dr. Saleeby suddenly springs on us a new definition of his terms. Monogamy equals the conditions of the home. Polygamy equals the conditions of the harem. This is not scientific reasoning: it is mere association of ideas. There is no necessary connection between monogamy and the home, polygamy and the harem. One asks at once, what sort of home? Is it the complete ideal domesticity of the family living all in one room, eating there, sleeping there (all in one bed), bearing children there, each always under the loving protecting eye of all the rest? Or is it the home in which the parents' address is Mayfair, the boys' address some communal institution at Eton or Harrow, Oxford or Cambridge, and the girls' address another communal institution in Bournemouth or Eastbourne, Girton or Newnham? As to the harem, what has it to do with polygamy? The Turk with only one wife calls her department his harem. The Christian monogamist Spaniard considers that you insult him if you inquire how his wife is. The professed polygamists of Salt Lake City had no harems. Dr. Saleeby might as well define England as roast beef and France as stewed frogs.

But I have neither time nor patience to go further. Dr. Saleeby does not know the contemporary facts, does not know their history, and, as far as I can judge, could not reason upon them to any purpose if he did. He is the latest example of what I have been pointing out for so many years: namely, that no human mind can survive the process of initiation into the medical profession. The ridiculous ease with which I have been able to turn him inside out would encourage my Socialist friends if it were not for the sufficiently notorious and deplorable fact that most of them are much more on Dr. Saleeby's side in the matter than on mine. Dr. Saleeby says that "the present advocates of polygamy propose to destroy not only monogamy, but the home and family." We may accept his assurance; but will he kindly give us the address of these people? Who are they? Where do they live? In what halls do they meet? In what pulpits do they preach? What is the name of their organization? What is the title of their newspaper? Can he possibly mean the Sociological Society, of which he is, like myself, a member?[2] It certainly discusses polygamy as it discusses every other social institution. But it does not advocate it. We are all, I presume, marriage reformers in one degree or another. Of course there are Mormons about, and Agapemonists, and "Varietists," and stirpiculturists and so forth. Mr. George Meredith proposed a time limit to marriage. George Eliot lived with a man who was separated from his lawful wife. Ruskin was divorced. Dr. Saleeby hints politely that if the truth were known my own private conduct will not bear investigation. I implore him to prove it; for I am almost ruined by the persistence with which the critics declare that I am a bloodless, passionless intellectual machine, incapable of realising the splendid delights of dramatic adultery. A scandal would rehabilitate me: I court it: I say not a word in my own defence. But what has all this to do with the Socialist movement? Dr. Saleeby did not mention the Socialist movement by name. Neither did he mention me by name. Perhaps he did not mean the Socialist movement, and did not mean me? If so, then his article loses all its topical interest; and I apologise. Can a gentleman do more?

Yours, &c.,
G. Bernard Shaw

II

[10 December 1907.]

Sir,—Since Doctor Saleeby seems to be in some doubt as to why I "went for him," I may say now that I did so because he made an absolutely unprovoked and scandalous attack on me and on another equally innocent writer. I seized the opportunity to give some useful instructions to the readers of the "Pall Mall Gazette" as well as to remind Dr. Saleeby that the ordinary courtesies of debate need not be suspended in discussions of sex.

Dr. Saleeby need not worry about Westermarck. I have read Westermarck, and have no reason to doubt that Dr. Saleeby has read him with equal care, as our statements concerning him agree perfectly. It is true that when I accepted Dr. Saleeby's statement, he immediately yielded to an irresistible impulse to contradict it;

[2]Shaw was a founding member of the Sociological Society in 1903; Saleeby and Westermarck were members of its council.

but the public will not blame him for a momentary loss of presence of mind.

Now for the real purpose of this letter, which is to help Dr. Saleeby in his work as a Maternalist. Dr. Saleeby is quite wildly misled by maternalist sentiment when he assumes in the matter of State protection of children that "the State sinned and the State repented: the mothers were motherly all the time if they had had the chance." As a matter of fact, the mothers furiously resisted the State when it rescued the children from them. At this very moment, the proposals to carry the work of rescue a step further by raising the age of the half-timers in the northern factories is being so resolutely opposed by the parents that the reform will have to be carried over their heads by the constituencies in which the question does not arise. Dr. Saleeby's rhetoric about "shallow, and cruel and brutally untrue libels upon mothers" does credit to his feelings; but he will be of no practical use as a maternalist until he gets rid of these sentimental illusions. He will find when he comes down to practical work as a maternalist that neither the rich mothers nor the poor mothers will act up to his expectations. The rich mothers will not take care of their children at all: they will not even suckle them for fear of spoiling their figures. The poor mothers he will find divided roughly into three classes about equal in numbers. One of these classes is so utterly unfit to be trusted even partially with the care of children that there is nothing for it but to take their families completely out of their hands. The women of the second section are incapable of managing for their children; but if the State takes the management off their hands, they will give them some affection and such home care and influence as any normally kind-hearted adult can exercise. The third section will help to keep Dr. Saleeby's faith alive by taking care of their children quite capably whilst they are out of school, and bringing them up as well as their means will permit. As far as I am able to ascertain, these are the hard facts of the existing situation.

But all this has nothing to do with the larger proposition which I put before the country in Man and Superman, and which I referred to at the meeting of the Sociological Society in the words quoted by Dr. Saleeby as expressing what he calls "a literally hateful conception of fatherhood."[3] The overwhelming social difficul-

[3]Saleeby and Shaw probably are referring to Shaw's remarks after reading a paper by Francis Galton on "Eugenics: Its Definition, Scope and Aims"; both the

ty we are in at present is that the mere growth of population has produced political problems which are completely beyond the mental grasp of the human units who have to deal with these problems as voters. Dr. Saleeby may pour forth dozens of dithyrambs to fatherhood and motherhood and marriage and monogamy; but still he has to face the fact that marriage has not yet produced a capable citizen even for village purposes. Civilisation after civilisation has collapsed through the fundamental weakness; and there is every symptom that our civilisation is going to go the way of the others. I need not repeat here the reasoning which led me from this undeniable fundamental fact to the conclusion which so shocked Dr. Saleeby at the Sociological Society. All I need say is that before Dr. Saleeby can persuade me to sacrifice the future of human society to his maternalism he will have to tackle me with harder weapons than the indignant enthusiasm of a young man's mother-worship.

Yours, &c.,
G. Bernard Shaw

REGICIDE AS "ACCIDENT DE TRAVAIL"

[On 1 February 1908 King Carlos and Crown Prince Franco of Portugal were assassinated in Lisbon. Shaw's letter to the *Saturday Review* appeared on 8 February.]

Sir,—Would it not be well for some journal in the position of the *Saturday Review* to initiate a serious correspondence on the subject of regicide? For obvious reasons the circulation of such a correspondence had better be restricted to readers with intellectual interests and some historic training; and the subscribers to the *Saturday Review* probably answer to that description as closely as is possible under existing circumstances.

The appalling frequency of political assassinations, successful or attempted, has made kingship a conspicuously "dangerous trade"; and the public seems to think that when it has raised an hysterical clamour of sympathy with the relatives of the victims, and solemnly described the obvious devotion and courage of the

paper and Shaw's remarks were published in *Sociological Papers*, vol. I (1905). Shaw had said that what society needs "is freedom for people who have never seen each other before and never intend to see one another again to produce children under certain definite public conditions, without loss of honor."

assassins as dastardly cowardice, everything has been done that the most exacting monarch can expect. I must say that if I were a king I should feel very little reassured by such futilities. Sympathy will not stop bullets nor damp bombs; and if a man has courage enough to kill a king at the cost of his own life, he is quite brave enough for the king, however loudly our sub-editors may assure the survivors that he was a coward. Such clamour rather increases the danger than otherwise by investing regicide with the fascination of morbid sensationalism; and our royal families might well point out, with some bitterness, that if all the royal personages who have been attacked or slaughtered since Alexander II. of Russia had been auctioneers, the Auctioneers' Institutes of Europe would long ago have forced our Governments to consider the peril seriously.

Our own position is a delicate one, because we are historically on the side of the assassins. We had our Carlos and our Franco; and we set the world the example of Liberal regicide. Our statue of Cromwell stands nearer to Westminster Hall than our statue of Charles. The French followed our example. The thing was done, it is true, under forms of law; but I am trying to look at it now from the king's point of view; and will anyone pretend that Charles or Louis would have admitted any constitutional distinction between their trials and executions and the comparatively merciful method of the Portuguese assassins?

The real question we have to face is, What were the Portuguese to do? The same question was raised in Germany in 1861 by the Kaiser's grandfather, when, by the advice of Bismarck, he expelled his Parliament from their chamber by military force, and announced that he would rule autocratically for the good of the people. Ferdinand Lassalle, the Socialist, solved the problem without regicide. He first explained, in reply to the Liberal complaints of the King's action as unconstitutional, that the real constitution of a country was not what the Liberal newspapers chose to say it was, but the actual effective forces then operative in the country. If the King can despotically turn the Parliament out, then, said Lassalle, the real Constitution is a despotic one, no matter what it is called. This pleased the Court party; and Lassalle was well spoken of in the Court papers until he went on to advise the Liberals to withdraw from all public activity and leave the King to do his work despotically as best he could in the face of European public opinion.

So far, this is the only alternative to regicide now before the public. And it has lost much of its force because European public opinion is no longer Liberal, no longer even constitutional. Bismarck himself formally inaugurated the "blood and iron" phase of public opinion—if a huge aggregate of the ignorant private rancours and prejudices and romancings of politically uneducated people can be called public opinion; and the difficulties of civil war (the alternative to assassination) have been greatly increased by modern weapons. As Lassalle had ascertained experimentally, the ordinary citizen neither understands nor values his constitutional rights sufficiently to fight for them: he would sell Magna Charta, the Bill of Rights, and the Habeas Corpus Act as waste paper to oblige a good West End customer. What then are the few men who do understand the magnitude of the issues to do?

Let me try to bring the question home to England. For two hundred years our monarchs have run no risks except the risks (serious enough, unfortunately) which all conspicuous persons run from lunatics. Our kings have accepted the Liberal position so completely that we have forgotten that it is still possible for kings to do what the late King of Portugal did. Our revolutions have been general elections swinging the pendulum between Whigs and Tories, whose differences were superficial. But the twentieth century brings a new force into the field—Socialism. Private property, at present supreme over both King and Parliament, may within the lifetime of many now living be defending its last ditch. Suppose the next four general elections show such a steady increase of the Socialists in Parliament as to make it a practical certainty that the fifth general election will place them in a majority! Suppose the only way of averting that will be the repeal of the last two great Reform Acts, or the introduction of the three-class system, with the establishment of a Strafford-Franco[1] dictatorship to suppress public demonstrations against these measures! Suppose the propertied classes and the Government of the day compel the reigning monarch to countenance these proceedings! Suppose that he, having taken his political bias, not, like King Edward, in the heyday of Victorian Liberalism, but in the heyday of Jingo Imperialism, were to throw himself heart and soul into the attack on Democracy! What should we do? What would be our remedy against the King? The English answer, so far, is, Kill him. The

[1]Shaw conflates Sir Thomas Strafford, the adviser to Charles I in England, who urged despotic acts, and Franco, who assumed the dictatorship of Portugal in 1900 as King Carlos tried to defuse popular opinion.

French answer, so far, is, Kill him. The Russian answer, so far, is, Kill him. The Portuguese answer, so far, is, Kill him. The ancient Roman answer, glorified to the utmost of his power by our greatest poet, is, Kill him. No sane and humane person can be satisfied with that answer; but it stands, and will continue to stand, until a better one is found.

Can the readers of the *Saturday Review* find the better answer?

Yours, &c.,
G. Bernard Shaw

SHAW EXPLAINS HIS RELIGION

[*The Freethinker,* 1 November 1908.]

Sir,—May I explain myself to the younger members of your flock—if you will allow me so to describe the readers of *The Freethinker*—who may otherwise be discouraged in their adventure into Freethought by the taunt that so conspicuous an atheist as myself recanted as soon as he was old enough to know better?

I have never changed my mind about popular religion in this country. I do not claim that this is a merit on my part: on the contrary, a genuine Freethinker should change his mind as often and as carefully as he changes his linen. But as a matter of fact, to be deplored or applauded as the case may be, I loathe the mess of mean superstitions and misunderstood prophecies which is still rammed down the throats of children in this country under the name of Christianity as contemptuously as ever. And in my opinion the blackest spot in English public life is the cowardly dishonor in which our public men leave the Blasphemy Laws unrepealed, and imply, in all their utterances on religious education and imperial organization, that they worship the savage idol in the tale of the bears sent to eat the children who mocked Elisha's baldness; that our Mahometan, Buddhist and Hindu fellow subjects are walking in darkness whilst our Glassites and Agapemonites and Plymouth Brethren and Countess-of-Huntingdonians are bathing in celestial light; and that Mr. Edmund Gosse's[1] father was a

[1]Poet and man of letters, librarian 1904–14 to the House of Lords, who introduced Ibsen to the English public. His father Philip, a zoologist and Plymouth Brother, was the central figure in his autobiographical book *Father and Son* (1907).

more enlightened man than Matthew Arnold. We may congratulate ourselves on the fact that the present Government contains only one man stupid enough to institute a prosecution for blasphemy; but what are we to say to that other fact that though every one of his fellow ministers who is of sufficient importance to make his opinions ascertainable, would, if the Blasphemy Laws were sincerely and impartially carried out, be an ex-prisoner legally incapable of holding his office, they all cowered shamelessly before the superstition of that colleague, and virtually committed themselves to the opinion that a man should be ruinously punished with the vilest criminals for refusing to believe that the birth of Jesus was parthenogenetic.

Your younger readers will now ask why, if these are my views, I am regarded by so many Secularists as an apostate. When I spoke on Progress in Freethought at the Hall of Science after the death of Bradlaugh,[2] why was I received with a burst of fury such as no clergyman need have feared there? Why do the congregations of the City Temple and Westbourne Park Chapel, with their famous pastors in the chair, make much of me, whilst the National Secular Society, after two trials, had to drop me as an intolerable blasphemer whose lectures would drive away the old guard on whose subscriptions the Society depended?

The answer is that I am contemptuously and implacably antirationalist and anti-materialist, and that the Secularism of the National Secular Society, in spite of your leadership, is crudely rationalistic and materialistic. When I called myself an atheist years ago in order to make it clear that I was on the side of Bradlaugh in his fight with the House of Commons, I meant that I had exactly the same opinion of what his persecutors called God as Mahomet had of the stones which the Arabs worshipped before he converted them. I used a negative term to express a negative position. I repeatedly and publicly repudiated the term Agnostic (logical as it was), because an Agnostic was then understood to declare, with regard to the existence of God (which then meant Jehovah), that he did not know. I said I could not take that position, because I *did* know that there was no such person. When questioners asked how I could prove a negative, I asked them how they could prove that there was not a blue horse with green wings

[2]The radical MP, who had led the National Secular Society, died on 30 January 1891. Shaw's lecture "Free Thinking, New and Old" was delivered before the society on 22 February.

capering at that moment on the roof of St. Paul's Cathedral, and what they would think of my intellect and character if, merely because I had not been to Ludgate Hill to make sure, I hesitated to deny, dogmatically and flatly, that there was such a horse so occupied.

So far, the Secularists regarded me as one of themselves. But neither Secularists nor anyone else can live on negations, any more than vegetarians can live on mere abstention from meat. When the account given in Genesis of the origin of the universe held the field, the man who said "Rubbish!" made an important contribution to Freethought; and our consciousness of that made us all say "Rubbish!" with an earnestness and eloquence which now seem ridiculous. For, very unexpectedly, Genesis fell before us like the walls of Jericho. And from that moment the Freethinkers, instead of being met with angry assertions of the actual existence of the Garden of Eden, found themselves eagerly and respectfully invited to explain the universe by people who quite agreed that the Bible story was impossible. The Agnostic reply, "I don't know," meant simple extinction of the Freethinker as a leader of thought. It may be a frank answer and a true answer; but so is the answer of the man who says "I don't know" when you ask him the way to Putney. You do not question his honesty; but you take no further interest in him.

When, as Nietzsche-Zarathustra put it, "God is dead," Atheism dies also. Bible-smashing is tedious to people who have smashed their Bibles. I do not say that there is no work left for atheists and Bible-smashers among people who remain steeped in the crude idolatry that is still all that religion means to large masses of the English people, though I doubt whether the line can be drawn higher now than at what the Roman Catholic Church gives up as Invincible Ignorance. But that is not my job. I prefer positive work; and, indeed, whether we like it or not, we all have to face positive work if we are to retain any hold of the pioneering section of the public. When you said, very penetratingly, in your article on my City Temple sermon that God is in process of manufacture, you put Atheism aside just as a man puts his gun aside when he has shot the tiger and must set to work with his spade. The clearing away of false solutions is not a clearing away of problems: quite the contrary: it brings you face to face with them. Denial has no further interest: you must begin to affirm.

Under this pressure there arose Neo-Darwinism, or the explanation of all phenomena as the result of Natural Selection. The world, according to this view, is only a purposeless accident, interesting only because of its amazing simulation of design and the ingenuity of its explanation. Opposed to this stands the 1790–1830 theory of Evolution as the struggle of a creative Will or Purpose (called by me the Life Force) towards higher forms of life—God in process of manufacture, as you put it. Neo-Darwinism is a materialistic theory. Evolution is a mystical one.

The Secularists embraced Natural Selection rather because it was the opposite extreme to Jehovah-worship than from any serious grasp of it and its ghastly implications. I took my own side, the mystical side, which at once brings me far nearer to Mr. Campbell, to Dr. Clifford,[3] to the late Samuel Butler, than to any Neo-Darwinian atheist. I cannot force any man to use my term Life Force to denote what he calls God; but if we both mean the same thing, and if the Neo-Darwinian atheist means something profoundly different, I had better be taken to be on the theologian's side against the atheist. Only, I prefer my own term, as it suggests none of the attributes of the ridiculous old *deus ex machina* to whose stuffed shoulders we used to shift all our responsibilities. If you ask me to shew you my "god's" head I shew you my own head (or your's). If you doubt the strength of its hands I tell you that it has no other hands than ours. And I solemnly warn you that if the present failure of our heads and hands to make a higher life possible continues, it will assuredly evolve some creature (it may not be even a Superman: it may be a Supersnake) who will clear us out as ruthlessly and completely as we have cleared the bison out of America, keeping only a few of us in the Zoo for the amusement of its young. That will certainly happen if, by taking to Neo-Darwinism, we all become, what so many Neo-Darwinians already are, a mob of futile cowards, seeking the elixir of life by vivisection because they have not the courage to seek political liberty by dynamite.

No doubt all this is obscure to people who imagine that Darwin invented Evolution, and who conclude, when I say that Mr. Campbell's Christ is, apart from a few inessential survivals of the

[3]Respectively, the Reverend Reginald John Campbell, a longtime Fabian, from 1903 to 1915 minister of the City Temple; and Dr. John Clifford, pastor of the Praed Street Baptist Church and the most influential figure in the Nonconformist churches.

old legend, as credible and interesting a person as Mr. Keir Hardie,[5] that I am preaching the doctrine of the Atonement. What I said at the City Temple was a simple statement of fact. I have always said that it was obvious to me as a professional expert in literature that the gospels are fictions and the epistles documents. I do not object to the gospels on that account any more than to the dramas of Euripides or Shakespeare; nor do I admit that a fiction is less true than a document—quite the opposite, in fact. There are no lies in *Hamlet;* and our bluebooks are mostly full of lies. But I regarded Jesus as a fictitious character exactly as I regard Shakespeare's Henry V. as a fictitious character. There may have been an actual preacher named Jesus (or seven or eight Jesuses, as Mr. J. M. Robertson[6] once contended) just as there was undoubtedly a king called Henry V.; but there was so much less evidence, and the point was so unimportant in view of the fact that neither the Evangelist nor Shakespeare were engaged in the senseless work of reproducing mere biographical facts, that it was not worth making any reservations. Mr. Campbell, however, has reconstructed a credibly historical Jesus with such success that I am now quite prepared to entertain the proposition that he existed in the Post Office Directory sense, and that some of the most fantastic utterances recorded in the gospels may be accepted as genuine traditions in the light of Mr. Campbell's view of Christianity as a movement that dates from several centuries before Christ. This no more implies a change in my religious opinions than if Mr. Campbell had convinced me that there actually was once a patriarch who saved his tribe and his farm stock from an inundation by means of a raft and houseboat, and that his name was Noah. You will appreciate the irony of the fact that whereas the religious papers have quite understood this secularist explanation of my position, the Secularist papers persist in taking the old-fashioned evangelical view of it as the return to the fold of a lost sheep.

I have once or twice before been on the point of writing to the *Freethinker* to explain the situation. Dare I say why I refrained? Well, it was because I feared to force you into the position of having either to lose some of your oldest subscribers, or else pretend to be as bigotedly materialistic as some of them are. My convic-

[4]Founder and editor of the *Labour Leader,* a Welsh miner who became an independent Labour MP in 1892 and in 1906 the first leader of the Labour Party in Parliament.

[5]Shaw had lectured on "Literature and Art" on 8 October 1908.

[6]British journalist, politician, Shakespeare scholar, and freethinker.

tion that you would not hesitate to speak your mind on that account was only an additional reason for not creating the dilemma. But now I think it better to get the explanation off my mind, leaving it open to you to treat this letter (of which I have kept no copy) as a public or a private one just as you think fit.

Yours, &c.,
G. Bernard Shaw

THE DEMONSTRATION AGAINST THE TSAR

[British relations with Russia, often strained and usually complex because of British interests in Asia that potentially conflicted with Russian ones, appeared to improve with a series of Anglo-Russian agreements commencing in 1907. King Edward and Tsar Nicholas met at Reval in 1908 and Cowes in 1909. Those who objected to the agreements usually did so on the basis of the tsar's despotism. Shaw's letter, in the *Saturday Review* on 17 July 1909, concerned a mass meeting called by the Labour Party in Trafalgar Square on Sunday, 25 July, "To protest against the Czar being received at Cowes in the name of the people of Great Britain. . . ." Among those participating, besides Shaw (who represented the Fabian Society), were Keir Hardie, J. Ramsay MacDonald, H. M. Hyndman, Margaret Bondfield, Ben Tillett, and George Lansbury.]

Sir,—In your issue of the 10th, commenting on the announced Trafalgar Square demonstration of the 25th July, you say that you can hardly believe that I am going to be one of the performers, adding that no man knows better that British indignation against Russian policy, especially on social questions, is either ignorance or hypocrisy.

I have to observe on this that there is no such thing as British indignation, one and indivisible. Certain Britishers loathe the Russian policy, just as certain other Britishers loathe Mr. Lloyd George's fiscal policy. The only way in which these sections can make their sentiments known, and thereby get counted in that estimate of public opinion which statesmen must have continually before them, is to demonstrate. There is to be a tremendous demonstration in the Solent[1] in favour of the Tsar. If there were to be no counter-demonstration the Government would be justified in concluding that the nation was unanimously in favour of the Solent demonstration. The object of the Trafalgar Square demon-

[1]The region around Cowes abutting the western part of the channel (called the Solent) between the Isle of Wight and the English mainland.

stration is to make such a disastrous and dishonourable inference impossible.

Nothing is more natural and proper than that I should take part in such a demonstration, as I happen to believe that all England's advantages over Russia depend on the fact that when kings behave in England as the Tsar behaves in Russia we either cut their heads off or replace them by their nearest well-behaved relative.

You are, I think, a little unjust to your own country in implying that it is as bad as Russia. It is quite true that England behaves in Ireland, Egypt, and India as the Tsar behaves in Russia; but Ireland, Egypt, and India are conquered countries, held in that position by simple force, exactly as England would have to be held if conquered by Ireland, Egypt or India. That would be no excuse for the tyranny of an English king over his own country; and it gives no countenance to the abominable tyranny of which the Tsar is the representative. The Englishman who neglects this opportunity of throwing a brick at him (metaphorically, of course) is utterly unworthy of his country and its traditions. I hope the *Saturday Review* will charter a canal barge, paint its name in bold white letters on both sides of it, hang it with Union Jacks surmounted by caps of liberty and black flags of mourning for the Tsar's victims, and place it well in evidence in the Solent on the day of our national disgrace.

Yours, &c.,
G. Bernard Shaw

GENERAL MOURNING: AN OVERLOOKED HARDSHIP

[Edward VII died on the night of 6 May 1910. Shaw's letter appeared in *The Times* on 12 May.]

Sir,—So much solicitude has been shown in the highest quarters to prevent any suffering among the working classes from the general mourning that I am emboldened to put in a plea on behalf of the class which, if not the poorest in the kingdom, perhaps suffers most from pecuniary anxiety. Take the case of a man with a professional or business income of a few hundreds a year, with three daughters at the nearest high school. The school is compelled to go into mourning. The dresses provided for the season have to be discarded, and new black dresses have to be bought. To a Court official it may be inconceivable that so trifling an expense could be a hardship to any one. By those who know what life on a small income is to people who have to keep up a social position above that of the working class it will be more justly appreciated as a calamity. The remedy is to drop the vague expression "decent mourning," and to define the wearing of a violet ribbon as the appropriate mourning for Royalty. This would be correct, inexpensive, and pretty. Why our schools should be deliberately made hideous with black because an honourable public career has come to its natural close in all peace, fulfilment, and cheerful memory is not apparent to any healthy-minded person.

I hope also that it will be understood that people who, like myself, abhor mourning, and have never worn it for their own nearest relatives, making it, indeed, a point of honour to discourage what we regard as a morbid attitude towards death, are as susceptible as any of the mourning wearers to the sympathy which goes out quite naturally and spontaneously to those to whom the late King's death brings too intimate a loss to be felt for the moment otherwise than as a keen personal grief.

Yours, &c.,
G. Bernard Shaw

THE CULT OF THE CORPSE

[When a controversy in the *Pall Mall Gazette* on cremation as a means of disposal of the dead diverged into a discussion of the effect of cremation on the detection of crime, the editor of the paper, Frederick J. Higginbottom, invited views from several prominent men. Shaw's response was published on 18 August 1910.]

Sir,—It is inexcusable carelessness to get hanged at present. A brief study of our system of death certification will enable any intelligent person to commit such murders as he (or she) may desire with impunity and with perfect consideration for the feelings of the relatives and the credit of his (or her) own family. Probably most of the deaths now occurring are, if not murders, at least deaths in which Nature is assisted. At all events, nobody can prove the contrary.

The public does not acquire an inside knowledge of cemeteries until it dies and is buried. If it did interment would be prohibited by law within a month of the discovery. The objection to burial is not that people are occasionally buried alive; on the contrary, buried people are quite unobjectionable whilst they survive. It is dead bodies that matter. How much they matter can only be grasped by those who know something of the real working of a graveyard. Our attachment to the practice of interment is not sentiment or respect for the dead, but superstition, stupidity, and slavery to the wrong sort of imagination—the imagination that conceives unseen things as they are not and cannot be as distinguished from the imagination that sees things as they are and must be.

Yours, &c.,
G. Bernard Shaw

TOO LONG STORIES

[*Westminster Gazette,* 13 September 1910.]

Sir,—In my opinion fiction should be sold by the pound, as Blue-books[1] are. I attribute a good deal of the steadiness of my own market to the fact that I have always thoroughly understood that people have to lay in a household store of reading, just as they have to lay in a household store of tea or cheese, and that they expect four-and-sixpence worth of it to last a certain time. I should like to take this opportunity of informing my customers that my next volume[2] will contain three complete plays and three prefaces comparable to Royal Commission Reports on subjects of universal interest. It will keep an average man of business in active reading for a fortnight, and will last the family fully a month; and it will bear reading over again once every eighteen months for life. This estimate does not include reading in bed; but it will be found under rather than over the mark with fair reading. You save money by buying my books. Books are like boots: if only they are readable and fit comfortably, those which last longest are the best. Mr. Heinemann[3] was the first publisher to grasp this fact, though it had long been familiar to every man of moderate means with a

[1]Official reports of Parliament and the Privy Council.
[2]An edition, published by Constable in February 1911, of the plays *The Doctor's Dilemma, Getting Married,* and *The Shewing-up of Blanco Posnet* with their prefaces—a total of five hundred pages for six shillings.
[3]William Heinemann, who founded his house in 1890, built much of his success on fiction. Among the novelists who appeared prominently in his lists were Henry James, Joseph Conrad, H. G. Wells, and such big money-makers as Hall Caine, Sarah Grand, and William De Morgan.

houseful of daughters all clamouring for something to read. Hence the 100,000-word novel.

Yours, &c.,
G. Bernard Shaw

THE METRIC SYSTEM

[A letter captioned "A Plea for the Metric System," signed "M. P.," was published in *The Nation* on 1 October 1910. It elicited correspondence from a number of contributors, including a letter from Alfred Watkins on 15 October. Shaw weighed in a week later.]

Sir,—You have had the usual exasperating letter demanding the establishment of the decimal metric system from a novice; and you have also had the unusual but valuable and entirely sound setting-right of the novice by an expert, Mr. Alfred Watkins.[1] May I now take up the discussion at the point to which Mr. Watkins has brought it. That point is, that in any practical metric system we must count, not in tens, but in fours or multiples of four. He suggests eights or sixteens. If we take eights, our figure notation would be 1, 2, 3, 4, 5, 6, 7, 10, 11, 12, 13, 14, 15, 16, 17, 20, &c., &c.; and a boy asking a greengrocer for 20 apples would be handed what we call 16. If we take sixteens, we shall have to write 16 as 10, and rename all the numbers from our 10 to our 15—thus, 1, 2, 3, 4, 5, 6, 7, 8, 9, ∀, ꓭ, Ɔ, ᗡ, Ǝ, Ⅎ, 10, 11, 12, 13, 14, 15, 16, 17, 18, 19, 1∀, 1ꓭ, 1Ɔ, 1ᗡ, 1Ǝ, 1Ⅎ, 20, 21, &c. Now the introduction of six new and unfamiliar digits is a large order; yet if we therefore reject sixteens and fall back on eights, we avoid, it is true, any new digits, but we run into three figures at our 80 instead of at our 100, into four figures at our 800, and so on, which is incompendious. Besides, as I shall shew presently, the complete avoidance of new digits is a mistake. The best plan, and the most familiar one, is to count by twelves and introduce two new digits. Call them, for illustration's sake, tee and ee, and note them as ⊥ and Ǝ. Then you count one, two, three, four, five, six, seven, eight, nine, tee (our 10), ee (our 11), ten (our 12), eleven (our 13), twelve (our 14), thirteen (our 15), fourteen (our 16), fifteen (our 17), sixteen (our 18), seventeen (our 19), eighteen (our

[1]Antiquarian, naturalist, and photographer as well as mathematician, Watkins would later publish a plea against the decimal system, *Must We Sell in Tenths?* (1919).

20), nineteen (our 21), teeteen (our 22), eeteen (our 23), and twenty (our 24). You would, of course, recast your multiplication tables and pence tables, and so forth, accordingly. When the boy asks for ten apples he will get what we call twelve; and when the greengrocer buys a hundred he will get what we call a gross (144). The notation will be just as convenient as that of the decimal metric system: thirty-four pence will be three and fourpence, and percentages will be calculated by a simple shift of the duodecimal point. And you will be able without fractions, not only to halve and quarter your standard quantities and coins, but to third them, which is often very convenient. You cannot do this with eight or sixteen.

The introduction of the two new digits would have the important advantage of making the new arithmetic unmistakable for the old. If a column of figures represented a new system without any visible new characteristic, its appearance would be simply that of the old system, with the sum wrong, just as all those proposals for simplified spelling which avoid new letters break down because they produce the effect of ludicrous misspelling in the manner of Artemus Ward or Mr. Dooley.[2] The new system should proclaim itself emphatically to the eye of the generation which would have to struggle through the confusion of the change, and to resist the impulse to write to The Times complaining that a Liberal Postmaster-General was charging one and fivepence for fifteen penny stamps.

Mr. Watkins is entirely right in his contention that the decimal system is psychologically repugnant as well as physically inconvenient. Give a cabman eighteenpence, and he thanks you for having given him more than a shilling. Give him a florin for the same ride, and he despises you as no gentleman, because you have filched sixpence from his half-crown. The double florin has perished because it was nothing but a spurious five-shilling piece. If instead of these detested coins a silver six-and-eightpence had been introduced, it would probably have been as great a success with the general public as with solicitors.

The original mistake we made was in not evolving six digits on our hands and feet. When we had to count up to ten, we count-

[2]Both Ward (the pseudonym of Charles Farrar Browne) and Mr. Dooley (a character created by Finley Peter Dunne) were popular expressions of American humor and personal favorites of Shaw.

ed on our fingers. Even up to twenty we could count the second ten on our toes. But beyond that we had to make a mark somewhere to show how many times we had counted ten; and that led us to a decimal notation. Had we had six digits on each hand we should have made our notation duodecimal. As it was, we made it decimal; but the practical need for quartering quantities led us to a duodecimal market practice. The French have attempted to alter the duodecimal practice to suit the decimal notation, but without real success. The right way is to alter the notation to suit the practice. No doubt we are too stupid and lazy to do it; but at all events, we had better know what we ought to do, lest we be landed at last in all the trouble, cost, and confusion of a change, only to find that we have changed to the wrong thing after all.

Yours, &c.,
G. Bernard Shaw

P. S.—Those who find the above figures puzzling must bear in mind that the figure 10 does not, like the lower figures, denote a fixed quantity, but simply one batch, no matter how many units the batch contains. 11 means one batch plus one, 12 one batch plus two, and so on. The fact that we keep accounts by batches containing as many units as we have fingers and thumbs leads us to associate the figure 10 with that quantity; but it is applicable to any quantity we may choose to count by. If we counted by threes we should write 1, 2, 10, 11, 12, 20, 21, 22, 30, &c.; and a family of 21 children would be what we call a family of 7.

DOG VS. MOTOR

I

[*The Car,* 22 February 1911.]

Sir,—Mr. Plunket Greene's[1] letter is not one for which anyone who likes dogs and appreciates their friendship will blame him; yet I, who claim to be in that position myself, have acted precisely as those two gentlemen, whom Mr. Plunket Greene calls

[1]Harry Plunket Greene, a bass baritone with an established reputation in concert halls, became professor of singing at the Royal Academy in 1911. In a letter in *The Car* on 15 February, he had complained of the caddish conduct of a motorist who sped away after killing his children's pet dog.

heartless cads, acted. I have more than once run over a dog and driven away as if nothing had happened, and on every such occasion there has been a lady in the car. Will Mr. Greene tell us what he would do in the same circumstances? I take it that a good deal depends on the lady. If she is a heartless cad, no doubt the correct thing is to stop the car, so that she may enjoy the "ghastly business of some minutes' duration," and perhaps laugh at the distress of the dog's owners. But suppose she is a humane and sensitive person, very fond of dogs, and likely to suffer acute distress for some days after witnessing ghastly businesses—what then? Is it so clear, as Mr. Plunket Greene thinks, that it is the duty of the driver, who can do no earthly good to the unfortunate animal, and whose apologies are much more likely to lead to a painful and undignified scene than to be of much comfort at such a moment, to stop and call the attention of his lady passenger to what has happened?

It is so far from being clear to me that I am quite sure that if Mr. Plunket Greene is ever inconsiderate enough to act once as he suggests, he will not do it twice. When I have had nobody's feelings to consult but my own and those of my *chauffeur,* I have stopped, and the experience I have gathered in this way does not justify me in advising other people to follow my example. When you are unfortunate enough to kill a dog, and can neither restore the dead to life nor achieve an extraordinary display of tact in consoling people who, for the moment, loathe you, by far your best plan is to withdraw as rapidly as possible, especially if you are disposed to resent being treated as if you did it on purpose.

How unreasonable people can be when they are upset by the loss of a pet animal is shown by Mr. Plunket Greene's complaint that the Andover motorists who killed his dog "left to his children all that remained of it." If they had carried it off, he would hardly have regarded that as an extenuating circumstance. If they had stopped, and Mr. Plunket Greene had appeared on the scene, does it not seem at least possible that in his distress he might have said things to them—perhaps even done things to them—that would have convinced them that it is impossible to undo or mitigate a really painful accident by a few polite speeches, however sincere they may be?

Besides, what is the motorist to say? If he says it was not his fault, his exculpation irritates the owner by implicating the dog. And he can hardly be expected to say that it *was* his fault. No doubt he might simply say the right thing. But the man who can say the right thing at the right moment under agitating and probably provocative circumstances is a man in ten thousand. For the other nine thousand nine hundred and ninety-nine, the safest rule is, "If you can do no good, hold your tongue and clear out." If you stop to apologise you will presently find yourself stopping to argue; and that is not likely to improve matters. You begin by saying that you are extremely sorry. You end by pointing out that if people choose to allow their dogs to stray about the roads they must take the consequences; that you have already apologised, and that you have heard as much of the affair as you are disposed to stand.

Mr. Plunket Greene says that he has failed to identify the owners of the cars which killed his dogs. Suppose he succeeds in doing so, what will happen? He will presumably make a claim for the value of the dogs. The car owners will have done for their cars what he should have done for his dogs—insured them. They will refer his claim to the insurance companies. The insurance companies will inform Mr. Plunket Greene that since it is not suggested that the slaughter was malicious or intentional, the owners of the cars are not liable in any way—that though, if a dog which is not under proper control causes damage to a motor-car which *is* under proper control, the dog's owner is actionable, the converse does not hold good. And Mr. Plunket Greene will have had his trouble for nothing. He has absolutely no case as a matter of law, and the object of this letter is to show that the motorists may have a very strong case as a matter of feeling.

I hope I am not showing any want of sympathy with Mr. Plunket Greene. If I had run over his dog, I should have felt miserable about it for a considerable time afterwards. Many motorists would feel the same. But our sympathy must not lead us into hypocrisy. The flat truth is that the slain dog for which a motorist stops is his first dog. No man stops for his tenth dog unless the circumstances are unusual, or he can do something more to the purpose than making sympathetic speeches, whilst politely but firmly refusing to admit that he is responsible, pecuniarily, legally, or morally, for the casualties which are inevitable as long as carriageways for fast traffic are used as fowl-runs, pastures, and playgrounds for pet animals, and even for infants. Every good-natured motorist will do what he can to avoid these casualties, for the sake of his own feelings as well as those of others; but he will kill a dog rather than a child, and a hen rather than a dog; and though to the end he will make more allowances for a puppy than for a dog, there will inevitably come a time (usually after about his twelfth act of involuntary slaughter) when he will think a little less of the need for motorists to train their drivers to avoid dogs, and a little more of the need for dog owners to train their dogs to avoid motors.

I may mention that when my driver, by a miracle of address, saved the life of a huge black collie in an Irish village last year, the inspector of police reproached him strenuously for losing an opportunity of extirpating a brute that flew at everything, and was a terror to the whole place.[2] The public sympathy is not always with the dog. Mr. Plunket Greene's dogs, however, were not savage black collies. One of them was an Aberdeen, the other a dachshund. Now if there is one dog that is less to be trusted to take care of itself in traffic than an Aberdeen, it is a dachshund. Both are slow, and almost invariably preoccupied. And the moral is that they had better be kept off our main roads. The motorist cannot always avoid them, and when he kills them it is useless to expect him to stop and apologise.

Although I am exceptionally squeamish about hurting animals, and for that reason cannot endure shooting, fishing, or hunting, I can recall at least thirteen cases in which cars in which I was seated (sometimes at the wheel) have gone over dogs. In one case I stopped, and the owner of the dog, a little girl, went into violent hysterics when I spoke to her. I bought her a new dog.[3] In another, when a poor man's sheep dog was the victim, I did not stop; but I sent a postal order from the next town to provide a substitute. In another, I managed to extricate an old retriever whimpering from beneath the car, and to pet him back into good humour, before restoring him with no bones broken to his proprietors, a couple of ladies, who scolded him energetically. In the remaining ten cases, I behaved like the "heartless cads," of whom Mr. Plunket Greene complains; that is, I left the slain on the field, and fled on, either concealing the accident completely from my

[2]Shaw later told this story in delightful detail in "Touring in Ireland," published in *The Car* on 5 April 1916, reprinted in *The Matter with Ireland,* ed. Dan H. Laurence and David H. Greene (1962).

[3]On 31 December 1910, Shaw's chauffeur had accidentally killed the pet dog of an eight-year-old child while driving Shaw through Lancashire to a lecture.

lady passengers (most men would do as much for their wives, I hope), or persuading them that nothing very dreadful had happened. And in the one or two cases in which this was impossible, the distress caused was quite sufficient to impress me with the undesirability of adding to the number of sufferers for no other purpose than to make a display of good manners and bad sense.

Again, may I express my desire to avoid any appearance of demurring unsympathetically to an expression of grief and anger, which I can thoroughly understand, and to which I myself might easily be provoked in similar circumstances. But since there is another side to the case, it had better be frankly stated. We hear so much abuse of the runaway motorist that it is as well to make it clear that he may have both humane and common-sense reasons for his apparent callousness.

Yours, &c.,
G. Bernard Shaw

II

[*The Car,* 15 March 1911.]

Sir,—May I reply on the whole debate, which has now, I presume, exhausted itself?

First, let me deal with the writer of "Automobile Notes" in the *Times*. His words carry weight and deserve it; and he has put it to me that if my argument justifies flight after running over and killing a dog, it equally justifies flight after running over and killing a child. Certainly it does, even *a fortiori*. If the feelings of the custodians of the child are alone to be considered, then there cannot be the slightest doubt that every motorist who is unfortunate enough to run over and kill a child should vanish at the top of his speed. I will assume that the circumstances are the most painful conceivable; that the person in charge of the baby is the mother, and that she has seen it slain before her eyes. I assume, further, that the case is not one of Hagar and Ishmael in the wilderness, that there are bystanders or neighbours to render assistance, as there usually are within the compass of a baby's walk. Now what is the irreducible minimum of grief and trouble for the mother? She must suffer the loss of her child and the horror of seeing it slain. Nothing can recall that. She must attend a coroner's inquest, and describe the scene over again, recalling every detail to answer questions. But if only the motorist has got clean away, that is all. Those who come to her assistance in the road and carry the child away will be guiltless of its blood, and full of sympathy both with her grief and with her detestation of the fugitive motorist. In the coroner's court every question asked her will be a sympathetic question; and the inquest will be made as little painful for her as possible. And afterwards nobody will ever remind her of her tragedy.

Now let us see what will happen if the motorist stops. First, she has to endure his expressions of regret. It may even be, if she has fainted, that she finds herself actually in the hands of the man who has killed her child. At the coroner's court she sees him again, and is also confronted with his lawyer, plying her with questions to entrap her into admitting that it was all the baby's fault or her own. If she is very lucky the verdict may be one of misadventure; but it is quite as likely to be one of manslaughter. Just when time is healing her wound a little, she is dragged to another court, a much more terrifying court, where she has again to recall the scene, and again be heckled, harder than before, by a counsel who now has to save his client from a possibly ruinous sentence of imprisonment. From beginning to end the difference made to her by the presence of the motorist is a difference to the bad; so much that any woman who could foresee it all would implore the motorist himself to take his apologies, and his sympathy, and his gentlemanliness to the end of the world, relying on her to do everything in her power to prevent his being traced and identified.

Do I then advise the motorist to run away? Certainly not. There are limits to the self-sacrifice that can be demanded even from a motorist who has run over a child. As long as juries are thoughtless enough to regard flight on such occasions as evidence of callous ferocity, no motorist can be advised to attempt it under existing circumstances, because successful evasion is impossible. In the case of a dog it is easy enough; the distracted dog owner, and the bystanders, look at the dog instead of at the motorist's number; and the police will not trace a fugitive who has committed no crime, it not being their business to apprehend persons in order that they may be sued in the county court. But as the killing of a child involves an inquest, which may result in a verdict of manslaughter or even murder, the whole national machinery for the apprehension of criminals will be turned upon the motorist. His attempt to spare the feelings of the mother by flight will fail; he will be ignominiously dragged from his hiding place, and brought to trial; and the mother will be dragged to court to testify against him, and face his counsel, just as if he had surrendered at once. He will have accomplished nothing, except the loss of all hope of being considerately dealt with. His flight may have been well meant and chivalrous; but chivalry that does more harm than good is Quixotism, and I cannot recommend Quixotism as a rule of the road.

On the whole, when you kill a human being, stop. Do not apologise, nobody will trouble themselves about your gentility at such a moment, but give your name and address, and, heartless as it may seem, call attention to any facts that may tend to put the deceased in the wrong. I do not say that the rule has no exceptions. If I killed a tramp fifty miles from anywhere, and there was nobody about, I might perhaps bury him and say nothing for the sake of saving trouble; but even this, though natural, would be extremely imprudent.

As to the dog, the correspondence has left me not only unshaken in my opinion, but strongly confirmed in it. I repeat, if you can do no good—nay, if you can do no good that cannot be done equally well by the bystanders—do not stop. I have already given my reasons, and only two sections of your correspondents have taken any position that I did not deal with in my first communication. Let me deal with these two briefly now.

The first section claims that it is the duty of the motorist to put the moribund animal out of pain. I picture the motorist descending from his car, and returning on foot to his victim and his victim's owner, with his cap in one hand and a tyre lever in the other. Between each sentence of apology he delivers a smashing blow on the skull of the dying friend of man. And when he has battered its head to pieces he says, in his gentlest accent, "I think I can assure you that your poor pet no longer suffers." Now I do not deny that this course might save the dog some useless suffering. But I cannot pretend to think that it would make a good impression. People are not always reasonable about these things. I shall not try to dissuade any motorist from trying it if he likes; but I shall not try it myself. After all, the owner can always borrow a poker, and if he shrinks from using it, he is more likely to know the way to the nearest veterinary surgeon than the motorist. I should not leave a maimed and lonely dog to his fate in a desert, out of reach of assistance; but, as a matter of fact, lonely dogs do not occur in deserts, any more than babies do.

The second remonstrant section points out that the motorist who runs away loses an opportunity of demonstrating that he is a gentleman, and thereby defeats the main purpose for which, in the opinion of many respectable Englishmen, the universe was created. I confess I have no answer to this. I even recommend the deliberate pursuit and slaughter of dogs as an effective means of providing occasions for these displays of *bon ton*. But let nobody suppose that the test of good breeding will be a light one. Gentlemen who rehearse imaginary comedies of exquisite good manners as they sit at home reading *The Car* may easily find, when their romance becomes reality, the owner of the dog, instead of listening in gentle distress to the hero of the piece until his or her tears give way to grateful and comforted smiles, taking a tone so unjust, so unappreciative, perhaps so grossly abusive, not impossibly even so violent, that the easy-chair dream of gentility may come untrue to the extent of anything from a deplorable altercation to several rounds of personal combat.

To the lady who protests against the assumption that women are more squeamish than men, I protest that I never meant to imply that they were. I drive off to spare the feelings of my male passengers quite as much as those of the female ones. But it happens that the complaint which opened the correspondence laid stress on the fact that there was a lady in the car. That was why I dealt with it from the lady's point of view.

Finally, I appreciate the forbearance and kindliness of Mr. Plunket Greene's references to myself. But since he still feels strongly that the motorist should have shown some special consideration for the two children, may I again refer to my own experience? Under circumstances of some difficulty in traffic my car was confronted by two dogs each intent on one another. My driver succeeded in avoiding both; but a third, running across to join the other two, got under the car and was killed. Its custodian was a little girl. I felt about her as Mr. Plunket Greene feels; and I stopped. What was the result? When the begoggled monster who had just killed her dog approached her, possibly with the intention of continuing his fell work, she went into screaming hysterics; and I was glad to hand my card to a bystander for her; and hurry off as fast as I could. My behaviour was entirely correct and gentlemanly; but was it really considerate? Would I have acted as I did if I had used my imagination and seen the matter from the little girl's point of view? Is Mr. Plunket Greene quite sure that if the

Andover driver had stopped and descended and tried to console his children they would have understood his intentions? Was it so very thoughtless to leave them to their nurse?

About thirty years ago, at an obscure public meeting in London, a humble anarchist (the harmless variety) rose, and began an impassioned address with the words, "Oh, Mr. Chairman and Comrades and Brothers, let us not be respectable, let us not be ladies and gentlemen." This correspondence has convinced me that there is more to be said for that exhortation than I quite grasped when I heard it uttered.

Yours, &c.,
G. Bernard Shaw

THE DRAMA OF DISCUSSION

[A leading article, "The Drama of Discussion," in *The Times* on 13 November 1911, commented on Shaw's address "The Novelty of the New Drama," delivered before *The Times* Book Club on 9 March. Shaw's response to the leading article was published in *The Times* on 15 November.]

Sir,—Your article on this subject in Monday's issue is disabled by an odd mistake. It assumes that I described the human race as having outgrown the drama and reached a phase in which it cares only for platform discussion. The improbability of any sane mortal putting forward such a proposition is enormous. In my case it is not only improbable, but impossible. It is quite true that pure platform discussion is extremely popular. For example, Mr. Gilbert Chesterton is to debate with me[1] at the Memorial Hall on the 30th of this month, and though not a single advertisement has been issued, every seat in the hall has been sold for some time past and asked for five times over since: a phenomenon which I may safely challenge the most profusely-advertised theatrical performance to equal if it can. We have therefore already arrived at the point of finding a good debate more attractive than nine out of ten plays.

But what I actually said was that every individual playgoer passes through three phases. First, the phase of childish illusion, in

[1]The debate was on Shaw's resolution "I assert that a Democrat who is not also a Socialist is no gentleman."

which the Fairy Queen seems really a Fairy Queen, and the policeman in the harlequinade a real policeman. Second, the phase in which the play is known to be a play and the persons on the stage to be actors, but in which all the old theatrical situations seem fresh and thrilling and the principal actors fascinating and lovable. Third, the phase in which the old situations have become the dreariest of platitudes, and in which the once admired and beloved actor or actress (now a little older) is, on the whole, less attractive than the domestic fireside or the club smoking-room. Now the English people, being mostly in the third phase, does not go to the theatre, though it does go to discussions when it gets the chance. The theatre at present lives on the young, the ignorant, and the fanciers of divorce cases. The bulk of the nation occupies itself with business, politics, religion, and open-air sport, with a dash of music and pictures, and leaves the theatre aside as the most expensive and worst ventilated way to boredom and influenza.

My contention is that, if you are to tempt the adult, married, sensible Englishman from his comfortable house (and if you cannot you will have no real national drama), you must give him plays in which life is presented, not as a string of imitations of incidents from the sensation columns of the daily papers, with actors pretending to fight duels and actresses pretending to have their feelings hurt, and both pretending to kiss one another in transports of simulated passion, but as an enormously interesting mass of problems of conduct which every member of the audience has or may have to solve for himself or herself. In order to raise such problems "things must happen," as your article very properly insists. Also, they must happen to credibly human beings. I may have omitted to mention these two conditions in my address. I omitted many things: for example, I did not remind the audience that there are milestones on the Dover road. I was vain enough to think that any one who had ever been inside a London theatre would give me credit for knowing the rudiments of my own business and being incapable of such a contradiction in terms as that "a play should be no play, but a discussion." Let me ask now, as to this cry of "things must happen," What things? When a brick falls on a man's head, is that something happening? When a doubt falls into his soul as to whether he may not be wrong on a point on which he has hitherto felt confidently right, is that something happening?

Well, people over 30 will not go to the theatre to see an imitation brick weighing half an ounce fall on an imitation scalp made of strong pasteboard. They *will* go to the theatre to see doubts attack the soul. And unless the actor is skilful enough to convey the conflict in his soul by making faces at the audience (which would seem to be the ideal of the critics who object so strongly to "talk" in a play) I am afraid the doubts must be discussed, even if the result be that "drama of discussion" practised by Euripides, Aristophanes, Molière, Shakespeare, Goethe, Ibsen, Tolstoy: in short, which is the invariable symptom of the highest dramatic genius.

But even on the plane of childish make-believe it is ungrateful to reproach me for lack of physical action. Why, in one of my plays [*Misalliance,* 1910] an aeroplane comes down and smashes a greenhouse. What more can you possibly want?

Yours, &c.,
G. Bernard Shaw

GETTING DIVORCED

[In the second of a series of "Letters to the Well-Known" in the Westminster *Gazette,* the pseudonymous journalist "Proteus" had challenged Shaw's liberal views on divorce as expressed in the preface to *Getting Married.* The open letter and Shaw's answer were published on 22 November 1911.]

My Dear Proteus,—

You are a hopeless fool—probably unmarried.

Academically and foolishly speaking, nothing but indissoluble marriage can protect you from the solicitation of the person who says "Get divorced; and marry me"—if you really desire to be protected from a possibility which has an altogether salutary effect on disagreeable mates, and may be your only means of escape from a miserable and lifelong slavery. Practically and sensibly speaking, dissoluble marriages, and even marriages that are legally no marriages at all (for example, the marriages with deceased wife's sisters before they were legalised) act just as effectually as indissoluble marriages in announcing that the choice of the parties is made, and that they are no longer in the marriage market. In fact, the dissoluble marriage is the better shield of the two; for a libertine can approach the victim of an unhappy indissoluble marriage with the certainty that he or she can never be called on to make good his or her vows of attachment by marriage, whereas under the conditions which I advocate no libertine could make proposals to a married person in the open character of a libertine because any serious and honourable overture would have to take the shape of a proposal for divorce and remarriage. The familiar libertine's opening "You are not happy in your marriage. Forgive me; but I cannot bear to see you suffering. I also am unhappy. I love you, &c., &c., &c.," would be at once met by an inquiry whether the sympathiser's intentions were honourable: that is, whether he or she intended marriage after the divorce. Many ladies and gentlemen who now play the cuckoo in indissoluble households in an entirely selfish spirit would be unmasked if the legal obstacle to the happiness they profess to long for were removed.

If the purdah is introduced by jealous wives and husbands, as a consequence of reasonably dissoluble marriage, the simplest remedy will be for the victims to open the window and scream for the police.

I apologise to the public for having to state such very obvious considerations in reply to a romantic alarmist who is afraid of being locked up by his wife in a harem. I really do not see that you would be any safer if marriage were again made indissoluble.

Yours, poor wretch, compassionately,
G. Bernard Shaw

INDUSTRIAL MALINGERING

[*Saturday Review*, 16 March 1912.]

Sir,—You ask "Is Mr. Shaw prepared to shoot malingerers of the industrial army?" Of course I am. I am prepared to push the analogy between the militant and the industrial army (suggested long ago by Professor Beesly)[1] much farther than that. In countries where the militant service is decommercialised by being made compulsory and general, the malingerer may plead defective sight, weak heart, feeble mind and the like; but he never dreams of pleading the possession of a thousand a year. He would be told very properly that the possession of a thousand millions a year no more exempted him from the duty of defending his country than from the duty of obeying the Ten Commandments. And when we establish not only compulsory military service but compulsory

[1]Edward Spencer Beesly, professor of history at the University of London and editor of the *Positivist Review*, was a leader of the English positivist movement.

civil service in the fullest industrial and professional sense, we shall not tolerate idling either from Weary Willie the tramp or Dreary Dolly the millionaire. If he says "I have £40,000 a year: why should I not loaf?", we shall reply "Why should you not murder, steal, ravish, bear false witness, or commit any of the minor crimes that hurt society far less than the crime of the parasite who begs his way, or, worse, pays his way, without working for what he begs or buys? The reason bluntly is that if your sense of honour does not answer the question we shall assume that you have none, and will therefore proceed to shoot you, as the *Saturday Review* very naturally suggests, in order to weed the nation of cads." Even if the creature shrieked for mercy and offered to set to work at once, I should shoot him all the more for being a coward as well as a cad and for offering to work without conviction. Perhaps just for one generation we might allow the plea of inculcation. If the malingerer were to say "How could I see the matter from the point of view of a gentleman? My parents were cads; my schoolmasters were cads; my schoolfellows were cads and the sons of cads; the parson who prepared me for confirmation was a cad; the bishop who confirmed me was a cad; the doctor who vaccinated me was a cad; the daily papers I read were owned, edited, and written by cads: we were all cads; and so we agreed, when a gentleman did by chance turn up, to shout that he was a cad and that we were the gentlemen. I never had a chance; and it's not fair to shoot me," the simple truth of such a plea would be irresistible. But, as I have said, it would lose its force in one generation of honour and patriotism.

Yours, &c.,
G. Bernard Shaw

THE TREASON TRIALS

[Trades Union leader Tom Mann and the editors of the journal *The Syndicalist* had been sentenced to imprisonment at the Manchester Assizes for publication of an article by Mann that purportedly incited the armed forces to mutiny. Shaw's letter appeared in the *Daily News* of 25 March 1912.]

Sir,—In the report of the Syndicalist trial in *The Times* it is stated simply that the prisoners were found guilty. But in your report a very different conclusion is reported. It is there stated that three questions of fact were put to the jury; and that the answers were in the form of three separate verdicts of guilty. Now, in the absence of a complete verbatim report, it is impossible for me to say exactly what this means. If the Judge directed the jury that all they had to do was to ascertain the facts, he misdirected them, and there should be an appeal on this ground. A jury has two distinct duties. One is to ascertain whether prisoner at the Bar actually committed the acts set forth in the indictment. That is clearly an indispensable preliminary to the discharge of the really solemn part of their duty—the part for which alone juries exist. That part is to decide whether the prisoner is an innocent or a guilty man. Thoughtless jurymen are apt to think that there is no difference and judges are tempted to encourage them in this error, because its effect is to take the case out of the hands of the jury and leave it in that of the Judge. A few instances will show how profound the difference really is.

It is a crime to break a stranger's windows without his permission: Mrs. Pankhurst[1] is at present in prison for doing it. But whenever there is a fire in London the members of the Fire Brigade commit this unlawful act openly and impudently. They are not indicted for it, not through any sympathy on the part of the Government with window-breaking, but because it is certain that if a fireman were so indicted, the jury would first decide among themselves that he had committed the act, and then find him "not guilty," with, probably, a rider expressing high commendation. If they did anything else, they would be sent to a lunatic asylum.

It happens that the very case now in question brings out this distinction between the verdict and the mere ascertainment of fact in the most startling way. No crime known to the law is more severely punished than the crime of murder. The act involved in murder is the act of killing a human being. Yet every civilized country has to keep an immense body of men both on land and sea expressly equipped and trained for this very act, and sedulously impressed on every possible occasion with the conviction that such killing is their most sacred duty. We actually go so far as to make a law under which any person can be indicted and, if found guilty, subjected to ruinous penalties, for asking the members of these forces to refrain from such killing. Under this law any Christian preacher, any publisher of the Bible, the works of Tolstoy, or Carlyle's "Sartor Resartus," or any painter-decorator who writes

[1]Emmeline Pankhurst, woman suffragist and founder of the Women's Social and Political Union in 1903.

up the Sixth Commandment on the wall of a church open to soldiers, may be indicted and punished. Yet painter-decorators do these things as openly as firemen break windows, and for the same reason: they know perfectly well that if they were indicted for incitement to mutiny any sane jury would first decide that they had actually committed the act, and then, exactly as in the hypothetical case of the fireman, find them not guilty, and commend their industry and piety.

Now I have no means of knowing whether the jury yesterday, when they had duly ascertained the undoubted and unquestioned fact that the prisoners actually committed the acts alleged in the indictment, proceeded to deal with the entirely separate question of whether the prisoners were guilty or innocent. But it seems to me at least possible that they misunderstood their duties, and imagined not only that they were bound to answer three questions as to facts (which nobody had any right to put to them except as a matter of curiosity appealing to courtesy for information) but that an affirmative reply to these questions committed them in law to a verdict of guilty. If that is so, the Court of Appeal should at once order a new trial, for it is impossible to conceive an error more hideous in its practical consequences, and more utterly subversive of every principle of constitutional law, than this. If it were admitted in theory there would be no sense in having juries at all. If it were carried out in practice there would soon be no law in England except the law of the revolver, which has already too many apologists in high places for the comfort of long-sighted people.

Yours, &c.,
G. Bernard Shaw

THE TITANIC: SOME UNMENTIONED MORALS

[To the *Daily News,* London, May 1912: a controversy between Shaw and Sir Arthur Conan Doyle concerning a bylined article by Shaw; reprinted in Hesketh Pearson, *Conan Doyle: His Life and Art,* 1943.]

I

[14 May 1912.]

Why is it that the effect of a sensational catastrophe on a modern nation is to cast it into transports, not of weeping, not of prayer, not of sympathy with the bereaved nor congratulations of the rescued, not of poetic expression of the soul purified by pity and terror, but of a wild defiance of inexorable Fate and undeniable Fact by an explosion of outrageous romantic lying?

What is the first demand of romance in a shipwreck? It is the cry of Women and Children First. No male creature is to step into a boat as long as there is a woman or child on the doomed ship. How the boat is to be navigated and rowed by babies and women occupied in holding the babies is not mentioned. The likelihood that no sensible woman would trust either herself or her child in a boat unless there was a considerable percentage of men on board is not considered. Women and children first: that is the romantic formula. And never did the chorus of solemn delight at the strict observance of this formula by the British heroes on board the *Titanic* rise to sublimer strains than in the papers containing the first account of the wreck by a surviving eye witness, Lady Duff Gordon.[1] She described how she escaped in the captain's boat. There was one other woman in it, and ten men: twelve all told. One woman for every five men. Chorus: "Not once or twice in our rough island story," etc., etc.

Second romantic demand. Though all the men (except the foreigners, who must all be shot by stern British officers in attempting to rush the boats over the bodies of the women and children) must be heroes, the captain must be a super-hero, a magnificent seaman, cool, brave, delighting in death and danger, and a living guarantee that the wreck was nobody's fault, but, on the contrary, a triumph of British navigation. Such a man Captain [E. J.] Smith was enthusiastically proclaimed on the day when it was reported (and actually believed, apparently) that he had shot himself on the bridge, or shot the first officer, or been shot by the first officer, or shot anyhow to bring the curtain down effectively. Writers who had never heard of Captain Smith to that hour wrote of him as they would hardly write of Nelson. The one thing positively known was that Captain Smith had lost his ship by deliberately and knowingly steaming into an ice field at the highest speed he had coal for. He paid the penalty; so did most of those for whose lives he was responsible. Had he brought them and the ship safely to land, nobody would have taken the smallest notice of him.

Third romantic demand. The officers must be calm, proud,

[1]Lucy Sutherland Wallace, wife of Sir Cosmo Duff Gordon, fifth baronet.

steady, unmoved in the intervals of shooting the terrified foreigners. The verdict that they had surpassed all expectations was unanimous. The actual evidence was that Mr. Ismay[2] was told by the officer of his boat to go to hell, and that boats which were not full refused to go to the rescue of those who were struggling in the water in cork jackets. Reason frankly given: they were afraid. The fear was as natural as the officer's language to Mr. Ismay: who of us at home dare blame them or feel sure that we should have been any cooler or braver? But is it necessary to assure the world that only Englishmen could have behaved so heroically, and to compare their conduct with the hypothetic dastardliness which lascars or Italians or foreigners generally—say Nansen or Amundsen or the Duke of Abruzzi[3]—would have shown in the same circumstances?

Fourth romantic demand. Everybody must face death without a tremor; and the band, according to the Birkenhead precedent, must play "Nearer, my God, to Thee," as an accompaniment to the invitation to Mr. Ismay to go to hell. It was duly proclaimed that thus exactly it fell out. Actual evidence: the captain and officers were so afraid of a panic that, though they knew the ship was sinking, they did not dare to tell the passengers so—especially the third-class passengers—and the band played Rag Times to reassure the passengers, who, therefore, did not get into the boats, and did not realise their situation until the boats were gone and the ship was standing on her head before plunging to the bottom. What happened then Lady Duff Gordon has related, and the witnesses of the American inquiry could hardly bear to relate.

I ask, What is the use of all this ghastly, blasphemous, inhuman, braggartly lying? Here is a calamity which might well make the proudest man humble, and the wildest joker serious. It makes us vainglorious, insolent, and mendacious. At all events, that is what our journalists assumed. Were they right or wrong? Did the Press really represent the public? I am afraid it did. Churchmen and statesmen took much the same tone. The effect on me was one of profound disgust, almost of national dishonour. Am I mad? Possibly. At all events, that is how I felt and how I feel

[2]Joseph Bruce Ismay, son of the founder of the White Star Line, was chairman and managing director at the time, thus owner of the *Titanic*.

[3]Noted contemporary explorers: Roald Amundsen and Fridtjof Nansen (Norwegian) and Luigi Amedeo, Duke of the Abruzzi (Italian).

about it. It seems to me that when deeply moved men should speak the truth. The English nation appears to take precisely the contrary view. Again I am in the minority. What will be the end of it?—for England, I mean. Suppose we came into conflict with a race that had the courage to look facts in the face and the wisdom to know itself for what it was. Fortunately for us, no such race is in sight. Our wretched consolation must be that any other nation would have behaved just as absurdly.

G. Bernard Shaw

II

[20 May 1912.]

Sir,—I have just been reading the article by Mr. Bernard Shaw upon the loss of the Titanic, which appeared in your issue of May 14th. It is written professedly in the interests of truth, and accuses everyone around him of lying. Yet I can never remember any production which contained so much that was false within the same compass. How a man could write with such looseness and levity of such an event at such a time passes all comprehension. Let us take a few of the points. Mr. Shaw wishes—in order to support his perverse thesis, that there was no heroism—to quote figures to show that the women were not given priority in escape. He picks out, therefore, one single boat, the smallest of all, which was launched and directed under peculiar circumstances, which are now matter for inquiry. Because there were ten men and two women in this boat, therefore there was no heroism or chivalry; and all talk about it is affectation. Yet Mr. Shaw knows as well as I know that if he had taken the very next boat he would have been obliged to admit that there were 65 women out of 70 occupants, and that in nearly all the boats navigation was made difficult by the want of men to do the rowing. Therefore, in order to give a false impression, he has deliberately singled out one boat; although he could not but be aware that it entirely misrepresented the general situation. Is this decent controversy, and has the writer any cause to accuse his contemporaries of misstatement?

His next paragraph is devoted to the attempt to besmirch the conduct of Capt. Smith. He does it by his favourite method of "suggestio falsi"—the false suggestion being that the sympathy shown by the public for Capt. Smith took the shape of condoning

Capt. Smith's navigation. Now everyone—including Mr. Bernard Shaw—knows perfectly well that no defence has ever been made of the risk which was run, and that the sympathy was at the spectacle of an old and honoured sailor who has made one terrible mistake, and who deliberately gave his life in reparation, discarding his lifebelt, working to the last for those whom he had unwillingly injured, and finally swimming with a child to a boat into which he himself refused to enter. This is the fact, and Mr. Shaw's assertion that the wreck was hailed as a "triumph of British navigation" only shows—what surely needed no showing—that a phrase stands for more than truth with Mr. Shaw. The same remark applies to his "wrote of him as they would hardly write of Nelson." If Mr. Shaw will show me the work of any responsible journalist in which Capt. Smith is written of in the terms of Nelson, I will gladly send £100 to the Fabian Society.

Mr. Shaw's next suggestion—all the more poisonous because it is not put into so many words—is that the officers did not do their duty. If his vague words mean anything they can only mean this. He quotes as if it were a crime the words of [Fifth Officer Harold Godfrey] Lowe to Mr. Ismay when he interfered with his boat. I could not imagine a finer example of an officer doing his duty than that a subordinate should dare to speak thus to the managing director of the Line when he thought that he was impeding his life-saving work. The sixth officer [James P. Moody] went down with the captain, so I presume that even Mr. Shaw could not ask him to do more. Of the other officers I have never heard or read any cause for criticism. Mr. Shaw finds some cause for offence in the fact that one of them discharged his revolver in order to intimidate some foreign immigrants who threatened to rush the boats. The fact and the assertion that these passengers were foreigners came from several eye witnesses. Does Mr. Shaw think it should have been suppressed? If not what is he scolding about?

Finally, Mr. Shaw tries to defile the beautiful incident of the band by alleging that it was the result of orders issued to avert panic. But if it were, how does that detract either from the wisdom of the orders or from the heroism of the musicians? It was right to avert panic, and it was wonderful that men could be found to do it in such a way.

As to the general accusation that the occasion has been used for the glorification of British qualities, we should indeed be a lost people if we did not honour courage and discipline when we see it in its highest form. That our sympathies extend beyond ourselves is shown by the fact that the conduct of the American male passengers, and very particularly of the much-abused millionaires, has been as warmly eulogised as any single feature in the whole wonderful epic.

But surely it is a pitiful sight to see a man of undoubted genius using his gifts in order to misrepresent and decry his own people, regardless of the fact that his words must add to the grief of those who have already had more than enough to bear.

Arthur Conan Doyle

III

[22 May 1912.]

Sir,—I hope to persuade my friend Sir Arthur Conan Doyle, now that he has got his romantic and warm-hearted protest off his chest, to read my article again three or four times, and give you his second thoughts on the matter; for it is really not possible for any sane man to disagree with a single word that I have written.

I again submit that when news of a shipwreck arrives without particulars, and journalists immediately begin to invent particulars, they are lying. It is nothing to the point that authentic news may arrive later on, and may confirm a scrap or two of their more obvious surmises. The first narratives which reached us were those by an occupant of a boat in which there were ten men, two women, and plenty of room for more, and of an occupant of another boat which, like the first, refused to return to rescue the drowning because the people in it were avowedly afraid. It was in the face of that information, and of that alone, that columns of raving about women and children first were published. Sir Arthur says that I "picked out" these boats to prove my case. Of course I did. I wanted to prove my case. They did prove it. They do prove it. My case is that our journalists wrote without the slightest regard to the facts; that they were actually more enthusiastic in their praise of the Titanic heroes on the day when the only evidence to hand was evidence of conduct for which a soldier would be shot and a Navy sailor hanged when later news came in of those officers and crews who did their best; and that it must be evident to every reasonable man that if there had not been a redeeming feature in the whole case, exactly the same "hogwash" (as Mr. Cunninghame Graham[4] calls it in his righteous disgust) would have been lavished on the veriest dastards as upon a crew of Grace Darlings.[5] The captain positively lost popularity when the deliberate and calumnious lie that he had shot himself was dropped. May I ask what value real heroism has in a country which responds to these inept romances invented by people who can produce nothing after all but stories of sensational cowardice? Would Sir Arthur take a medal from the hands of the imbecile liars whom he is defending?

Sir Arthur accuses me of lying; and I must say that he gives me no great encouragement to tell the truth. But he proceeds to tell, against himself, what I take to be the most thundering lie ever sent to a printer by a human author. He first says that I "quoted as if it were a crime" the words used by the officer who told Mr. Ismay to go to hell. I did not. I said the outburst was very natural, though not in my opinion admirable or heroic. If I am wrong, then I claim to be a hero myself; for it has occurred to me in trying circumstances to lose my head and temper and use the exact words attributed (by himself) to the officer in question. But Sir Arthur goes on to say: "I could not imagine a finer example of an officer doing his duty than that a subordinate should dare to speak thus to the managing director of the line when he thought he was impeding his life-saving work." Yes you could, Sir Arthur; and many a page of heroic romance from your hand attests that you have often imagined much finer examples. Heroism has not quite come to that yet; nor has your imagination contracted or your brain softened to the bathos of seeing sublimity in a worried officer telling even a managing director (godlike being!) to go to hell. I would not hear your enemy libel you so. But now that you have chivalrously libelled yourself, don't lecture me for reckless mendacity; for you have captured the record in the amazing sentence I have just quoted.

I will not accept Sir Arthur's offer of £100 to the Fabian Society for every hyper-Nelsonic eulogy of the late Captain Smith which stands in the newspapers of those first days to bear out my

[4]R. B. Cunninghame Graham had been, among other things, a Socialist MP, a world traveler, and the author of travel sketches and tales of Scotland.
[5]Grace Horsley Darling, a lighthouse keeper's daughter on the Farne Islands, rescued five people from a steamboat wreck in 1838.

very moderate description of them. I want to see the Fabian Society solvent, but not at the cost of utter destitution to a friend. I should not have run the risk of adding to the distress of Captain Smith's family by adding one word to facts that speak only too plainly for themselves if others had been equally considerate. But if vociferous journalists will persist in glorifying the barrister whose clients are hanged, the physician whose patients die, the general who loses battles, and the captain whose ship goes to the bottom, such false coin must be nailed to the counter at any cost. There have been British captains who have brought their ships safely through icefields by doing their plain duty and carrying out their instructions. There have been British captains who have seen to it that their crew knew their boats and their places in their boats, and who, when it became necessary to take to those boats, have kept discipline in the face of death, and not lost one life that could have been saved. And often enough nobody has said "Thank you" to them for it, because they have not done mischief enough to stir the emotions of our romantic journalists. These are the men whom I admire and with whom I prefer to sail.

I do not wish to imply that I for a moment believe that the dead man actually uttered all the heartbreaking rubbish that has been put into his mouth by fools and liars; nor am I forgetting that a captain may not be able to make himself heard and felt everywhere in these huge floating (or sinking) hotels as he can in a cruiser, or rally a mob of waiters and dock labourers as he could a crew of trained seamen. But no excuse, however good, can turn a failure into a success. Sir Arthur cannot be ignorant of what would happen had the Titanic been a King's ship, or of what the court-martial would have said and done on the evidence of the last few days.

Owing to the fact that a member of my family was engaged in the Atlantic service, and perhaps also that I happen to know by personal experience what it is like to be face to face with death in the sea,[6] I know what the risk of ice means on a liner, and know also that there is no heroism in being drowned when you cannot help it. The captain of the Titanic did not, as Sir Arthur thinks, make "a terrible mistake." He made no mistake. He knew perfect-

[6]Shaw's maternal uncle, Walter J. Gurly, was for many years a medical officer on ships of the Inman line. Shaw had experienced a near drowning at Llanbedr, Wales, on 12 August 1907. For his description of the occurrence, see his letter to H. G. Wells, 14 August 1907, in *Collected Letters 1898–1910* (1972).

ly well that ice is the only risk that is considered really deadly in his line of work, and, knowing it, he chanced it and lost the hazard. Sentimental idiots, with a break in the voice, tell me that "he went down to the depths": I tell them with the impatient contempt they deserve, that so did the cat. Heroism is extraordinarily fine conduct resulting from extraordinarily high character. Extraordinary circumstances may call it forth and may heighten its dramatic effect by pity and terror, by death and destruction, by darkness and a waste of waters; but none of these accessories are the thing itself; and to pretend that they are is to debase the moral currency by substituting the conception of sensational misfortune for inspiring achievement.

I am no more insensible to the pity of the catastrophe than anyone else; but I have been driven by an intolerable provocation of disgusting and dishonourable nonsense to recall our journalists to their senses by saying bluntly that the occasion has been disgraced by a callous outburst of romantic lying. To this I now wish to add that if, when I said this, I had read the evidence elicited by Lord Mersey's[7] inquiry as to the Californian and the Titanic's emergency boat, I should probably have expressed myself much more strongly. I refrain now only because the facts are beating the hysterics without my help.

G. Bernard Shaw

IV

[25 May 1912.]

Sir,—without continuing a controversy which must be sterile, I would touch on only one point in Mr. Shaw's reply to my letter. He says that I accused him of lying. I have been guilty of no such breach of the amenities of the discussion. The worst I think or say of Mr. Shaw is that his many brilliant gifts do not include the power of weighing evidence; nor has he that quality—call it good taste, humanity, or what you will—which prevents a man from needlessly hurting the feelings of others.

Arthur Conan Doyle

[7]John Charles Bigham, Baron (later first Viscount) Mersey, a judge, was a commissioner of the inquiry into the disasters. Among the questions dealt with was why the nearby ships, including the *Californian*, had been unable to help more quickly.

HYMN SINGING

[A journalist, Raymond Blathwayt, had marked the six-hundredth performance of *Fanny's First Play* on 24 October 1912 by publishing in the *Daily Citizen* an article "Bernard Shaw at a Salvation Meeting: How He Conducted the Hymns." Shaw gently chided him for inaccuracy in a letter in the *Daily Citizen* two days later.]

Sir,—My friend Mr. Blathwayt, an inveterate romanticist, has spoiled the story of my singing at the Salvation meeting. I took on myself the duty of leading the singing in my box, being of opinion that hymn-singing, when the tune is a jolly one (and the Salvation Army has enough genuine religion in it to specialise in jolly hymn tunes), is a highly enjoyable, healthy, and recreative exercise. Now the art of leading a choir, or an orchestra, or anything else, consists, not in being "carried away," but in carrying other people away; and this I did with such success that a young lady in the Army bonnet took my hands as we left the box at the end of the meeting, and said, with moist eyes, "*We* know, don't we?" And really I think we did; so I refrained from explaining to the lady that the *Daily Express* habitually paralyses its readers with horror by describing me as an atheist, and that I would have sung just as lustily to Allah in a mosque, or to Brahma in a temple if the music had been equally inspired.

Mr. Blathwayt did not appreciate the story, or else he forgot it. I suspect him of considering religion as a sort of drunkenness of the soul (many Englishmen do), and therefore of misunderstanding my conviction that it is the intensest sanity and sobriety of the soul. The religion that carries people away is not my religion. My religion brings them to their senses. Hence, perhaps, its unpopularity.

Yours, &c.,
G. Bernard Shaw

SUFFRAGE AND MARTYRDOM

[In early 1913 the suffrage movement, led by the redoubtable Emmeline Pankhurst and the Women's Social and Political Union, entered a new and militant phase; a substantial amount of property was destroyed by burning, cutting, bombing, and window smashing. Mrs. Pankhurst was tried for "inciting to commit a felony," a charge that permitted the state not to have to prove a specific act. Found guilty and sentenced to "three years' penal servitude" in Holloway Prison, she promptly went on a hunger strike—at which point the government invoked the recently enacted "Cat and Mouse Act," which provided for the temporary release from imprisonment of a hunger striker, who was, however, subject to rearrest at such time as her health improved sufficiently to enable her to serve the rest of her sentence. Mrs. Pankhurst's sentence provoked an outbreak of guerilla warfare. On 12 April, she was released under the provisions of the act, rearrested on 26 May, released again on 30 May, rearrested on 14 June, and released again on 17 June. The last arrest prevented her from attending the funeral of the suffragist Emily Wilding Davison, killed when she disrupted a race at Epsom by seizing the bridle of the king's horse and was crushed by the animal. Among the measures introduced in Parliament was a Women's Suffrage Bill sponsored by the Liberal W. H. Dickinson, defeated in 1913; Prime Minister Herbert Henry Asquith was among those who spoke against it. Shaw's letter appeared in *The Times* on 19 June 1913.]

Sir,—I am quite confident that when I say that the moment chosen for the arrest of Mrs. Pankhurst on Saturday last made the proceeding a revolting one I am giving expression to the feelings of a large body of your readers. There was no necessity to rearrest her until after the funeral. Any official or Minister realizing the situation would, if he had a spark of decent feeling, have taken care to order a postponement. As no such order was given, we must conclude that the Government does not yet realize the situation.

May I call attention to two new considerations? The first is that it is now clear that the plan of the Home Office is, first to relieve the worst tension of public opinion by turning Mrs. Pankhurst out of prison, and then, by rigidly imprisoning her in the house in which she has taken refuge, produce all the effects of the closest confinement whilst escaping the responsibility which would attach to those effects if they occurred in prison. It is alleged that Mrs. Pankhurst's condition is very serious. It is quite clear that it cannot be very favourable, as Mrs. Pankhurst is not made of iron. Suppose Mrs. Pankhurst dies! Will the Government, merely because it has contrived that she shall die out of Holloway, still cry "Don't care," as it did by arresting Mrs. Pankhurst before Miss Davison's funeral instead of after it [?]

The second point is the newly-declared attitude of the Prime Minister. In the debate on the Dickinson Bill Mr. Asquith for the first time opposed the franchise for women explicitly on the ground that woman is not the female of the human species, but a distinct and inferior species, naturally disqualified from voting as a rabbit is disqualified from voting. This is a very common opinion. Mahomed's efforts to discredit it 14 centuries ago were lost on many Arabs as completely as on Mr. Asquith. But it makes the position extremely uncomfortable. A man may object to the proposed extension of the suffrage for many reasons. He may hold that the whole business of popular election is a delusion, and that votes for women is only its reduction to absurdity. He may object to it as upsetting a convenient division of labour between the sexes. He may object to it because he dislikes change, or is interested in businesses or practices which women would use political power to suppress. But it is one thing to follow a Prime Minister who advances all, or some, or any of these reasons for standing in the way of votes for women. It is quite another to follow a Prime Minister who places one's mother on the footing of a rabbit. Many men would vote for anything rather than be suspected of the rabbit theory. It makes it difficult to vote for the Liberal Party and then look the women of one's household in the face.

The situation, then, is that if Mrs. Pankhurst dies public opinion will consider that the Government, for which Mr. Asquith is in effect finally responsible, will have executed her. Mr. Asquith will not be moved by that: in his opinion it will matter just as much as killing a rabbit. I cannot convince him that he is mistaken, but I can assure him that a very large section of the public will not agree with him.

I suggest that the authorities, having had to let Mrs. Pankhurst out of prison, should now let her alone. There was something to be said for not letting her out; there is nothing to be said for pursuing her, now she is out, with a game of cat-and-mouse that will produce on public feeling all the effect of vindictive assassination if she, like Miss Davison, should seal her testimony with her blood.

Yours, &c.,
G. Bernard Shaw

MORALITY AND THE THEATRE

I

[Press disclosure that Baron Sandhurst, the Lord Chamberlain, had received letters from the Bishop of Kensington and other clerics complaining of the play *A la Carte* at the Palace Theatre and, particularly, of some suggestedly promiscuous stage business involving the actress Gaby Deslys, was followed by indignant rebuttals from Miss Deslys and the theatre's managing director Alfred Butt. On 30 October 1913, *The Times* disclosed that the Bishop had again written to Sandhurst to indicate that it was not particulars of the performance that were at issue but what he deplored as "the atmosphere of immorality and the suggestion of vice" that pervaded the entire production. When the Bishop reiterated these sentiments in a letter in *The Times* on 6 November, Shaw responded with a letter, published two days later, in which he wielded as his principal cudgel a quotation from *Revelation,* 22:11.]

Sir,—May I, as a working playwright, ask the Bishop of Kensington to state his fundamental position clearly? So far, he has begged the question he is dealing with: that is, he has assumed that there can be no possible difference of opinion among good citizens concerning it. He has used the word "suggestive" without any apparent sense of the fact that the common thoughtless use of it by vulgar people has made it intolerably offensive. And he uses the word "objectionable" as if there were a general agreement as to what is objectionable and what is not, in spite of the fact that the very entertainment to which he himself objected had proved highly attractive to large numbers of people whose taste is entitled to the same consideration as his own.

On the face of it the Bishop of Kensington is demanding that the plays that he happens to like shall be tolerated and those which he happens not to like shall be banned. He is assuming that what he approves of is right, and what he disapproves of, wrong. Now, I have not seen the particular play which he so much dislikes; but suppose I go to see it tonight, and write a letter to you to-morrow to say that I approve of it, what will the Bishop have to say? He will have either to admit that his epithet of objectionable means simply disliked by the Bishop of Kensington, or he will have to declare boldly that he and I stand in the relation of God and the Devil. And, however his courtesy and his modesty may recoil from this extremity, when it is stated in plain English, I think he has got there without noticing it. At all events, he is clearly proceeding on the assumption that his conscience is more enlightened than that of the people who go to the Palace Theatre and enjoy what they see there. If the Bishop may shut up the Palace Theatre on this assumption, then the Nonconformist patrons of the Palace Theatre (and it has many of them) may shut up the Church of England by turning the assumption inside out. The sword of persecution always has two edges.

By "suggestive" the Bishop means suggestive of sexual emotion. Now a Bishop who goes into a theatre and declares that the performances there must not suggest sexual emotion is in the position of a playwright going into a church and declaring that the services there must not suggest religious emotion. The suggestion, gratification, and education of sexual emotion is one of the main uses and glories of the theatre. It shares that function with all the fine arts. The sculpture courts of the Victoria and Albert Museum in the Bishop's diocese are crowded with naked figures of extraordinary beauty, placed there expressly that they may associate the appeal of the body with such beauty, refinement, and expression of the higher human qualities that our young people, contemplating them, will find baser objects of desire repulsive. In the National Gallery body and soul are impartially catered for: men have worshipped Venuses and fallen in love with Virgins. There is a voluptuous side to religious ecstasy and a religious side to voluptuous ecstasy; and the notion that one is less sacred than the other is the opportunity of the psychiatrist who seeks to discredit the saints by showing that the passion which exalted them was in its abuse capable also of degrading sinners. The so-called Song of Solomon, which we now know to be an erotic poem, was mistaken by the translators of the 17th century for a canticle of Christ to His Church, and is to this day so labelled in our Bibles.

Now let us turn to the results of cutting off young people—not to mention old ones—from voluptuous art. We have families who bring up their children in the belief that an undraped statue is an abomination; that a girl or a youth who looks at a picture by Paul Veronese is corrupted for ever; that the theatre in which *Tristan and Isolde* or *Romeo and Juliet* is performed is the gate of hell; and that the contemplation of a figure attractively dressed or revealing more of its outline than a Chinaman's dress does is an act of the most profligate indecency. Of Chinese sex morality I must not write in the pages of *The Times*. Of the English and Scottish sex morality that is produced by this starvation and blasphemous vilification of vital emotions I will say only this: that it is so morbid and abominable, so hatefully obsessed by the things that tempt it, so merciless in its persecution of all the divine grace which grows in the soil of our sex instincts when they are not deliberately perverted and poisoned, that if it could be imposed, as some people would impose it if they could, on the whole community for a single generation, the Bishop, even at the risk of martyrdom, would reopen the Palace Theatre with his episcopal benediction, and implore the lady to whose performances he now objects to return to the stage even at the sacrifice of the last rag of her clothing.

I venture to suggest that when the Bishop heard that there was an objectionable (to him) entertainment at the Palace Theatre, the simple and natural course for him was not to have gone there. That is how sensible people act. And the result is that if a manager offers a widely objectionable entertainment to the public he very soon finds out his mistake and withdraws it. It is my own custom as a playwright to make my plays "suggestive" of religious emotion. This makes them extremely objectionable to irreligious people. But they have the remedy at their own hands. They stay away. The Bishop will be glad to hear that there are not many of them; but it is a significant fact that they frequently express a wish that the Censor would suppress religious plays, and that he occasionally complies. In short, the Bishop and his friends are not alone in proposing their own tastes and convictions as the measure of what is permissible in the theatre. But if such individual and sectarian standards were tolerated we should have no plays at all, for there never yet was a play that did not offend somebody's taste.

I must remind the Bishop that if the taste for voluptuous entertainment is sometimes morbid, the taste for religious edification is open to precisely the same objection. If I had a neurotic daughter I would much rather risk taking her to the Palace Theatre than to a revival meeting. Nobody has yet counted the homes and characters wrecked by intemperance in religious emotion. When we begin to keep such statistics the chapel may find its attitude of moral superiority to the theatre, and even to the public-house, hard to maintain, and may learn a little needed charity. We all need to be reminded of the need for temperance and toleration in religious emotion and in political emotion, as well as in sexual emotion. But the Bishop must not conclude that I want to close up all places of worship: on the contrary, I preach in them. I do not even clamour for the suppression of political party meetings, though nothing more foolish and demoralizing exists in England to-day. I live and let live. As long as I am not compelled to attend revival meetings, or party meetings, or theatres at which the sexual emotions are ignored or reviled, I am prepared to tolerate them on reciprocal terms; for though I am unable to conceive any good coming to any human being as a set-off to their hysteria, their rancorous bigotry, and their dullness and falsehood, I know that those who like them are equally unable to conceive any good coming of the sort of assemblies I frequent; so I mind my own business and obey the old precept—"He that is unrighteous, let him do unrighteousness still; and he that is filthy let him be made filthy still; and he that is righteous let him do righteousness still; and he that is holy let him be made holy still." For none of us can feel quite sure in which category the final judgment may place us; and in the meantime Miss Gaby Deslys is as much entitled to the benefit of the doubt as the Bishop of Kensington.

Yours, &c.,
G. Bernard Shaw

II

[The Bishop replied to Shaw in *The Times,* 10 November 1913, claiming that his principal objection was to "altering sketches or pieces after they have been officially sanctioned" by the Lord Chamberlain. Shaw's rejoinder appeared in *The Times* on 15 November.]

Sir,—I note the Bishop of Kensington's explanation that in his recent agitation against the Palace Theatre he has been concerned not with public morals but solely with a technical infraction of the Lord Chamberlain's regulations. In that case I have nothing more to say, partly because the management of the Palace Theatre strenuously and indignantly denies that the infraction has occurred, partly because Lord Sandhurst is quite well able to take care of himself, but mainly because this astonishing episcopal reply to an earnest demand for a statement of principle sends me reeling into a dumb despair of making any Englishman understand what political principle means or even persuading him that such a thing exists.

It is useless for me to repeat what I said in my former communication. If the Bishop was unable to grapple with it yesterday, there is no reason to expect that he will be able to do so to-morrow. But lest I should seem to fail in patience, I will comment on one or two points of his letter. I am very glad he has pointed out that the Lord Chamberlain has no real control over performances, and that the guarantee of decency which the Censor's licence is supposed to carry is illusory. I have pointed that out so often that I cannot but feel encouraged when a Bishop repeats it. I am glad that he agrees with me also that the power of influencing people for good is inextricably involved with the power to influence them for evil. But if this is so, why does the Bishop still imagine that he can suppress and destroy the power for evil without also suppressing and destroying the power for good? An evil sermon—and there are many more evil sermons than evil plays—may do frightful harm; but is the Bishop ready to put on the chains he would fasten on the playwright, and agree that no sermon shall be preached unless it is first read and licensed by the Lord Chamberlain? No doubt it is easier to go to sleep than to watch and pray; that is why everyone is in favour of securing purity and virtue and decorum by paying an official to look after them. But the result is that your official, who is equally indisposed to watch and pray, takes the simple course of forbidding everything that is not customary; and, as nothing is customary except vulgarity, the result is that he kills the thing he was employed to purify and leaves the nation to get what amusement they can out of its putrefaction. Our souls are to have no adventures because adventures are dangerous. Carry that an obvious step farther and the Bishop of Kensington will be gagged because he might at any moment utter false doctrines. He will be handcuffed because he might smite me with his pastoral staff. The dog-muzzling order will be extended to the muzzling of all priests and prophets and politicians. The coward in all of us will seek security at any price.

But this does not touch the present issue. I repeat that there is no consensus of opinion as to what is objectionable and what is desirable in theatrical entertainments. Mr. Butt's audiences are as big as the Bishop's congregations, and they pay him more than they pay the Bishop. If the Bishop may say to these people, "You shall not go to the Palace Theatre, or, if you go you shall not see what you like there, because I do not consider it good for you," then these people may say to the Bishop, "You shall not preach the doctrine of the Atonement; for in our opinion it destroys all sense of moral responsibility."

I need not again elaborate the point; but I will point out

something that the Bishop may not have thought of in this connexion. Not only is art, or religion, a power for evil as well as for good; but the self-same exhibition or sermon that effects one man's salvation may effect another man's damnation. The placing of the Bible in the hands of the laity by the Protestant Catholics produced great results; but it also produced all the horrors that were predicted by the Roman Catholics as their reason for withholding it, from an epidemic of witch-burning to the political excesses of the Anabaptists and Puritans, and the sour misery of 16th century Scotland. The case against the freedom of the Palace Theatre is as dust in the balance compared with the case against the freedom of the Bible Society. Is the Bishop, having attacked the Palace Theatre, going to attack the Bible Society *a fortiori?* Of course not, because he can see the overwhelming argument in favour of scriptural freedom which he is unable to see in the case of the theatre, because the theatre is the Church's most formidable rival in forming the minds and guiding the souls of the people. Well, he must compete with fair weapons, not with the bludgeons of official tyranny. He cannot dissect out the evil of the theatre and strike at that alone. One man seeing a beautiful actress will feel that she has made all common debaucheries impossible to him; another, seeing the same actress in the same part, will plunge straight into those debaucheries because he has seen her body without being able to see her soul. Destroy the actress and you rob the first man of his salvation without saving the second from the first woman he meets on the pavement.

It is reported that the Bishop of London, preaching on Sunday in the church of St. Mary Magdalen, Paddington, dealt with this subject. Far be it from me to accuse any man of the fantastic things our reporters put into all our mouths; but I can believe that he proposed "a vigorous campaign for a clean, pure life." If by this he means, as I may without offence assume that he does, life according to the highest conception his lights can show him, then he is on the right tack, though, if his conceptions are at all lofty, he will get more kicks than halfpence for his pains. As long as he sticks to the propagation of noble impulses and aspirations he cannot go far wrong. But if once he turns aside from that honourable work to the cheap and rancorous course of persecuting the people who do not share his tastes under pretext of weeding out evil, he will become a public nuisance. He is reported to have declared that, "It has been said that no Christian Church has any right to criticize any play in London." It may be that there exists some abysmal fool who said this. If so, he was hardly worth the Bishop of London's notice. The Christian Church ought to criticize every play in London; and it is on that right and duty of criticism, and not on the unfortunate Lord Chamberlain, that the Christian Church ought to rely, and, indeed, would rely without my prompting if it were really a Christian Church.

Finally, may I thank the Bishop of Kensington for alleging as a reason for persecuting the Palace Theatre (for he does not, after all, combat my demonstration that his action was persecution) that I should probably disapprove of the entertainment myself? As to that, I can only say that, if the Bishop sets out to suppress all the institutions of which I disapprove, he will soon have not one single supporter, not even

Yours, &c.,
G. Bernard Shaw

THE MADNESS OF THIS WAR

[Published in the *Daily Citizen,* 1 August 1914, on the day Germany invaded France and Luxembourg. England declared war on Germany on 4 August.]

Sir,—A symposium on the madness of war at this moment is about as timely and sensible as a symposium on the danger of damp sheets would be if London were on fire.

If war is madness, we should have thought of that before. It is no use piling up armaments and blustering for years and then, when the first shot is fired, suddenly joining the Quakers. We have made our bed and must lie on it.

To us and to Western civilisation the worst calamity that can occur is a war between France and Germany, or between either of them and England. All our diplomacy and all our power should be directed to its prevention. And to that end there is only one thing that our diplomacy can do, and that is to represent that, in such a war, England must take her part and is ready to take her part with the object of making a speedy end of it at the expense of the aggressor.

If it is quite clear that our intervention is certain and will be resolute, a Western war will not be undertaken except as a last resource and at an appalling risk. With that responsibility on us, those of us who have nothing more helpful to do than to sing Christmas carols had better hold their tongues.

But it is important that our statesmen and diplomatists should understand that there is a strong and growing body of public opinion to which all war is abhorrent, and which will suffer it now only as a hideous necessity arising out of past political bargains in which the people have had no part and the country no interest. The alliance between the revolutionary Government of France and the reactionary Government of Russia is a monstrous and unnatural product of cosmopolitan finance. One of its threatened consequences at present is the forcing by circumstances of England into the ranks of Russian despotism in defence of a Servian assassination. That is not a position of which we can feel proud, though it serves us richly right for allowing it to be brought about by our political apathy and stupidity.

We muddled our way in and we may have to fight our way out. The best of us will consent to the inevitable, sullenly and angrily; and this had better be taken carefully into account by statesmen and journalists who may feel tempted to deck this horrible emergency in the rhetorical trappings of enthusiasm and patriotism.

Yours, &c.,
G. Bernard Shaw

CALL YOU THIS DISCIPLINE?

[Shaw published *Common Sense about the War* as a thirty-two-page supplement to the *New Statesman* on 14 November 1914. It produced an enormous outcry. His subsequent letter to the *Daily Citizen,* a moderate Labour paper sponsored by the Trades Union Congress, was published on 26 November.]

Sir,—Your reception of my "Common Sense About the War" in your issue of the 23rd raises an extremely serious question.

The difficulty which a war presents at present to the Labour and democratic cause is the natural patriotic tumult which makes it so hard to keep the interests of the working classes distinct from those of autocratic secret diplomacy, commercial intrigue, professional military interests, and the policy of Divide and Govern. We are placed in such a position that without the most careful tactics we shall be either ruined and discredited by a defeat for which our opposition to the capitalist Government will be blamed, or brought absolutely under the heel of the governing and military classes by a victory of which they will take all the credit.

Properly handled, this war can be led to a victory, not only for the Allies over Germany, but for democracy over its worst enemies both at home and abroad. And when I say democracy I do not mean Mr. Asquith's pseudo-democracy, which uses Mutiny Acts in time of peace to imprison Labour leaders and muzzle the Labour Press, but genuine working-class democracy. Well, I have put many weeks of very hard work into this job of disentanglement. I have shown that there is a tremendous case for pushing this war to a victory over Prussia from the Labour point of view, and that it is being spoiled by the official case, which is a very bad one.

I have shown that the official mistrust of the people, which led the diplomatists to conceal their plans from the nation with a completeness which may be gauged by a reference to Mr. Gardiner's[1] article in support of non-intervention in the *Daily News* (a Government organ) *before* Sir Edward Grey[2] owned up to having practically already declared war by engaging the co-operation of the Fleet to France without asking the leave of the House of Commons, was unnecessary as regards the people of England, who were perfectly willing to go to the rescue of France and fight Potsdam on the respective merits of Republicanism and Potsdamnation without any lawyer's excuses, and most mischievous as regards Germany, where the concealment of our intentions and preparations produced an impression of treachery which has cost many an Englishman his life and done no good whatever.

I have stood for a brave and straight democratic fighting case; for open democratic diplomacy, for full civil rights, and a fair livelihood for the soldier and his dependents, for clean hands and clean mouths, and the discarding of the dirty lies and rancours that are invented and fomented to take the attention of our people off speculators in shoddy khaki and refreshment contractors who bribe sergeants to wink at the supply of uneatable food even to our troops in training at home (with what effect on recruiting can be imagined), and for an energetic pushing of the in-

[1]A. G. Gardiner, a supporter of Asquith's conduct of the war, was editor of the *Daily News*.
[2]Liberal MP for Berwick-on-Tweed, 1885–1916; foreign secretary, 1905–16.

terests of Labour and democracy now that a formidable emergency has at last given serious men the opportunity of making themselves heard above the din of party twaddle.

In short, I have put my best brains and skill at the service of the Labour cause, with no other defence against the inevitable storm of capitalist and official abuse than the support of those for whom I did the work.

And the result is that the *Daily Citizen,* the organ of the Labour movement, promptly proceeds to show its loyalty to the Foreign Office and its support of conscription under military law and its abhorrence of Socialists and Labour agitators and its general entire agreement with the *Daily Express* and the *Globe* and the *Times* by an article displaying, applauding, exulting in, and reproducing the ravings of my poor friend Blatchford,[3] accompanied in another column by a rehash of the stale personal gibes with which the capitalist Press tries to discredit me because I am on the side of Labour.

Now Mr. Blatchford does not matter: he has had Germany on the brain for years, and the strain of the war has obviously upset him. Besides, his paper is not a representative paper in the sense in which the *Daily Citizen* is a representative paper. When I am repudiated by the *Daily Citizen* I am repudiated by the Labour Party and the Trade Union movement; and it becomes open to the anti-Labour papers to declare that I am utterly ignorant of the aims and sympathies of democracy; that the Labour movement is wholeheartedly in favour of Sir Edward Grey and his foreign methods and of Mr. Asquith and his home methods; that Labour makes no claim for representation at the War Office and has no objection to the system, imported from Prussia, under which soldiers are denied all ordinary civil rights; and that when our men in the trenches have won the victory with their blood and our substance we shall be perfectly content to have the terms of peace settled behind our backs by Sir Edward Grey and to go on humbly and obediently until he sends us to the trenches again without consulting us.

Now, before I sit down under all this with my usual patience I should like to know whether those who read the *Daily Citizen,* those for whom it is understood to speak, and those by whose efforts and sacrifices it was established and is being carried on

[3]Robert Blatchford, editor of *The Clarion,* had called for censorship of Shaw.

under great difficulties, really mean all this, and approve of my being stabbed by their paper in the back when I am making a stand for them at a crisis when such stands, never very easy to make, are exceptionally difficult and even a little dangerous?

If so, I know where I am, and can continue to cry in the wilderness without making any pretence that the contemptuous estimate of my personal character and the angry detestation of my aims and opinions expressed by the baser sort of capitalist papers are not thoroughly shared by the working classes and even by the Socialists.

If, on the other hand, I have some support in the Labour movement, now is the time for my supporters to protest against the attack on me. I do not expect any man to commit himself to every sentence I write, because I cannot expect every man to spend as much time and thought over that sentence as I, or to know the world as I know it. But my conclusions are stated clearly enough; and if a man agrees with my conclusions I expect him in such a moment as the present to say so with some show of resolution and conviction, and not treat me to a grudging admission that there may be something in what I say and that it is rather plucky of me to say it, but that he objects to my parting my hair in the middle and thinks I ought to eat a little meat.

In my 30 years' public work I have seen man after man in the Labour movement sell out because he could not trust his future to the loyalty of the workers; and I should perhaps have had to sell out myself long ago if I had not possessed certain powers as a writer which made me a little more independent than others.

I suggest that the treatment I am meeting now from the *Daily Citizen* is not such as to encourage any man with a talent for public life, who may be hesitating between the Labour and the capitalist causes, to come down on the right side.

Yours, &c.,
G. Bernard Shaw

SUPPRESSED BY *THE TIMES*

[Ramsay MacDonald had resigned the leadership of the Labour Party on 5 August 1914, when the executive committee of the party refused to form an opposition to the ruling Liberal government in spite of having opposed its policies before the outbreak of the war. Speaking out against those policies, MacDonald called Sir Edward Grey, the foreign secretary, "a menace to the peace of Europe for the last eight years." Shaw entered the fray with a letter that attacked various efforts to unify the country and justify the British position. Rejected by *The Times,* it was published in the *Labour Leader* on 26 November 1914 as "The Bernard Shaw Letter Suppressed by 'The Times.' "]

Sir,—The "contemptuous indifference" with which you are devoting your choicest columns day by day to Mr. Ramsay MacDonald emboldens me to point out that the publication of his opinions in Germany may prove of considerable use to this country later on, just as his visits to India have probably helped to gain for us that popular support as against Germany which we most certainly do not owe to the utterances of his political opponents. When we have finished our fight with Germany, we shall—unless we are utter cads—shake hands with her; and in that hour it will be important that the Germans should know that British organised Labour, when it "rallied splendidly and unanimously to the national cause" (I am quoting Mr. Prothero)[1] was not for a moment rallying to the proceedings of our Foreign Office, of which it was kept in a state that went perceptibly to the other side of complete ignorance until the war had to all intents and purposes already begun.

The nation does not regard the war as needing the slightest excuse: it wants to fight Germany just to show that it *can* fight Germany; that England counts for as much in the field as she did a hundred years ago under Wellington and two hundred years ago under Marlborough; and that all this military bugaboo with which the diplomatists of Europe have been terrifying themselves and one another for the last forty years is such an insufferable nuisance that it is time for brave men to take it by the scruff of the neck and teach it manners and common sense.

[1]Rowland Edmund Prothero, land agent for the Duke of Bedford and Conservative MP for Oxford University, was shortly to become president of the Board of Agriculture. Shaw is quoting from his letter to *The Times*, published on 1 October.

The Foreign Office has exactly the opposite opinion: its views are to be found in the pages of General Von Bernhardi,[2] whose British programme (published, of course, as a warning to Germany) it has carried out to the very letter by manoeuvering Germany into the present war. Thus the Foreign Office and the nation are at war for entirely different reasons. The nation's reasons are fit for publication. The Foreign Office's reasons have to be concealed at any hazard. Hence all this nonsense about Belgium, and the fancy picture of a bloodthirsty Kaiser selecting the hour at which Russia, France, and England were leagued against him as the psychological moment to make war. If Mr. MacDonald is not imposed on by these unnecessary and unpopular child's excuses, may not the reason be that his party has nothing to conceal and nothing to be ashamed of, that he has read the White Papers, and that he is a Scotchman with brains, and not a rabbit?

It is natural for Sir Valentine Chirol,[3] as an old Foreign Office man, to supply us with a set of official excuses for being at war with Germany; but suppose we don't happen to consider our conduct in need of any excuse and very strongly resent the Foreign Office assumption that we should never have dared to attack the Prussian bogey if Sir Edward Grey had not led us blindfold up to the guns?

Why should Mr. MacDonald not make the Germans understand that we are not all hypocrites, that we are not afraid of them, and that we are at war with them for far better reasons than the official ones, which are not borne out even by the official publications?

Yours, &c.,
G. Bernard Shaw

[2]The Prussian General Friedrich von Bernhardi was in charge of the German war effort; his book *Germany and the Next War* was published in English translation in 1911.

[3]Journalist and former member of the foreign department of *The Times*, who had in his youth been a clerk in the Foreign Office. A letter from him also appeared in *The Times* on 1 October.

"INSENSATE MALICE"

[Perhaps the most violent response to *Common Sense about the War* was Robert Blatchford's leading article ("Blatchford's Reply to Pro-German Outburst"), which occupied a full page in the *Weekly Dispatch* on 22 November 1914. While Blatchford commenced with a general discussion of the need to support the government, he yet injected his own objections to its policies, among them the imposition of "arbitrary censorship." This, however, drew him to Shaw's polemic, about which his indignation made him virtually incoherent. He grew irate over Shaw's "pamphlet," his Irishness, his "perverse love for the role of Devil's Advocate," his alleged attacks on Shakespeare and Lord Nelson, and especially his "cynical falsehood" about human emotions. Shaw, he illustrated, "would tell an old friend that his dog was not full bred" and thus miss the point that what the friend "saw best and loved most [was] the love-light in the dear old doggie's eye." When Blatchford at last turned to Shaw's "blatant and disingenuous attack upon the country in which he has lived his life," he attempted to undermine Shaw's view of Anglo-German history and then concluded: "I have given enough space to this piece of insensate malice and dirty innuendo. It is the meanest act of treachery ever perpetrated by an alien enemy residing in generous and long-suffering England." Shaw's reply appeared a week later in the *Weekly Dispatch*.]

Sir,—I wonder whether there is on the earth's surface a more ridiculous chap than my friend Blatchford, if I dare call him so before the war is over. Is there another man alive who, being offered a whole page of *The Weekly Dispatch* to write a serious article on the war, would sit down, with Rome burning round him, and discourse sweetly on Sterne and Goldsmith and lovers meeting in a lane, and finally turn on his own right tank man and assail him with frantic abuse in the face of the enemy because he did not "see the love light in his dear old doggy's eye"! How on earth could I see the love light in his dear old doggy's eye when I never set my own eye on the animal in my life?

Then I am reviled for preferring Wellington to Nelson (I never said I did, by the way); as Mr. Blatchford dislikes Wellington because if Mr. Blatchford had talked to him as he talks to the unfortunate readers of *The Weekly Dispatch*, the Iron Duke would have said, as usual, "Sir, don't be a damned fool," whereas Nelson would have wept over the dear old doggy and offered Robert five shillings to drink his Majesty's health.

Well, it is all very funny, and in war time we make haste to laugh lest we should cry; but unless a joke makes for friendship and discipline, or carries a little earnest with it, or at least does not mislead anybody, it had better be kept until the situation is a little less serious.

Now let me state clearly the views I stand for; so that the readers of *The Weekly Dispatch* may judge for themselves whether they like them or not. First, I will give my view of the war; and then my view of the political scandal which the war has brought to light, as war always does bring political scandals to light.

1. I contend that although France, Russia, and England on the one side (the Entente) and Germany and Austria (the Alliance) on the other were leagued against one another in two distinct camps, as they had a perfect right to be in pursuance of current militarist theories as to the necessity of maintaining a balance of power, yet the Kaiser was not justified in attacking France when Russia attacked him. Mr. Blatchford, in repudiating my view, commits himself to the contrary militarist view that if the Kaiser had not attacked France, France would have attacked him in the rear while he was fighting Russia, and that England, in pursuance of Sir Edward Grey's secret arrangements with France, would have joined her. If Mr. Blatchford can show any third course that was open, let him do so, and stop palpitating between calling me a jaundiced liar and telling me what I would do if I came upon "a pair of of happy lovers in a flower-scented lane" (my custom on such occasions is to look the other way and steal off as quietly as possible). But to put the Kaiser in the wrong I have had to take an extreme democratic position, abhorrent to "we militarists and Jingoes," as Mr. Blatchford describes himself. I contend that the Kaiser's business was to have kept the peace until Russia actually attacked him, and to have exposed his western frontier fearlessly to an attack by France, simply trusting to the public conscience of western democracy in France, England, and America to make such a cowardly and unjustifiable act impossible. It is difficult to see how France could have attacked him under such circumstances. It is certain that we could not have joined in such an attack, and that public opinion would have been so strongly on his side that we might even have had to come to his rescue. I grant that such a bold and liberal policy would have required some nerve and knowledge of public human nature. But if a man has not these qualities he has no right to be in control of the armed forces of a nation or any other dangerous forces. It was on the

cards; it was the right policy; and only by pointing to it as the proper one can we support our contention that Germany put herself in the wrong by attacking France. What has Mr. Blatchford to say to that? I ask him not to put me off with his enjoyment of the scent of the hawthorn and his wonder at the beauty of the moon. I can enjoy both these natural phenomena at the proper time and place; but for the present I want to know whether he agrees with me as to what the Kaiser ought to have done; and, if he does not, to be good enough to let us all know what he is quarrelling with the Kaiser for not doing.

2. I contend that when Germany attacked France, we were bound to stand by France, not because of the secret diplomatic agreement to do so that had been made behind our backs, but on broad human grounds of neighbourliness and the common interest of all good democrats in resisting and mastering autocratic militarism. I contend that Sir Edward Grey struck the right note for the first time when he said that we could not stand by and see France, our friend and neighbour, bombarded and battered, and that it was for this that the House of Commons rose enthusiastically at him and that the nation followed the House of Commons. I know that Mr. Blatchford thinks the nation rose at the articles in which he himself expressed his wild hatred and fear of Germany; but I quite simply and flatly do not agree with him. I do not believe that this nation in the lump hates Germany, or is a bit afraid of her, or thinks that all Englishmen are angels and all Germans demons; it just is not going to be walked over by Germany or to stand by and see her walk over France and Belgium. And I tell Robert that that is the real British attitude, and that he got *his* attitude from his Italian grandmother (or whatever relation it was) and not in the Dublin Fusiliers.

3. Also, I say that I wish England and France had taken on Germany by themselves, and left Russia out of it. I do not like the Russian Government, and am not surprised to hear that it cares so little for public opinion here that it has just abolished the Finnish Constitution in our face, and that its commanders in Galicia have told the Poles that when they conquer Austrian Poland there will be no Polish language and no Polish institutions, but thorough Russianisation. Still, I am not sorry to have the two most formidable militarist and Prussian autocracies in Europe (for the Czardom is as thoroughly North German as the Kaiserdom) fighting against one another instead of combining against us. None the less I hold

to it that events have proved that the policy I advocated last year and the beginning of this was the right one. That policy was, that we should arm to the teeth, leave Russia out of the question, and tell Germany that if she attacked France we should attack her, offering her as a fair equivalent the assurance that if France attacked her we should help her against France. And if Robert Blatchford can show me any other policy that will not make Russia master of the European situation I will listen to him with eager interest and promise faithfully never "to tell an old friend that his dog is not full bred, that its muzzle is turning grey, and that it has blunt teeth." But I very much doubt whether Robert has a policy. He has a temper, but we cannot afford to sacrifice hundreds of thousands of men to gratify his temper. My policy is better worth fighting for.

4. I have demanded several things for the soldier which Mr. Blatchford also demands, and two things that he has not demanded. One is that our soldiers should not be deprived of their civil rights in the Prussian manner. The other is that men of Mr. Blatchford's opinions concerning religion should be enabled to enlist without having their consciences outraged by being forced to take an oath in which they do not believe. Anybody but Robert Blatchford would be grateful to me for standing by him. But Robert regards it as a liberty on my part to meddle. I am sorry; but I shall go on meddling.

5. I think an Englishman who kills a German because he hates him is guilty of murder. I think that an Englishman who kills a German in self-defence or in defence of his home and his folk is entitled to a verdict of Justifiable Homicide. But the Englishman who kills a German, not hating him, for the sake of principles which he believes to be as important to the German as to himself, or to defeat principles which he believes to be as disastrous to the German as to himself, is the only noble warrior; and I believe I could get more and better recruits out of any town in England on that gospel than on the gospel of fear and hatred that Mr. Blatchford has let the Kaiser frighten him into. We hear nothing of Mr. Blatchford's sort of talk from the men in the trenches. And if the worst came to the worst I would rather see an Englishman die like a gentleman than win like a blackguard.

6. I declare that the most dangerous people among us at present are the frightened people, the scaremongers. The one thing that a French officer dreads more than anything else is the sudden

cry among his troops "Nous sommes trahis"—"We are betrayed." Well, that is exactly the scare that Robert Blatchford has succumbed to here. When soldiers are caught that way, they turn frantically and cut down their own comrades, as Blatchford is trying to cut me down. It does not matter to me, because I am now comfortably seated on Robert's head, and he is very sorry he spoke; but it may not always end so happily; for everybody is not proof against the contagion of panic as I am. We have got to keep our heads, continue to smile and crack our jokes and throw an occasional friendly packet of cigarettes into the German trenches between the shells; and when somebody's nerve breaks down and he "starts hollerin" like Robert, we have to put him to bed gently until he is himself again.

And now as to the political scandal. We are informed by Sir Edward Grey (not, as Mr. Blatchford seems to think, by me) that in 1906 an arrangement was made with France by which provision was made for placing the British Army under the command of the French military authorities, and the British Navy became virtually the North Sea squadron of the Anglo-French Fleet. The object of this combination was defence against the Triple Alliance of Germany, Austria, and Italy (Italy has since backed out). Russia was also a party to the combination. But this is not the scandal. You may think, as I do, that it was not the right combination, and that, for the present, the East had better fight its own battles without dragging in the West. But if Sir Edward Grey did not think so, he was quite right to form the combination he thought best for his country. What is more, the scandal was by no means the secrecy of the combination. Much as I and my fellow-democrats object to secret diplomacy, it is an established institution in England and is quite in order until it is formally abolished, as in America.

Where, then, is the scandal? Well, when the combination was made, the diplomatists who made it solemnly said to one another: "Will you please understand and take note that this does not bind us to anything?" And they all said: "Certainly not," and winked at one another as they went for their hats. On the strength of that little comedy Mr. Asquith and Sir Edward Grey reportedly assured the British nation that "this country is not under any obligation not public and known to Parliament which compels it to take part in any war. In other words, if war arises between European Powers there are no unpublished agreements which will restrict or hamper the freedom of the Government or of Parliament to decide whether or not Great Britain should participate in a war." The scandal was that when, after Sir Edward Grey had virtually declared war without consulting the House, he had to reveal the existence of the combination, three members of the Government resigned, and many persons considered that Mr. Asquith's and Sir Edward's previous declarations, though covered verbally by the comedy, had had the effect of deceiving them and the nation. I happen to be one of those persons; and I happen also to agree with our Allies, the French Ambassador and the Russian Minister for Foreign Affairs, that Sir Edward Grey should have declared to the Kaiser from the beginning that if France were attacked England was bound in honour to come to the rescue of France. And that, in which probably 99 per cent. of the readers of *The Weekly Dispatch* will heartily agree with me, is what Mr. Blatchford is screaming at as "insensate malice and dirty innuendo," and "the meanest act of treachery ever perpetrated by an alien enemy residing in generous and long-suffering England," nay, as an act possible only to a man who could not see "the lovelight in his dear old doggy's eye."

Yours, &c.,
G. Bernard Shaw

"THE PRO-GERMANISM OF BERNARD SHAW"

[*Daily Dispatch,* Manchester, 7 December 1914.]

Sir,—As the letter which appeared in your columns under the above heading, signed I. Hubert, seems to have misled some of your readers, will you allow me to warn you against giving currency to that gentleman's statements until the war is over? I have not the pleasure of his acquaintance; but the contents of his letter show that he is one of the unhappy people who have been driven by the excitement of the war into a craze for writing to the Press about documents they have not read and persons of whom they knów nothing. The following passages contain the gist of his letter:—

> There are some among us with whom the thought rankles bitterly that, had we been better prepared, the tragedy of Belgium might have been averted. But who is Mr. Shaw to throw this at us? Shaw, the pet of the peace-at-any-price party! That party the fear of whose criticism was the cause of any shilly-shallying our Governments may have shown, and for which Mr. Shaw now reviles them.

> The men who had warned us of the German menace, and whose teachings have been proved up to the hilt, indulged in no recriminations. They wasted no time saying: "I told you so," but did their best to help when the catastrophe occurred. It has been left to Mr. Shaw hypocritically to reproach us with a condition which his special school of thought has helped to bring about.

My views about armaments are quite well-known to those who have read my utterances on the subject; and they have been repeated in what Mr. Hubert calls "the scurrilous pamphlet by G. B. Shaw," which he has clearly not read, being, as he modestly explains later on, in a condition of "strengthened allegiance to the old-fashioned virtues of truth and loyalty, honour and sacrifice." I can only say that if Mr. Hubert goes on in this way when his sense of truth is artificially strengthened, one rather wonders what he used to write to the papers when it was in a merely normal state.

In the middle of last year and at the beginning of this, in two long communications to the *Daily Chronicle* and the *Daily News*[1] respectively on foreign policy, I urged, as I have always urged, that the clamour against armaments on the score of expense was absurd in the face of our huge resources; that our armaments might well be doubled or trebled without trenching on a single man that we were not already employing to much less advantage; and that the right policy for us was to arm to the teeth and enter the field of European diplomacy with positive demands of our own instead of continually leaving the initiative to other Powers and explaining that we must do so-and-so, not because we wanted to do it, but because some other Power was doing something that left us no alternative. And the positive policy I proposed was that we should tell Germany that if she carried out her well known military programme of attacking France lest France should attack her first, we should throw ourselves on the side of France, fully armed and prepared. And that we should at the same time assure Germany that if France attacked her we should throw our armaments on the side of Germany, as we were determined to keep the peace of the West of Europe, by arms if necessary, without regard to any engagements that might have been entered into further East. I could see no other way of controlling the situation without

[1]*Daily Chronicle,* 18 March 1913: "Armaments and Conscription: A Triple Alliance Against War"; *Daily News,* 1 January 1914: "The Peace of Europe: and How to Attain It."

making ourselves dependent on Russia, and involving ourselves in the strained relations of that country with Germany's ally.

Nobody ventured to tackle that proposal in public. In private it was said that such a declaration might provoke war. I was strongly of opinion that the absence of a declaration of some positive sort was far more likely to end in a war of general mutual fear and mistrust than the boldest and most explicit declarations of the terms on which we should fight and of the terms on which we should remain friendly. I claim now that events have borne me out precisely. And as both our French and Russian Allies begged us so strongly up to the very last moment to declare that we would fight (as the Government had secretly bound us in honour to do) if France were attacked, it will be seen that I was not alone in my opinion as to which course was the more dangerous.

As to the general reception of my pamphlet, I wish that those who, like Mr. Hubert, denounce it without having read it, would make up their minds firmly as to whether I am a negligible person or not. If I am, the sensible course is to neglect me, not to fill columns with all sorts of fussings about me, from demands that I should be shot (apparently for high treason to Russia) to mere abuse. If, on the other hand I am a writer of some importance, it is clearly a direct playing into the hands of the enemy to announce in all directions that my pamphlet is a justification of Germany and a declaration that she is in the right in this war. Even if this description of my essay were true, it would be stupid to circulate it. If a German journalist were to tell the truth, which is, that my pamphlet contains not only the strongest case against Germany that has yet been made out, but for the first time shows what Germany could and should have done, all the idiots in Germany would shriek at him as a traitor and a pro-Englander. But several English journalists are claiming all my weight for the Germans in an insane determination to damage me at any cost, even that of circulating manifest falsehoods, preventing people from recruiting (many young men who regard me, rightly or wrongly, as an oracle, have thus been persuaded that I am "against the war"); and obscuring the vital necessity for averting a military triumph for the Prussian system.

I am, of course, aware of the cause of this. Many of our journalists and breakfast-table and club-fire patriots spent the three months before my pamphlet appeared in blowing bladders which my analysis of the situation remorselessly pricked. Naturally, they did not like being made to look like fools. When I ridicule them and expose them, they say I am ridiculing and exposing the British Empire. If they were the British Empire no man would risk his thumbnail in its defence. I shall continue to suggest, with all possible good humour, that there is something better worth fighting for than their personal susceptibilities; and they, no doubt, will continue to make the enemy a present of my reputation and influence, such as they are. I cannot help that. I can write anti-Potsdam pamphlets, but I cannot prevent foolish and frightened people from assuring the world that they are anti-English because they are necessarily anti-idiot. And when I see reputable newspapers allowing the Archbishop of York[2] to be pilloried by all the cads and blackguards in his diocese because he has followed the impulse of a Christian and an English gentleman in paying his personal tribute to our enemy at the right moment, as an example and rebuke to the rabble who are disgracing their country before the world by their vituperation, I am glad to remember the speech made by M. Marmande[3] in London on Thursday last, in which he told us with genuine admiration how much he had been struck by the fact that the British soldier at the front never said a word against the man he was fighting; never made a wounded German prisoner feel that he was otherwise than safe and among men who bore him no malice; and, when angry civilians talked about Huns and brutes and the like, always said "No: they are soldiers like ourselves." That is the way to make our enemies respect us. The way to make them despise us is the way of the foul mouth and the lying tongue and the distraught terror that sees a spy at every corner and a Zeppelin in every cloud.

Worse than the abusive people are the vainglorious people. They seem to believe that this war is going to be settled by Englishmen shrieking to the four corners of the earth that they are the flower of the human race, and the Germans the dregs of creation. I do not think that Krupp's guns will take the slightest notice of these glowing testimonials to ourselves. This war is going to be settled by blood and iron; and the blood on our side must be the blood of men deeply imbued with the popular British tradition of life, and implacably resolved that the Prussian Junker tradition shall not prevail against it either in England or anywhere in the

[2]Cosmo Gordon Lang, later Archbishop of Canterbury.

[3]R. de Marmande, a French political scientist interested in the working classes, was the author of *Les Intellectuels devant les ouvriers* (Paris, 1907).

world, even in Prussia itself, if they can help it. Official cases and disputed points of international law are poor fare to recruit on: they will never carry us beyond the point at which the diplomatists and generals will be quite willing to patch up a peace until they are ready to begin again. Not until we have convinced Prussia that the militarist game is not worth the candle will it be time to stop; for not until then shall we have reaped the harvest of our blood and tears. We are not out, I take it, to wrangle over a scrap of paper; and, in my opinion, when the Germans put that question to us, our official people, instead of looking shocked and pained, should have told the Imperial Chancellor flatly that he was up against something much more serious than 1839[4] stationery, and that we should have defended Belgium and France against his assault if there had never been such a thing as a treaty in the world.

Yours, &c.,
G. Bernard Shaw

THE VALUE OF NEUTRALITY

[In its leading article "Why Nations Go to War," the *Morning Post* on 23 February 1915 "notice[d] that Mr. Bernard Shaw is again railing at what he calls British hypocrisy because we persist in suggesting that the violation of the Neutrality of Belgium was a main reason for going to war. Mr. Shaw's raillery is amusing; but on this occasion it proceeds from an entire ignorance of British history. . . .There is no hypocrisy in the matter." Shaw's reply appeared on 27 February.]

Sir,—Your entire agreement with me as to the real nature and object of the war policy of our Foreign Office emboldens me to press my point as to the worthlessness of guarantees of neutrality or of independence (you treat the two, quite rightly, as coming to the same thing as far as Belgium is concerned). If this is lost sight of we shall have the Treaty of Peace, whenever it comes, padded with such guarantees, with the result that we may be fooled into purchasing a farthing's worth of waste paper at the price of substantial concessions.

The word "neutral" is being used daily in different senses, to

[4]At the London Conference of 1838–39, the "perpetual neutrality" of Belgium was promised by the major powers, including Prussia, and a final Dutch-Belgian separation treaty was signed in 1839.

the confusion of the public mind. Sometimes it means simply "not at war," like America. Sometimes "neutral State" means independent buffer State, as in your article. Only occasionally does neutral mean subject to treaties guaranteeing neutrality, as in the cases of Belgium and Switzerland; and in these cases it means not neutral but, on the contrary, subject to interference by foreign Powers, limiting the State's diplomatic activities and threatening that any invasion by the armed forces of any foreign Power will be a casus belli for the foreign signatories if they choose to treat it as such. Obviously this is not neutrality at all, and such treaties can neither have nor acquire any ethical sanction. That is why the 1839 treaty failed not only to protect Belgium but to convince the Germans that we would fight for it. Also why the Germans were no more bound by it morally than we by the Act of Algeciras.[1]

As to what you call my raillery, meaning, I take it, that "chastening of morals by ridicule" which is the classic formula for my profession, its importance has been greatly heightened by the perils of war, and you may depend on my carrying on business as usual.—Yours, &c.,

G. Bernard Shaw

THE NEED FOR CRITICISM

[*Everyman*, 16 July 1915.]

Sir,—In your issue of June 25th a letter from Mr. D. H. Charles contains the following sentence: "Just as it is wrong, I admit, to criticise publicly the conduct of the Government in the midst of a great crisis, even though such criticism contain a substantial element of truth, so it is equally wrong to defend the enemy from any point of view or on any subject."

May I beg Mr. Charles not to spread this curious ethical paradox just at present in England. In Germany it may pass, because the Germans are disciplined idealists, and the best results for Germany may be obtainable in an emergency by trusting to the idealism of the German rulers, and the *Treue* of their subjects. In England such counsels point straight down the road to ruin. We

[1]A treaty signed by the major European powers and the United States on 7 April 1909, designed (at the instigation of the Kaiser) to limit French influence in Morocco by introducing an effective local administration.

are not idealists; we hate discipline; and our governing class is so incorrigibly addicted to muddling, slacking, and jobbing that even when their country's peril makes them sincerely anxious to do their best for her, they cannot change their habits or learn new methods at a moment's notice. The result is that if the English people stop the fiercest criticism of their rulers on Monday, the soldiers will be in brown paper boots on Tuesday; munitions will run short on Wednesday; and before Saturday ten thousand men will lose their lives unnecessarily. At the beginning of this war, I had not forgotten what happened in the Crimean War until Florence Nightingale, Russell[1] and Dickens attacked the Government as nobody had ever dreamt of attacking the Russians. It was fresh in my recollection that in the South African War we were both disgraced in the field and swindled in the Commissariat until Queen Victoria, in desperation, insisted on sending out Lord Roberts and getting rid of the worn-out and hopeless incapables whom the mob were cheering as madly as if they had been so many Nelsons and Napoleons. I took the lesson to heart, and attacked the War Office and the Government vigorously without waiting for supports. But instead of following me, our patriots took the easier and safer line of attacking me. Months elapsed before my critical line was taken, except by Mr. Austin Harrison,[2] who knew the difference between official England and official Prussia. Probably twenty thousand men have been killed or maimed in Flanders because the Government was assured every day that no matter what it did or neglected, Mr. Charles's rule that "it is wrong to criticise publicly the conduct of the Government in the midst of a great crisis" (that is, when criticism is needed as it was never needed before) would be religiously observed, and every Minister and general praised daily in terms that would have provoked a remonstrance from the flatterers of Canute.[3] What was the result? We are now told without contradiction that not only were private engineering firms snubbed when they of-

[1]John Russell, first Earl Russell, Whig MP, who became prime minister in 1865, demanded and carried into effect a separation (1854) of the war and colonial departments. He was openly critical of the government's policies both before and after the Crimean War.

[2]Journalist and political writer who became editor of the *English Review*.

[3]Danish king of England, 1016–35. The story is told in Holinshed's *Chronicles* (VII.13) of Canute rebuking his flatterers by showing them his inability to hold the rising tide.

fered to produce munitions, but that the Woolwich plant was so scandalously underworked that machinery capable of turning out ten thousand cartridges in a given time was turning out four thousand only. Mr. Lloyd George[4] announces an immense multiplication of the output, and his audiences cheer delightedly instead of going black in the face with rage and asking him why in the name of all things Englishmen swear by when they are really angry the measures he has just taken were not taken ten months ago. Is it not clear that they would not have been taken even now if the Conscriptionist Press had not at last plucked up courage or been driven by terror to attack the War Office much more severely than I attacked it?

I hope now that we have begun to grumble like Englishmen Parliament will be soundly walloped into taking the war seriously, and we shall hear the last of "the united front" of frightened civilians huddling in a corner. The world will not see what England can really do until her rulers are waked up by the methods of the old-fashioned fighting mates of our merchant marine. These men had to get their ships to port, and no doubt they would have been only too glad to do it by flattering and indulging the British sailor. But as they found by experience that the effect of this gentlemanly behaviour was that the ship stayed still in fine weather and drifted on a lee shore when the wind got up, they kicked and swore and punched. The experience of the first year of the war has shown that the old characteristics of the British mercantile marine still persist strongly in the British bureaucracy and the British Cabinet. And unless the Press and the Opposition lay on much more vigorously than Macduff we shall be on the rocks before we have stopped cheering Mr. Asquith's resolution to fight to the last drop of his blood, forgetting in our aesthetic delight in his splendid patriotism that when a man is bleeding he dies long before he comes to the last drop, and is too exhausted to fight long before he comes to the point of dying.

So far from its being "wrong to defend the enemy from any point of view or on any subject," it is the most sacred duty of the representatives of art, literature and science during a war to keep these subjects high above the level of the war as supernational things, and to lose no opportunity of exchanging courtesies with their representatives in the hostile country. When all politicians

[4]David Lloyd George, later prime minister, was in July 1915 minister of munitions.

become statesmen and all journalists become gentlemen any attempt to question this ancient and honoured view will be repudiated as an outrage on the fair fame of this country.

Yours, &c.,
G. Bernard Shaw

ILLUSIONS OF WAR

[Following Shaw's Fabian lecture on "The Illusions of War" in the King's Hall on 26 October 1915, his fellow Fabian and longtime friend Sir Sydney Olivier wrote a letter to the *New Statesman,* published on 30 October, in which he accused Shaw of an "ecstatic amblyopia" on the subject of the war, most particularly on the question of England's real responsibility to Belgium. Shaw's response was published in the same journal on 6 November.]

Sir,—I owe Sir Sydney Olivier and all the rest of my audience an apology for having laid out my lecture on a scale too extensive for the time available. I had to finish as best I could without developing my criticism of what I called the ecstatic vision of our relations with our allies and the neutrals. I will not attempt to fill up the hiatus here; but I will indicate a point or two relevant to Sir Sydney's letter.

1. My ancient insistence on the danger of the torrents of virtuous indignation in which we indulged over the scrap of paper and the breach of neutrality was, as I made quite clear at the time, caused by the probability that before we were done with the war we or one of our allies would have to do the same thing. The event has justified me: we have violated the neutrality of Greece, and Russia has violated the neutrality of Persia.[1] I actually mentioned Serbia as an example of a country which was inaccessible except through the territory of other Powers. We had better have kept on

[1]Despite efforts of Greece's King Constantine to keep his country neutral, allied forces invaded Salonika in 1915 to establish "a peaceful blockade," eventually establishing a rival Greek government, which declared war on the Central Powers and deposed Constantine. The Triple Entente (Britain, France, and Russia) had several years earlier carved Persia into three "protective" spheres of influence, with Russia occupying the oil-rich north. The Persian government, though under heavy pressure from its co-religionists the Turks, and from German diplomats in Teheran, to enter the war on the side of the Central Powers, struggled to maintain strict neutrality. Combat between occupying and invader forces, however, plunged the beleaguered nation into war as effectually as if hostilities had been formally proclaimed.

sincere human ground until the discoveries at Brussels made it possible for us to acknowledge our more direct obligations.

2. I do not think the Belgians will, or ought to, regard an acknowledgment of our direct obligation as superfluous on the ground that we are willing to see them through as a matter of honour. If I owe a man money for value received, I have no right to refuse him a bill for it on the ground that I sympathise with him so much that he can depend on me. If *he* proposes to put it on that footing, well and good (though even then I should probably not care to take advantage of his generosity or inexperience); but the proposal should certainly not come from me.

3. The view that "On her own dignity and of her own spirit Belgium took up arms to resist a German invasion" is one which may very honourably and proudly be insisted on by the Belgians; and I quite appreciate the feeling which has moved Sir Sydney Olivier to put himself in their place and utter it for them in a context which makes misunderstanding impossible. But he will admit that if I had made such an assertion on behalf of England, I should have been understood as saying to the Belgians, in effect: "Remember that you went into this war on your own account; and you must bear the consequences yourself: don't try to put them on us." I could hardly find a better example of the danger I was warning my audience against: the danger of being so preoccupied with our own point of view and our own good intentions that we are utterly unconscious of how very differently our attitude may be interpreted from the other end. I must add, moreover, that my insistence on our obligation is most certainly not superfluous on the ground that it is admitted by everybody. On the contrary, every attempt to admit it has been angrily resented and denounced as pro-Germanism. What there has been is a very general and indignant demand that Germany shall be compelled to compensate Belgium to the utmost farthing. No Belgian has yet asked, "Suppose you fail to do anything more than compel Germany to evacuate Belgium, incidentally smashing up what is left of our towns in the process, how about our compensation then?" Suppose some Belgian does ask that, is the reply to be my reply or not? Sir Sydney will see my point. It is the right of the Belgians to be heroic about Belgium. It is not our right to be heroic for them, especially when the heroics take the form of exonerating us from our obligations to Belgium.

4. I cannot for the life of me see what claim civilians have to exemption from the risks of war. Civilians clamour for war, pay

for war, send soldiers to war, express hostile sentiments and do hostile things (I gave painful illustrations) which would make a good soldier sick, and exult when their army and navy rain bombs on enemy civilians. Under such circumstances I persist in thinking that the contrast between our shrieks over the deaths of a few civilians and our spectatorial enjoyment of the carnage at the Gallipoli landing[2] must appear selfishly inconsiderate to our troops, which was my point on Tuesday.

5. Finally, concerning Miss Cavell.[3] As what she did and suffered was done for us, it is right and natural that she should be a heroine to us; and it would be disgraceful of us to dishonour her memory by cinematographic claptrap, or merely break her coffin into sticks to beat the Germans with. There is a way in which we can pay our debt to her, and test the sincerity of her loudest champions. We cannot complain of the denial to her by military law of all the safeguards of human justice, because we have shot ten people ourselves without any of those safeguards under the same law. We cannot plead her sex, because our own criminal law, civil and military, makes no distinction between men and women; and no woman asks that it should, any more than Edith Cavell did. We cannot vapour about chivalry, because if she had come back alive to demand the political rights granted to the meanest of men, and had broken a shop window to compel attention to her claim, she would have been mobbed, insulted, and subjected to gross physical violence with the full approval of many of the writers who are now canonising her. What we can do is very simple. We can enfranchise her sex in recognition of her proof of its valour. The Bill might gracefully be introduced by Mr. McKenna in the Commons and Viscount Gladstone in the Lords.[4] If this proposal is received in dead silence, I shall know that Edith Cavell's sacrifice has been rejected by her country.

Yours, &c.,
G. Bernard Shaw

[2]In April 1915, at Winston Churchill's urgence, the Allied Expeditionary Forces landed troops on the Gallipoli peninsula in the Dardanelles, to relieve pressure on a Russian army that had suffered astronomic losses in battles with the Turks. The campaign was a disaster, its cost in bloodshed enormous.

[3]Edith Cavell, an army nurse, had been executed by the Germans in Belgium as a spy; a monument was erected to her in London after the war.

[4]Reginald McKenna, at present chancellor of the exchequer, was a banker and longtime Liberal MP. Viscount Herbert Gladstone had been a Liberal MP for Leeds and home secretary, 1905–10.

AMERICAN PREPAREDNESS

[*Intercollegiate Socialist,* New York, December 1915.]

Sir,—I have no intention of visiting the United States this year. If I did, I am afraid you would hesitate to welcome me to your platform. I should strenuously recommend the United States to build thirty-two new dreadnoughts instead of sixteen, and to spend two billion dollars on its armament program instead of one. This would cost only a fraction of the money you are wasting every year in demoralizing luxury, a good deal of it having been in the past scattered over the continental countries which are now using what they saved out of it to slaughter one another.

If the United States wishes to stop war as an institution; that is, to undertake the policing of the world, it will need a very big club for the purpose. It is possible, however, now that the belligerents are bleeding to death so rapidly that the only question to be decided is which side will be first exhausted, that the United States might not only induce them to state the terms on which they will consent to make peace, but even to co-operate in establishing supernational institutions which will provide an alternative to war, and even deal with war as a crime.

Until then, the United States can decline to enter the race for the biggest armament only at the risk of finding itself where Britain would have been to-day if it had refused to keep ahead of the German fleet. It is true that at present the Pacifism of America is the hope of the world; but it is because America is powerful as well as pacific that she will be listened to.

If I were an American statesman, I should tell the country flatly that it should maintain a Pacific navy capable of resisting an attack from Japan and an Atlantic navy capable of resisting an attack from England, with Zeppelins on the same scale, a proportionate land equipment of siege guns and so forth. And until the nations see the suicidal folly of staking everything in the last instance on the ordeal of battle, no other advice will be honest advice.

Yours, &c.,
G. Bernard Shaw

THE CASE AGAINST CHESTERTON

[This correspondence grew out of Shaw's review of Julian West's *G. K. Chesterton: A Critical Study,* published under the above caption in the *New Statesman,* 13 May 1916. References to another recent book, *The Servile State* (1912) by Hilaire Belloc (an associate of Chesterton who frequently joined him in "debates" with Shaw), and to Beatrice (Mrs. Sidney) Webb, author of the Minority Report on the Poor Law (1909), inform the controversy.]

I

[3 June 1916.]

Sir,—Mr. Bernard Shaw, in his very genial criticism, suggests that I should reply to it in *The New Witness*[1]—and in a more general way I shall certainly do so. But since he puts to me certain particular questions before your particular public, I hope you will allow me to answer them as honestly as I can, and therefore, I fear, at some length.

(1) He asks me what I would do with Jo,[2] the poor guttersnipe in "Bleak House." I would give him money; until I could effect a revolution to give his family private property. I am certain that Dickens denounced the right honourables, as I should denounce them, for tolerating a society in which Jo or Mrs. Jo (to give his mother a name) have no private property, no domesticity, and no money. I deny that Dickens's Utopia would have been either the Socialist State Mr. Shaw would like to promote, or the Servile State which he is promoting. I need not dwell on the extraordinary effort to make something out of the success of the two Dickens heroines in comforting the cottager's wife. The identity of Mrs. Webb and Esther Summerson does not strike me; nor am I surprised that Mrs. Pardiggle still thinks she is quite different from Mrs. Pardiggle. But the facts in the Dickens case are easily tested. Mr. Shaw expresses his distrust of Mrs. Pardiggle by calling her "an uninspected inspector." Am I to understand that Esther Summerson was an inspected inspector? In fact, of course, she was

[1]Publication edited by G. K. Chesterton's brother, Cecil, to which both Chesterton and Hilaire Belloc were regular contributors.
[2]Like all of the Dickens characters mentioned in the letters—Jo's mother, Esther Summerson, Mrs. Pardiggle, Sir Leicester Dedlock, Snagsby—Jo is a character in *Bleak House.*

trusted by the poor because she helped them in exactly the same personal, patchy, and exceedingly practical way in which they help each other, doing day and night the difficult things that are desperately wanted, while Mr. Shaw (in a turret in Adelphi Terrace) is trying to figure out on paper whether 25 or 33 per cent. of them have the more rudimentary rights of human beings. This fact, that the right way is the poor's own way, is actually emphasized by Dickens in the text, for anyone to see less blind to facts than a Fabian. I say, then, that—pending a revolution—I do not believe in any sort of direct personal action except direct personal charity; and this I say, not merely because I have "a feeling heart," but because I have a thinking head, and perceive that this is the one and only way which Mrs. Webb and the social organisers have not already turned into a trick for selling Jo into slavery. If Mrs. Jo were there I would give money to Mrs. Jo; and under no possible circumstances would I give it to Mrs. Webb. Giving it as I do, I am quite aware that Mrs. Jo may use it badly; I am also aware that Mrs. Webb must use it badly; and could not now by any possibility use it well. The reason is that her school of sociology, and Mr. Shaw in so far as he is the dupe of it, are driven by a diseased and slavish social theory; and far less to be trusted with Jo than Jo to be trusted with money.

And if Mr. Shaw asks me why, I convict him out of his own mouth. By his own account, his "feeble-minded person" is not the exception, but practically the rule. In his own explanation he slides quite calmly from the half-wit to Jo, who was not a half-wit, and then to Jo's mother, whom there is no earthly reason for supposing a half-wit, and then to some three-quarters of the English populace. By his own confession his coercion threatens only the poor, and almost any of the poor. I will give no expression to the anger and contempt which a democrat must feel for all this; it would be unjust, for Mr. Shaw has never disguised the fact that democracy is almost the only thing he really regards with bitterness. I merely claim that he himself warns all democrats that he would not leave a vestige of it remaining. Nor is this surprising, considering the moral standard of which he gives us a glimpse. He says elsewhere that nearly everybody must be feeble-minded, because the world is at war. Taking his words at their lightest value, they must mean that challenging pain and death for the good name of a nation is something in the direction of irresponsibility. If a child shows a sneaking admiration for valour in the field, or begins to show a morbid interest in the credit of his country, the mental specialist will at least keep an eye on him. This sounds very absurd; but it is Mr. Shaw who is absurd and not I. He does seriously think feeble-minded exactly what everybody else thinks strong-minded, and regards as the hardest and most heroic of the duties of a citizen. He claims to know the proportion of irresponsible people; and this (good heavens!) is the sort of test he will apply!

(2) Mr. Shaw also says: "Does Mr. Chesterton, like Mr. Houston Chamberlain,[3] really think, that Jew, *qua* Jew, is a worse man than himself? Mr. West has clearly a right to know." Mr. West is welcome to know, though I cannot promise that he will understand. The answer to the question itself is that I have a mystical timidity about feeling confident that any man is a worse man than myself. That individual Jews are much better than myself I know in my private life; but I cannot even imagine what this has to do with the Jewish Problem or anything I ever said about Jews. Mr. Shaw startles me with a life-like impersonation of his young sentimentalist in "Man and Superman," and gravely invokes Macaulay. Macaulay, he observes, said that red-haired men could be as easily arraigned as Jews.[4] Macaulay also said that Socialism was absurd, and the main evil of competition beyond the cure of government. He said a great many things of that kind. But it is as easy to prove him wrong about red hair as about competition. Show me that red-haired men have married red-haired women to keep their type separate for two thousand years; that all this time they worshipped a Red Bull with appropriate customs and commandments, while everybody else worshipped the sun or moon with quite different customs and commandments; that, by whatever cause or fault, no red-haired man ever touched a spade or a plough or became native in nations wholly agricultural; that from every age and land, from the farthest Caucasian hamlet to the farthest Californian camp, came the one unvarying human tale

[3]Houston Stewart Chamberlain, British-born political philosopher, wrote his later works in German. His *Foundations of the Nineteenth Century,* translated into English in 1910, used racial theories to propound the quality of "Germanism" which would bring a new order to Europe.

[4]In a review of *Statement of the Civil Disabilities and Privations affecting Jews in England* (1829) in the *Edinburgh Review* of January 1831, Macaulay argued that the "English Jews are, as far as we can see, precisely what our government has made them" and then invoked the analogy of "gentlemen with red hair."

of the red-haired man who lent money to the poor and ruined them; that (to take a last out of an endless list) one powerful red-haired family was so utterly international that the brothers and nephews of it were banking and wire-pulling in all the chief capitals of Europe—show me anything like this and I will consider the comparison between the Red Hair and the Red Shield. But I appeal to Mr. Shaw, as the most eminent red-haired man of the age, to testify that no such features adorn the family history. Really, of course, Macaulay believed (with other provincialities) that the Jew was distrusted in the Middle Ages for some reason as fanciful as red hair. He was distrusted for usury; and for initiating certain international intrigues of the Marconi type.[5] We do not blame Jews more than their Gentile beneficiaries, like Mr. Lloyd George; it is because that sort of finance is a Jewish tendency or tradition; and to deny it, because it captures individual Gentiles, is exactly as realistic and sensible as to deny that the gipsies are vagrants because Mr. Belloc slept in a wood.

There is also a question about Votes for Women; but as the reply would be both longer and less urgent, I will not further strain your courtesy except on a further demand; the answer will be found in the sections about crowds and hanging in my book "What's Wrong with the World?" But finally, may I ask Mr. Shaw a question—only one? When Jo, or Jo's mother, or the required number of mothers, have been deprived of self-direction as a practical measure, what guarantee can he give me that those who are doing it intend *ever* to restore any sort of liberty to them or their descendants? Where is there the sign, or the sign of a sign, that his favourite social reformers mean to "abolish poverty," except in the sense of feeding the people as slaves have always been fed?

Apologizing, and thanking you in anticipation, I am,

Yours, &c.,
G. K. Chesterton

[5]Charges in 1913 that members of the government had been speculating in Marconi Company shares led to a parliamentary inquiry, which exonerated the ministers involved in the scandal. Their political integrity, however, remained compromised.

II

[10 June 1916.]

Sir,—Mr. Chesterton has asked me a question to keep me going. "When Jo, or Jo's mother, or the required number of mothers, have been deprived of self-direction as a practical measure, what guarantee can Mr. Shaw give me that those who are doing it intend *ever* to restore any sort of liberty to them or their descendants?"

Now, if Mr. Chesterton had asked me what guarantee I could give him that if an Act for the protection of Jo were passed it would really be enforced, or even left unrepealed by the next plutocratic Parliament, I could understand his anxiety. But why should he ask for a guarantee that Jo, once snatched from the pit of neglect and destitution, should be thrown in again, as if his rescue were an insult to society to be apologised for and undone at the earliest opportunity? I do not want to deprive Jo's mother of self-direction: I am not a distiller. I want to deprive her of Jo-misdirection; and if Mr. Chesterton imagines that I long to restore it to her, or intend that it shall ever be restored to her, world-without-end, he little knows his man.

Mr. Chesterton's opinion that "the right way is the poor's own way" is Pangloss[6] *in excelsis*. It is certainly not the opinion of the poor themselves, who know too well that their way is not their will, but a backway of squalid necessity into which they are forced by iniquitous circumstances. The opinion of the poor is that "the poor in a lump is bad"; and a very sound opinion it is, too. If the right way is the poor's own way, then all is for the best in this best of all possible worlds, wherein four out of every five are made poor by skimming off them all that could rescue them from poverty and heaping it on the fifth, who is cursed by Mr. Chesterton and will burn with Dives in hell.[7] And, incidentally, the Fabian Society, with its impious challenge, "Why are the many poor?" is a mischievous mistake, founded on "a diseased and slavish social theory," as Mr. Chesterton puts it. And, incidentally, I am the greatest fool alive, and Sir Frederick Banbury[8] the wisest of the wise. The poor are far too prone to believe that the right

[6]The pedantic old tutor, optimistic in the face of all evidence, in Voltaire's *Candide*.
[7]The rich man in the parable, *Luke* 16:19.
[8]Conservative MP for the City of London, 1906–24.

way is the rich's own way, which is a more rational, if not less damnable error than the other. In any case they have to give in to it, as the rich are the only people who can afford to choose that way at all, or whose views are attended to; and even their freedom to choose is an illusion. There is no way in a wilderness.

Private charity is the remedy of Sir Leicester Dedlock and of Snagsby. There is no more biting satire in literature than the story of the poor little law stationer helplessly watching Jo dying of a socially preventible disease (lest his mother's self-direction should be compromised) and piling useless half-crowns on the table to relieve his futile compassion whilst he idiotically babbles "*Our* Father" to the child who is gasping his life out because nations have never been taught to say "Our Children." Mr. Chesterton "sees himself," as the actors say, as Snagsby. I do not. I feel half tempted to give Mr. Chesterton a terrible lesson by bribing some journalist to publish a personal paragraph in this style:—

> Mr. Gilbert Chesterton, or G.K.C. as his friends affectionately call him, is cut off by the war from his palace in the Dolomites, and is now in residence at—[*address in full*], where he is known as The Angel Millionaire. A tale of distress is the surest introduction to Mr. Chesterton and the shortest way to his heart and purse. No applicant ever turns from his door empty-handed. He keeps a special account at his bank for charity and it is said that a book of one hundred cheques lasts him barely a week. Even in the depth of winter he is frequently seen making for home entirely nude, having given all his clothes to some shivering waif by the wayside. He is adored by the poor; and his greatest delight is to sit in his veranda and hear the air humming with the prayers of grateful widows and orphans. His famous fleet of motor-cars includes a Rolls-Royce bequeathed to him by a begging letter-writer who boasted that during the last ten years of his life he had done business with Mr. Chesterton exclusively, assuming no less than two hundred and thirty different characters, of whom over a hundred had permanent pensions.

I venture to predict that within a fortnight from the appearance of that paragraph, Mr. Chesterton will be cured for ever of his faith in private charity, except as a sentimental luxury, although most of the appeals with which he will be overwhelmed will be genuine enough.

Democracy in the sense of government of the people for the people by the people is only tyranny in (let us hope) its last ditch. For the poor man there is no freedom; and poverty can be got rid of only by legislators who not only want to get rid both of poverty and riches, but who are also very highly qualified as lawyers and economists, and are, to put it roughly, just the sort of brainy, conscientious, "dry" people the trueborn Englishman loathes from the bottom of his soul. There is no more dangerous humbug than the demagogue who declares that the voice of the people is the voice of God, and that "it is for you to decide, gentlemen," knowing full well that the response will be, "Hear, hear, governor: tell us what to decide." If plays were written for the people by the people, nobody would go to the theatre unless they were compelled (as they probably would be); yet it is easier to write a good play than to make a good law, and the penalty of failure is less severe. For playmaking and for lawmaking you must go to the abnormal people who have the specific talent which these exercises of human faculty require; and if you consider that this necessity constitutes "the Servile State," you must just put up with the servility. You cannot help yourself. For if the alternative were to go without plays and laws, we could at least embrace it, and live like savages sooner than face this bogey which Herbert Spencer bequeathed to Hilaire Belloc; but as the actual alternative is to have abominably dull plays and ruinous laws, the choice is Hobson's choice: that is, no choice at all. Mr. Chesterton would not have Mrs. Sidney Webb's Minority Report; so he got Mr. Lloyd George's Insurance Act. Mrs. Webb offered him such safeguards against maladministration as are possible. He threw in his weight against her; and he now has a real "servile state" in which every power, from boundless exploitation, insult, abuse, personal violence and blood-poisoning to the direct power of killing has been quite unnecessarily conferred on the people's masters without a single safeguard, and he has to persuade himself that he likes it because it means "challenging pain and death for the good name of a nation." In his inculcated and unnatural and uncharacteristic phobia of legislation to protect the feebleminded, he is keeping the strongminded under the thumb of those who have no minds at all. He is frightened by a mere alliteration even out of his appetite for romance. The battle of St. George with the Dragon is sordid and prosaic beside the battle of Mrs. Sidney Webb with Lord George Hamilton[9] for the souls and bodies of the children of the poor. Like Florence Nightingale's battle for the Crimean soldiers with the Panglosses and Panjandrums of her day, it continues the tradi-

[9]Chairman of the royal commission on poor law and unemployment, 1905–09. The struggle within the commission is told in chap. VII of Beatrice Webb's *Our Partnership* (1948).

tion of Joan of Arc, in which the most extravagant romantic heroinism touches the sternest realities; yet Mr. Chesterton, of all men, has nothing to say except that Mrs. Webb *must* use money badly. And all because Mrs. Webb probably classes him as feeble-minded in practical politics. He will not be her dupe, he says. But if he must be somebody's dupe (which seems to be the position) why be Herbert Spencer's? It is true that Mrs. Webb is not like Esther Summerson. If she began to resemble that pre-Ibsenist ideal of her sex, Mr. Chesterton would be the first to implore her on his knees to retrace her steps ere it were too late. Esther left the brick-makers to their fate and to their freedom and to "the way of the poor." Even Mrs. Pardiggle had more social conscience than that. Esther's idea of helping them was to put her handkerchief over the face of a dead baby. Its father subsequently sold the handkerchief to Esther's mother and drank the proceeds. Mrs. Webb keeps her handkerchiefs and looks the dead babies in the face, swearing that they shall not die if she can help it, and does not idealise their fathers as "the poor" and their ways as "the right way." After all, it may be possible to combine the whirlwind social activity of Mrs. Pardiggle with the sympathy and goodwill of Esther. But no combination will be of any use without experience, an arduous study, and a tremendous documentation. Mrs. Webb worked in a sweater's den, collected rents in an East-end tenement property, lived with the poor in a factory district, married the omniscient Mr. Webb (a fearful adventure), sized up the rich, the official, and the ecclesiastical, produced the first books to which we owe any exact and comprehensive knowledge of the history of labour as distinct from the romancings of philanthropists, and fought like the very devil all the time to extort better conditions of life for the poor and plan our production and distribution in their interest. And Mr. Chesterton, instead of sending her a ten-pound note, and interposing his formidable person and trenchant pen between her and our troublesome political street boys, assures the world that she is not to be trusted. Perhaps nobody is to be trusted beyond a certain point; but everyone is entitled to a reasonable loyalty and friendly assistance, or at the very least a respectful neutrality, when they have given such proofs of goodwill as are within human possibility.

The Jewish question I must leave to Mr. Zangwill.[10] I do not

[10]Israel Zangwill, novelist and playwright, a Jew who had forsaken his religion but not his racial heritage, was a zealous advocate of Zionism.

mind an exhibition spar with Mr. Chesterton; but I will not cut him to pieces. That about worshipping the Red Bull while everyone else worshipped the sun and moon, for instance! What Sunday School was Mr. Chesterton sent to? But I refrain; it is too cheap a gambit to be played between such champions.

Yours, &c.,
G. Bernard Shaw

III

[17 June 1916.]

Sir,—I thank Mr. Shaw for his letter, which is great fun; but really I would suggest, as a friend, that he hurts his repute with the rising generation by playing about with the simple thesis of the Servile State, and either pretending not to understand it or not thinking it worth while to try. He does indeed begin by an attempt to answer my question, or part of it. I do not understand the answer; and as I never indulged the cant of calling him a mystifier, I can only suppose he does not understand the question. Perhaps it would help him if he read the rest of it, which ran, "Where is there the sign, or the sign of a sign, that his favourite social reformers mean 'to abolish poverty' except in the sense of feeding the people as slaves have always been fed?" Obviously Jo's mother, as an individual with certain alleged defects, will not be with us "world without end" in any case. The question is whether Mr. Shaw hopes that Jo or his descendants can be trained and fed into comparative health and skill by being more directly controlled by richer people; and, if so, hether their health and skill are to be controlled for the profit of those people. This is not the question Mr. Shaw answers; it is only the one I asked him.

Each of Mr. Shaw's arguments is easily disposed of in turn by simply stating what the Servile State is. Thus, he recites the old arguments for an aristocracy, the answer to which is as obvious as they are. Who decides who is superior, or whether Mr. Webb is a pioneer or a dodgy slave-dealer. There are only two tests possible, apart from the supernatural. The best may be those most trusted, however passively, by the community. If so, we are to accept democratic opinion so long as it is negative and lazy opinion. If not, they must be those most trusted by themselves. In which case we must obey all the lunatics out of asylums, under a cryptic high priesthood of the lunatics in asylums. That is the answer to Mr.

Shaw and aristocracy; but aristocracy is not the Servile State. Mr. Shaw says: "For playmaking and for lawmaking you must go to the abnormal people who have the specific talent which these exercises of human faculty require; and if you consider that this necessity constitutes 'the Servile State' you must just put up with the servility." I do not consider that the Servile State. I consider that snobbishness, or that specially craven form of it the French call *snobisme.* The whole phrase is full of the notion that a free man must always bow to the temporary idol of the Intelligentsia, an idol so dead and wooden that it is very properly called "the thing." If you want to know what such things very rapidly become when the popular breath has never been in them, go where owls and ivy inherit the halls of the poor old Ibsen Club in *The Philanderer.*[11] Certainly the wit of Shaw has survived the wisdom of Ibsen; and obviously it is abnormal, in the sense of unusual, to be able to write his plays, as it may be to write Mr. Webb's calculations. I never said the State had no use for clerks. But if the plays and laws do not appeal to and perpetuate the normal, they go into the dustbin with all the million mad sects and dead Utopias that failed to appeal to it in the past. But all this has no more to do with the Servile State than with the South Pole. The definition of the Servile State is economic; and if my economic claims be humble, as they doubtless are, it is all the more surprising that I can state it as economics and Mr. Shaw can only answer it with rhetoric. The Servile State is a condition in which the law enforces labour upon a defined number of people, and guarantees the surplus wealth, or profit, of that labour as the private property of another and equally defined number of people. It has the corollary that any legislation which guarantees the adequate support of the employee as such, without either allowing him the profit or allowing him to refuse the work, is legislation directed to this end and to no other—*e.g.*, compulsory arbitration without complete confiscation of profits is slavery. What we want to know is whether Mr. Shaw, Mr. and Mrs. Webb and others, admit that they are working for this or not; and if not, whether they can point to the minutest particular in which they are working against it, or working for anything divergent from it—such as Socialism. This is quite a plain definition and quite a plain question. And when Mr. Shaw only answers it by talking at random about bogies, demagogues

[11]Shaw's second play, written in 1893 and first performed in London in 1905.

and panjandrums, he is behaving to us exactly as the most blustering Anti-Socialist of his youth behaved to him when they refused to discuss Socialism as the socialisation of the means of production, and insisted on discussing it as Anarchism, Free Love, red ruin and the breaking-up of laws.

Again, Mr. Shaw says: "For the poor man there is no freedom, and poverty can be got rid of only by legislators who not only want to get rid both of poverty and riches, but who are also very highly qualified as lawyers and economists, and are, to put it roughly, just the sort of brainy, conscientious, 'dry' people the trueborn Englishman loathes from the bottom of his soul." But this is just where my question holds him up. Let us grant that the dry and brainy (what a crew!) do want to get rid of poverty, in the very limited sense of anarchic and accidental starvation; in short, that they do want to "feed the people as slaves have always been fed." But where is the shadow of a sign that they want to get rid of riches? Mr. Shaw can only show that by pointing to some Collectivist expropriation of the rich. He cannot do it. Until he does, I fear his priceless remark about the Fabian Society and "its impious challenge, why are the many poor?" will be received by our young friends with rather irreverent mirth.

It is so again about Mrs. Webb, who is now apparently cast for a yet more romantic part. "The battle of St. George with the dragon is sordid and prosaic beside the battle of Mrs. Sidney Webb with Lord George Hamilton for the souls and bodies of the children of the poor." May I suggest that we are supposed to know what St. George did with the dragon; and we are trying to find out what Mrs. Webb proposes to do with Lord George Hamilton. So far as we can see, she proposes that an endless procession of princesses should pass into the dragon's power, on condition that he does not eat them for food, but makes them work to produce it for him. It is so when Mr. Shaw, missing the point again, suggests that an army is a Servile State. It is not, by the economic definition. Militarism is not slavery, any more than Socialism is slavery, though either might be tyranny. A regiment will not be servile until it produces a surplus which goes to the Colonel or the Major. Here one must notice what can only be called the startling ignorance of classing our case with Herbert Spencer's. Spencer (meaning to bring a moral charge of tyranny) said something to the effect that Socialism is slavery. I fail to find any connection, except a flat contradiction, between this and Mr. Belloc, who points out that Socialism is not slavery. It is his whole point that Fabians are working for slavery and not for Socialism.

There is one point also that may as well be cleared up. Mr. Shaw comes a curious logical cropper when he says, "If the right way is the poor's own way, then all is for the best in this best of all possible worlds." Surely I can say that during the Russian retreat the Grand Duke's way was the best way,[12] without saying that all was for the best. I think both rich and poor have suffered in the horrible modern schism, but I think the poor have more of the pain but less of the poison—that is to say, less of the perverted nonsense that Mr. Shaw talks against patriotism and the family, and all the ideals which are as fruitful as his are sterile. On these things I flatly and confidently disagree with him; but who is to judge between us, unless it be God or the people?

By the way, I think he is unwise in brandishing his quite innocent imitations as superiorities. In his article he claimed to know all about wine from a childish memory of ginger-beer. In his letter he refers me to a Sunday School for the settlement of the Jewish problem. Certainly on that subject he writes, not only as if he had been to a very Evangelical Sunday School, but as if he had never been anywhere else.

Yours, &c.,
G. K. Chesterton

IV

[24 June 1916.]

Sir,—Mr. Chesterton is righting himself gradually, as he was bound to do if left to his own wits and his own honesty. But there is no reason why he should waste his time in doing over again the drudgery of mere investigation that has already been done by the Fabian Society, and without which, though he may work out abstract definitions and propositions in sociology, he cannot possibly identify the real working protagonists of the movements he wishes to support or oppose. Why not start where the Fabian So-

[12]Grand Duke Nicholas commanded the Russian army until he was packed off by the tsar to a lesser command in the Caucasus in September 1915. His dictatorial rule in the war areas and impossible demands on the work force resulted in heavy military casualties, severe hardships for civilians, and Jewish pogroms in Poland.

ciety has left off in the work of ascertaining the facts, even if he wishes to make a quite different use of the facts?

"The Servile State," says Mr. Chesterton, "is a condition in which the law enforces labour upon a defined number of people, and guarantees the surplus wealth—or profit—of that labour as the private property of another and equally defined number of people." But this is what we have already. It is not what Herbert Spencer called "the coming slavery," but the slavery already come.

What Mr. Chesterton suspects, not without good grounds, is that this servility could be much more scientifically organised than it is; and what he fears is that the more scientifically it is organised the more formidable it will become. Also he sees the fact—though, as I think, without yet seeing through it—that the political and industrial machinery of Socialism is equally efficacious as a machinery of scientific Servilism, exactly as a rifle in the hands of an employer is just as deadly as a rifle in the hands of an employee. It is a machinery devised to control the distribution of the national product; and it can be adjusted to effect a distribution in the proportion of a thousand to one between the Duke of Portland[13] and the scavenger on whose work the habitability of the Portland Estate depends, or the equal distribution which I advocate. Thus you get the ironical circumstance that since both the Scientific Servilist and the Socialist can achieve their ends only by complete control of distribution, each is compelled to work at the construction of the machinery that will defeat him if his opponent captures it, precisely as we have to go on devising Dreadnoughts and submarines with the full knowledge that Germany will copy everything we devise. It is accordingly quite true that the Fabian Society and Mr. Sidney Webb are engaged in the construction of a machinery which can be used to fortify the Servile State if the Servilists can collar it and are intelligent enough to understand its handling. But it is equally true that the scientific Servilists are engaged in the construction of a machinery which can be used to abolish servility if the serfs can, and will, collar it. Mr. Chesterton is naturally looking for a machinery that will work only one way—his way. But the nature of the case does not leave room for a *tertium quid.* Until Mr. Chesterton can breed a sort of sheriff who can levy exe-

[13]While Shaw may be referring to one of the most famous of inherited estates, William John Cavendish Bentinck-Scott, fifth Duke of Portland, is best remembered for his restoration of the family estate, Welbeck Abbey.

cution for income-tax, but becomes paralysed when a writ for privately appropriated rent is put into his hand, he will have to put up with sheriffs who will distrain upon Mr. Belloc as effectively as upon Lord Northcliffe.

Now comes the practical question: Who are the people who are doing what Mr. Chesterton wildly accuses Mr. Webb of doing: that is, organising Servilism instead of Socialism? The Servilists of the hour are, I should say, the apostles of Scientific Management. Their gospel was very competently reviewed in the *New Statesman* last week by one who shall be nameless (not me). If they get hold of Mr. Chesterton they will double the number of words per minute he can write, by placing his ink-bottle three point seven inches nearer to him, and tracing the exact path his elbow must take when he reaches out for it. Then there are the profit-sharers, who offer the worker a percentage of the profits on the speculation that he will immediately sweat himself hard enough to increase the total profits by double that percentage. There is Mr. Henry Ford, who combines the two methods so ably, and, one must in fairness add, so philanthropically, that he claims to be able to make a workman "worth" a pound a day, and to pay it to him.[14] There are, or were, the Positivists, who proposed to moralise the capitalist, and who fought that point out with the Fabian Society thirty years ago. There is the very able and influential group of young men whose organ is *The Round Table,*[15] who are the real heirs to Positivism, and who must be highly amused at the spectacle of Mr. Chesterton too busy fighting his own side to notice *The Round Table*'s existence. And there are the disciples of the early phase of John Stuart Mill: the advocates of the Peasant Proprietor panacea. If Mr. Chesterton were to be cut off now in his prime (which Heaven forfend!), history would say only, "*Que diable allait il faire dans cette galère?*";[16] for peasant proprietorship happens to be the one part of the political machinery of Servilism for which Socialism has no use, though the happy dweller under Socialism will not lack "the little house on the hill" desiderated by Morris, in whose *News from Nowhere,* by the way, there is not a trace of a peasant property, and men sow and reap

[14]Ford had recently instituted his "$5 a day" wage for automobile workers, in 1914.

[15]A group of young Liberals had founded this political quarterly in 1910.

[16]A famous line, translated as "What the devil was he doing in that galley?," in Molière's *Les Fourberies de Scapin* (1671).

on the land they all belong to (instead of its belonging to them) for the fun and the health of it; and the French, Italian, and Irish peasant proprietor of to-day, who will not dig an irrigation channel to fertilise or drain his own field until you can convince him that his next-door neighbour will not be a farthing the better for it, is not only unknown but inconceivable.

Mr. Chesterton is, I think, misled by the stability of certain poor forms of marginal production which are not yet worth the direct attention of capitalists, not to mention the simple stability of human activity, which will keep men walking and talking long after the motor-bicycle and the dictaphone totter on the brink of perfection. Mr. Chesterton's articles, whether written with Nature's quill, or with the detestable Brummagen steel nib, or the gold and iridium fountain pen, or clattered on a typewriter, or dictated to a servile secretary, or bawled into a receiver, will remain wholly unaffected in their relation to Socialism or Servilism, because the economic problem of Socialism and of Servilism alike is one of distribution. Production decides how much you have to distribute, but not how it is distributed. The village blacksmith persists, though his son becomes a steel smelter, just as the annual fair and the country town market day persist along with Tattersall's and The Baltic.[17] But if Mr. Chesterton thinks that the village blacksmith gets his share, he had better go and ask him—just to make sure.

Finally, it must always be borne in mind that compulsion to work was not invented by Mr. Sidney Webb, but by Nature, and that this compulsion also has to be distributed. What is Mr. Chesterton's solution of that little problem?

Yours, &c.,
G. Bernard Shaw

V

[15 July 1916.]

Sir,—Though I missed, by an unavoidable accident, the last two issues of your paper, I hope you will allow me to reply once more to Mr. Bernard Shaw, especially as the reply can now, by comparison, be very simple and short.

[17]Tattersall's was the first Australian lottery, founded in 1881; The Baltic was a shipping exchange.

I am only too pleased that we are back at the point at which we started; since Mr. Shaw is prepared to see the point. I think it of so much practical importance that I will not dwell on many other things that I could say. I could point out, for instance, that when he repeats my definition of the Servile State and adds "But this is what we have already," he makes a slip. It is very arguable that what we have already is something much worse. But the definition contains the important phrase "by law," which is the stamp of literal slavery as distinct from capitalism tending towards it. I could speculate on what Mr. Shaw can possibly mean by saying that I am gradually righting myself. If I am right at all in holding any of the views here expressed, I have been right for many years. I could point out the absurdity of calling peasant ownership, the stability of which he is obliged to admit, "a poor form of marginal production." Does he think the French War Loan, or the indemnity of 1871, could be raised on poor marginal production? The wealth of France has always been largely a thing of peasant proprietorship; and the proprietorship has been stiffened, not loosened, by the French Revolution and every step in French historic reform. But all this, as I say, I will willingly subordinate to the one practical and even personal question which I asked at the very beginning, and which I ask again.

The important point mentioned by Mr. Shaw in his last letter, and by me in my first, is in his two sentences which run as follows: "It is accordingly quite true that the Fabian Society and Mr. Sidney Webb are engaged in the construction of a machinery which can be used to fortify the Servile State if the Servilists can collar it and are intelligent enough to understand its handling. But it is equally true that the scientific Servilists are engaged in the construction of a machinery which can be used to abolish servility if the serfs can and will collar it." Very well. Now can Mr. Shaw give me any indication anywhere that Mr. Sidney Webb, or the Fabian Society in so far as he represents it, is *not* constructing with the Servile object, and *is* constructing with the Anti-Servile object? Can he tell me one thing they are doing which a Servilist might not do as much as a Socialist? Let it be supposed, if you will, that we are weak and of little faith. Let it be imagined that the reckless republican idealism that flames from Mr. Webb has left us cold; that we underrate his ardour for abstract equity and equality; that our morbid fancy imagines him capable of settling down in a comfortable and humane Servile State. Still, if anyone sets out to answer us, this is the doubt he has to answer. And the only possible way of answering it, on Mr. Shaw's own showing, is to find some point where the Socialist and Servile plans diverge, and to show that Webbism at that point diverges from Servilism. Where is there such a point? Where has any Fabian helped any serf to collar any part of this new machinery, admittedly so double-edged a tool? As for the Servilists, they have no need to collar it; they are simply the Capitalists, and have collared it long ago. Therefore any Socialist increase in the powers of the State means in itself only an increase in the power of the Capitalists, who hold the State—and the statesmen.

I hope it is unnecessary for me to say that I accuse Mr. Shaw himself, in his capacity of champion of Webbism, of nothing worse than that Quixotic and even fantastic fidelity which he always denounces and I always admire. Personally, moreover, I am sure he is serious in offering to be satisfied with the most austere equalisation of income, for I think him a man not only disinterested, but unworldly. But if I am asked to extend such confidence to Fabianism as a tendency of to-day, I would put it to his private sense of humour whether it is not the fact that Mr. Herbert Samuel[18] has given valuable assistance and sympathy to the cause? Am I asked to believe that Mr. Samuel will use a machine admittedly useful to plutocracy for the purpose of a Jacquerie[19] of the serfs? It is as well to know about these things.

Yours, &c.,
G. K. Chesterton

VI

[22 July 1916.]

Sir,—The scales have fallen from my eyes. Mr. Chesterton's question devastates my whole public life. I have been duped, misled, gulled, wasted. Why did I never think of it before? How simple it is! Listen to it. "Now can Mr. Shaw give me any indication anywhere that Mr. Sidney Webb, or the Fabian Society as far as he represents it, is *not* constructing with the Servile object, and *is*

[18]In his capacities as postmaster general and home secretary in 1915–16.
[19]Peasant insurrection in France (1358), named for the archetypal French peasant, "Jacques."

constructing with the Anti-Servile object?" I cannot. I simply cannot. Oh, the artfulness of Webb! How this man has taken me in! I see it all now: the career begun in the Colonial Office in the undemocratic upper division of that centre of tyranny over servile races, the continual demand for more regulation under cover of protecting the workers against sweating, the hideous theory that the man who works under 366 rules is more free than the man who works under 365, the clamour for political programmes, consisting always of more rules, the setting up of an idol called The Common Rule, worshipped according to a ritual called Collective Bargaining, the ridiculous economic paradox that it is better for the country that men should work eight hours by law than twelve in freedom, the monumental series of books all with the same Servile moral of More Regulation, the sinister marriage with a notoriously regulative lady, the Minority Report designed to snatch from the unemployed their one consolation of being free, the chairmanship of the Technical Education Board, culminating in the destruction of the Board Schools and the establishing of the Thirty-nine Articles over the freedom of thought of half the children in the country: these, and much more, would surely have opened anybody's eyes but mine, as they have opened Mr. Chesterton's, to the true character of this arch-conspirator against liberty, this industrial Ignatius Loyola, this—this—this—I can find no epithet stinging enough; but I could just kick myself for my "quixotic and even fantastic fidelity" to such a monster.

And now that I come to think of it with my mind cleared and cured of its Webbist delusion, can I feel sure that I am the only victim? Is it not rather curious that Mr. Webb, or, as Mr. Cecil Chesterton would call him, "Webb," has never replied to or resented the repeated and fierce attacks made on him by Mr. Gilbert Chesterton? It is impossible that he can be really indifferent to them: no man can afford to ignore so tremendous an antagonist unless there is between them a secret confederacy, and the attacks are only part of the game. Take the two great Servile strongholds: the Church and the Liquor Trade. It has never been possible for Mr. Webb to support these openly: the slightest hint of such support would cost him the position of confidence among the organised workers of the country into which he has wormed himself. But such is the craft and guile of this born seducer of honest men that he is quite capable of corrupting Mr. Chesterton, by the specious arguments of which he is a master, to undertake the defence of the rectory and the public-house. I do not say that he got at Mr. Chesterton directly: he is too wily to make so crude a frontal attack. But he could always get at him through Hilaire Belloc. Can Mr. Chesterton give me any indication anywhere that Mr. Sidney Webb, or the Fabian Society in so far as he represents it, is *not* tampering with Mr. Belloc with Servile objects? What is the avowed method by which the Servilists have tried, not without success, to use the war for the purpose of smashing the Trade Unions and bringing the workers into complete subjection? Dilution of labour. Always dilution. In view of that, is there no significance in the fact that Mr. Belloc, by his writing, has made a war fortune for a journal with the aggressively Dilutionist title of *Land and Water*?[20] Is Webb the real owner of *Land and Water*? If not, where are the indications of his innocence? There is something extraordinarily Webbian in the policy of that journal. With every air and profession of being ultra-patriotic it in effect directs the strategy of the enemy. The reverses which our Italian ally has so fortunately retrieved were caused by the Austrians acting on the brilliant demonstration in *Land and Water* of the vulnerable place in the Italian position by Mr. Belloc. But how could Mr. Belloc do that unaided? He is but a simple soldier of one year's experience, a man of the pious peasant type, incapable of involved plans. Webb, an ex-volunteer, descended from a family of hereditary riflemen, and himself a qualified marksman (may not this throw light on some of the assassinations of the last thirty years?), is a born strategist, with the unmistakable Napoleonic profile. Belloc would be as wax in the hands of such a man: he would, in all good faith, prompt Hindenburg and Company at every step of their campaigns, and act as a conduit for the poison of Webb to the mind of Chesterton.

Webb is a notorious nobbler of the Press. We have seen how he captured *Land and Water*. The *New Statesman* is suspected to have been his own idea from the beginning. But the obviousness of his connection with the latter would make it necessary for him to control another paper through which he could work in the dark. With the clues we already possess, it is not very hard to place our fingers on this insidious organ. The Chestertons would write for it. Belloc would write for it—perhaps edit it for the first year. It would attack Webb on every possible occasion, but—

[20]Belloc wrote military commentaries for this journal during 1914–18.

mark this—always on grounds that would not take in a baby. It would concentrate a sort of burlesque fire on the men it wished to advertise. I, poor dupe, would be too easily tempted without any prompting to undertake Webb's defence. I ask, is there such a paper? It is useless for Mr. Chesterton to prevaricate, to equivocate, to deny. The *New Witness* corresponds to the description at every point.

But I have further evidence that amounts to absolute proof. Webb was the man who first raised the warning against premature peace. Webb was the man who insisted that Democratic Control of diplomacy is an impossibility, and that you can stop war only by putting the whole world under supernational regulation—for his mad appetite for regulation goes beyond frontiers and oceans. Having these opinions he would naturally regard Mr. Morel[21] with a hatred that knew no bounds. Well, what is the explanation of Mr. Cecil Chesterton's attacks on "Morel" in the *New Witness?* Why should Mr. Cecil Chesterton hate Mr. Morel? He loves Frenchmen—is always cracking up the French; and Mr. Morel is a Frenchman. He is devoted to Mr. Belloc for the sake of the French half of him. Mr. Morel is perhaps the most ardent and powerful exponent of that revolt against the corruption of politics and diplomacy to which Mr. Cecil Chesterton has consecrated his life. Why should he not only attack Mr. Morel, but go to the insane length of demanding, on the very morrow of his protest against the shooting of President Pearse, that Roger Casement[22] shall be executed, not as a traitor, but as a former colleague of Mr. Morel? There is only one possible explanation of such an extravagance. The pen is in Mr. Chesterton's hand; but the mind that guides it is Webb's. Webb is *Land and Water,* Webb is the *New Witness,* Webb is the *New Statesman,* Webb is not only Shaw, but Belloc, the Chestertons, and the German General Staff of the Central Empires. Let him who would deny it—if so impudent a mortal exists—give me any indication that he is *not.*

Yours, &c.,
G. Bernard Shaw

[21]E. D. Morel, a crusading writer critical of imperialism, whose *Morocco in Diplomacy* had just appeared.
[22]References to the recent Easter Rebellion of 1916; both Patrick Henry Pearse, Irish educator (whom Shaw alone was calling "President"), and Roger David Casement, Irish nationalist, were executed.

VII

[29 July 1916.]

Sir,—I am, as may very well be imagined, entirely satisfied with the result of this discussion. I wanted to find out a certain thing for certain; and I have found it out. It is, of course, the fact that Mr. Webb and the Webbites do not now stand for Collectivism at all, but for the reform and renewal of Capitalism. Mr. Shaw's last heartily exhilarating digression depends entirely on the notion that I merely asked him to prove a universal negative, and say why Webbism should not be servile. As he said about me, I always admire him as a fantastic artist; but unfortunately for the joke, I did not merely ask him to prove the negative, but the positive. He himself quotes me as asking for evidence that Mr. Webb "*is* constructing with the Anti-Servile object." In other words, I ventured to ask a professed Socialist whether he even pretended to be doing anything for Socialism. Mr. Shaw passes over this question entirely; and his silence is very eloquent. For my purposes, in fact, his silence is the last word. I am satisfied for an exceedingly simple reason; that I know very well that if so fine and forcible a debater as Mr. Shaw had been able to answer that simple question, he would not have filled nearly two columns with amusing fairy-tales about everything that neither he nor anybody else believes. He would simply have said, "In such and such a case Mr. Webb wants to take such and such capital and capitalist power from such and such capitalists"; and I should have been answered. He does not give me such a case, because there is no such case. Of course I really knew it before; and the number of those who know it already is increasing every day. But I am sincerely grateful to you for your courtesy in allowing me to bring the fact before your readers.

Yours, &c.,
G. K. Chesterton

SHAW'S JESUS

[On 3 June 1916, Desmond MacCarthy published in the *New Statesman* (of which he was the drama critic) a review of Shaw's latest volume of plays, *Androcles and the Lion, Overruled,* and *Pygmalion.* Since the plays were already known, it was the preface Shaw wrote for the volume—"on Christianity and its founder"—that MacCarthy really reviewed, calling it "the worst piece of work he has done." What especially evoked MacCarthy's ire was the passage in which Shaw described the Christ of the Gospels as Shaw imagined him—"highly-civilised," "cultivated," "convivial," "jocular," a man who "breaks the Sabbath," "is impatient of conventionality," "has no modest affectations": "He is, in short, what we should call an artist and a Bohemian in his manner of life." MacCarthy accused Shaw of "an egotistical delusion latent in this picture: all men are *really* like me." Furthermore, Shaw's "interpretation of Christianity is fundamentally wrong, because it is the interpretation of a man who is a prophet of a State conception of life." Shaw, MacCarthy argued, thinks religion "is a mystical impulse tending towards social progress. His religion is a religion only of the conscience." Hence, individual feeling and contemplation are missing from Shaw's sense of Christianity as MacCarthy understood it.

In the next week's *New Statesman* (10 June), MacCarthy's view was endorsed by the Reverend Cavendish Moxon, who protested that Shaw's Jesus "is a gross offence against historical truthfulness" because "He obviously belongs to the twentieth century."

Shaw's reply to both commentators, which appeared in the same journal on 17 June, began with a dismissal of the idealized portraits of Christ in two immensely popular late Victorian works, Marie Corelli's *Barabbas* and Frederic William Farrar's *The Life of Christ.*]

Sir,—I really must protest against the portraits of Jesus left to us in the gospels being described as fancy portraits by me. It is true that the three very distinct portraits by Matthew, Luke and John have long ago been combined into a composite portrait, and overlaid by nearly 2,000 years of painting, sculpture, legend, homily, theology, idealism, and sentimental fiction culminating in Miss Corelli's *Barabbas* and Farrar's *Life.* So deeply have these repaintings affected our consciousness of Jesus that it is almost impossible now to read the gospels without reading into them all the mediaeval conceptions, the Renascence conceptions, the capitalistic conceptions, and, in this country, the purely snobbish conceptions which are as anachronistic in them as a telephone in the Garden of Eden. In the "dry" States of America, a teetotal conception is so insisted on that Churchmen write pamphlets to prove that the miracle of turning water into wine is founded on a Jacobean mistranslation of a Greek word which really means ginger beer.

I have done my best to disentangle the gospel biographies from their modern adulterations; and I am not surprised that Mr. Desmond MacCarthy cannot express his contempt for the result. I was somewhat taken aback myself, though my emotion was not one of contempt. But it is useless to blame me for the shock. If I had chosen to write in the style of John Knox, I could have fortified with a text every sentence of the passage quoted by Mr. MacCarthy. The ascetic Jesus, the virginal Jesus, the austerely moral Jesus, the beautifully dressed and scrupulously clean Jesus, the teetotal Jesus, like the snob Jesus of Anthony Trollope's parsons, is simply not in the gospels. He is absent not merely by default but by the express repudiation of Jesus himself, whose assertions of his kindly anti-ascetic view of life against that of John the Baptist I have sufficiently emphasized.

As to the notion that I have drawn Jesus in my own image, I do not see why Mr. Desmond MacCarthy should deny us the fellowship of the Holy Ghost as the crown of our common humanity. Of course, Jesus was as like me as any one man is like another. Did Mr. MacCarthy expect me to assume that one of us was a unicorn? I may go further, and claim that as we were both led to become preachers of the same doctrine in spite of different circumstances and by independent ways, I may reasonably be considered a little more like Jesus than, say—well, perhaps I had better name no names. At all events, whether Jesus be placed in a sub species or in a super species, it is a species to which I apparently belong philosophically.

But beyond this I cannot see that I have gone. I am not a faith healer. I am a teetotaller and vegetarian. I am reviled, not as a gluttonous man and a wine-bibber, but as what Mr. Chesterton calls a Puritan. My appearances at rich men's feasts are so rare that my extra-domestic "evening dress," though more than thirty years old, is still in excellent preservation. If any attempt is made to crucify me (and my dislike to blatant pseudo-patriotic nonsense may yet get me into trouble) I shall most certainly not submit as to a fatal ordeal and undertake to rise after three days. I could make out a better case for half a dozen of our public men as models for what Mr. Cavendish Moxon calls "my Jesus" (that in the critic's but a choleric word which in the author is flat blasphemy)[1] than can be made out for me. Still, I shall not affect to regard the comparison as uncomplimentary. It is not in modest deprecation that I insist that "my Jesus" is not mine at all, and not one and indivisible, but the three Jesuses of the gospels: the harsh, bigoted, vituperative, haughty Jesus of Matthew, the charming, affable, woman-beloved Jesus of Luke, and the restlessly intellectual debater, poet, and philosophic genius described by John. None of these may be the pet Jesus of the individual reader's idealising vision; but I was not dealing with the various pet Jesuses any more than with the various pictured Christs of Van Eyck, of Dürer, of Raphael, of Leonardo, of Michael Angelo, of Guido, of Rembrandt, of Rubens, of Noel Paton or Holman Hunt, of Burne-Jones, and of Von Uhde.[2] All these are different; and the finest of them to my taste are repulsive to people who regard those which seem to me contemptible as official and authentic. In any case, it is clear that anyone writing about the historical Jesus must not write about Raphael's "Transfiguration" or Guido's "Ecce Homo" or Burne-Jones's figure in the east window of Speldhurst Church, but about the Christs of Matthew, Luke and John, and must face the fact that most readers will be astonished and scandalised at the restoration.

Your correspondent, Mr. Cavendish Moxon, is incredulous because "Mr. Shaw's Jesus" is not a damaged antique. He probably believes that Venus rose from the sea with her arms broken off; that Coeur de Lion lived in a ruin; and that Handel's harpsichord was worm-eaten and made a noise as of jangled bell wires. I will not attempt to disturb his belief in Progress, in the Twentieth Century, and in a lightning evolution which has reduced the preacher of 1916 B. Coxon to the intellectual rank of a remote barbarian. I will say, however, that until Mr. Cavendish Moxon can master the elementary distinction between a sacrifice and a martyrdom he had better let "Mr. Shaw's Jesus" alone.

[1]Shakespeare, *Measure for Measure,* II.ii.130: "That in the captain's but a choleric word,/Which in the soldier is flat blasphemy."
[2]Of the painters listed, perhaps the least known are the last four: Joseph Noel Paton, who turned to religious subjects in his paintings after 1870, was also a poet; William Holman Hunt and Edward Coley Burne-Jones were both strongly associated with the Pre-Raphaelite movement; Friedrich Karl Hermann Uhde, known as Fritz von Uhde, painted cold religious paintings and was head of the Munich Secession.

Mr. Desmond MacCarthy's simple and true observation that we cannot love ourselves is quite admirable; but I embrace its consequences. Am I to understand that Mr. MacCarthy regards them as a *reductio ad absurdum*?

Yours, &c.,
G. Bernard Shaw

"I HAVE NOTHING TO WITHDRAW"

[*The Star,* 25 October 1916.]

Sir,—I am not qualified to contribute to your series of confessions by people who talked nonsense about the war when it began. If the series is to be complete, you will have to enlarge the paper very considerably.

I made a carefully considered statement on the European situation about fourteen months before the war, and again seven months before. Three months after I made a further statement, equally carefully considered. And I have made several statements since then.

Everything that has occurred has confirmed even my conjectures with a precision that has startled me. I have nothing to withdraw, and no changes of opinion to record.

As I was violently abused for my utterances during our Reign of Terror, I suggest that you should invite contributions from the writers who frantically attacked my Common Sense About the War. They will have plenty to confess, and are doubtless anxious to apologise.

Yours, &c.,
G. Bernard Shaw

DEMOCRACY'S SALUTE TO FREED RUSSIA

[Under the banner head "Democracy's Salute to Freed Russia: Striking Messages of Welcome from Well-known Men and Women," the editor of the *Daily Chronicle* reported on 5 April 1917 that a "request was received . . . from the Provisional Committee of the Duma, inviting us to obtain articles from leading British authors and expressions of opinion from representative public men and women on the new Russian democracy," following the February revolution under Kerensky. Among the messages provided to the editor, which had been "published throughout the Russian Press," was the following by Shaw.]

No bad news that could possibly come to us, not even that of the most terrifying German victory, could be so frightful as the news that the work of Petrograd and Moscow and the army had been undone by the ignorance of the peasants, and that there was danger of a restoration. The very stones in our cities would cry out against such a horror. I doubt if even the Hohenzollerns would dare, in the face of democratic public opinion in Germany, to aid the Tsar in a counter revolution; for his Government has made royalty stink in the nostrils of the world. Nobody but a madman, or a peasant besotted by ignorance and superstition, could dare to thrust Russia back into the pit from which she has just struggled up into the sunlight.

At all events, neither madmen nor peasants nor courtiers must be allowed to turn back the clock. If Russia must have her La Vendée[1] and her noble emigrants, she must crush them with one hand whilst with the other she sets Germany free by crushing the Hohenzollerns. Already the German soldier is blessing the Russian, because the mere echo of the Russian trumpets of liberty has broken the savage Prussian discipline and set his officers persuading him that he, too, is free. By overthrowing the Romanoff Russia has for the first time earned the right to overthrow the Hohenzollern without hypocrisy. There can be no turning back now; if the Romanoffs returned, having learned nothing and forgotten nothing, it would be to take a vengeance for the Revolution so bloody and cruel that the work of the Revolution would have to be done again with a ruthlessness that hardly bears thinking of.

The Revolution must not fail either at home or in the field.

[1]A reference to the rising of royalists against the French republic (1793–95) in the western department of La Vendée.

Germany, with her revolution still before her, and now made inevitable by the Russian example, still believes that she owes her military prestige to the Hohenzollerns. The German armies have seen that, in spite of the devotion of the Russian people, the slaves of the Romanoffs cannot stand against them. They have yet to learn what a revolutionary army of free Russians can do. Russia is on her trial in this matter; but nobody in the West doubts the result if Russia will hold together until the Hohenzollerns can no longer dream of conquering her. Let us do justice to the Romanoffs. Even they, many of them, perceive that the one supreme need of Russia to-day is unity, singleness of purpose, and indomitable resolution. The courtier who would upset the Revolution to-day is more royalist than the Tsar, and less patriotic than the Grand Dukes, who accept the Revolution. They must have swallowed many a bitter prejudice before they made this sacrifice. The Russian people must sacrifice something for the sake of unity and victory also. The Socialist must not try to force his programme on the Liberal, nor the Liberal on the Socialist at the cost of a division of forces in the face of the common enemy. Russia and liberty must be saved first. When both are secure, the questions that divide Russian from Russian, Frenchman from Frenchman, Englishman from Englishman, and, let us not forget, German from German, will have their turn. For the moment, the questions that unite must stand before those which divide; and men must sacrifice their party cries as they sacrifice their lives and goods for the common welfare of their country.

A REPUBLICAN SOCIETY FOR GREAT BRITAIN

I

[A letter from H. G. Wells, in *The Times*, 21 April 1917.]

Sir,—Will you permit me to suggest to your readers that the time is now ripe, and that it would be a thing agreeable to our friends and Allies, the Republican democracies of France, Russia, the United States, and Portugal, to give some clear expression to the great volume of Republican feeling that has always existed in the British community? Hitherto that has neither needed nor found very definite formulation. Our Monarchy is a peculiar one; the general Republican feeling has found satisfaction in the assertion that the British system is in its essence a "crowned Republic";

and it is very doubtful whether even in Ireland there is any considerable section disposed to go beyond the implications of that phrase. But it will be an excess of civility to the less acceptable pretensions of Royalty and a grave negligence of our duty to liberal aspirations throughout the world if thinking men in the British community do not now take unambiguous steps to make it clear to the Republicans of Europe, Asia, and the American Continent that these ancient trappings of throne and sceptre are at most a mere historical inheritance of ours, and that our spirit is warmly and entirely against the dynastic system that has so long divided, embittered, and wasted the spirit of mankind.

The need extends beyond even the reassuring establishment of a common spirit with the French, Russian, American, and Portuguese Republicans. The ending of this war involves many permanent changes in the condition of Eastern Europe and Western Asia. In particular there is the question of the future of the reunited Polish people. The time has come to say clearly that the prospect of setting up some puppet monarch, some fresh intriguing little "cousin of everybody," as a King in Poland is as disgusting to liberal thought in Great Britain as it is to liberal thought everywhere else in the world. We have had two object-lessons in Bulgaria and Greece of the endless mischief these dynastic graftings cause. Bulgaria is by nature a peasant democracy as sturdy and potentially as pacific as the Swiss. A King has always been an outrage upon the ancient Republican traditions of Athens. So long as Russia chose to be represented by a Tsar and to permit an implicit support of the Greek monarchy through him, so long were British publicists debarred from a plain expression of their minds in this connexion. But now the case is altered. It is, I am convinced, a foolish libel upon a disinterested and devoted monarch to hint that the preposterous "Tino"[1] has now a single friend at Court among the Allies. The open fraternization of the British peoples and the Greek Republicans is practicable, necessary, and overdue.

For the demonstration of such sentiments and sympathies as these, for the advancement of the ends I have indicated, and for the encouragement of a Republican movement in Central Europe some immediate organization is required in Great Britain. To begin with, it might take the form of a series of loosely affiliated

[1]The overthrown Constantine I, King of the Hellenes (1913–17, 1920–22), Eleutherios Venizelos having forced the abdication and formed a republic.

"Republican Societies," centring in our chief towns, which could enrol members, organize meetings of sympathy with our fellow-Republicans abroad, and form the basis of more definitely purposeful activities. Such activities need not conflict in any way with one's free loyalty to the occupant of the Throne of this "crowned Republic."

Yours, &c.,
H. G. Wells

II

[A letter from Shaw to *The Times,* datestamped as received 22 April 1917; unpublished.]

Sir,—

I congratulate The Times on having the courage to publish Mr Wells's letter. I have tried in vain to find the same courage in much more Radical quarters. I am not, however, in the slightest degree convinced by the leading article in which you undertake to demonstrate that clever men can sometimes write very foolishly. What you have proved is that able editors can sometimes handle a difficult situation very prudently. The moment has not yet come for The Times to convulse the country houses and the clubs by throwing over the monarchy. The monarchy is a popular and convenient institution. The persons who now represent it are perhaps the most blameless it has enjoyed since the reign of Alfred the Great. Nobody says a hard word against the King; and everybody speaks well and kindly of the Heir Apparent. Only a very small group of people, all resident within a few square miles of Buckingham Palace, have the faintest suspicion of how powerful the monarchy is, or are personally subject to its pleasure and displeasure. The people whom you call the "half educated" all believe that England is more republican than the republics, and will endorse your article line for line as "what they always say." You are absolutely right in your view that "republican feeling has never been general in those countries." You might have gone further and said that public feeling has never been general in them. There is no more feeling against the monarchy than there was five years ago against voluntary military service. Nevertheless it has been necessary for the Government to take the extremely unpopular and inconvenient step of instituting compulsory service. If we discard the monarchy it is quite likely that the change will be as unpopular as it will be in some ways inconvenient. He who imagines that therefore it will not be taken knows little either of human nature or English history. If Mr Wells stood absolutely alone in England as an individual with a personal taste for a republican constitution and a personal dislike for thrones, his letter, which contains all the essential truths of the immediate situation created by the war, would not shake the throne any the less. His contemporary history is very much to the point. Can you say as much of your courtly academic sketch of our constitutional history?

You say that the King has far less personal power than the President of the United States. I feel quite sure that when the King read that bit of your article on Saturday morning, he winked at the Queen. Whilst London Society is organized by the Court, and whilst politicians' sons want careers and politicians' wives want to make good matches for their daughters, you may give the Cabinet all the power you boast of its having, and give the people all the votes and all the initiatives and referendums and democratic safeguards that you can devise, leaving the King no ostensible powers at all; and you will yet find it easier to induce a Cabinet minister to tear five million nobodies from their firesides and places of business, and send them to freeze under fire in the trenches, than to cut a single button from the livery of a palace page boy. The Prime Minister is a powerful person; Lord Northcliffe[2] is a powerful person; Sir William Robertson[3] is a powerful person; but I should like to see any of them dare tell the King that he is a clever fool with absurd, half-educated views. Sooner than be suspected of the least coldness to monarchy, they would follow you to the desperate length of saying all that about Mr Wells, who is perhaps in his way a greater power than any of the three.

There is every reason why a President should have more power for four years than Franz Josef had when he was a dangerous dotard and threw the match into the European powder magazine. It is a commonplace of politics that a democratic ruler's word is better than an autocrat's bond, and that an agreement for four

[2]Alfred Harmsworth, Viscount Northcliffe, proprietor of the newspaper *The Times*. Beginning in the Great War, he became famous as a leader of public opinion.

[3]Later first Baronet, a field marshal who became chief of the imperial general staff in December 1915.

years can be made more stringent than an agreement for forty. When you say that the Crown is the keystone of the Empire, and that "It binds the whole of the vast fabric together as no other institution does or can do," our minds go back to George III, the keystone of the Empire that once included the realm of President Wilson, and to Abraham Lincoln, the Keystone of the United States which held where the Empire broke. But it is idle to appeal to history in this matter. I could, I think, make a far better case for monarchy than your case, which comes to no more, after all, than that it really doesnt matter, as the King is a nobody. Among the heap of trumped-up special pleadings that are called history I know none thinner than the Liberal case for limited monarchy. It is not half so well supported by facts as the crude statement that republican revolutions have mostly replaced monarchical governments by governments of thieves and assassins. But neither testimonials nor indictments and recriminations will settle the matter. The fundamental case against monarchy is that it rests on a basis of idolatry that can no longer be maintained. When you say, as in effect you do in your criticism of Mr Wells, that a king, far from being any wiser and fuller of divine grace than a President, is really to be bolstered up because he is not even a President but only the puppet of the Cabinet, you not only insult the King's manhood to an extent that for the moment rallies me, an inveterate republican, to his side in pure human revolt and indignation, but give your whole case away and allow Mr Wells a walk-over. When a king cannot even cut off the head of an editor who pleads such an unkingly case for him, it is time to put up the shutters in the palace; sell the crown to the theatrical costumier; and welcome King George as member, elected by an overwhelming majority, for the once royal borough of Windsor, free at last to tell Cabinet ministers and editors what he thinks of them and knows about them, and to speak with Mr Wells in the gate as man to man. The home truths would not then be all on one side, I think.

The immediate case for Republicanism, as far as it can be packed into a nutshell, is that political homogeneity has become a necessity of that international organization which war has forced on the most powerful existing empires. Not one of them has been able to stand alone. Germany has had the advantage of monarchical homogeneity; whilst we and the French have been horribly embarrassed by the heterogeneity of Russian and British monarchy and French and American republicanism. The revolution in Russia has not only eased the situation prodigiously, but swept away the last hope of the survival of monarchy as a typical modern form of the State. I for one am therefore prepared to part with the throne on terms which will proclaim the most cordial relations with its occupant. I am a regicide, not a homicide. I hope His Majesty will talk it over with Mr Lloyd George; it is obviously not a business for societies and public meetings and public opinion and the like.

Yours truly
G. Bernard Shaw

PLAYWRIGHTS' TEXTS

[A letter to the editor, signed "S." (M. H. Spielmann), relating to a recent discussion on "the text of Shakespeare's plays," appeared in the *Times Literary Supplement* on 25 October 1917. "Believing," said Spielmann, "that the fundamental principles by which our leading dramatists are guided when preparing their plays for the stage and the press cannot greatly differ from those of Shakespeare and his contemporaries, I have asked three of our most eminent playwrights to set forth each his own methods, while expressing an opinion, briefly stated, on the merits of the controversy. I begged for details whereby we might estimate their views in the light of their methods, of changes (if any) made during rehearsal or progress of the play, of preparation for the press, with regard to corrections and emendations, when the manuscript text of their plays was being turned into 8vos (modern parallels to 4tos)." Shaw's statement, reproduced below in full, followed briefer statements by Sir Arthur Pinero and Henry Arthur Jones.]

I cannot give you a general answer covering all the plays. When I began I could not get my plays acted in this country at all. I therefore proposed to publish them as books. Heinemann, whom I consulted, told me that plays were not read in this country; those which were published sold in batches according to the number of characters in the play: one copy per character and one for the prompter, shewing that they were purchased for the rehearsing of amateur performances and for no other purposes. He allowed me to see an actual ledger account to satisfy me on the point.

I contended that the business was in a vicious circle: that plays were issued in unreadable acting versions, with revolting stage directions like telegrams with all the definite articles left out, and peppered with technical prompter's terms that insulted the human imagination: for example

SIKES—Take that, damn you [*strikes her with bludgeon*].

NANCY—Oh, God forgive you, Bill [*staggers—business with eyes—dies*].

SIKES—Now to escape the police [*takes hat from table R. C.; brushes it with elbow, grinding teeth; crosses L. C. up; sees ghost; shrieks; back to R. C. and exit R. U. E.*].

I asked whether anyone could read Oliver Twist if Dickens had written it in this way; and I made a resolution, which is still unbroken, that no play of mine, however full its stage directions, should ever mention the stage or use any technical term that could remind the reader of the theatre or destroy the imaginative illusion. Grant Richards, who was then starting in business, published two volumes of plays [Shaw's *Plays Pleasant and Unpleasant*] written in this manner; and their success practically re-established the public habit of reading plays, though I am sorry to say that my system of stage direction is so little understood that even burlesques of it often include references to "the centre of the stage," and such specifications as "to the right of the stage, a small table," &c., &c. Naturally, what my parodists overlooked is not noticed by authors generally; and though I am followed purely as a fashion, the point of my fashion is missed, and telegram English and references to the theatrical mechanism will survive, and still make people prefer novels to plays as instruments to produce illusion.

This by the way. What you are concerned with is the fact that whereas my earlier plays were printed first and acted afterwards, my later ones were "produced" by me, and acted, years before they were collected into volumes, to be finally revised for press in the light of my practical stage experience of them, and prefaced by essays to which they had no more relation (if so much) than a text has to a sermon.

Let me illustrate the consequences by an example. My Caesar and Cleopatra was written and published before it was acted. It was, except for the old copyrighting farce which has no importance and is now abolished by the last Copyright Act, first produced in Berlin. During the rehearsals it was discovered that I had forgotten to remove one of the characters, Apollodorus the Sicilian (the hero of the carpet incident) from the stage in the third act. I had accordingly to write in a speech or two to dismiss him; and this speech of course appears in the later editions and is not in the earlier ones.[1] Later on, when Forbes Robertson,[2] for whom the part of Caesar was written, was at last able to take it up, he said one day at rehearsal that the scene with Septimius in the second act, which is one of the great acting points in the play, required a little more explanation and additional preparatory ferment to enable him to make the most of it; and I immediately wrote in about a dozen speeches to get it right for him. An edition printed from Forbes Robertson's prompt copy would contain those speeches, which I regret to say I have been too lazy to have inserted in my own editions.[3]

But there is a further complication. The great length of Caesar and Cleopatra led to several expedients to shorten it. I first cut out the third act; but the fascination of this episode of fun for the actors, and its success in Berlin, produced a rebellion against the author; and it had to be restored. To make room for it I struck out the first scenes of the first and fourth acts, and replaced them by a prologue to be spoken by the god Ra. But the difficulty was that this tremendous exordium required another Forbes Robertson to deliver it; and the English stage produces only one at a time. But several ambitious actors tackled it, and established this version for a time on the stage. Now suppose some XX century Heminge and Condell print in folio a version of the play from the authentic prompt copies used by our Burbage, the original Caesar; and take my editions as the equivalent of the Shakespearian quartos. The quartos will have scenes omitted in the folio; and the folio will have an entirely different opening and several passages omitted from the quartos. The *Literary Supplement* of that day will be able to keep a correspondence going for months about the discrepancies.

Man and Superman has also had its vicissitudes. If its texts had to be put together from prompt books and scene plots, the materials would be, first, a three-act comedy, and second, a piece of an indescribable *genre* entitled A Dream of Don Juan in Hell,

[1]An added exit speech for Apollodorus was inserted near the end of act IV (not III) in the 1904 second English impression of *Three Plays for Puritans*.

[2]Leading tragedian of his generation, who first performed the rôle of Shaw's Caesar in 1906.

[3]First added to the published text in the French translation by Augustin and Henriette Hamon, 1926; later inserted into the revised text of the Collected Edition, 1930.

the connexion between them being discovered by the documents of later performances in which this Dream, with an additional scene to explain its introduction, was performed as the third act of the comedy.

From John Bull's Other Island to Pygmalion, the prompt copies and the printed editions should be identical because the plays passed through the furnace of production by the author before they were passed for press; but they are not quite so. I made revisions of no great extent, but of importance (as such things go) in many of them. And further changes are possible. The rehearsals of future revivals may suggest changes to me. An actor at a loss for his line may improvise one happy enough to be annexed by an author who has always taken his goods where he found them and been thankful. The passage that was just [right] for one actress may be just wrong for another, and may be modified accordingly. The changes need not be improvements: they may be adaptations to inevitable circumstances. The more skilful an author is, the more apt he is to adapt his work to the conditions instead of quarrelling with them.

You must consider also that an author may make a change and neglect to make the contingent changes it involves. Shakespeare's Julius Caesar is played to this day with alternative scenes containing the revelation of Portia's death retained together. Probably Shakespeare never dreamt that any producer would be unobservant enough to see that the Brutus-Cassius quarrel scene, evidently written in later to strengthen the end of the play, involved the omission of the earlier version; but he may have forgotten all about it. In Fanny's First Play the third act was written as two acts with an interval of a month between; but I hate these violations of the very valuable unity of time; and finally I ran the two acts together as they now stand. But, if you please, I never took the trouble to make the contingent alterations; and the act now presents the phenomenon called "double-time," like A Midsummer Night's Dream, which is both a night and a week, my act being both an afternoon and a month.

The long and the short of it is that any play that has passed through the hands of the author in several successive theatrical productions and literary editions may present wide variations, all equally authentic, and that the alterations, if their order of date can be established, are not necessarily intended as refinements and improvements (except in the literary versions) but may be adaptations to theatrical circumstances more or less favourable. And, I repeat, it is not the ablest author who stands most obstinately by his original text, and can produce his effect only in one way: on the contrary the able author has to check a tendency in himself to play about with his work and perform *tours de force* of mere adroitness at the risk sometimes of overlooking serious damage to his original inspiration.

You may of course use this letter as you please. Excuse its haste, it is only a rough and ready memorandum to assist you.

Yours, &c.,
G. Bernard Shaw

"It will be seen," concluded Spielmann, "that even so finished and deliberate a writer as Mr. Bernard Shaw, whose 'copy' is amazingly 'clean,' revises his plays for the press 'in the light of his practical stage experience of them'; and, as he shows, there is abundant evidence of variations in certain of his plays the cause of which not the most intelligent and ingenious bibliographers could even guess at from the text before them, or would accept as probable, unless they had direct information or proof of the complicated facts."

LUTHER AND THE FABIANS

[*Everyman,* 9 November 1917.]

Sir,—Luther was in an impossible position logically. As against the Pope he was an anarchist. As against the peasants who took him at his word he made Popes of all the princes. But what could he do? As a sane politician he could not hand Germany over to Munzer and crude theocrats like John of Leyden and Cnipperdolling.[1] As an inspired prophet he could not relapse into Augustinian monkery and bid the world crawl back to the footstool of Leo X. In the face of Tetzel[2] and the trade in indulgences he could not preach justification by works and leave the keys of heaven and hell in the hands of the Church. In the face of the Anabaptists who claimed justification by faith for murder and arson and anarchy

[1]John of Leiden and Bernhard Knipperdolling were both religious reformers (the former Dutch, the latter German). Fanatical leaders of the Anabaptists, they were tortured and put to death as heretics in 1536. Thomas Münzer, an earlier Anabaptist, executed in 1525, was a leader in the Peasant War.

[2]Johann Tetzel, a Dominican monk, was appointed (1517) commissioner of indulgences for all Germany. His scandalous sale of indulgences for sins not yet committed came under fierce attack by Martin Luther.

he had to bawl for the police. And he, the arch-iconoclast, could hardly idolise the elect Tom, Dick and Harry like the democratic Calvin. Do not blame the man for not anticipating the Fabian Society; he did his best in the dark.

Yours, &c.,
G. Bernard Shaw

GENERAL MAURICE'S ALLEGED BREACH OF DISCIPLINE

[Major-General Sir Frederick B. Maurice, director of military operations for the imperial general staff, 1915–18, was moved by conscience to write a letter to the press in which he claimed that answers given in the House of Commons on 23 April 1918 by Bonar Law, leader of the House, to questions put by members as to the extension of the British front in France were "mis-statements which in sum give a totally misleading impression of what happened." These statements, Maurice insisted in a letter published in the *Daily Chronicle* on 7 May, as well as earlier inaccuracies given out by the prime minister, David Lloyd George, on 9 April, "are known by a large number of soldiers to be incorrect, and this knowledge is breeding such distrust of the Government as can only end in impairing the splendid morale of our troops at a time when everything possible should be done to raise it. I have therefore decided, fully realising the consequences to myself, that my duty as a citizen must override my duty as a soldier, and I ask you to publish this letter in the hope that Parliament may see fit to order an investigation into the statements I have made."

British newspapers, especially the *Westminster Gazette*, the *Daily Telegraph*, and the *Daily Chronicle*, which had been charging that the government's censors had supplanted "censorship" for military reasons with "suppression" of facts for political reasons, made much of General Maurice's charges, and Lloyd George, raging that Maurice was "trampling upon King's Regulations, setting examples of indiscipline to the whole Army," was confronted by the opposition with a motion in the House to appoint a committee of inquiry into the allegations. Maurice instantly retired from the service, emerging on 15 May as the *Daily Chronicle*'s new military correspondent. Shaw's letter of 19 May, captioned as above, was rejected reluctantly by Robert Donald, editor of the *Daily Chronicle*, because Maurice, "desperately anxious to maintain an ultra-correct attitude" (British Library), did not wish it to be published.]

Sir,—

May I, as a member of the general public on whose behalf General Maurice has committed professional suicide, ask, in common gratitude to a brave and public spirited soldier and citizen, what crime he has committed. Mr Orage,[1] an editor whose independence of all party considerations and vulgar political ambitions cannot be doubted, writes calmly of "the just opinion that General Maurice transgressed his duties as a soldier." And Mr Gilbert Chesterton, also above suspicion of axe grinding, pours a broadside of his heaviest metal into Mr Lloyd George (incidentally implying a defence of General Maurice) with a very curious comment. Dealing with the current cant that if Mr Lloyd George is not to be trusted he should be turned out, but if he is not turned out, let him be trusted, Mr Chesterton adds that this "in itself sounds very reasonable; and in nine cases out of ten it would be very reasonable." I ask, in bewilderment, how? why? what is there reasonable about such rubbish? In Mr Chesterton's place I should have written "this in itself sounds drivelling nonsense; but in one case in a thousand it might be the best we could make of a bad job."

I never yet heard of a political constitution in which the appeal to Caesar was not open to everyone. In a democracy public opinion is Caesar; and if General Maurice may not appeal to it, we are not democrats, and our profession of fighting Germany in the democratic interest is bunkum.

An autocratic or oligarchic government may ask the people to trust it or to overthrow it: in fact these are the only possible alternatives. But a democratic government is by definition one that asks for no trust and would not get it if it did, accepting the test of making good under the freest criticism and the strictest public audit. Mr Chesterton warns us not to trust Mr Lloyd George. I dont; but I owe it to Mr Lloyd George, in mere civility, to assure him that my mistrust is not peculiar to him, and that as a democrat I would not trust the Angel Gabriel himself any further than I could see that he was proving equal to the occasion.

General Maurice's letter to the Press contained nothing that any Englishman has not a right to say to the English people and their Allies on democratic assumptions. On any other assumptions he has no personal rights at all, and neither have I nor has anyone else. I must repeat that during war there are two forces balancing and steadying one another in every belligerent country: the military force making unlimited demands for men and material, and the civil force keeping these demands within the limits of

[1]Alfred Richard Orage, a Fabian, was editor of the *New Age.*

economic and vital solvency. No one disputes the complete freedom of the civil minister to tell the country at any moment that the military command is not doing its best, or is asking too much, and even to disgrace the commanders by giving them the sack in the face of the public. But can anything be more monstrous than the assumption that the military command should not be equally free to tell the public what it thinks of the civil government, to defend itself against attacks, to correct inaccurate or malicious statements, and to appeal directly to the nation to sack its government?

If this democratic freedom is denied to the soldier, how far is his slavery to go? When a certain weekly journal [*The Nation,* issue of 7 April 1917] was confined to these shores by the Government, the House of Commons was officially informed that this step had been demanded in a private letter by Sir Douglas Haig, leaving it to be implied that the Commander-in-Chief has the temperament of an operatic tenor and was piqued by a compliment paid to General Hindenburg on the skill with which he had withdrawn his troops from a dangerous salient.[2] It appeared subsequently that Sir Douglas Haig had not written any such letter. The statement was one of those acts of devotion to the Government by which ambitious Englishmen secure office under all circumstances whilst their party remains in power. As such acts of devotion are considered allowable, and do not fail of their reward, it is clear that they may be stretched to any extent. The generals who were accused last year of writing ridiculous letters may be accused this year of taking bribes, of taking morphia, of taking six wives, of taking holidays during offensives, of taking to their heels, of taking fire by spontaneous combustion and being ignominiously extinguished by the killfires of their chauffeurs, or, worse still, of any of these subtler deviations from the path of honor and duty which might conceivably be made by a good man under the strain of war. Are they to allow themselves to be broken in silence, and to have that silence taken as an admission of guilt? If they seek a spokesman in parliament, is their case to be made the subject of a vote of confidence instead of a verdict on their merits? I do not care who calls this discipline: I call it lunacy. It is like telling me that M. Clemenceau's publication of the Emperor Karl's letter

[2]Former field marshal Haig was thus complaining about the efforts of his counterpart, the German chief field marshal General Paul von Hindenburg.

was a breach of etiquette.[3] If Emperors choose to make communications of European importance, and Prime Ministers choose to bring indictments against the British Army in the face of jealous Allies, it is the idlest trifling to suppose that they can hide themselves behind private or professional conventions.

As nobody disbelieves the statements of General Maurice, and nobody need on that account doubt any statement made by Mr Lloyd George when sidestepping him, and as, furthermore, the General will certainly find himself far more powerful as war expert to The Daily Chronicle than he was at Versailles, there is perhaps no great harm done to the two gentlemen in question; but the democratic rights of the army should be none the less emphatically affirmed; and General Maurice should be assured that no one with a grain of common sense conceives his action as a misdemeanor, or takes it otherwise than as a signal service to the community.

yours truly
G. Bernard Shaw

THE DOMINIE—NEW STYLE

[A "dominie" in Great Britain is a schoolmaster or pedagogue. Shaw's letter appeared in *The Bookman,* November 1918.]

Sir,—I am indebted to Mr. George Sampson's[1] review in your columns under the above heading for an introduction to the collection of essays entitled "The New Teaching," edited by Dr. John Adams.

The New Teaching is nothing but the practice of teachers who really teach. These men are continually struggling against the competition of men who are not teachers but simply schoolmasters. They do not teach: they set lessons and beat or otherwise torture children who do not learn them. They may be, and often are, callous ruffians, as cruel as they are lazy and incompetent. At best their work is no more skilled work than the work of a prison

[3]On 14 April 1918, Clemenceau had given to the press a letter from the emperor of Austria, Charles I, in which Charles had conceded the legitimacy of French claims to Alsace-Lorraine.

[1]An elementary school teacher, later a headmaster, who became London County Council schools inspector.

warder. If they were police constables they would be unable to take the beats which require sense and tact rather than the assertion of brute force and the maintenance of the crude terrors of the law. Of these I have said that thirty shillings a week and the status of dog-trainers represent the market value of their labour and their manners; and I have protested against the genuine teachers being dragged down by their competition to this level. I have never lost an opportunity of insisting on the value and dignity of genuine teaching, and denouncing the masquerade of mere boy farming and child taming as education in so-called schools which are merely prisons in which children are locked up to keep them from worrying their parents. In this I have the support of every genuine teacher and educationist in the country, a support generously expressed in their correspondence with me.

Yet most people are so unaccustomed to make any distinction between a mere schoolmaster and a teacher that Mr. George Sampson, in the very act of reviewing a book in which the strenuousness of real teaching is impressed on him, calmly adds: "These (the genuine teachers) are the people to whom that great educationist Mr. Bernard Shaw proposes to give thirty shillings a week and the status of dog-trainers." He then adds—and I confess he extorted the laugh he played for, even from me, its victim—"The bilious buffoon who has ceased to draw is a common object of the circus." Now I protest I am not bilious; I have obviously not ceased to "draw" Mr. Sampson; and the buffoon who has ceased to draw is not a common object of the circus, because he cannot get an engagement there. There is no truth in Mr. Sampson's statement, and no sense in his comment.

I do not answer such stuff when it appears, as it mostly does, in *The Schoolmaster;* but in *The Bookman* it might mislead people whose esteem and support is of importance to me on public as well as personal grounds.

I am therefore reluctantly driven to stand Mr. Sampson in the corner. It is, I grant, a poor pedagogic method; but if I cannot reform Mr. Sampson, I must at least be allowed to make him ridiculous.

Yours, &c.,
G. Bernard Shaw

"THE CROAKING RAVEN DOTH BELLOW FOR REVENGE"

[The Great War ended on 11 November 1918. Shaw's letter was published in the *Manchester Guardian* on 21 November under a caption borrowed from *Hamlet,* III.ii.264.]

Sir,—It is only to be expected that the innocent civilian who understands little of peace and less of war should continually cry out against the operations of war as crimes demanding punishment. And as it was thought necessary that those who wrote at first-hand about the war should, under official instructions, dwell on the ferocities of the enemy, passing over everything harsh and shocking in our own proceedings, the same civilian is led to imagine that his own country must come spotless out of any subsequent judicial investigation, whilst the enemy must emerge covered with infamy, with many of his officers marked out for condign punishment. Accordingly, our party politicians, with an election [on 14 December] toward, are promising in all directions that the peace negotiations will consist largely in making police court cases of the incidents of the war, and postponing the problem of the resettlement of Europe to a demand for sentences to be passed on individual Germans for individual assaults on members of our Seamen's and Firemen's Union. It therefore behoves those of us who are not candidates to declare that this is all childish nonsense, and that a general raking up of the incidents of the fighting is even less possible after the present war than it has proved in former wars, when there was the same clamour, and the same horrors to provoke it.

First, in order to head the indignant citizen off a hopelessly wrong turning, it must be understood that the objection to bringing offenders to account is not in the least that they are innocent or that their crimes are exaggerated or were not committed. On the contrary, it may be confidently assumed that for every atrocity yet recorded in the present war several hundreds have never been mentioned and never will be mentioned. Even if not one complaint had been made it would remain statistically certain that more foul play than the human heart could bear the narration of must have formed part of the proceedings of the last four years. When millions of men are in question, crime, even horrible crime, may be assumed without any specific evidence whatever.

This applies to peace as much as to war. When we say that an

Englishman is incapable of cruelty, treachery, rapine, theft, and murder, we are speaking of the respectable Englishman. We know quite well that we have to keep prisons and gallows to deal with disreputable Englishmen who are capable of all these crimes, and that the very judge who sentences them, as in the case of Jeffreys,[1] is sometimes a more cruel scoundrel than the people he sends to the stake. We know that we have had to set up a Society for the Prevention of Cruelty to Children to restrain certain Englishmen and Englishwomen from behaving to their own children like incarnate fiends. They are, of course, not typical Englishmen and Englishwomen; but in every million of English people there is a certain percentage of them.

Now it is our just boast that this percentage is smaller in England than in Germany. But it is also smaller than in America, France, Italy, Russia, and Portugal, to say nothing of Senegal and other "non-adult" countries whose inhabitants have fought for us. I ask any candid man to think of what the worst compatriot he knows is capable of. I ask him to remember that the soldiers for whose conduct the Allies are responsible number between seventeen and twenty millions. Our own population is forty millions; and in peace-time we convicted one another annually of 13,000 crimes, 50,000 indictable offences, and 800,000 non-indictable offences, these last including a good deal of conduct that might be roughly classed as drunken blackguardism. This means that, even if all our allies were as virtuous as we, the normal allowance for all the Allied troops for the last four years is about 6,500 crimes, 25,000 offences, and 400,000 regrettable incidents per annum. We should therefore have to make the Germans an allowance of at least half the misconduct represented by these figures before we could feel sure of coming out of a searching investigation with a larger credit balance than could be accounted for by the fact that an invading army, with every native hand against it and no law to protect it, always has to resort to terrorism: that is, to do much more horrible things than the army of friendly defence.

We must, it is true, beware of assuming that the criminal classes do more mischief in war than in peace. On the contrary, in war they live under conditions of discipline, comradeship, public opinion, and exemption from poverty, which make many of them

[1]George Jeffreys, who became lord chief justice in 1682, is mostly remembered as the brutal judge at the "Bloody Assizes" after Monmouth's Rebellion of 1685.

into honest men and good soldiers. When they return they do not improve: they relapse. Already our magistrates, after trying sentimentality for a while on discharged soldiers, have had to announce sternly that not even a Victoria Cross will secure immunity for a soldier if he breaks the law, no matter how satisfactory his character may have been in the army. No man can be as bad in a regiment as he can be in a slum; for bayonet-fighting uses up the superfluous energy and irritability that might vent itself at home in savage assaults. But if criminals behave better as soldiers than as civilians, honest men, unfortunately, often behave much worse. Many honest men serving in this war are not highly civilised men. They are men who have formed part of lynching mobs. In moments of excitement and inflamed imagination they saturated live men's skins with kerosene and compelled women to set them on fire. Some of them are Africans and Indian tribesmen. Among the white men there are backwoodsmen who are not, to say the least, penetrated with a sense of the right of a surrendered prisoner of war to life and humane treatment. Even from the highly civilised white men who have never been roughened by the backwoods, the camp, or the battlefield, have we not had letters in the newspapers clamouring for retaliatory cruelty with a ferocity that would have revolted Captain Kidd? How would such people come out of an impartial investigation of atrocities? Is it credible that any commander, knowing what war is, and what must happen on all sides in all wars, will consent to such an orgy of recrimination and raking up of horrors as is demanded by the simpletons who imagine that twenty million Englishmen, Frenchmen, Italians, Americans, Indians, and Africans of all sorts are an army of angels and Germany a hell of unredeemable fiends?

It is not my business to go on to help the Germans to state their case. I am concerned only with the case they could make against us. But I am bound to warn our Vindictives that some of the specific charges which have been most sensationally exploited to rouse and sustain civilian feeling in England against the enemy would break down technically in a court of justice, and can therefore never be pressed with the consent of our military authorities. I am sorry to have to add that the recklessness of our Jingo journalism has robbed us of some of the moral advantages we might have claimed on the bare facts of the case. For example, there is no substantial evidence that the French used poison gas in the war before the Germans. But the Germans, on the authority of the

English press, are able to allege that they did. At the beginning of the war the sort of journalist who invented the "Nearer, my God, to Thee" fable about the Titanic set to work to invent a terrible gas discovered by Monsieur Turpin,[2] and to write descriptions of trenches full of dead German soldiers standing stiffly to their arms just as they had stood when the deadly gas smote them. Our papers published these tales and exulted in them. And now all such tales and exultations, idle romances and blitherings though they were, will put us out of court if we arraign the Germans for actually doing the thing our journalists imagined and suggested. I shall be asked whether England is to be held responsible for the fancies of a few thoughtless idiots. I reply simply, yes. We cannot help ourselves. What we can do is to take care that these same thoughtless idiots shall not wreck the settlement of the war by screaming for a Sulla proscription[3] to console them for the cessation of their accustomed daily dose of blood and destruction.

The punishment of Germany will be, and indeed already has been, terrible enough to satisfy all except parochial persons who can understand some vindictive retaliation on an individual with a name and address, but to whom the downfall and failure of a Great Power mean nothing. In truth the consequences of the war must be so appalling for the Central Empires that our business is not to rub them in, but rather to see how civilisation can be saved now that the bottom has suddenly fallen out of Europe. Having knocked Germany off her feet, the most pressing thing we have to do for her is to set her on her legs again; for nobody who is not a political lunatic can face the prospect of a European chaos. When we break a German's leg with a bullet and then take him prisoner, we immediately set to work to mend his leg, to the astonishment of our idiots, who cannot understand why we do not proceed to break his other leg. We shall have to act on the same principle with the German nation. We have broken its back, and now we have to get its back mended again somehow. The alternative is to kill it; and that is not a practicable alternative.

Those who attempt to introduce unnecessary complications

[2]François Eugene Turpin invented the high explosives Melinite and Turpinite; the poison gas rumor was unfounded.

[3]Lucius Cornelius Sulla, a Roman general and politician who was dictator of Rome 82–79 B.C., proscribed many of the leaders of the Marian party, most of whom were exterminated.

into the settlement should remember two things. The first thing is that now that we are no longer under the spell of pressing and deadly peril the vogue of panic-stricken fools is over. It has been one of the worst tyrannies the war has brought on us; and the reaction from it will put the fools in their places pretty roughly. The second is that Prussia is not even yet so completely down and out as she was in the last year of the Seven Years War. Frederick could not defeat the Allies; but he could and did wait until they quarrelled and saved him. Now if the alliance between Britain, France, and the United States is dominated by their fools, who are nothing if not quarrelsome, it may fly to pieces and enable the Germans to attach themselves to one of the quarrelling sides and snatch the honours of war out of the jaws of defeat and political dissolution. Moral: Muzzle the fools; and make clean work of the settlement whilst all the circumstances are still propitious to us.

Yours, &c.,
G. Bernard Shaw

BURY THE HATCHET

[*Manchester Guardian,* 3 February 1919.]

Sir,—It is within the recollection of the nation that during the war very material assistance was given to the enemy by the diversion of men from the front to useless activities at home, and of administrative energy to bogus domestic problems by noisy persons who would have been suspected of being in the enemies' pay if it were not unfortunately too well known that we have always with us plenty of people who will help our enemies for nothing, with a firm conviction that they are rendering priceless assistance to their country and getting on with the war at a tremendous rate.

Their zeal found various outlets. Sometimes they looted the shops of bakers with what they conceived to be German names, such as Duval, Lamberti, Petersen, Strachan, Macmurdo, and the like. Sometimes they abolished German competition in their own businesses (pianos, for example) without the trouble of producing a better article. But these operations were intelligent because they were remunerative to the operators. Mostly they did unmitigated mischief to themselves and everyone else except the Germans. They sowed dissension and mistrust in the nation by declaring that our Government was really a conspiracy of "hidden hands" to deliver us over to our foes; they kept Lord Haldane, our ablest European statesman and War Minister, out of office; they clamoured for the imprisonment or so-called repatriation of the harmless and productive people who are technically "enemy aliens." I have never been able to understand why so much attention was paid to this clamour; for those who raised it would not in time of peace have inspired even the weakest Government with the most momentary tremor; but during the war there was a good deal, even in high places, of that kind of nervousness which starts from the banging of a door as affrightedly as from the exploding of a bomb, and hears a Zeppelin in every country postman's motorbicycle. And there was the same inability to distinguish the voice of any hysterical creature bawling from a second-floor window, either through sheer terror or a desire to call attention to his own importance, from the voice of public opinion. A good deal of senseless cruelty was the result. It was not very cruel in its incidence on Germans who were really foreigners and sojourners and whose spiritual or material home was the Fatherland. It was horribly cruel and unspeakably silly in its incidence on the "aliens" who were not aliens at all.

Early in the war I came upon the case of an English woman, a domestic servant, who in her youth had married a German and been deserted by him after a fortnight's honeymoon. She had placed her savings in the Post Office Savings Bank. Her savings were sequestrated, and she was ordered to "repatriate" herself; that is, to throw herself, an English woman not speaking a word of German, into a foreign and hostile country to starve under the fire of the soldiers of her own country. This barbarous absurdity was not pushed to the latter extremity in her case, for the authorities are, as a rule, only too glad to find excuses for not doing their worst, and "repatriation" was not then always practicable; but the threat, like the sequestration, was strictly in order. Side by side with such cases were those of English women who had lived as the wives of Germans and were fairly open to suspicion of having strong German sympathies, but who were able to receive the agents of the "Hidden Hand" agitation with the thumb to the nose by simply explaining that they were not legally married to their reputed husbands. Sarah was cast out; Hagar went free; Ishmael supplanted Jacob.

I could fill columns of your paper with instances of the ridiculous anomalies and tragic injustices which the operation of the law as to nationality has produced. Take for example the prisoners of Ruhleben.[1] When, having at first suffered nothing worse than an obligation to report to the police, they suddenly became the victims of an "Intern them all" stunt in the German press, and were all sent to that famous camp, they naturally expected to find themselves among their own countrymen, or at least in the company of their allies. To their astonishment and dismay they found themselves in a colony recruited from all the nations of the earth, but predominantly German. The "alien enemies" of Germany were no more English then the "alien enemies" of England are German. They were people who had acquired a technical English nationality under all sorts of fantastic pretexts and accidents, and had clung to it to escape military service. Many of them could not speak a word of any Allied language. For genuine English company the English prisoners had to fall back on the Wagner worshipper captured at Bayreuth, the British criminal flying from British justice, and the British detective who shared his fate. If a return had been made of the number of relatives the Ruhleben prisoners had serving in the Allied and the German armies respectively it would have been found that the German army had by far the greatest claim on the family affection of the camp.

Now turn to that shockingly overcrowded house of sorrow, the Alexandra Palace,[2] where our "enemy aliens" have found their Ruhleben. There, too, the prisoners know the horrible irony of the telegram from the War Office regretting to inform them that their sons have fallen gloriously fighting for their (the sons') country against their (the parents') country. I may be wrong as to the wording. It may be that the War Office is logical enough to wire: "You will be glad to hear that your son has been slain by the defenders of your official country of origin." But being human rather than logical, they probably put it the other way. Then there are the soldiers who are not killed. They come home on leave, some of them with Victoria Crosses and the like, and are permitted to visit the Alexandra Palace and see for themselves how the country for which they have fought is treating their innocent parents. If this was monstrous when we were at war, what is it now

[1]A racetrack on the edge of Berlin that was the internment camp for four thousand British civilians for the duration.
[2]On the outskirts of London, in which the British established their internment camp.

when all the troops of Armageddon are demobilising, such demobilisation being the reality, and the only reality, of peace?

Take the comparatively straight cases where the victims are adult immigrants, born in some territory that was before the war subject to the Central Empires. Many of them had rather less sympathy with Potsdam than a Kerry Sinn Feiner has with Dublin Castle; they had actually come to England, as the Kerry man often goes to America, to escape from a Government they detested. I know one case of a woman of Polish extraction and tradition, a native of Silesia, who has been settled in London for ten years, and has been occupied all that time in nursing (like Edith Cavell) her "enemies."[3] She is now under orders to hand over all she possesses to the Public Trustee except £10, which she is to spend in repatriating herself at her own expense on a coast of the Continent as remote from her birthplace as Toulouse is from Edinburgh, to live there, presumably, on such share as she can get of the twenty millions we have just had to send out of this country to feed Germany. To our credit be it said, she was treated with complete consideration during the war. Yet now that the war is over we proceed to ruin her. Why? I am convinced that no official or responsible person in the kingdom can be forced to push the regulations to extremity if only decent public opinion will refuse to allow itself any longer to be shouted down by people who, now that the war is over, find themselves sinking back into the obscurity from which its terrors most inadvisedly lifted them. And yet hers is a very mild case compared to thousands that could be cited.

If the proposal were to take all our "alien enemies" and shoot them—("Hear, hear," from all the noisy nobodies)—there would be some sort of sense in it, for "stone dead hath no fellow." If they are really dangerous, why not make an end of them now that our vanquished foes can no longer retaliate? But to send them back to Germany, with all their friendly feeling towards us turned to bitterness and hate, or to keep them here eating their heads off and their hearts out in overcrowded camps about which there will presently be a pro-German scandal, and which obviously cannot be kept going for ever, and this, too, at a moment when the birth-

[3]This was Eva M. Schneider, resident in London since 1908, who was companion and nurse to Shaw's invalid sister Lucy. By Shaw's efforts, the order for her expatriation was subsequently rescinded.

throes of the League of Nations make it enormously important that we should set the world an example of consideration for vanquished enemies is, to say the least, excessively stupid. At Versailles the great ceremony of burying the hatchet is drawing the attention of the entire world. But there are two ways of burying the hatchet. One is to bury it in the skull of the prostrate enemy alien. The other is to establish that peace for which nine hundred thousand of our young men went to their graves like beds. Is it not time that we should begin to enjoy the peace they died for? Or is peace to be nothing but the vilest spite and unreason of war without its braveries, its heroisms, its patriotisms, its chivalries, and the dangers that give reality to these noble words? Are the very spoils to be to the camp-followers instead of to the victors?

Finally—to end on a note of hard fact—let us not forget that the League of Nations has now to settle the very thorny question of general human rights of entry, of travel, of sojourn, and of way for all men in all lands. The war raised these questions in an acute form, first in Belgium and then in Greece. They were already burning questions in California, Australia, and South Africa. We are ourselves, both as exporters of capital and born travellers, explorers, and adventurers, the chief penetrators (both peaceful and warlike) of the world. If the old formula, "He's a stranger; heave half a brick at him" be adopted as international law by the League of Nations, more British heads will be broken than German ones. It is our business to see that we give no countenance to it. The sooner every "alien" who can pay his way here is set free to pay it, and the mass of our people who are not wasting their time in nurse-tending him in one way or another set free to do productive work the better.

Your, &c.,
G. Bernard Shaw

SITTING ON OUR SPURS

[*Daily News*, 19 February 1919.]

Sir,—Mr. Lloyd George's election agent secured his seat at Carnarvon against the attack of Mr. Austin Harrison by the appeal "Vote for Lloyd George and No Conscription." This was good, sound pacifism; but even the election agent did not venture so far as "Vote for Lloyd George and Immediate Disarmament."

As far so I know, not a single candidate on the Government side said a word about disarmament. I am told that no less than a hundred and thirty-one "commercial" candidates, all now safely in the House of Commons, are pledged to disarmament, and received material support in their contests on the strength of that pledge. But nothing was said about it in public; and the electorate certainly did not intend to bring about instantaneous disarmament any more than it intended to achieve, as it actually did achieve, the most convincing reductio ad absurdum of our pseudo-democracy on record.

The tactic of saying nothing about it, but doing it, will justify itself by its success, if it be successful. In fact, it has more than half justified itself already, because the disarmament is more than half accomplished. But had we not better consider a little before we go through with it?

In the early days of the war, now forgotten as everything that happened more than a fortnight ago always is forgotten in this land of political trifling, our men at the front, when hard pressed by the enemy's shells, would telephone to our artillery the whereabouts of the strafing battery, and beg that it might be wiped out. And the answer would be: "We can spare you only one shell a day." The artillery might have added: "And we shall have to pay twice as much for that one shell as it costs to produce at a reasonable profit." Before that, when we were drilling our recruits with broomsticks instead of guns, we were told that we should have as many rifles as we pleased in eleven months, or fifteen months, or whatever was the nearest guess at the time needed to provide the plant for a rapid multiplication of rifles; and in the meantime the British soldier, acutely aware that under such circumstances the enemy does most of the sticking, poured forth his feelings to his parents when he was on leave; and thus we came to know the bitterness of disarmament; for that was the reality of disarmament. The sources on which we had relied for our war supplies on land are now shown to have been equally incapable of rising to the occasion by sea.

Those sources were summed up under the imposing name of Private Enterprise by the sources themselves, and as profiteering by the public. For my part, I should not have grudged the profits if the profiteers could have won the war. As a matter of fact, they all but lost it; and they actually did lose scores of thousands of our lives and limbs because their Private Enterprise, relatively to the national need, was only Private Piffle. The situation was saved by our taking the business in hand ourselves and building national factories and shipyards, organising our labour in them, and allowing the Private Pifflers to help only under national direction and control.

The result of our change of system was that at the end of the war we had more guns than we needed, more shells than those guns could fire, a fleet fully equipped with anti-submarine craft, and our shipping organised in such a way that nationally controlled ships were carrying three cargoes for every one they had carried before under Private Enterprise.

In short, the difference between armament to superfluity and disarmament to disaster is the difference between Public Enterprise and Private Enterprise. And the way to change from armament and victory back again to disarmament and "We can spare you only one shell a day" is to wreck National Enterprise and sell its plant to the Private Pifflers by that sort of auction known as a knock-out. That is the real Knock-out Blow for the British Empire; and that is precisely what the Government is now busily trying for, regardless of the warnings and protests of Marshal Foch and M. Clemenceau that the war is not necessarily over yet, and that Germany still commands an army of three millions, doubtless very tired of war, but still not so tired as to take lying down Mr. Bottomley's[1] proposal to exploit them commercially at the lowest German competition wages until we have extracted ten thousand million pounds from them.

I learned from the Saturday column of A. G. G.[2] that the Coalitionists received Mr. Bottomley's proposal very favourably, and even showed a disposition to take on the United States as well as the Central Empires any day of the week if they go too far in poaching on the preserves of British Private Enterprise. I am afraid they will some day have to take on the United States, poaching or no poaching, with Heaven knows what alliances against us, if they do not study foreign policy a little more and private enterprise a little less; but what are we to think of a House which cries: "Come the four quarters of the world in arms, and we shall shock them," whilst reducing the Empire to an armament supplied by

[1]Horatio Bottomley was a controversial and unscrupulous journalist, financier, and MP whose enterprises led to imprisonment in 1922.
[2]Alfred G. Gardiner, editor of the *Daily News*.

the local ironmonger as per samples dated 1914–15? Such insanity would shock anybody. Mr. Bottomley is one of the ablest men in the present House; and in my opinion he is its natural leader. Indeed, I gather that that is the opinion of A. G. G. also.

If Sir George Younger's[3] crowd (I do not know what else to call it, as it is in no sense a political party) wants a Napoleon, Mr. Bottomley is the man for its money. But I ask Mr. Bottomley whether he would care to be a Napoleon without an army, or worse still, with an unarmed army. It is easy to stand in the House of Commons, a towering figure with one foot rhetorically on Berlin and the other on Washington. But Napoleon reminds us of Egypt; and Egypt reminds us of a jest of our French Allies, which is not recorded in the Gallipoli books. Pointing to the old guns of Omdurman with which we proposed to repeat the exploits of Alexander, and parodying our old watchword of "One Man, One Vote," they cried "One Gun, One Shot."

When we have completed the scrapping of the national factories and shipyards, Germany may snap her fingers at us. She has just elected a Government committed to Public Enterprise as its main principle. We have done just the reverse. That was not clever of us. The policy of the resultant Government, so far, is to wreck our public enterprise, disarm us, demobilise our troops and provoke them to civil war by denationalising the industries we had nationalised as a reply to the miners who demand, very reasonably, that the mines shall be nationalised, keep all the Germans we have captured eating their heads off at our expense instead of sending them home, and then bully both Europe and America as if we had kept our forces at home and abroad at the highest pitch of efficiency and were ready for anything.

In short, having gloriously won our spurs, we now proceed, as usual, to sit on them.

Yours, &c.,
G. Bernard Shaw

[3]A brewer who was a Conservative MP and chairman of the Unionist Party organization.

THE LEAGUE OF NATIONS

[Shaw's *Peace Conference Hints,* published on 12 March 1919, was reviewed by William Archer (the early champion and translator of Ibsen, an author and drama critic) in the *Daily News* on 12 April. Shaw's proposal for a "supernational tribunal" and "legislature" was agreeable enough to Archer, except for his objection that "for the moment the superstition of sovereignty may block the way." Archer disputed Shaw's point that the "difficulty in forming a League of Nations is not to get every nation into it, but to keep the incompatible nations out of it" and Shaw's position that all nations are "incompatible" except those "between the Carpathians and the Rocky Mountains"—that is, all excepting Europe and America. Shaw's reply appeared in the *Daily News* on 15 April.]

Sir,—Mr. Archer has mistaken my point as to the League of Nations. He says that I look forward to a world of Spartans and helots, and that it will not work. I am afraid that he has laid himself open to the retort that it has worked so well (for the Spartans) hitherto, that the onus of proof of the practicability of any other system lies with the helots. But I thought I had made it plain that what I looked forward to was neither a single Spartan Superstate nor a single obviously unworkable and unstable League of All Mankind from China to Peru,[1] but several combinations, psychologically homogeneous within themselves, all equally interested in keeping the peace in their own way. There might be a yellow combination, a Latin and Spanish-Indian combination, a couple of Eurasian combinations, in which Russia and India might find their moorings, and a certain number of unplaceable units which the combinations could keep in order as far as war is concerned. Between these integrations there will be all sorts of mechanical links, beginning with the postal link. Of course Mr. Archer or any of us could make a much shorter and neater job of the business if it could be left in our hands; but it will not. Things must happen as they do happen, in spite of the Spanish nobleman who thought he could give the Almighty a few hints.[2]

[1]Echoing the opening couplet of Samuel Johnson's "The Vanity of Human Wishes" (1749): "Let Observation, with extensive view, / Survey mankind, from China to Peru."

[2]Alfonso X (1226?–84), King of Castile and León, known as "the Wise," is alleged to have said, after studying the Ptolemaic system, "Had I been present at the creation, I would have given some useful hints for the better ordering of the universe."

One thing is, however, beyond all question. If any nation enters into the business assuming that some other nation consists of foreign devils whom God has commissioned it to smite as the Amalekites were smitten, we may just as well drop the whole project and prepare for the next war. I do not know whether Mr. Archer's sly quotation from Pickwick means that we are to understand that it is Serjeant Buzfuz[3] who is speaking, and not the unofficial Archer; but I am sure that the last foe to be overcome is the Pharisee, to whatever nation he may belong.

Yours, &c.,
G. Bernard Shaw

EPSTEIN'S CHRIST

[An exhibition of the young sculptor Jacob Epstein's statue of Christ in London in 1920 led to harsh criticism of the statue by the press, the clergy, artists' associations, and other groups. Father Bernard Vaughan, a Jesuit priest and ardent social reformer fanatical on the subject of the "sins of society," published an attack, "Is It Really Christ?" in *The Graphic* on 14 February. Father Vaughan's judgment: "I feel ready to cry out with indignation that in this Christian England there should be exhibited the figure of a Christ which suggested to me some degraded Chaldean or African, which wore the appearance of an Asiatic, American or Hun, which reminded me of some emaciated Hindu or badly grown Egyptian." Shaw replied to Father Vaughan in *The Graphic* on 20 March.]

Sir,—Father Vaughan is an unlucky man. He has a genius for mistaking his profession. The war tore off his cassock and revealed the spurs, the cartridge belt, the khaki beneath. And now that he is demobilised, his wandering star leads him into the profession of art critic.

When I was last at Lourdes I saw a cinema representation of the Passion. I think that Christ would have pleased Father Vaughan. He looked like a very beautiful operatic tenor. I have seen Victor Capoul[1] and the late Lord Battersea;[2] and he was as Christ-like (in Father Vaughan's sense) as both of them rolled into

[3]Serjeant (Officer of the Court) Buzfuz was barrister for Mrs. Bardell in her alienation suit against Samuel Pickwick in Dickens's *Pickwick Papers*.
[1]French tenor heard in London from 1871 to 1879.
[2]Cyril Flower, first Baron Battersea, was Lord of the Treasury under Gladstone, a Liberal MP, and a noted art collector.

one. He was more the gentleman than the Christ of Oberammergau, who was in private life a wood-carver. The Church is so powerful at Lourdes that I do not think this exhibition would have been possible without its approval. That the approval was obtained is not to be wondered at. The Church knows its business at Lourdes. And the cinema actor knew *his* business, which was to study the most popular pictures of Christ, and to reproduce their subject in his own person with the aid of his make-up box. He purchased the ambrosial curls and the eyebrows, and put them on with spirit gum. If his nose was not the right shape, he built it up with plastic material. The result was very pretty, and quite satisfactory to those whose ideal Christ is a stage lover. I did not care for it myself. The stage has no illusions (of that sort) for me; and I feel quite sure that Christ was no more like a modern opera singer than he was like Henry Dubb,[3] the modern carpenter.

Now that Father Vaughan is going in for art, many terrible shocks await him. Imagine him in Bruges, looking at the Christs of the Netherland school (he can see some, by the way, in the National Gallery). He will almost forgive Mr. Epstein when he sees how Dierick Bouts and Hans Memling and Gerard David made Christ a plain, troubled, common man. Or he may go to Tunbridge Wells and walk to Speldhurst Church, where he will see a magnificent Morris stained window in which Burne-Jones, departing utterly from the convention which he himself had so often exploited, made the figure on the cross a glorious Greek God. Michael Angelo did the same in his Last Judgment. Holman Hunt, after representing The Light of the World as an excessively respectable gentleman with a trim beard and a jewelled lantern, knocking at a door with the gesture of a thief in the night, lived to be reviled by the Vaughans of his day for representing Him in "The Shadow of the Cross" as a Syrian—actually as a Syrian Jew instead of an Oxford graduate. Raphael's unique Christ in His Transfiguration is a Tyrolese peasant. Rembrandt's Christ is a Dutchman. Von Uhde's Christ is a poor man who converses with men in tall hats, and women in nineteenth-century bonnets and shawls.

[3]A laborite generic name, identified by R. H. Tawney in *The Attack* (1953) as "the common, courageous, good-hearted, patient, proletarian fool, whose epic is contained in the well-known lines, 'We go to work to earn the cash to buy the bread to get the strength to go to work to earn the cash,' etc., and who is worth, except to his modest self, nine-tenths of the gentilities, notabilities, intellectual, cultural and ethical eminences put together."

But there is no end to the varieties of type to be found in the Christs of the artists. We are only waiting for an advance in African civilisation for a negro Christ, who may be quite as impressive as any of the Aryan ones. The shallowest of all the Christs is the operatic Christ, just as the shallowest of the Virgins is the operatic Virgin. Father Vaughan, obsessed with the Christs of Guido, Ary Scheffer, Muller & Co., and with the Virgins of Sassoferrato and Bouguereau, was staggered by Epstein's Christ, just as he would be staggered by Cimabue's gigantic unearthly Virgin. He will soon know better. And if he will only read the Gospels instead of the despatches of the war correspondents, he will find that there is not a trace of "tenderness, calmness, and sweetness" in St. Matthew's literary portrait of Christ, and that the operatic Christ was invented by St. Luke.[4]

All the Christs in art must stand or fall by their power of suggesting to the beholder the sort of soul that he thinks was Christ's soul. It is evident that many people have found this in Mr. Epstein's Christ, and that Father Vaughan has not. Well, Father Vaughan will find his Christ in every Roman Catholic Church in the land, and in all the shops that furnish them. Let him choose the statue that is nearest his own heart; and I have no doubt that Mr. Cecil Phillips[5] will place it beside Mr. Epstein's and leave every man to judge for himself which of the two is the more memorable.

Yours, &c.,
G. Bernard Shaw

THE BLUSHING BARRISTER

[*Daily News,* 28 January 1921.]

Sir,—As a member of the male sex, will you allow me to protest indignantly against the proceedings reported by you in your issue of the 26th as having occurred in the Divorce Court on Tuesday last?

The jury consisted of six men, married and unmarried, of various ratepaying ages, and of six women, married and unmarried,

[4]Shaw's comments are repetitive of the views expressed by him in the preface (1916) to *Androcles and the Lion* and in the letter to the *New Statesman* of 17 June 1916 ("Shaw's Jesus," pp. 204–207 above).
[5]A director of the Leicester Galleries, in which the statue had been exhibited.

of various ratepaying ages. The case began with a discussion between the Bench and the Bar as to the effect on the jury of certain love letters described as abominable and beastly, and certain presumably obscene picture cards.

The conclusion arrived at seems to have been that as all men are familiar with abominable and beastly letters and obscene picture cards, they should examine these documents and tell the innocent women what they thought of them. Now I am a married man in my sixty-fifth year; and I solemnly protest that I am entirely guiltless of this alleged male habit of reading abominable and beastly letters and gloating over pornographic pictures.

Sir Edward Marshall Hall's[1] assumption that my sensibilities in this matter are less delicate than those of women is not only unfounded, but extremely offensive. It was part of his case that these "exhibits" had passed between a man and a woman. Then why in the name of common sense did this blushing barrister exclude the six jurymen from the apology which he thought it necessary to make for presenting them to the six jurywomen?

I need not emphasise the gross absurdity of referring Miss Lilian Barker,[2] whose extraordinary record as a welfare worker during the war, to say nothing of her present responsible employment, makes her judgment more valuable in any question of domestic morality than that of the whole British Bar and Bench, to the nearest juryman, possibly a bashful novice of twenty-two, for instruction as to what she should think of an improper picture.

But I declare that it is monstrous that any woman or any man having a public duty of this kind to perform, should have his or her name published as having on such-and-such a day been engaged in the examination of "abominable and beastly" documents. What would be said if hospital nurses could not assist at unmentionable operations—as they have to every day—without having their names published in connection with disgusting descriptions of their work? Why is the sense of decency which protects nurses and surgeons from such repulsive reports suspended in the case of jurymen and jurywomen?

If the published letters are fair samples of the "abominable

[1]The former Conservative MP was a well-known advocate in divorce and libel actions.

[2]An elementary school teacher who became a penal officer. In 1935, she was appointed assistant commissioner and inspector of H. M. Prisons.

and beastly" documents, I can say without fear of contradiction that nothing in the case was half so shocking to sensible delicacy as the unfortunate discussion with which it opened. If the leaders of the Bar are really as sensitive as Mr. Silas Wegg,[3] with his "Not before Mrs. Boffin, sir," then I suggest that it will be on the whole less socially inconvenient for them to change their profession, or confine themselves to Admiralty practice, than for Parliament to repeal the Act in deference to their bashfulness.

Yours, &c.,
G. Bernard Shaw

IMPROVING LONDON

[*Architecture: Journal of the Society of Architects,* January 1923.]

Sir,—Why don't you send a competent young man round London to suggest improvements in existing ugly public buildings, and to mark the hopeless ones for demolition? For example, the Houses of Parliament could be made almost presentable by removing the top storey; and a list of the tombs which should be cleared out of Westminster Abbey would be very useful to a Bolshevik leader in the event of a dictatorship of the proletariat being established. That would give a practical turn to much pointless grumbling and sniffing.

Yours, &c.,
G. Bernard Shaw

STATE RECOGNITION OF BETTING

[*Manchester Guardian,* 17 April 1923.]

Sir,—The object of betting is to obtain money without working for it. All respected and influential people hold and acquire property with this in view; and the more they succeed the more they are respected and the greater becomes their influence. The State organises, legalises, and protects their operations with all its might. The poor man cannot afford this method: he backs horses,

[3] A ballad-monger hired to read books to the wealthy but illiterate Mr. and Mrs. Boffin, in Dickens's *Our Mutual Friend.*

takes shares in sweepstakes, and (abroad) buys lottery tickets. It is obviously invidious that the State should organise the rich man's method and persecute the poor man's method. In equity there should be a bookmaker's counter in every post office and a totalisator[1] in every railway station. In villages the rector might act as bookmaker for the labourers to counterbalance his extra-clerical support of the squire. Sir Alfred Mond has given all the reasons for encouraging the betting spirit in the community, and the House of Commons has voted with him.[2]

Personally I am of opinion that to live, or attempt to live, either by private property or by betting, or to evade or attempt to evade the primal social duty of producing all that one consumes, and more, by any method whatsoever, should lead straight to the lethal chamber. When it leads, as at present, to the House of Lords, it also leads finally, and inevitably, to the collapse of civilisation.

Yours, &c.,
G. Bernard Shaw

EVE'S "REPUGNANCE"

[Eve's reaction to the Serpent's revelation of the method of sexual reproduction in Shaw's *Back to Methuselah* was a subject of discussion by Herbert Farjeon in an article on 1 March and by T. V. Taylor in a letter on 22 March 1924, in the *Weekly Westminster*. Shaw's response appeared in that journal on 5 April.]

Sir,—Eve's wry face is simply a criticism of the *method* of reproduction, which offends her sense of human dignity and decency. Making all possible allowance for the artificiality of civilised prudery, it remains true that if the extraordinary emotion and intensification of life which makes reproduction so irresistible could be dissociated from a physical procedure which is common

[1]A machine employed, in parimutuel betting, for registering wagers and for computing the odds and payoffs as the wagers are placed.

[2]Alfred Moritz Mond, later first Baron Melchett, a chemical industrialist and financier, was a Liberal MP for Swansea (1910–23) with a sympathetic attitude toward Labour. The chancellor of the exchequer had contemplated a tax on betting in March but was discouraged from pursuing it by the debates in Parliament in which Mond took an active role. The proposal was set aside on 13 April.

to mankind and the lower forms of evolutionary creation, we should no longer be so ashamed of it that no sober person can be induced to face it in the presence of a third party.[1]

Yours, &c.,
G. Bernard Shaw

A SHAVIAN EXPLANATION

[*Morning Post,* 6 December 1924.]

Sir,—Why does the *Morning Post* always go to Moscow for its news about me? On November 26, at Kingsway Hall, in London, I spoke for over an hour, mainly on the Russian question.[1] The usual accommodation was provided for the Press, and reporters were present. Apparently it never occurred to the *Morning Post* that my very carefully considered utterances were of any public interest, for it left its readers in utter ignorance that the Shavian oracle had spoken. But nine days later the *Morning Post* announces that its Russian correspondent, on whom I gather it relies for its London news, states that the Moscow and Petrograd papers have reported my speech. I submit that this proves that the Moscow and Petrograd papers know their business better than the London ones.

The twenty-one lines of Russian translation re-translated into English naturally give only a very faint notion of the ten thousand words or so uttered by me. I spoke far more strongly than anyone would suppose from reading these lines. And, of course, the argument is telescoped into nonsense here and there. But the report is as accurate as most Press reports; and my only complaint is that it gives no idea of the force and completeness of my indictment of the absurdity, the savage arrogance, and the reckless defiance of

[1]D. H. Lawrence reacted to this point of view in chapter XII of *Lady Chatterley's Lover* (1928): "After all, the moderns were right when they felt contempt for the performance; for it was a performance. It was quite true, as some poets said, that the God who created man must have had a sinister sense of humour, creating him a reasonable being, yet forcing him to take this ridiculous posture, and driving him with blind craving for this ridiculous performance. Even a Maupassant found it a humiliating anti-climax. Men despised the intercourse act, and yet did it."

[1]Shaw's lecture, sponsored by the Fabian Society, was entitled "Some Observations from Experience."

the public opinion of the world shown in the drafting of the ultimatum to Egypt.[2]

I may add that full publicity was given in the *Daily News* and in America to my remark, made on the morrow of the General Election, that the verdict was, in effect, a declaration of war on the Soviet Government. It is odd that a pronouncement so extremely congenial to the *Morning Post* should have been ignored by it. What fault has it to find with it?

Yours, &c.,
G. Bernard Shaw

*This letter relates to the report, published in Russian journals, and reproduced by us with every reserve, of opinions expressed by Mr. Shaw on the Egyptian situation. It is now clear that our reserve was quite unnecessary. [*Ed., *M.P.]*

OUR "COMMUNISTS"

[The *Daily News* of 11 June 1925 published an article by Philip Snowden, Socialist MP and former chancellor of the exchequer, in which he observed that "the International Labour and Socialist movement" had often been "wrecked" by one "fanatical minority" or another. The latest version of this problem, Snowden suggested, was the British Communist Party, which "has maintained its organisation and supported its press and propaganda by funds supplied from Bolshevik sources." Snowden urged the Labour Party to dissociate itself from "Communist propaganda." Shaw's reply was published on 12 June.]

Sir,—Mr. Philip Snowden's article sets me asking can nothing be done to clear up the confusion created by assumption of the term Communist by the extreme Left Wing of the Labour movement, and its rash acceptance as a reproach and a hissing by the Labour Front Bench.

When Mr. Snowden is as much a Communist as Plato, or William Morris, or myself, it is rather bewildering to hear him denounce "the Communists" as the worst enemies of Labour. When he is obviously on the side of the Russian Revolution as

[2]The "ultimatum to Egypt" and the editor's appended reference to "the Egyptian situation" relate to the recent murder of the Sirdar of Egypt (British commander-in-chief of the Egyptian army), Lt. Gen. Sir L. O. F. Stack.

against Mr. Winston Churchill and Lord Birkenhead,[1] what is the general reader to make of his vituperative use of the word Bolshevik?

We must really get this thing straightened out if the distinction between a Labour Party in Parliament and a vaguely Liberal Opposition is to be maintained in the public consciousness. It is as if a sect advocating violently unchristian doctrines had arisen and called its members Followers of Christ, and the bishops had fallen into the trap and begun to denounce Christianity and its nominal head with all their powers of invective. The end of that would be that Christians would lose all confidence in bishops, and get hopelessly muddled as to what Christianity is and which side they were on.

What are the people whom Mr. Snowden denounces as Communists, and whom he would not denounce if they really were Communists like himself? They are a very mixed lot. Some of them are so ignorant of political etiquette and void of British national self-respect that they take money from Russia without knowing that they thereby place themselves on the footing of our own secret service agents abroad, whom we should certainly sack if they were silly enough to form societies for the purpose of showing their hands.

Why the Russian Government does not sack them—if the money is really Government money—I cannot imagine. If it is not Government money, then they are simply missionaries, and should call themselves the Society for the Propagation of the Gospel of Marx according to the Russian Orthodox Church in Partibus Infidelium. That would be both accurate and imposing.

Others, independent of Russia, are Labour Fascisti. Like Signor Mussolini and the King of Spain, they are fed up with Parliamentary shuffling and compromising, and are for Direct Action: that is, the seizure of power by a coup d'etat by those who, like Mussolini or the Spanish Military General Staff, can pull it off, promising to rule by main force in the interests of the Proletariat.

Some of them are simple Anarchists, primitive souls who, having been convinced by their observation and experience that our parliaments and courts of justice are occupied mainly in rob-

[1]Frederick Edwin Smith, first Earl of Birkenhead, was at this time lord chancellor.

bing and oppressing the poor, conclude that the world would be a happy place but for its parliaments and policemen.

Some of them are free and independent Britons (in theory) who, without reasoning about it, object to be governed at all.

Some of them are men and women with an intense pity for suffering and horror of cruelty. No matter what party they support they turn against it the moment it accepts power and responsibility, because a party in that position finds itself immediately obliged to hang or imprison somebody; and from that moment they declare that it has betrayed the cause of humanity.

Some are Communists credulous enough to believe that all the people who call themselves Communists are Communists, a delusion almost as extravagant as that all the people who call themselves Christians are Christians, and even know what Christ taught.

And then there are the political prentice lads, always against the political machine because it is so slow, and because the capitalist forces have such a knack of making it work their way.

What sense is there in calling a Left Wing made up in this way Communist? It is a darkening of counsel by words without wisdom. Surely Mr. Snowden's business is to insist that he and his colleagues are holding the fort of Constitutional Communism against political pirates who are not Communists at all, and who, if ever they get to close quarters, will haul down the red flag and hoist the Jolly Roger of Fascism, Syndicalism, Anarchism, and Dictatorship.

The Labour Party is right to hold the fort; but it must not hoist the white flag of the bourgeoisie, because in a Labour fort the white flag is the sign of capitulation, and might as well be a white feather. This is all the more important now as there are forces in existence which are tending to detach Labour from Socialism (including Communism) and make it frankly trade unionist in the sense in which trade unionism is simply working class capitalism, or democratic Liberalism.

As to whether that is desirable or not I need express no opinion in this connection. The sole purpose of my letter is to show that the present absurd use of the word Communist as an abusive epithet by Communists and as an authentically descriptive one by people who are much less Communist than Mr. Baldwin,[2] is mud-

[2]Stanley Baldwin at this time was the Conservative prime minister.

dling the public and compromising the Labour Front bench to an extent that may make the next election as silly a misunderstanding as the last.

Yours, &c.,
G. Bernard Shaw

THEATRE APPLAUSE

[*Daily Telegraph,* 6 February 1926.]

Sir,—As far as serious work in the theatre is concerned, I should put applause during the performance on the footing of brawling in church.

The first condition of an artistic performance is that the players should be able to forget the audience and the audience to forget itself. The moment the audience makes an uproar, and the players are compelled to stop and wait until silence is restored, there is an end of the artistic conditions which have been established in the uninterrupted silence of rehearsal with great care and labour. Also the time occupied by the entire performance is being prolonged, which means, if the play is timed at rehearsal to the classical and popular limit of from three hours to three hours and a half, that the end of the play is spoiled, because half the audience is agonising about its last train or 'bus, instead of listening free from care, which is the only condition in which a play can be enjoyed.

One of the great services that wireless is rendering to mankind is that it is accustoming performers to do without applause, and at the same time making an audience hear what a horrid noise it makes; for when an opera is broadcast, not from the studio but from the theatre, the applause at the fall of the curtain comes as a detestable and unbearable din from a den of savages. People are at last beginning to understand why Mr. Arnold Dolmetsch[1] at his concerts asks the audience not to clap, on the simple ground that it makes a disagreeable noise and shatters the impression made by the music.

The only entertainments at which loud laughter and applause should be countenanced are those which have laughter and ap-

[1]A French musician resident in London who specialized in performances of obscure compositions on archaic musical instruments of his own construction.

plause for their object. Therefore, what I have said does not apply to clowning or to political oratory. As you pay a clown to make you laugh, it would be ridiculous to deprive yourself of the thing you have paid for. At political meetings no man would dare to talk as political orators are expected to do (I am one myself) unless the audience encouraged him and intoxicated themselves by dervishlike uproar and antics. But when a drama is being enacted, no matter how amusing it may be, there should be no applause; and the actors should never appear out of character to take calls.

As to the customary author's call, it is an outrage, because the audience should never remember—indeed, the happiest playgoers do not know—that there is an author at all.

Yours, &c.,
G. Bernard Shaw

NOT A FILM SNOB

[*Daily News,* 26 February 1926.]

Sir,—In your issue of the 23rd you say that "if distinguished and imaginative writers like Mr. Shaw would cease to look on the moving picture contemptuously as a vulgar class of entertainment not worthy of their genius or literary dignity" certain beneficial results would follow.

I assure you I am entirely guiltless of any such senseless snobbery. I have recognized from the first the enormous importance, both artistically and morally, of the film, and I have never said or done anything inconsistent with that recognition.

But it does not follow from my appreciation of the possibilities of the dumb drama that I should become a dumb dramatist.

If Michael Angelo were now alive I have not the slightest doubt that he would have his letterbox filled with proposals from the great film firms to consecrate his powers to the delineation of Felix the Cat[1] instead of painting the Sistine Chapel; but I think you will agree with me that his duty would lie in the direction of frescoe and sculpture rather than of Los Angeles.

Why can you not pardon me for thinking that a master play-

[1]A popular film cartoon character created in 1919 by Pat Sullivan, an Australian.

wright of seventy is better occupied in writing complete plays than fumbling with scenarios as a beginner?

Mr. Harry Warner's[2] public complaint of my inaccessibility is partly responsible for your misunderstanding. But Mr. Warner went on to describe how, regarding me as a National Institution ("your Mr. Shaw"), which no doubt I am, he took the phrase so literally that, instead of simply writing to me, he approached the Foreign Office.

I regret that the Secretary of State for Foreign Affairs was too much occupied with Locarno[3] or the proposed additions to the League of Nations to arrange a meeting for us; but, really, it was hardly his business. A frontal attack may prove more successful.

Yours, &c.,
G. Bernard Shaw

"BLIND LEADERS OF THE BLIND"

[*Daily Herald,* 17 August 1926.]

Sir,—In your issue of July 31 I am accused of gross professional misconduct as a journalist in having, it is alleged, hoaxed the editor of the *Financial News* with a spoof article on the French franc.[1] The evidence is that I wrote:—

> "The British Government has, by inflation, practically repudiated half the War Loan,"

the truth, according to your financial expert, being that

> "The British Government, by deflation, almost doubled the value of War Loan Stock."

Did it? Then I lost a rare opportunity of selling out. "To be exact," your expert goes on, "those who bought War Loan have their property increased by 85 percent." Well, I bought War Loan as an original subscriber. Careless as I am about such matters, I think I should have noticed it if I had become so much richer.

[2] Harry M. Warner was president of Warner Bros. Pictures Inc., founded in 1923.

[3] Sir Austen Chamberlain participated in the peace conference at Locarno in 1925.

[1] "The Franc and Mr. Bernard Shaw. Back to Gold," 29 July 1926.

What actually happened was this. The Government said to me: "If you have any spare subsistence on hand at present, hand it over to us for our soldiers; and for every quantum of it that is measured by £100, we will give you every year a quantum of the year's production measured by £5." I took the offer, and handed over my spare subsistence. The Government then inflated the currency until the yearly quantum measured by £5 was only half what it had been when the bargain was struck.

In figures the Government still acknowledged an indebtedness to me of £100, and paid me £5 a year interest. In goods it acknowledged a debt of £50, and paid £2 10s. interest. Your expert, being a man of figures, is taken in by the transaction. I, being a man of facts, and the victim in the transaction, am not. That is why he was so scandalised when I said what I now repeat, that the British Government, by inflation, practically repudiated half the War Loan.

Please observe that if the Government had expropriated me openly in the proper way, by increasing its taxation and super-taxation of my whole income, I should, as a Socialist, have had no ground for objection.

As to your expert's blunt assertion that "the British Government, by deflation, almost doubled the value of War Loan stock," I can only gasp and put the following questions to him:—

1. Can he give me the name of any stockjobber who will "make me a price" for my War Loan stock which will bear out his statement?

2. Can he produce any Stock Exchange quotation to the same effect?

3. Will he buy any of my War Loan from me at 400?

4. Can he indicate any market where I can purchase twice as much for my money as I could when I subscribed to the War Loan? (This question is of intense interest to the readers of the *Daily Herald,* as if any interest will buy double, so will a workman's wages.)

5. Will he come with me to the Bank of England, and induce the Governor to give me sovereigns or bullion for my treasury notes at the pre-inflation gold standard rate?

6. If he cannot answer all these questions in an affirmative sense, does he still wish your readers to believe that my contribution to the *Financial News* is ridiculous nonsense, and the editor of that paper an ignorant gull?

Your expert, after the manner of financial experts, throws out the imposing remark that "in March, 1920, our National Debt was equivalent to 2,400 millions of gold sovereigns. It is now equivalent to 4,500 millions." Now the war debt is just exactly what it was when it was borrowed, not half a loaf, nor a tin of bully beef, nor a high-explosive shell, more or less; but our currency has been so debased (inflated is the polite term), that a loaf or a tin of bully costs nearly twice as much in paper money as it did. But this had happened before 1920. Therefore, if your expert's valuation is correct, gold must be nearly twice as cheap as it was in 1920. How much gold is your expert prepared to sell to me at this rate?

I should, however, have made one notable qualification of my statement that the Government had practically repudiated half the War Loan. The Government could borrow shillings from me, and, by the magic of inflation, turn them into sixpences. But it could not borrow dollars from the United States and turn them into half-dollars. Consequently it has to pay the United States in gold values, whilst it pays me in paper values. As I happen to hold a little United States Liberty Loan Stock, I am hit both ways—by inflation at home and deflation of the dollar exchange. And your expert thinks I am nearly twice as rich as I was. I can only say that if he goes speculating on his calculations he will soon be on the "dole."

The orgy of State and financial swindling which has raged since the war under such deep terms as Inflation, Devaluation, Extension of Credit, demands for a reduction of the Bank Rate and so forth, must be stopped, or we shall all crash in bankruptcy or rebellion after reducing the purchasing power of wages to zero. All the writers of city articles should be re-employed as racing tipsters. It would be cruel to hang them.

Yours, &c.,
G. Bernard Shaw

"MR. SHAW OFFENDED"

[The BBC declined to broadcast a speech by Shaw, delivered at a dinner on his seventieth birthday (the full text of which appeared in the *New York Times* on 15 August 1926), on the grounds that it would be politically controversial and therefore officially prohibited by the government. The occasion itself was judged to be "partisan," a dinner under the auspices of the Parliamentary Labour Party, presided over by J. Ramsay MacDonald. The *Manchester Guardian,* in a commentary on 2 August, concurred with the BBC's decision. Shaw's reply was published on 17 August, with a response by the editor.]

Sir,—Your article of the 2nd, headed as above, has overtaken me here [at Stresa, Italy] and filled me with consternation. From the mass of modern newspapers one expects neither any defence of popular rights nor, indeed, any conception of their existence. If at the next general election the Government were to place its agents at the doors of every polling station to exclude everyone who did not sign an undertaking to vote for its candidates, I believe that the great majority of our present editors would accept that arrangement as perfectly fair, obvious, and natural. It would be left to the *Manchester Guardian,* and perhaps one or two other great provincial dailies with traditions, to cry "To your tents, O Israel!"[1] Why, then, has the *Manchester Guardian* on this occasion lain down under the Government steam roller like any doormat in Fleet Street?

The answer is that, owing to the peculiar conditions of newspaper work, editors have not yet discovered the enormous political significance of wireless. They know it only rather contemptuously as a string of entertainment programmes for which they have to find space. They have never had the headphones on, nor ever been exhorted by a loud speaker, because at the hours when the ether is vibrating with party politics, controlled and selected and censored by the Postmaster General, and referred in special cases (mine, for instance) to the Prime Minister, the editors are too frantically busy with their night's work to attend to anything else short of an earthquake.

That is how the *Manchester Guardian,* so vigilant in its scrutiny of the written word, came to write, print, and publish, under the heading and on the date aforesaid, the shattering, staggering,

[1]The Biblical call to revolt: *1 Kings,* 12:16.

swoon-inducing remark that, "in the perfectly intelligible interests of a service which is not a political agency, speeches which may be controversial in the political sense are not distributed."

Great Scott![2]

Bless your innocence, within the few weeks preceding my claim to have my speech broadcast, my loud-speaker shouted acutely controversial political speeches at me from the Prime Minister, the Home Secretary, Lord Grey, Lord Balfour,[3] and Mr. Lloyd George, to say nothing of unattached orators. They called the nation to arms as special constables against the trade unions in defence of an alleged breach of the British Constitution. When the general strike was called off they compared the peril from which they had rescued the country to that of 1914. They handed one another bouquets which would have seemed overcoloured in the garden of Klingsor,[4] and implied that their critics were enemies of the human race. They licensed an unnamed orator to praise their Great Deliverance to a musical accompaniment of a choir singing [Charles Hubert H.] Parry's setting of Blake's "Jerusalem." When the scare was over they let themselves go on the coal strike, on the neglect of science by our employers (a literally burning question finely handled by Lord Balfour on the platform of a scientific society), on the right of the clergy to intervene in political issues, on Pacifism *versus* Imperialism, on the League of Nations, on Anglo-Italian relations (Sir Austen Chamberlain[5] at a banquet in honour of our friend Signor Cippico[6]); in short, on every controversial topic of the moment without the smallest restraint.

Can anyone be so simple as to believe that these gentlemen were asked to promise that they would not be controversial, or so cynical as to believe that they gave such promises and then deliberately broke them? Is it conceivable that the Postmaster General dared to propose to Lord Balfour, for instance, that he should commit the sin of Esau[7] (without the mess of pottage) by surren-

[2]A jesting allusion to the *Manchester Guardian's* illustrious editor, Charles Prestwich Scott.

[3]Arthur James Balfour, prime minister 1902–05, was now the Conservative leader in the House of Lords.

[4]The wicked knight in Wagner's *Parsifal.*

[5]Foreign secretary, 1924–29, who had negotiated the Locarno Pact (1925) and was awarded the Nobel Peace Prize in 1925.

[6]Conte Antonio Cippico, Italian literary critic and poet.

[7]Esau sells his birthright, in *Genesis,* 25, for a "mess of pottage."

dering that right of free speech which every British citizen should hold as a sacred trust, or that, if he had, Lord Balfour would not have refused, as emphatically and indignantly as I did when this infamous proposal was made to me?

Does nobody see the gravity of the issue? Or am I, as has been suggested, simply mad with self-conceit? At former general elections and platform campaigns I have always exercised the right of free speech on equal terms with the Cabinet. From Joseph Chamberlain at Glasgow to Mr. Baldwin[8] at Newcastle I have followed or preceded our Parliamentary leaders on the same subjects, the same platforms, to equally crowded audiences, without let or hindrance. Had an attempt been made to muzzle me, the *Manchester Guardian* would have been the first to vindicate my right. The largest audience Mr. Baldwin and I could reach then was five thousand, mostly noisy political partisans. To-day we can address five millions of unselected and therefore really representative citizens. And immediately Mr. Baldwin seizes me by the throat and says, "I and my friends shall address the five millions as we please; but you shall not address them politically at all, except on conditions dishonourable to yourself, and not only impossible to be observed, but not binding on me and my supporters."

I must leave it at that. If, now that I have opened your eyes to the facts about wireless, you can still see nothing more important at stake than "Mr. Shaw Offended," then you cannot see the sun in the heavens. Your concluding lines were, I know, written in good faith. You wrote:

> The embargo is not an embargo against Mr. Shaw; it is a general embargo against controversial politics in the middle of an ordinary wireless entertainment. To be hurt because this rule, which affects everybody, was not specially waived in the case of one individual seems a particularly curious reaction in the case of a good Socialist.

The only possible defence of the embargo would be that it was an embargo against me personally, and not a general embargo against controversial politics. But in that case it should be applied by a court of law. The plain truth is that it is not a general embargo: it is an embargo on criticism of the Government. It is waived automatically in the case of members of the Government and their friends, and specially applied to the Labour Opposition and its

[8]Stanley Baldwin was in the second (1924–29) of his three terms as prime minister.

friends. It is a shameless abrogation of the British right of free speech, and is, for any other purpose, blank nonsense. And—incidentally—but for it I should not have mentioned the Government in my speech on July 26.

Yours, &c.,
G. Bernard Shaw

. . . . *So far from no one but Mr. Shaw being alive to the difficulties of the rule, those difficulties were being discussed long before that birthday party threw its chief guest into such distress of mind; and it is now understood that the rule will be relaxed and that "a moderate amount of controversial matter, provided that it is of high quality and distributed with scrupulous fairness," will be permitted when the new governing body of our British broadcasting service comes into existence. . . . But we are quite sure that neither the Commissioners nor anybody else would dream of applying to our admirable "G. B. S." for advice on what is likely to be admissible material for "controversial" broadcasting. For years he has specialised from time to time in a kind of controversy which lays itself out to be perverse rather than persuasive, and, as his letter which we publish this morning shows, his pen has lost little of its self-destructive cunning.* [Ed., *M. G.*]

NOT A BLACK SHIRT

[*Daily News*, 26 November 1927.]

Sir,—I must apologise to your reporter for having misled him completely by my Fabian lecture on Democracy[1] on Wednesday evening. I am very conscious of the shortcomings of my performance; and I quite understand that to compress the 9,000 words or so which I must have uttered into 200 was an impossible task. I think, however, I can put the propositions which puzzled him into a few lines. They were, first, that Socialism, like Capitalism, is independent of forms of government, and can be recommended to a despot (say, to Marcus Aurelius) as confidently as to a British Labour Prime Minister; and second, that a British Prime Minister in office, being election-proof for five years, or an American Presi-

[1]Shaw's lecture on 23 November 1927, "Democracy as a Delusion," was the last in a series of six Fabian Society lectures on "Political Democracy: Will It Prevail?"

dent for four years, is a Dictator for that period with an effective monopoly of the initiation and control of legislation and foreign policy.

To summarise these two incontrovertible propositions by the scare-head "Socialism Must Get a Dictator," and describe my attitude by the epithet "Black Shirt," is, to put it as mildly as possible, to miss both my points.

Whilst fully admitting that my presentation of an elaborate analysis of democracy left much to be desired (I was conscious of making a shocking muddle of it), I think your reporter must have been suffering from the prevalent Mussolinian obsession. The word dictator brings on a violent attack of this distressing complaint; but I had to use it.

Yours, &c.,
G. Bernard Shaw

THE PRESS

[A series of articles, "The Future of the Press," by St. John Ervine, Rebecca West, and Wickham Steed, appeared in *Time and Tide* between 10 February and 9 March 1928. Shaw's response was published in *Time and Tide* on 23 March.]

Sir,—Mr. Wickham Steed[1] has put his finger on the flaw in the old-fashioned political journalism when he says that events have an unhappy knack of making political criticism obsolete before there is time to write it. During the war I asked a military chief how far strategy could be kept ahead of actual warfare. His reply was: "half a kilometre ahead of the front line." When the war began I wrote an article about it.[2] It took me two months to hunt up and read the necessary documents and consider and solve the problems involved; and it was fast work at that. Once started I tried to keep up, but could never finish an article radically enough to be of any use before the war left it far behind. Meanwhile the papers had been rushing out dozens of editions every day; and people had been feverishly reading them. Their leading articles

[1]Henry Wickham Steed, an English journalist, formerly editor of *The Times*, was proprietor and editor of the *Review of Reviews*.

[2]*Common Sense about the War*, published as a supplement to the *New Statesman*, 14 November 1914.

and specials and news from the front (the Fleet Street front) had the character and value of the cacklings of a flock of chickens charged by a fast motor-car.

But what could the writers do? Consider the situation. Russia, the most backward country in Europe, had mobilized against Germany, the most elaborately civilized. In any natural course of events, England and France, being on the German plane of western European civilization, should have at once rallied to the defence of Germany and forced Russia to demobilize. Yet they combined with her to crush Germany. It would have taken a first-rate historian, a first-rate philosopher, and a first-rate statesman many weeks to straighten out this monstrous tangle and produce a really competent *Times* leader on it. But every journalist on the editorial staff was supposed to be able to do it without assistance in an hour.

The war was only an extreme case of what is happening every day. The reports come in with the news from hour to hour. And the leader writer is expected to supply the verdict of history on the news as fast as it comes in. To put it another way, the reporter is a reporter and the news is news; but the leader writer is an imposter and his judgments are tosh. Accordingly, the leader writer has to develop a power of rapidly stating problems in so imposing a way that his readers are too much impressed to notice that he never solves them. After some years of this the leader writer becomes incapable of doing anything else: hence the familiar phenomenon of the journalist who can write better than most authors and yet cannot for the life of him write a book.

The first-rate political journalist goes beyond this. He also has no time to solve the basic problems raised by events; but he can make pithy comments on the news of the week. He can referee party fights, and pick a brilliant critical staff. Such a one is born to edit a good weekly. As he has a week to turn in, he can make his leading article much less of a sham than it would be if he edited a daily and had only a few hours to turn in. A weekly paper in capable hands shews journalist political criticism at its best; but capable editors are very rare, because they must have ability enough and to spare for literature, and yet deliberately prefer journalism to literature as an occupation.

The moral is that the business of a journalist is news and not political philosophy. The dawning recognition of this limitation involves the disuse of the old-fashioned leading article in which the Fleet Street leader writer penned portentous nothings about Lord Palmerston and the Eastern Question (a foreign policy front article was *de rigueur*), and will yet involve the disuse of the sham political leader altogether; but this is not in the least because people do not like long articles and long sermons and long speeches on the platform and on the stage when they are interesting. What they cannot endure is the pompous oracle with nothing to say, the noodle's oration, the twaddler's pulpit platitude, and the ranter's tirade. They prefer snippets because the snippets are usually much better. But let anyone come along who can supply the real thing, and the public cannot have enough of it.

Note also, as to daily papers, that their offices are prisons in which the cleverest editor will soon lose touch with the world, being cut off as he is from political meetings, scientific lectures, concerts, and even dinners by the hours during which he has to work. A daily paper should have at least three editors, each having one day on and two days off. At present the papers are twenty years behind the times, because the editors are recluses. Lighthouse keepers with wireless sets know far more of what is going on in the world.

In estimating the influence of a paper it must be remembered that nobody but a lunatic or a railway traveller held up for two hours at a junction reads a newspaper through. I never read the sporting news; and those who do read it never dream of reading political articles. This is the secret of the ridiculous political ineffectiveness of the big circulations rightly insisted on by Mr. St. John Ervine.[3] When a bye-election comes we see some enormously circulated paper excitably putting its shirt on a candidate who is presently ignominiously defeated. To the readers of that paper politics are what the calculus is to a goose or what the Cup Ties are to me. They simply skip them.

This explains also my recollection of the beginning of the *Daily Mail*. As I remember it Northcliffe began by doing his best to make it a good paper on the old assumptions. It did not succeed. To lessen the strain of competition he bought a moderately popular evening paper, and put in an editor with instructions to kill it by filling it with trivialities and trash. The circulation of the victim immediately shot up to an unprecedented figure. Northcliffe took the hint, and set the *Daily Mail* to cater for people with

[3]Irish playwright, journalist, and dramatic critic of *The Observer*.

shallow views and trivial tastes, with the same result.[4] I do not blame him. Shallow and trivial are relative terms; and people who are (relatively) shallow and trivial must have their papers like other people. It was in that direction that there was room for enormous expansion; and the Northcliffe press expanded accordingly. It did not degrade its proper customers: on the contrary it probably informed and elevated them, though the highbrow spectator thought it was demoralizing them. When the *Daily Mail* theatre critic of that day[5] wrote long notices of my plays Northcliffe refused to print them on the ground that he was not going to advertise a damned Socialist. This was very amateurish journalism; but it proved that he was not politically unscrupulous, and that he was sufficiently up-to-date to know my opinions, thereby stamping himself as an exceptional genius in Fleet Street. He had the right qualities and the right ignorances and deficiencies for the occasion. Before the paper settled down it used to take my breath away by its blunderings, which were brought to my doorstep often enough by its young men. But it really did what all newspapers begin by professing to do: it supplied a want. It was not my want, nor Mr. Ervine's want, nor Miss Rebecca West's[6] want, nor Mr. Wickham Steed's want; but it was the want of many people to whom we are reluctantly obliged to concede the right to live; so let us put a smiling face on it and let it rip.

Yours, &c.,
G. Bernard Shaw

THAMES BRIDGES

[*The Times,* 3 May 1928.]

Sir,—The letter addressed to you by the London Society is really more than I can endure in silence. For 30 years I lived with Waterloo Bridge under my study windows; and my hatred of its

[4]Shaw appears to be in error here. Lord Northcliffe acquired the *Evening News* in 1894, two years before he founded the *Daily Mail,* which is described in the *DNB* as "an elaborately planned halfpenny morning newspaper, which was his greatest achievement in creative journalism and opened [a] new epoch in Fleet Street."

[5]Two theater critics, S. F. Brookfield and (from 1903) James Waters, shared the job in the early years of the *Daily Mail.*

[6]A pseudonym assumed by Cicily Fairfield, astute journalist, critic, and novelist, after the character in Ibsen's *Rosmersholm.*

incurable ugliness and fundamental wrongness increased during all that time. I now live with Charing Cross Bridge under my study windows; and every glance I give at it convinces me more completely that it is a model of what a river bridge should be.[1]

Waterloo Bridge, originally designed as a string of nine canal bridges end to end, is a causeway with holes in it, blocking the view of the river hopelessly, and all but blocking its navigation, which is no doubt its recommendation to people who have no eye for a great river, and so little sense of art that they can write or read themselves into believing that Rennie[2] was one of the great architects of the world. Charing Cross Bridge is a roadway through the air, supported by pillars which do not hide the river, and which reduce the obstruction of the waterway to a negligible minimum. And that, precisely, is what a Thames bridge should be.

All that is needed for Waterloo Bridge is a sufficiency of dynamite, followed by a law making it a capital offence to make perforated causeways across the Thames.

The enthusiasts who are clamouring for its preservation can then find a new subject in those quaint Dicky Doyle[3] fantasies, straight from the titlepage of *Punch*, and painted with all the gay English colours of the Queen of Diamonds, which have sprung up by our dull roadsides to supply us with petrol. The cry for painting them dark green and dirty citrine as a prelude to abolishing them and substituting untidy piles of cans will prove a congenial occupation for our amateur art lecturers.

Yours, &c.,
G. Bernard Shaw

[1]Shaw's London residence at 10 Adelphi Terrace overlooked the Thames Embankment. In 1927 he removed to Whitehall Court.

[2]John Rennie, a Scottish engineer, designed Waterloo, Southwark, and London bridges.

[3]Richard Doyle, artist and caricaturist, designed the famed cover of *Punch*.

DO APES MAKE WAR?

[Dr. Serge Voronov, a Russian physician specializing in "rejuvenation" treatments involving gland transplants from monkeys, visited England in 1928. Dr. Edward Bach, a well-known physician, deprecated Voronov's theories in a statement quoted in the *Daily News.* Shaw's response to this appeared in the same paper on 29 May 1928, ascribed to "Consul Junior," a performing chimpanzee well-known to visitors at the Regent's Park zoo.]

Sir,—On behalf of my fellow-guests of the Royal Zoological Society, I must protest warmly against the audacious statement by Dr. Edward Bach[1] reported in your issue of last Saturday.

He declares, first, that "when the glands of an ape are grafted on to a human being, the characteristics of an ape are bound also to be transplanted," and, second, that "characteristics possessed in a high degree by the anthropoid ape are cruelty and sensuality."

The implication is that apes are more cruel and sensual than human beings; and that an operation tending to raise a man to the level of an ape would make him crueller and more sensual instead of less so.

We apes are a patient and kindly race; but this is more than we can stand. Has any ape ever torn the glands from a living man to graft them upon another ape for the sake of a brief and unnatural extension of that ape's life?

Was Torquemada an ape? Were the Inquisition and the Star Chamber monkey houses? Were "Luke's iron crown and Damiens' bed of steel"[2] the work of apes?

Has it been necessary to found a Society for the Protection of Ape Children, as it has been for the protection of human children? Was the late war a war of apes or of men? Was poison gas a simian or a human invention?

[1]Author of *Chronic Disease: A Working Hypothesis* (1925) and *Heal Thyself* (1931), Bach practiced medicine in Los Angeles.

[2]Line 436 of Oliver Goldsmith's "The Traveller" (1764). Goldsmith is referring to two famous torture executions. The "iron crown" refers to the punishment of György Dosza, leader of a Hungarian peasant uprising of 1514: he was forced to sit on a red-hot iron throne and wear a red-hot iron crown; his brother, Luke (it appears Goldsmith confused the two), was obliged to drink Gyorgy's blood. Robert François Damiens was a French fanatic who attempted to assassinate Louis XV at Versailles on 5 January 1757, for which he was horribly tortured and then executed.

How can Dr. Bach mention the word cruelty in the presence of an ape without blushing? We, who have our brains burnt out ruthlessly in human scientists' laboratories, are reproached for cruelty by a human scientist!

And the moment chosen is one in which even the iron hearts of men have been moved to protest against the horrors of the Ouran Outang trade as reproducing all the barbarities of the old trade in human negroes! It is an insult not only to us, but to history and common sense.

We leave Dr. Voronoff to demonstrate to Dr. Bach how crudely unscientific is his fear—which ought to be a hope—that men can acquire the characteristics of apes by stealing their glands.

We ourselves are not concerned with what men call science except as mutilated victims; but we are concerned with experience. We perceive that vaccination and anti-toxin inoculation have given to men neither the virtues of the cow nor the qualities of the horse.

Man remains what he has always been: the cruellest of all the animals, and the most elaborately and fiendishly sensual. Let him presume no further on his grotesque resemblance to us: he will remain what he is in spite of all Dr. Voronoff's efforts to make a respectable ape of him.

Yours, &c.,
Consul Junior
The Monkey House,
Regent's Park.

WHERE ARE THE DEAD?

[A discussion of "the eternal question 'Where Are the Dead?' " in the *Daily News* elicited a flood of correspondence from readers, including a letter from Shaw, captioned "Shaw Butts In," published on 6 June 1928.]

Sir,—I am butting into this controversy, not with any intention of settling it, but merely to suggest a variation of its method. I have noticed that the point under discussion is stated as whether "we" are immortal, whether "the dead" survive, or whether "the soul" perishes with the body.

The style is the leading article style, the royal style, or the style of Italian and Highland politeness, in which the individual is not you but she, the she denoting an abstraction of honour and excellency,as to which anything is credible and arguable.

This gives immense scope to the discussion and elasticity to its terms; but it takes our feet off the earth so completely as to enable the controversialists to prove that there may be such a thing as immortality without producing the faintest conviction that any particular Tom, Dick or Harry, Susan, Sophronia or Jane ever was or will be immortal.

What I propose is that your next few contributors shall discuss, not whether "we" are immortal, or whether the soul is immortal, or whether the dead are still seeking lodgings in infinite space, but whether I, Bernard Shaw, am going to persist to all eternity in a universe utterly unable to get rid of me, no matter how desperately tired it may become of the Shavianismus, or how intolerably bored I may be by myself. Can there never be enough of me? Never too much of me?

Also, am I myself to have any say in the matter? Am I or am I not to be allowed to hand myself back to my creator, and say "Will you be so kind as to pulp this worn out article, and remanufacture it, if possible, without any of the glaring defects which have made it so troublesome to myself and others?"

For the guidance of those who will undertake this discussion, I had better say that as far as I know no person has ever doubted that I did not exist before October 1855.

Now the arguments that prove that I cannot have an end seem to me to prove equally that I cannot have had a beginning. Many persons think that it would have been better if I could not have had a beginning. But I most certainly had a beginning. The event can be precisely dated.

I may be a brick made from the eternal clay: in fact, people to whom I have injudiciously lent money have sometimes called me a brick; but the brick, though made of the clay, is not the clay.

Nobody but a lunatic would maintain that a brick existed before it was baked, or will still be a brick when it has crumbled into dust. Consequently, all the arguments that prove that my non-existence is impossible must be ruled out.

As a matter of fact, I have non-existed; and the discussion must address itself to proving or disproving that the non-existence that was possible before 1855 can never be possible again.

With this hint I leave your contributors to their stupendous theme: an eternity of G. B. S. Imagine it, if you can! Millions upon millions of Shaw plays! Billions upon billions of letters to the Press, intensely irritating to many worthy citizens! To be "a fellow of infinite jest," not, like poor Yorick, figuratively, but literally!

Chesterton, too. He also will be bombinating for ever and ever, world without end. And Wells and Belloc in sempiternal controversy! How if we became really convinced of it—not on paper, where anybody can be convinced of anything, but genuinely in the centre of our life—and immediately went off our chumps, as I for one most certainly should?

Frederick the Great was very far from being in all respects a trustworthy guide; but when he said to the soldier who was running away, "Confound you, do you want to live for ever?" he said a mouthful.[1]

One word more. Let no controversialist try to evade the point by assuring me that I shall survive, not as myself, but as the just man made perfect. He might as well tell me that the chariot of Pharaoh survives in the Rolls Royce.

When I use the word "I" (as I frequently do) I mean myself, with all my imperfections (if any) on my head, and my eyebrows turning up, and not down like those of my friend Mr. George Robey.[2] I mean the celebrated G. B. S., almost unbearably individualised, with his consciousness and his memories, his tricks and his manners, complete and exact in his GBEssence.

Otherwise the controversy is about nothing, and had better be dropped for some of the issues at the next General Election.

Yours, &c.,
G. Bernard Shaw

RELICS

[*The Observer*, 24 March 1929.]

Sir,—In an article under the heading "Books and MS. for Sale" in your issue of the 17th I figure as one of the authors whose waste-paper baskets are proving gold mines to dealers in relics.

Now it does not seem to me to matter a rap to the purchaser

[1]"Ihr Racker, wollt ihr ewig leben?"—addressed to the Guards at Kolin, 18 June 1757.

[2]A popular low comedian and music hall performer of the period, who was called "The Prime Minister of Mirth."

of a relic whether it is genuine or not, provided he believes it is. But it may matter a little to the person thus venerated. If, for instance, a jawbone were sold as having played an authentic part in my platform eloquence, I should like it to be a healthy jawbone, and not one bearing evidence of diseases from which I have never suffered. If a manuscript poem, I should like it to be fairly up to my literary mark, and not to imply amatory personal relations which I have never enjoyed.

May I, therefore, beg my worshippers not to scramble too blindly for alleged Shaviana? Otherwise they may share the fate of one of their number in America, who has just paid £300 for a copy of Locke's "Essay on the Human Understanding," advertised in the sale catalogue as profusely annotated and underlined by me.[1] Before somebody else pays £600, or £6,000, for this treasure, I had better state unequivocally that I have never read Locke's Essay, and that I never disfigure books by underlining them, my practice, whether as a reviewer or a student, being to make a very light dot in the margin with the tip of a pencil, and note the number of the page on the end paper. When I make a marginal note, which happens perhaps once in twenty-five years, I write the letter *s* and the letter *r* in the ordinary way, and not as printed. The facsimile in the sale catalogue shows that the annotator of Locke used the printed forms for both letters. In short, the £300 treasure is worth about threepence in the book market, though intrinsically it is worth as much as, or more than, a commentary by myself.

Let me hasten to explain that the case is one of carelessness and credulity, not of deliberate forgery. The name of the annotator is actually written by himself in the volume. It is Horace Townsend, of Derry, County Cork. He was my wife's father, and he distinguished himself at his university, where, apparently, he was examined in the university manner in Locke, and had to mug up that philosopher accordingly. Hence the underscored passages and the marginal notes in his handwriting, which, I repeat, nobody with the smallest claim to expertness could possibly mistake for mine.

A remnant of my wife's inheritance of the Derry library was sold when we left Adelphi-terrace [in July 1927] and were compelled to unload an intolerable burden of books. Evidently the

[1]Purchased for $1,500 by the Brick Row Book Shop in the Thomas Hatton sale at the American Art Association, New York, on 26 February 1929.

Locke volume went with the rest, which it would not have done had either my wife or myself ever opened it.

I am sorry to disillude its latest purchaser, and can only suggest by way of consolation that if the present rage for relics continues it may easily happen that when all my own autographs are appropriated those of my father-in-law may command equally extravagant prices. Meanwhile, will dealers and collectors be reasonably critical and not repeat a mistake which only the prevalent mania can excuse?

Yours, &c.,
G. Bernard Shaw

WHY NOT INVITE TROTSKY?

[*Daily Herald,* 26 July 1929.]

Sir,—It is evident that the real reason for denying Mr. Trotsky's right of way in these islands is that given by Mr. Stephen Sanders:[1] namely, that he might be assassinated by some White Russian, to say nothing of White Englishmen. All the other reasons given are ridiculous: they would equally justify the expulsion of Mr. Winston Churchill and Lord Birkenhead,[2] and the suppression of the *Daily Mail.*

The difficulty about this particular reason is that as anybody may be assassinated anywhere and at any time, it would justify the exclusion not only of Mr. Trotsky but of the entire human race.

It is clear that his risk of assassination in England is not as great as the risk run by General Sir Henry Wilson, who actually was assassinated,[3] and by all those who were in any way respon-

[1]Fabian Society secretary, 1914–20, and thereafter honorary treasurer. In 1929 he was Labour MP for Battersea and took part in the July parliamentary debates over the government's decision not to grant Leon Trotsky, the former Bolshevik leader expelled from the U.S.S.R. in January, a visa to enter England in order to establish a domicile.

[2]Frederick Edwin Smith, first Earl of Birkenhead, was a controversial advocate and debater in the House of Commons who had, in spite of his sympathies with the Northern Provinces, assisted in the Irish settlement of 1921.

[3]Shot dead outside his London house on 22 June 1922 by two ex-British Army Irish soldiers; Wilson, chief of the Imperial General Staff in 1918 and appointed field marshal in 1919, had urged a policy of coercion in Ireland.

sible for the Black and Tan campaign in Ireland, the Amritsar massacre in India, the Denshawai incident in Egypt, and all the White Terrors which have devastated Europe in the social convulsions which followed the war.[4]

If Mr. Trotsky is willing to take the risk, who has any right to gainsay him? Every public man in England, from the King downward, takes it every day.

I hope Mr. Trotsky will be not only allowed, but warmly invited, to favour us with his very interesting presence among us. His opinion of our British Communists—he is almost as frank as Lenin—would probably be extremely palatable to Mr. Churchill.

Yours, &c.,
G. Bernard Shaw

DEMOCRACY AND THE SOVIET SYSTEM

[The publication in *The Times* on 11 August 1931 of a letter from C. R. V. Coutts, commenting on a report on 6 August of Shaw's talk to the Independent Labour Party Summer School, led to a controversy in the correspondence columns between Shaw, Ernest Barker, and C. H. St. John Hornby. Shaw's I.L.P. talk was published in *Platform and Pulpit,* 1961, as "The Only Hope of the World"; the correspondence was privately printed by Hornby in a pamphlet in 1946. The text reproduced here is that of *The Times.*]

I

[13 August 1931.]

Sir,—Mr. Coutts[1] must not be in too great a hurry for absolute equality of individual dividend in the distribution of the national income in Russia. Though, as I have demonstrated (apparently unanswerably), we must all come to this at last if we are to have permanently stable civilizations instead of ephemeral ones, as at present, we certainly cannot do it without making up our minds as to the figure at which we can afford to stabilize. Russia can hardly be expected to stabilize at the figure represented

[4]I.e., in any instance in which foreign governments attempt to affect the policies of other governments through acts of violence.

[1]C. R. V. Coutts was manager and actuary of the Provident Mutual Life Assurance Association and a frequent commentator on economic matters.

by the share of an unskilled labourer to-day. She has never for a moment since the revolution pretended or attempted to do so. A professional section—including practical professors of political science like Lenin and Stalin, diplomatists like Litvinoff[2] and Sokolnikoff,[3] generals like Trotsky, educational and artistic culturists like Lunacharsky,[4] with the rank and file of professional routineers, and the organizers of industry and agriculture—would be impossible at such a level; and, boundless as British credulity seems to be as to nonsensical impossibilities resulting from Russian Communism, nobody can suppose that these eminent men cost their country as little as unskilled labourers. I should guess, roughly, that they cost at least as much as the salary of a British back-bench member of Parliament, plus their official expenses. To be equally comfortable personally and socially in England would cost about ten times that modest sum.

Put it, however, at £400 a year. Russia's business for the moment is to stabilize at that figure, and to "liquidate" (in Russia liquidation means extermination) the unskilled labourer as fast as she can afford to, substituting for him a comparatively skilled worker capable of using delicate machinery and educated to the point of understanding the Russian political system and intelligently professing the religion which form the constitution of modern Russia. Lenin postulated this much as indispensable to a Communist State. To achieve it, a professional standard of life and, consequently, a professional share of the national income will be needed. But the process will take time; and, meanwhile, it is economically impossible to pay unskilled labour much more than enough to keep it alive, whilst its quality is being improved; and it is imperatively necessary to attract foreign skilled labour and professional direction by adequate pecuniary inducements. Equality of income will be reached by levelling up, not by levelling down. And at no point can the process produce the monstrous absurdities of distribution inherent in our private property system.

May I take this opportunity of repeating in print my spoken

[2]Maxim M. Litvinov was commissar of foreign affairs, 1930–39; with Lunacharsky, he entertained Shaw and the Astors during their visit to the U.S.S.R. a fortnight earlier.

[3]G. Y. Sokolnikov was commissar for heavy industry until the "Radek trial" of January 1937.

[4]Anatoli Lunacharsky was former commissar for education.

warnings that Communist Russia must be taken seriously? Most of our comments so far have been beneath the level of ghost stories. Russian Communism is neither Anarchism nor Syndicalism, both of which are called, and even call themselves, Communism in England. It is Fabian Socialism. Lenin, who studied the histories of trade unionism and co-operation by Lord and Lady Passfield, *ci devant* Sidney and Beatrice Webb, would, if our Spiritualists could ascertain his wishes as to a suitable motto for his cenotaph, choose The Inevitability of Gradualness. This obvious fact now provokes a peal of both Russian and British laughter; but the reason is not that it is true (truth is always amusing when accurately stated), but that political power in Russia was transferred from Capitalism to Communism by a sudden and sanguinary political catastrophe, whereas the Fabians, knowing that such catastrophes cannot be made to order, have had to confine themselves to British constitutional possibilities. But if we have a violent Socialist revolution in England, however complete the slaughter and expropriation may be, gradualness will be as inevitable the day after as the day before; and this the nature of things has forced on Russia, though Trotsky laughs at me for being a Fabian, just as Engels used to. Lenin had to shoot the Anarchists and Syndicalists quite as assiduously as Trotsky, with the help of 30,000 officers from the Tsar's Army, shot the White counter-revolutionists. The U.S.S.R. is really a Union of Fabian Republics; and the sooner we realize that as such it has the support of our most serious political students, and might even (if so disposed) claim these islands as its ideological and scientific fatherland, the sooner we shall cease incurring the present enormous contempt of its able statesmen for our intelligence by speaking and writing as if it were a transient orgie of drunken buccaneers. Russia is what we call a great country, making a great experiment to which we ourselves have led up through many empirical but steadily converging paths. She is led by men of impressive ability and unprecedented freedom of thought, operating a system from which the disastrous frictions of our continual conflict of private interests, and the paralysing delays of our Parliamentary engines of opposition and obstruction, have been ruthlessly eliminated. If we intrigue against them, as they all very naturally suspect us of doing, in an attitude of moral and intellectual superiority, we shall add dangerously to the series of very unpleasant surprises they have already given us. Even those to whom Russia is the enemy had better not underrate her.

Russia has not only political and economic strength: she has also religious strength. The Russians have a creed in which they believe; and it is a catholic creed. The Russian is not trained to regard himself as a Russian: he is a member of the international proletariat, which includes the British proletariat. The Russian carpenter, mason, or ploughman has no hostility to the British carpenter, mason, or ploughman, and will not fight him as such. But if the British capitalist says to the Russian Communist "For one or both of us the hour is come," he will find himself confronted with a ruthless, disciplined, and well-armed fanatic; and the famous Marxian law of historical development will be on the side of the fanatic.

At this, too, the Russians laugh as heartily as they do at being called Fabians. They have got rid of religion, they tell us, pointing to churches which are as empty as our London City churches, though who will may worship in them, as I have seen for myself. To call them religious, and the Third International a Catholic Church, seems to them a Shavian joke, as it may seem to some of our Catholics a Shavian blasphemy.

I refer both sides to the saying of Father Keegan in *John Bull's Other Island:* "Every jest is an earnest in the womb of Time."[5]

Yours, &c.,
G. Bernard Shaw

II

[14 August 1931.]

Sir,—There was a famous "Master of the Sentences" in the Middle Ages. There is a famous "Master of the Paradoxes" in this. It was dangerous to disagree with the Master of the Sentences. It is perhaps still more dangerous to disagree with the Master of the Paradoxes. But there is an exhilaration in danger.

The first Paradox. If we are to have permanently stable civilizations, we must stabilize—say, in a given case, at £400 each a year. So stated, the paradox becomes a commonplace, or even a tautology. But I take it that Mr. Shaw means something more. He really means that such a civilization would not only be stable, but also worth having—not only enduring, but also beatifying. Stabil-

[5]In act IV of Shaw's play.

ity we should all concede—the stability of an ancient Egyptian monument: the stability of a frozen sea. But beatitude? Would a world which was all on the level of a *petite bourgeoisie*—all in long streets of small villas (or perhaps, if we follow the Russian example, in great dormitories and refectories); all in the still and quiet peace of the Passivity of Sameness—be a world of beatitude? Not for me. I have been a member of a large family living on an income which I will not mention, because it would seem fantastically small. I have been a member of a small family, living on an income which again I will not mention, because it is only a vanished dream—but anyhow it was a great deal larger. I am now—where I am. And it has been something—indeed it has been much—in my life that it has had range (upwards and downwards); as I believe that it is something in every man's life that it should have the chance of range. In the same way it is something, and indeed a great thing, in the life of a national society that it should have range. Of course the range has gone, and still goes, far too low: of course it goes, and still goes (not so much as it did, for the State is very active), far too high. But every member of a national society benefits by the fact that *it* has range; and he benefits because he becomes the member of a society which is diversified and alive with the Activity of Diversity which is the process of life itself. I passed by Buckingham Palace the other Sunday morning and mingled with a happy crowd trooping to watch a show in front of that great building. I thought, "Perhaps we are children, and perhaps we shall always be children (why not?); but what an amount of fun this brave, various world can give us!"

The second Paradox. "Practical professors of political science, like Lenin." That stings; or at any rate it excites a professional interest—though I hasten to admit that I am (happily) only a theoretical professor of the subject. I have always wondered whether political science was a science or an art; but I have read Lenin on "The State and Revolution," and I will willingly concede, for the sake of argument, that it is rather an art than a science. In that case it is an art of doing or producing something. What? It has generally been held that the something might be defined as the preservation of a system of law and order, which gave each man a foothold of rights on which he could try himself out and feel his range. That was hardly Lenin's object. His political art was *imprimis* the art of making a revolution. I prefer my old master Aristotle, who devoted a book or so of his Politics to the art of avoiding revolution.

The third Paradox. Russian Communism is Fabian Socialism. I fail before this paradox. I understand, indeed, that Russian Communism, *after having made a revolution,* is being gradual and evolutionary. Naturally, because when you are not making revolutions, you do go gradually and you do evolve. But I had always thought that the essence of Fabian Socialism was to pursue a gradual evolution, without making any revolution—to attain all that you could get by revolution, and even more, without the blood and the sweat and the agony. Was I wrong?

The fourth Paradox. "To call them religious, and the Third International a Catholic Church, seems to them a Shavian joke." But is it not a commonplace, and how can a commonplace be a Shavian joke? I have said the same thing again and again myself (proof positive of its nature); and so have we all. Any passionate revolution—political, like the French; economic, like the Russian—proceeds to climb the pulpit and arrogate the pontificality of universality. That is its terror. Religion is not politics; it is not even economics, and when either of the two becomes a religion it is an insurrection of the Titans.

They who have made but superficial studies in the natural history of the human mind have been taught to look on religious opinions as the only cause of enthusiastic zeal and sectarian propagation. But there is no doctrine whatever on which men can warm that is not capable of the very same effect.

For myself, I confess to a profound and sympathetic interest in the great attempt which is being made in Russia to try out a new social order. If only that order was not advocated as a religion, which it is not and cannot be; if only it had some room for diversity, as every true social order must have; if only it left some interstices and breathing-places for liberty, as every true social order should!

And now I bow my head. I remember—for I was educated at a college where it was a saying, or a reported saying, of our master—that the paradoxes of one generation became the commonplaces of the next. But that, I am sure, is a fate which will never befall *all* of Mr. Shaw's paradoxes. For some of them, I suspect, are not really paradoxes. They are paralogisms.

Your obedient servant,
Ernest Barker[6]

[6]Noted historian and professor of political science at Cambridge University.

III

[15 August 1931.]

Sir,—Mr. G. Bernard Shaw's interesting and temperate letter on the Soviet in your issue of August 13 prompts one to ask what, if any, is his political creed. I hope that I am not doing him an injustice when I say that he probably calls himself a democrat. But in singing the praises of the Russian form of government he says that Russia

> is led by men of impressive ability . . . operating a system from which the disastrous frictions of our continual conflict of private interests and the paralysing delays of our Parliamentary engines of opposition and obstruction have been ruthlessly eliminated.

Not even Mr. Shaw would maintain that these supermen have been chosen to govern by the suffrages of the majority of their fellow-countrymen, so that we must presume that, whatever he may label himself, he is at heart an aristocrat and in favour of an efficient and self-imposed oligarchy. We who have been brought up to respect so-called democracy and the principles embodied in successive Reform Bills have been led to believe that these same "Parliamentary engines," of which Mr. Shaw speaks so slightingly, are the safeguards of the rights and privileges of the people. Though I do not agree with Mr. Shaw's views about Russia, I confess that I am at one with him in his implied view that democracy in our huge modern States has proved itself a comparative failure. But are we to gather from Mr. Shaw's letter that he is equally in favour of Fascism? Both the Soviet and the Fascist systems are imposed upon the mass of the people by a minority and both honestly profess to govern for the good of the governed. A popular vote, fairly taken, would probably upset both of them. Are both, in Mr. Shaw's opinion, right systems, or one of them only, and, if so, which?

I am rather inclined to suspect that Mr. Shaw only approves of a self-imposed oligarchy so long as that oligarchy is imbued with his own Fabian principles. Some of us who are not Fabians are also in favour of the same form of government, but by men holding different views from those of Lenin or Stalin. The unfortunate thing is that all such Governments are by their opponents invidiously dubbed tyrannies, and, as such, are eventually overthrown; for no one seems to believe in benevolent tyrannies. And so, *faute de mieux,* we fall back upon democracy and the popular vote, which, though they may not give us good government, at least give us the semblance, if not the reality, of governing ourselves; and most people seem to prefer governing themselves badly to being governed well by somebody else.

It will be interesting to see whether those countries which continue to "govern themselves" will be able to hold their own in the struggle for existence against those countries which are governed by oligarchies unhampered by "Parliamentary engines of opposition and obstruction" and by all the conflicting interests, real or imaginary, of individuals. The Russian experiment must, as Mr. Shaw rightly says, be taken seriously, and it seems to a humble observer like myself that the Soviet system, so long as it can maintain itself and, in Mr. Shaw's words, compel unskilled labour to accept a wage "not much more than enough to keep it alive," is economically a great and growing menace to the standard of living of the workers in all civilized States and may cause incalculable harm from which it will take a generation to recover. It is hard to believe that the system will be permanent, for the simple reason that, however beneficent its ultimate aims may be, it does not rest upon the expressed will of the people but is in effect a slave-driving system, and this very fact is the essential postulate of its success. Fabian Socialism might be an ideal system if men and women were perfect. But in view of the fact that human nature is imperfect and will probably remain so, and that it prefers adventure to the dullness of a drab uniformity, it would seem that individualism, with all its manifest imperfections and regrettable inequalities, makes in the end for a higher, and in every sense better, standard of life in all classes than a Socialism under which the great majority of men and women can only be induced to put forth their best efforts by a ruthless system of compulsion.

Your obedient servant,
C. H. StJ. Hornby[7]

IV

[20 August 1931.]

Sir,—I am divided between a grateful reluctance to abuse your generosity in the matter of space and the courtesy which owes some reply to your correspondents Professor Ernest Barker and Mr. StJohn Hornby. I will be as brief as possible.

[7]Founder and director of the Ashendene Press.

For Professor Barker I can do nothing. He says, in effect, that he cannot be happy or feel free unless he has more money—or is it less?—than other people. Until he states exactly how much more or less will satisfy him, and why he should be considered more or less than other people, the discussion is in the air and could only waste your space.

Mr. StJohn Hornby endorses an alleged general preference of adventure to the dullness of a drab uniformity, and maintains that it makes in the end for a higher, and in every sense better, standard of life. It may be so; but it does not make for civilization. Perhaps Mr. Hornby would be higher, and in every sense better, as a Pirate King than as the famous artist-printer he is; but he would be hanged in England and get at least three years' imprisonment in Russia all the same. The dullness of a drab uniformity of honesty, security, employment, sanitation, and established expectation of behaviour is the price he must pay for the peaceful prosecution of such bloodless adventures as the Ashendene Press Dante.

As to Democracy in the sense of responsible government in the interests of the governed, and not in those of any class or individual, that is what we all now profess to aim at. As a method of securing it we rely on a routine of adult suffrage and party electioneering. The Russians rely on a system called the Dictatorship of the Proletariat, by which the proletariat is much more effectively dictated to for its own good than under our system. It is a voting system; but the only way to obtain a vote is to show an unselfish interest in public affairs and a competent knowledge of the Communist constitution. It is found as a matter of experience that any group of associated workers—in a factory or on a collective farm, for example—will naturally secrete one or two exceptional individuals with these qualifications, easily recognizable by their voluntarily adding public work to their industrial or agricultural tasks, and by their writings or uttered sentiments. When they have given their proofs they are called technically a cell (in the physiological sense) and are accreted by the Communist Party and devoted entirely to public work with no other hold on their new position than their power of making themselves indispensable by their efficiency. They finally constitute the whole Communist Party and elect the committees, with their chairmen and secretaries, by which the government of Russia is carried on. Part of their work is to persuade and educate the workers to form factory and farm committees for criticism and complaint, and to give them such powers of control as they are capable of exercising, so that the Government may always know where and when the shoe pinches. The trade unions have quite a large say in the appointment of managers and general ordering of the industries which immediately concern them.

That is Russia's solution of the democratic problem so far. Obviously it does solve it far more effectually than our system. It excludes from official authority and from the franchise the ignorant, the incompetent, the indifferent, the corrupt, and the pugnacious and politically incapable masses who, though they revel in a party fight or any other sort of fight, can make no intelligent use of their votes, and are the dupes of every interest that can afford the cost of gulling them. Responsibility to such innocents is no responsibility at all. The threat of it kept the oligarchic statesmen of the nineteenth century in order; but the execution of the threat has proved its worthlessness; and now politicians who spend Monday in making promises, Tuesday in breaking them, and Wednesday in being found out are re-elected by enthusiastic majorities on Saturday. Responsibility to the Communist Party is real responsibility: its members know their business and cannot be humbugged. They are all under skilled criticism, and have not to waste their time and means "nursing" constituencies. Failures and recreants can be promptly scrapped. Party opposition for the sake of opposition is punished as sabotage; and attempts to paralyse the Government by "constitutional safeguards" against tyrannies that have long lost their powers are not tolerated. Pious fictions like "the people's will," [or] "public opinion" are not admitted as excuses for *fainéant* statesmen. Liberty does not mean liberty to idle and spunge. The political machinery is built for immediate positive use; and it is powerful enough to break people who stick ramrods into it. In short, it is much more democratic than Parliament and party.

Nevertheless to an average member of Parliament it seems the negation of Democracy, because he or she would not be organically secreted as a governing cell, but, on the contrary, convulsively excreted into private trade or *kulak*[8] farming under a suspended sentence of "liquidation" which might be executed at any moment. To such Unsocialists the Russian system is the Reign of Ter-

[8]In the Soviet system, a term of contempt for the well-to-do farmer who resisted collectivization.

ror which keeps Mr. Churchill awake of nights. But the nation does not consist of average M.P.s; and their terrors do not trouble it. When Lady Astor[9] asked a worker on a communal farm why he had returned from capitalist America to Communist Russia, he replied that he returned because he wanted freedom of speech. "But," said Lady Astor, "surely you are not free to advocate Capitalism here?" "Certainly not," he replied, "but then I don't want to advocate Capitalism: I want to denounce it." No earnest Government tolerates sedition; but the sedition of the Capitalist west is the constitutionalism of the Communist east and *vice versa.* Democratic freedom of speech means the freedom of normal people to say what they want to say and not suffer from compulsory hypocrisy. Who can pretend that our employees have much of this freedom? Freedom to speak one's mind at the cost of getting the sack is hardly worth dying for.

Only when Communism is conceived, as by Mr. Churchill, to be a tyranny which all its subjects would denounce if they dared, does it seem reasonable to believe that the Russians must be gagged to prevent them from clamouring to be reduced to the condition of the inhabitants of this highly perplexed island.

Yours, &c.,
G. Bernard Shaw

V

[24 August 1931.]

Sir,—Mr. Bernard Shaw's entertaining reply to my letter really amounts to this—that he is, as I suspected, a whole-hearted advocate of oligarchy, or perhaps he would rather call it aristocracy, as a system of government. He has therefore answered my question, though not so clearly and straightforwardly as I could have wished. His line of argument, however, leads to the inevitable conclusion that he has no fundamental objection to Fascism as such. He merely prefers the Bolshevist to the Fascist because he approves of the policy of the former and not of the latter.

Are we not all, or at any rate the sensible ones among us, at heart rather like Mr. Shaw? We all hanker after an aristocracy, or

[9]Nancy Lady Astor, Conservative MP for Plymouth, 1919–45, who had visited the U.S.S.R. with Shaw and her husband, Waldorf 2nd Viscount Astor.

government by the best, but unfortunately we cannot agree upon a definition of "the best," or upon the right way to choose them; nor can we see eye to eye as to what form of policy, socialist or individualist, will secure the greatest happiness of the greatest number, which is presumably what we all ought to aim at.

I cannot help smiling at Mr. Shaw's idea of freedom of speech as exemplified by his story of Lady Astor's talk with the returned prodigal from the United States. Does he really call this freedom, or is he writing, to use a rather mixed metaphor, with his tongue in his cheek? And is it quite fair to say that our English workmen dare not speak their minds for fear of "getting the sack"? I think not.

Mr. Shaw states that in Russia attempts to paralyse the Government by constitutional safeguards against tyrannies that have long lost their power are not tolerated. But how about the existing tyranny of the Soviet? What safeguard has the mass of the people in Russia against that? Perhaps Mr. Shaw will tell us. I seem to see underlying his argument the excuses and defences of all the tyrants of all time.

Mr. Shaw's obvious predilection for a drastic limitation of the franchise, which is apparently his idea of true democracy, is one which many of us share. We all want to get rid of the "ignorant, the incompetent, the indifferent, the corrupt, and the pugnacious and politically incapable masses." But, in order to secure this desirable end, who is to make up the list of voters—Mr. Shaw or myself? Whichever of us it may ultimately be, he is sure to be branded as a tyrant. Perhaps, therefore, as joint conspirators against the common weal, as variously defined, we had better shake hands and turn to our ordinary avocations, he to the writing of books and I to the more humble but not less useful task of printing them. Then, should I ever become the English Mussolini, Mr. Shaw shall be my Censor of Plays. Should he, on the other hand, one day be the English Stalin, I shall hope to be his State Printer. I might even forgo the idea of becoming a Pirate King if I had the chance of being appointed Printer in Ordinary to Mr. Shaw.

Your obedient servant,
C. H. StJ. Hornby

MORAL DETACHMENT

[*Bernard Shaw,* a biography by Frank Harris completed by Shaw upon Harris's death in August 1931, was reviewed in *Time and Tide* by Lady Rhondda (the journal's editor) on 28 November 1931. In the course of her discussion, she argued that what made the book interesting was the letters Harris had received from Shaw on sexual subjects, "giving his own views and something of his own experience, and amazingly interesting letters they are." She went on to quote one of the letters at length, in which Shaw claimed that "I never associated sexual intercourse with delinquency. I associated it always with delight, and had no scruples nor remorses nor misgivings of conscience." Shaw immediately hedged this statement considerably and used it to justify his views of marriage as needing "other considerations" than sexual ones for "permanence and seriousness." Nonetheless, he drew the wrath of the Reverend Edward Lyttelton, D.D., former headmaster of Eton (1905–16), whose remarks appeared in the next week's issue. Lyttelton, observing that Shaw in his youth "was often guilty of what was once called sensual sin," cited the judgment that such revelations were "amazingly interesting," and wrongly assumed that the journal itself (and not its editor, in her capacity as reviewer) was giving Shaw's remarks "a still wider publicity without a hint of disapproval. Do you not thereby lead your readers to suppose that you too look upon sexual lawlessness with cool impartiality, not as wrong, but merely as a sign of the times?" An editorial note appended to Lyttelton's letter protested against the "sexual lawlessness" charge; the next week's issue—12 December—contained a longer rebuttal by Shaw himself.]

Sir,—I am the unfortunate and far from innocent cause of a pontifical reproach addressed to you by Dr. Lyttelton for reviewing a biography of me without improving the occasion by denouncing me as a sensual sinner. My guilt from Dr. Lyttelton's professional point of view is undeniable. I am openly living with a woman whom I call my wife, and who calls me her husband, though nothing in the nature of a marriage ceremony has passed between us except a declaration by a lay registrar who has no claim to the apostolic succession, and whose authority in such sacramental matters no Churchman can possibly recognize or countenance. Even if there were nothing else against me this would justify Dr. Lyttelton in refusing me communion, and in calling on the editor of *The Church Times,* if not of *Time and Tide* (for neither time nor tide is Churchbound), to anathematize me.

But how if the Pope were to write calling you to account for publishing, without any expression of abhorrence, a letter from a person who scandalizes half western Christendom by parading himself as a married priest with children of whom he has not even the grace to be ashamed? This is sensual sin complicated by the most abandoned impiety. If I am to be put in the pillory, then I insist on Dr. Lyttelton standing there beside me. It would be an honor for me; and I may venture to hope, on the strength of an acquaintance which on my side at least has been a cordial and appreciative one, that he might find my company quite endurable.

But why should we two sinners be singled out in this fashion? What about the guests at the recent Round Table.[1] Are brazen polygamists and damnable idolators to pass unrebuked because they are Indian princes? Is the heathen half-naked rebel and traitor to the British Empire, Mahatma Gandhi, to have his seditious utterances spread without a word of personal condemnation? Turn from the Round Table to the Cabinet. Is Mr. Samuel,[2] who would be described by the more fervent members of Dr. Lyttelton's faith in Germany as a Godmurderer, never to be repudiated as a denier of Christ's divinity? Is Mr. MacDonald to be allowed to make bishops when his soundness on the subject of prelacy has never been established? Turn to literature. Is Mr. Chesterton to be reviewed without the sternest reminders that in Dr. Lyttelton's judgment he is an Apostate? Turn to science. Are atheists, materialists, mechanists, determinists, in whose every line a contemptuous denial of the authority of the Church is implicit, to be quoted and reported at a length and with a prominence denied to archbishops without a word of exhortation to them to flee from the wrath to come?

I need not multiply examples. If Dr. Lyttelton really believes on reflection that any paper, even *The Church Times* or *The War Cry,*[3] could be edited on the lines he proposes to the Editor of *Time and Tide,* all I can say is, let him try. He will be reduced to absurdity by the first paragraph he has to pass for press. Like King George, who is Defender of The Faith in an empire in which Christians number only eleven per cent. (and a very mixed lot at that), he will be compelled to admit that The Faith is wider than

[1]The Round Table Conference on India's autonomy was held in London from September to December 1931. Mohandas Gandhi was one of the delegates.
[2]Herbert Louis Samuel was (for the second time) secretary of state for home affairs in 1931–32 and leader of the Liberal Party in the House of Commons.
[3]The journal of the Salvation Army.

the thirty-nine articles of his little sect, and that he must be civil to people who are outside his communion.

Dr. Lyttelton must not understand me as having made any confession of sensual sin. I strongly resent a qualification of my conduct which is, from my point of view, properly applicable only to practices which are personally repugnant to me, and to intemperances which are the curse of many marriages. My theory of sexual ethics may seem merely wicked to Dr. Lyttelton just as his theory of original sin seems to me merely psychopathic; but as I have never called on an editor to treat him as a delinquent on the strength of our differences I am surprised and somewhat wounded at his taking this course with me. I recognize the obligation to defend both my views and my conduct against his challenge, provided we come into the lists on equal terms and the challenge does not beg the question; but our relative situations are so well understood (at least Dr. Lyttelton's is) that I think it would be a great waste of time; and the upshot could not cancel our human and kindly relations nor make it a whit more possible for editors to boycott us or lecture us on the perils of our views to our souls.

I am entirely unrepentant; and from what I know of Dr. Lyttelton I feel fairly sure that he will not take it in bad part if I add, familiarly, that if he doesn't like it he must lump it.

Yours, &c.,
G. Bernard Shaw

A LESSON IN THE "OBVIOUS"

[*The Observer,* 1 May 1932]

Sir,—May I volunteer my assistance to my friend, Professor J. B. S. Haldane,[1] in the difficulties mentioned in the report of his lecture ["Hereditary Transmission of Acquired Characters"] at the Royal Institution, which, to my great grief, I was prevented from attending by pressing business[2] at Stratford-upon-Avon. I am, among other things, a man of science. For more than seventy years, ever since I began to "take notice," I have made observations and experiments in the spacious laboratory of the world

[1]Biologist, reader in biochemistry at Cambridge (1922–32), and author, with J. S. Huxley, of *Animal Biology* (1927).
[2]The opening of the New Shakespeare Theatre.

with a marvellous portable apparatus compactly arranged in my head. My procedure has been quite genuine: I have never manufactured evidence in a secret chamber, nor argued from events which I had myself brought about and could control. I have sought for knowledge and studied error, postulating intellectual integrity as an indispensable quality in scientific work, and accepting fully the discipline of having to discover honorable and kindly ways of satisfying my curiosity as being better for keeping my faculties in training than the fool's claim to revive benefit of clergy, and commit any villainy he pleases provided he does it in the character of a man of science.

Among my many experiments was one which I tried on Professor Haldane. It was not what is called a laboratory experiment: it was done, like most of my experiments, in public. Mr. Haldane had been speaking to a large audience,[3] and had used the expression "men of science" repeatedly. I put a question to him. "What is a man of science?" I said. "Or, to get down to living examples, am I a man of science and is my friend, Mr. H. G. Wells, one?"

Professor Haldane's reaction to the first example was, as I knew it would be, a pure reflex: one of that collection of reflexes the establishment of which as an easy substitute for cerebration is the main effect of our educational system. He dismissed the notion that I could be a man of science as a bad joke, exactly as he must have wagged his ankle if I had clipped him across the knee. But over Mr. Wells he hesitated; and his brain began to work slowly and doubtfully. He could not, he said, feel quite sure about Mr. Wells. He could not pretend to an accurate knowledge of Mr. Wells's personal history; but he thought he had heard or read somewhere that Mr. Wells had in his youth attended lectures at the Royal College of Science and perhaps performed some laboratory experiments there. If that were so he could not deny to Mr. Wells the title of Man of Science.

If this answer had been made by a certified mental defective it would have appeared natural enough. But Mr. Haldane is rather on the excessive side mentally. He has outstanding mental ability, literary talent, a sense of humour, and a genuine and hereditary interest in science. As such he has been the subject of a most instructive experiment. You take a man with all these natural ad-

[3]Haldane had delivered a lecture, "The Place of Science in Western Civilization," under the auspices of the Fabian Society, on 25 October 1928.

vantages. You put him through Eton and Oxford, and make him a Cambridge professor. And the result is the reply which I have just quoted. This single experiment would fully justify an intelligent government in dynamiting Eton and Oxford to smithereens with their teaching staffs inside, and establishing a special hospital for the study and treatment of stultifying conditional reflexes. If I were to state publicly that Mr. Wells's intellectual credit rests wholly on his brief juvenile contact with the Royal College of Science, and were then discovered trying to solve the problem of evolutionary inheritance by snipping the shoots off tomatoes, I should be superannuated as hopelessly Ga-ga.

Let me come to the rescue of the tomatoes and solve Professor Haldane's problem for him. He must first get the Garden of Eden out of his mind once for all, and advance as far as the year 1790 to the conception of evolution, introduced at that date by a poet (of sorts) who had never been at the Royal College of Science. I am not forgetting that Mr. Haldane has heard of evolution, and even believes that he has grasped it and assimilated it. But he has not really advanced so far. I have. The proof of this is very simple. Nobody who has grasped the concept of evolution ever talks afterwards of acquired habits as distinct from other habits. If evolution is true all habits whatsoever are acquired habits. The difference between the most elementary speck of protoplasm and a sea urchin, or between a sea urchin and a human boy, is an accumulation of acquired habits and organs for their exercise. This is so obvious that I am half ashamed of thinking it necessary to state it. It is an equally obvious condition of evolution that all habits are either heritable (when new) or inherited. Yet here we have Professor Haldane, one hundred and forty years after Erasmus Darwin, lecturing at the Royal Institution, with the gravity of a second Archbishop Ussher,[4] on acquired habits and characters as if there were any other sort of habits and characters, and, whilst assuming by university reflex that acquired habits cannot be inherited, consenting to leave the question open until he has snipped some more tomatoes. He could produce exactly the same effect on me at less expense by putting straws in his hair.

The only question that remained open after 1790 was the rate at which habits and characters are inherited. I studied this prob-

[4]James Ussher was best known for his promulgation of a scheme of Biblical chronology that establishes 4004 B.C. as the time of creation.

lem scientifically in 1895 by making an experiment with a suitable apparatus. Not being under the influence of Dr. Watts as Mr. Haldane still is, it did not occur to me to go to the ant, the bee, or the tomato to learn from them something about myself.[5] There was no reason on earth why I should not learn about myself first hand. So I acquired a habit: the habit of balancing myself on a bar moving rapidly forward on two wheels tracking in tandem, the front wheel being deflectable. This feat was entirely impossible at first, and remained so for several days without the slightest improvement. Then one day it became so completely possible and automatic that I have never had to think about it since. The change from impossibility to facility was instantaneous and apparently miraculous, proving that my resolute purpose had started some process of organic creation which had consummated itself at the apparently miraculous moment and left me with a new faculty. I had by the acquirement of a new habit evolved from a pedestrian into a bicyclist.

All habits being heritable in the concept of evolution, I knew that the bicycling habit must be heritable. But in 1895 men had been bicycling for a quarter of a century; and it was already clear that their children were not born bicyclists. The son of a bicyclist was not perceptibly better able to balance himself on a bicycle than his father had been before bicycles were invented. However, this presented no great difficulty. The world was full of experiments on the subject for anyone with a mind sufficiently scientific to observe them. For instance, a moustache is a habit; but the son of Victor Emmanuel[6] was not born with an enormous moustache: he had to wait twenty years before he inherited it, although he had inherited other habits, such as breathing, yelling, suctional drinking, performing complicated chemical processes of digestion and excretion, and creating (called growing), all at or before birth, which meant that he had formed these habits and created the organs for their exercise within a period of nine months. Evidently, then, the process of inheritance is a timed process, and the timing is variable. The embryologists have established the fact that the accelerations are even more curious and startling than the retardations; for the habit of inheritance is in itself so inveterate that the

[5]Shaw is making a sly reference here to the Reverend Isaac Watts's *Divine Songs for Children,* 1715.
[6]King of Italy, 1900–46.

living subject cannot get rid of a habit even when it has to be discarded to allow of higher developments. But the process of acquiring and discarding can be accelerated to such a degree that the subject can at least acquire and discard an obsolete habit not merely in prenatal months, but later on presumably in prenatal moments.

The conclusion is clear to anyone whose mind is unhampered by reflexes manufactured at the public schools and universities on a foundation of Genesis plus the poems of Dr. Watts. A new habit is inherited at first by imperceptible increments, and the time rate of this process accelerates until finally the date at which the fully developed habit is completely inherited comes within the span of the subject's lifetime, and occurs earlier and earlier until it becomes prenatal. I need not elaborate this here. It gets rid of all the difficulties bothering Professor Haldane and wasting his time. It needs no tomatoes, only brains, and freedom from university reflexes and seventeenth-century theology.

I explained the matter publicly in a lecture on Darwin which I read at the beginning of the century to the same Society[7] to which Mr. Haldane made his answer about Mr. Wells. It is dealt with in my biological plays, especially in the preface to "Back to Methuselah," which is not a university text-book, and may therefore be relied on as an up-to-date scientific document. For some reason it is intensely annoying to the pseudo-scientists who have been for nearly half a century desperately struggling to banish mind from the universe (as that very remarkable scientist Samuel Butler put it); but that is a credential rather than an objection.

As a mathematician Professor Haldane will find the study of the accelerations interesting, especially now that Sir Arbuthnot Lane[8] has pointed out that skeletal changes which until quite recently were supposed to require millions of years for their evolution are as a matter of fact produced by functional adaptation in less than a couple of dozen months.

It is to be borne in mind that a heritable habit must be voluntarily acquired. A man can acquire a habit of murdering but not of being hanged. Professor Haldane's tomatoes will never acquire a habit of having their shoots snipped off. Traumatic mutilations

[7]Fabian Society, 23 March 1906.

[8]Well-known surgeon and advocate of social medicine, author of *New Health for Everyman* (1932) and several papers on anatomy.

are not the work of the evolutionary appetite, and therefore cannot produce evolution. Professor Haldane should study the evolutionary appetite.

Yours, &c.,
G. Bernard Shaw

NOT HYPNOTISED BY STALIN

[*Daily Express,* 25 June 1932.]

Sir,—Nobody seems, so far, to have taken in the full significance of Mr. Westgarth's[1] statement that when I visited Russia last year I saw, not the real Russia, but an elaborate show staged for my special benefit, like the operatic Russia staged for Catharine II. by Patiomkin[2] when she took a holiday tour through her dominions.

If Mr. Westgarth is right, then all I can say is that the Soviet Government has achieved a feat of which no other Government in the world is capable.

Just think of it!

According to Mr. Westgarth, the Russian Government, at a fortnight's notice (for my journey was unpremeditated), built two enormous cities, presumably of papier maché and painted canvas, each swarming with millions of inhabitants, all specially washed, dressed, and fed up for me; and passed off these two scenic impostures on me as Moscow and Petersburg (the name Leningrad is inappropriate and has caught on very imperfectly).

And this had to be done so thoroughly to avoid detection that I could not stop my motor-car without warning to step unexpectedly into a church or police court, or take a babies' crèche by surprise with Lady Astor, without finding in full swing a service of the Greek church, a couple of trials, and a supply of specially fattened babies ready for me.

But this was not all. I did roughly about fifty hours of day-

[1]J. R. Westgarth, a British engineer, who had worked for more than two years in the U.S.S.R., had recently written an article published in the *Daily Express* in which he suggested that Shaw had been deceived by the Soviet system of conducting carefully stage-managed tours for visiting VIPs.

[2]Grigori Patiomkin [Potemkin], Russian statesman and military leader, was chief court favorite of Catherine II.

light railway travelling in Russia. The Russian Government, to delude me, had to provide at all the stops, not only flourishing provincial towns and cities and villages, but crowds of sham passengers chaffering with sham peasants selling food, sham bystanders, and sham children, to mask the starvation and squalor of the real Russia.

When I say that I was completely taken in, it must be remembered that as a professional playwright of forty years' experience, I am an expert in theatrical illusion, and know all the tricks of the actor, scenepainter, property man, and producer inside and out.

To have deceived me is a triumph of Soviet administration.

One trick in particular completely beats me; and Mr. Westgarth makes no attempt to explain it. How did the Russian Government, with the Russian children and adults all starving, manage to fatten so many up for me at such short notice?

I did not see a single under-nourished person in Russia, young or old. Were they padded? Were their hollow cheeks distended by pieces of Indiarubber inside?

If this is the explanation of the absence of emaciation in the clothed people in the streets, how about the many hundreds whom I saw every day in Moscow at the centre of repose and culture, sun bathing and swimming in Lido costumes which revealed every possible degree of plumpness; or in the country as the train crossed the rivers, where the Soviet had tastefully introduced groups of figures, adult and juvenile, who were no doubt intended to be "noble and nude and antique," and were certainly nude and robustly muscular.

The children who were specially shown to me may have been washed and dressed up for the occasion, as Mr. Westgarth declares they were; but the boys had nothing on but the most exiguous bathing slips, and there was no getting over the fact that they had plenty of tallow on their ribs. The girls' ribs were not visible; but they could have lived for a fortnight on the chubbiness of their calves.

I photographed them, and my photographs, which were published in *Nash's Magazine* here,[3] are not in the least like the terri-

[3]Shaw's article "Touring in Russia," illustrated by himself, was published in *Nash's—Pall Mall Magazine,* London, January 1932, and in the same month as "What G. B. S. Found in Red Russia" in *Cosmopolitan,* New York, but with the substitution of photographs by Margaret Bourke-White.

ble photographs of English starved children which are sent to me every year with appeals for help from the English charities which have sprung up to rescue such little unfortunates from the worst horrors of Western capitalism and democracy.

How was it done? Is there a Red Magic that can produce illusions that are beyond the utmost art of Elstree[4] and Hollywood?

The most plausible explanation is that I was hypnotised, and only imagined what I saw. And yet there are difficulties in accepting even this.

I cannot think that Stalin hypnotised me; for I saw him only at the very last moment before I left; and as he is rather a busy man he can hardly have had time to pursue me in disguise through the streets making secret passes at me all the time I was there.

It is true that there may have been relays of hidden hypnotists at work; but if so, why did they not make a better show for me, since the utmost prosperity and magnificence would have cost them no more than commonplace shabbiness.

They might at least have made all the women beautiful and all the men's boots look new. They might have repainted all the shops. They need not have grotesquely overcrowded the trams nor put so many people to sleep in the same room. But perhaps that was only their artfulness, lest I should overdo my praises of the New Dispensation.

I am sorry for Mr. Westgarth. It is clearly not his fault that when he returned from Russia he found a literary market greedy for tales of starvation, squalor, and slavery in Russia.

Yet when we are forced to choose between believing that what I saw was either a colossally expensive theatrical imposture or a hypnotic delusion, and believing that Mr. Westgarth is simply telling our anti-Communist editors what they want and are ready to pay for, I am afraid some of the more cynical of your readers will take the line of least resistance.

For my own part, I am inclined to suspect that Mr. Westgarth's standards are so high that what seemed to my modest scale of expectation an enviably promising state of things seemed to him too miserable to be endured.

What he must feel as he contemplates the hard times we are

[4]British film studio, visited by Shaw two weeks earlier to witness location scenes for the film version of his *Arms and the Man*.

passing through in this unhappy country is something that no feeling heart can contemplate without tears.

Yours, &c.,
G. Bernard Shaw

INSANITY AND THE LAW

[Paul Doumer, president of France, was assassinated on 7 May 1932 by a Russian fanatic, Paul Gorgulov, who was convicted and guillotined for the crime. Shaw's letter of 15 September 1932 to *The Times,* declined by the editor, survives in the archive of that newspaper, unpublished until now.]

Sir,—Now that the unpleasant but necessary business of liquidating the murderer of President Doumer has been disposed of and is no longer *sub judice,* had we not better reflect awhile on the wild absurdity of the legal process by which he was brought to the guillotine, as the same absurdity would have been forced on us by our English law if the case had occurred here?

Gorgouloff was a madman of the most dangerous kind. His insanity was so obvious and its results so tragic that to doubt or question it would be in itself an act of extravagant lunacy. He could have been kept alive in a city only as a tiger is kept alive in Regent's Park; and, as he would have been of no legitimate interest as an exhibition, there would have been no excuse for wasting valuable lives in caging and keeping him. There was every possible reasonable ground for liquidating him, and none whatever for preserving him.

Yet the only way to achieve his destruction legally was by establishing the monstrous fiction that he was a sane man. His trial resolved itself into a struggle by his advocates to prove the perfectly obvious fact that he was mad, as against the efforts of the prosecution to make him out as sane as George Washington. As it was clearly necessary to guillotine him, the court had no alternative but to outrage commonsense by adopting the George Washington view. Surely this *reductio ad absurdum* of the inviolability of lunatics under our law calls for a change. There is not, and never can be, any question of punishing lunatics for their mischievous actions. We do not punish mad dogs for biting us: we simply put an end to their existence without giving ourselves any moral airs about it. What would be thought of us if we solemnly declared that a mad dog is sacred, and must be carefully preserved and tended in a special dogs' home, and that only sane dogs should be shot?

If we cannot yet get completely rid of our superstitions of expiatory punishment, purifying sacrifice, sanctity of madmen, retribution and all the rest of it, and inscribe "Judge not that ye be not judged" and "Vengeance is mine, saith the Lord" over our criminal courts, at least we can devise some honester way of getting rid of dangerous lunatics and hopeless undesirables than pretending that they are sane, or charging them with the latest murder and hanging them on absurdly hypothetical evidence. Lunatics are quite well aware of their queer privilege: "They can't kill *us*" is the word at Broadmoor. It is quite easy to find out how to simulate madness by a few simple and effortless tricks which are accepted as conclusive symptoms. If lunatics knew that though privileged to commit crimes, they were liable to polite but ruthless liquidation as intolerable public nuisances, they would be more careful about their conduct than other people instead of less.

We are now in the midst of an epidemic of crime. The police are demanding enlarged powers without knowing exactly what powers to demand; for they know that increased severity of punishment, which the uninstructed public always clamors for in a panic, is quite useless without increased certainty of detection, which is the only really effective deterrent. Every day they take a string of mischievous people to prison, only to find a string of equally mischievous people being let out to start mischief making again. I suggest that if the police could report people as being simply undesirable citizens, and thereby compel a careful enquiry into the truth of the report, with a possibility of the enquiry ending in the painless disappearance of its subject from the list of existing nuisances, our sense of social responsibility would be greatly heightened, and our conduct correspondingly improved. The execution of Gorgouloff is only a glaring proof that if we do not deal with such people in straight ways circumstances will compel us to do it in crooked ones.

Yours truly,
G. Bernard Shaw

THE PEACE LETTER

[The publication of Lord Riddell's *War Diary* in the summer of 1933 renewed the controversy about the late Lord Lansdowne's "Peace Letter," a proposal of peace published in the *Daily Telegraph* on 29 November 1917 after *The Times* had refused it. It had caused an immediate furor, recalled in *The Times* in August 1933 by various correspondents, who quarreled over whether or not Lord Balfour, then foreign minister, had advance knowledge of the proposal. Lansdowne, a former foreign secretary and viceroy of India, had argued that a peace might be negotiated if Germany understood the limits of British war aims; he was immediately denounced as a German sympathizer or worse. Shaw entered the fray in a letter published in the *Daily Telegraph* on 24 August 1933.]

Sir,—May I give expression to a sense of stupefaction induced by the recent correspondence in *The Times* about Lord Lansdowne, which I feel sure many of your readers must share? In 1917 he was the foremost of our Elder Statesmen on the side of our old monarchical order.

In the face of the passionate war fury of that dreadful time, he alone had the prescience and the courage to warn his party to stop the war on pain of pulling down its own house about its ears. How right he was from the point of view of his own party the world now knows only too well.

The only reward he got was a howl of execration from his own people, led by a then very militant Pacifist with a protest against "a German Peace Offensive,"[1] and an indignant refusal to publish his letter from *The Times*. It was then that the *Daily Telegraph* came to the rescue and gave Lord Lansdowne the publicity to which he was entitled by his eminence as a statesman and by the supreme importance of his warning.

Think of it! Three empires were at stake. Monarchy as the predominant form of government in the civilised world was at stake. The throne of Peter the Great has fallen far more abjectly and instantly than the throne of Henri Quatre and Le Roi Soleil in the eighteenth century. The Liberal provisional Government

[1]This appears to be an exaggerated allusion to Lord Robert Cecil (later first Viscount Cecil of Chelwood), parliamentary undersecretary for foreign affairs 1915–16, who wrote his own memorandum in partial contradiction to Lansdowne's 1916 private memorandum to the prime minister (Asquith) a year before his "peace letter" was published. Cecil, who was active in the creation of the League of Nations, was a pacifist who won the Nobel Peace Prize for 1937.

which succeeded it had crashed at a kick from Lenin, as if Lilburne the Leveller[2] had superseded Cromwell.

The Germans were beaten, and knew it; Alsace and Lorraine were to be had for the asking. The Apostolic Empire was cracking; and the Hohenzollerns were evidently done for if the war went on.

Lord Lansdowne saw all this, and knew what it meant for his party and his Cause. He gave the order to Cease Firing. It was disregarded; and he died, as fools thought, in disgrace.

And now, instead of expiating their folly by building a noble monument to him, they can do nothing for his name but squabble in the columns of the unrepentant *Times* as to whether he should have asked Lord Balfour's leave to open his mouth. And it is again left to the *Daily Telegraph* to show some public sense of the values involved.

Lord Lansdowne did not share my political opinions; but I feel bound to voice the feelings of those who, like myself, cannot acquiesce silently in so ridiculous an injustice to the memory of the wisest of my Conservative contemporaries.

Yours, &c.,
G. Bernard Shaw

THE MENACE OF JAPAN

[On 13 October 1933, the *Daily Dispatch* had published Sidney Campion's ostensible interview with Shaw in which Shaw is alleged to have attacked the Japanese code of *Kodo* (defined by the paper as "blind worship of everything Japanese" but more exactly meaning "blind or fanatical worship of the Imperial rule"), and expounded on the menace of the *Kodo* of all the dangerously armed Western powers. Shaw replied in a letter published in the *Daily Dispatch* on 17 October.]

Sir,—In your issue of the 13th you have featured certain utterances of mine under the heading of an interview with Mr. Sidney Campion.[1] The impression conveyed by this report is dangerously misleading, as readers unacquainted with the facts

[2]John Lilburne was a leading Leveller—a radical republican group in Cromwell's time that wanted to extend the franchise to "freeborn Englishmen."
[1]At this time a member of the Parliamentary Press Gallery staff, Campion's career encompassed the law, education, sculpting, and journalism.

must have inferred from it that I had made use of your columns to raise an unprovoked call to arms against Japan.

What actually happened was that I, with several other journalists, accepted an invitation to meet Professor O'Conroy[2] to discuss his book *The Menace of Japan* with him. What I said was not addressed to any particular newspaper or journalist.

The gist of my speech was that what Professor O'Conroy singles out as the Menace of Japan is equally the menace of all the heavily armed Western Powers; that British Kodo, American Kodo, French Kodo, Italian Kodo, and German Kodo are precisely the same poison as Japanese Kodo; that the conflict of them threatens the existence of civilisation; and—coming to a specific instance—that General Araki (the live wire in the Japanese battery, whose very genial and frank reception of myself left me with a most friendly personal impression),[3] in the Kodo-militarist speeches of his quoted by Professor O'Conroy, was echoing the sentiments of the late Field Marshal Lord Roberts when he was warning us that we must fight Germany. Within the last fortnight we have had broadcasts from Mr. Stanley Baldwin and Mr. Bryant on the English national character and destiny[4] which General Araki will probably adapt for Japanese use, quite unconsciously, before the end of the month.

I hastened to add, and now I repeat, that the only country in which there is the least excuse for Kodo is Germany; as everyone who is capable of seeing both sides of a political situation will admit that if we had been defeated in the war of 1914–18, and the victorious empires were treating us as the Allies are treating Germany, we should stuff every English child old enough to distinguish the right end of a gun from the wrong one with implacable Kodo until we were again our own master.

Yours, &c.,
G. Bernard Shaw

[2]Taid O'Conroy had lived in Japan for fifteen years, teaching at Keio University in Tokyo as well as at the Imperial Naval Staff College. *The Menace of Japan* had just been published.

[3]Shaw had taken tea with General Sadao Araki, the Japanese minister of war, during a visit to Tokyo on 7 March 1932.

[4]Baldwin, who had been prime minister twice, was presently lord president of the council in Ramsay MacDonald's government; Sir Arthur Bryant, the historian, had spoken on "What Is Our National Character?" on 2 October.

B.B.C. PRONUNCIATION

I

[*The Times*, 2 January 1934.]

Sir,—As chairman of the committee[1] which in the discharge of its frightful responsibility for advising the B.B.C. on the subject of spoken English has incurred your censure as it has incurred everyone else's, may I mention a few circumstances which will help towards the formation of a reasonable judgment of our proceedings?

1. All the members of the committee[2] speak presentably: that is, they are all eligible, as far as their speech is concerned, for the judicial bench, the cathedral pulpit, or the throne.

2. No two of them pronounce the same word in the English language alike.

3. They are quite frequently obliged to decide unanimously in favour of a pronunciation which they would rather die than use themselves in their private lives.

4. As they work with all the leading dictionaries before them they are free from the illusion that these works are either unanimous or up-to-date in a world of rapidly changing usage.

5. They are sufficiently familiar with the works of Chaucer to feel sincerely sorry that the lovely quadrisyllable Christemasse, the tryisyllable neighebore, and the disyllable freendes should have decayed into krissmus, naybr, and frens. We should like to vary the hackneyed set of rhymes to forever by the Shakespearian persever; and we would all, if we dared, slay any actress who, as Cleopatra, would dare degrade a noble line by calling her country's high pyramides pirramids. But if we recommended these pronunciations to the announcers they would, in the unusual event of their paying any attention to our notions, gravely mislead the millions of listeners who take them as models of current speech usage.

6. We are not a cockney committee. We are quite aware that Conduit Street is known in the West End as Cundit Street. Else-

[1]The B.B.C. Advisory Committee on Spoken English, of which Shaw was a member from 1926 and chairman from 1930 to 1937.

[2]Among the twenty-one members of the committee at this time were Lascelles Abercrombie, Lady Cynthia Asquith, Lord David Cecil, Sir Johnston Forbes Robertson, Daniel Jones, Rose Macaulay, and I. A. Richards.

where such a pronunciation is as unintelligible as it is incorrect. We have to dictate a pronunciation that cannot be mistaken, and abide the resultant cockney raillery as best we can.

7. Wireless and the telephone have created a necessity for a fully and clearly articulated spoken English quite different from the lazy vernacular that is called modd'ninglish. We have to get rid not only of imperfect pronunciations but of ambiguous ones. Ambiguity is largely caused by our English habit of attacking the first syllable and sacrificing the second, with the result that many words beginning with prefixes such as ex or dis sound too much alike. This usage claims to be correct; but common sense and euphony are often against it; and it is questionable whether in such cases it is general enough to be accepted as authentic usage. Superior persons stress the first syllable in dissputable, labratory, ecksmplary, desspicable, &c.; and we, being superior persons, talk like that; but as many ordinary and quite respectable people say dispūtable, laborratory, exemmplary, and despickable, we are by no means bound to come down on the side of the pretentious pronunciation if the popular alternative is less likely to be confused with other words by the human species called listeners-in.

We have to consider sonority also. The short i is much less effective than the long one; and the disturbance I created in the United States last April by broadcasting privvacy instead of prywacy was justified. Issolate is a highly superior pronunciation; and wind (rhyming to tinned) is considered more elegant in some quarters than wynd; so that we get the common blunders of trist (rhyming to fist) for tryst and Rozzalind for Rosalynde; but we recommend the long i to the announcers for the sake of sonority.

Some common pronunciations have to be rejected as unbearably ugly. An announcer who pronounced decadent and sonorous as dekkadent and sonnerus would provoke Providence to strike him dumb.

The worst obstacle to our popularity as a committee is the general English conviction that to correct a man's pronunciation is to imply that he is no gentleman. Let me explain therefore that we do not correct anyone's pronunciation unless it is positively criminal. When we recommend an announcer to pronounce disputable with the stress on the second syllable we are neither inciting him to an ungentlemanly action nor insinuating that those who put the stress on the first ought to be ashamed of themselves. We are simply expressing our decision that for the purposes and under the circumstances of the new art of broadcasting the second syllable stress is the more effective.

Yours, &c.,
G. Bernard Shaw,
Chairman

II

[*The Times,* 25 January 1934.]

Sir,—The correspondence on the subject of B.B.C. pronunciation has proved very amply that the pronunciation of the English language is not the simple matter, perfectly agreed among gentlemen, that most of your correspondents supposed.

Last Monday two broadcasters discoursed on literature and economics.[3] They used the words combated and inextricable respectively. I, who am just as good an authority on pronunciation as either of them, usually say cumbited and ineckstricably. They, being just as good authorities as I, said cmbatted (rhyming to fatted) and inixtrickably. Clearly neither they nor I can claim usage on our side. As cumbited is easily mistaken when atmospherics are raging for comforted I think I shall say cmbatted when next I broadcast, unless indeed I shirk the word I am no longer quite sure about. As to the other, go as you please. There are thousands of words which have no usage because they are not very often used. Thoughtless speakers always bounce at the first syllable and stress it: others have an instinct for the characteristic syllable. Sometimes the first syllable happens fortunately to be the characteristic one: only children say ludickrus instead of loodicrous. But what about exemplary?

My grandfather, an educated country gentleman, occasionally swore by the virtue of his oath. He said: "Be the varchew o' me oath!" He called lip salve sawve. The actors of his time called lute lewt and flute flewt; and their be and me for by and my lasted well into my own day. I can even remember when obleege was heard from old people as well as varchew; but the spelling beat that, as it always does in the long run except when the word, like would or could, is in continual use. Pronunciations are always obsolescing and changing. If the B.B.C. had existed a hundred years ago it

[3]On Monday, 22 January, the literary offering was a reading of part of Byron's *Childe Harold,* by Sheila Barrett; Commander Stephen King-Hall spoke on "Economics in a Changing World."

would have been reviled for recommending vertew and oblyge instead of varchew and obleege. To-day it has to deal with America, which would have it pronounce necessarily neseserrily, rhyming to merrily.

Then there is the trouble about accents. In choosing an announcer regard must be had to the psychological effect of his accent. An Oxford accent is considered by many graduates of that University to be the perfection of correct English; but unfortunately over large and densely populated districts of Great Britain it irritates some listeners to the point of switching off, and infuriates others so much that they smash their wireless sets because they cannot smash the Oxonian. The best English to-day is literally the King's English. Like his Royal grandmother before him King George is the best speaker in his realm; and his broadcasts are astonishingly effective in creating loyalty. If he delivered a single broadcast in an Oxford accent his people would rise up that very day and proclaim a republic.

How little the situation is appreciated is shown by the ridiculous extent to which this correspondence has been occupied with the trivial case of Conduit Street. The name of that street is either grossly misspelt or grossly mispronounced: I do not know which. I have no doubt that if one of the new streets made by the London University and the British Museum be appropriately named Pundit Street it will be solemnly labelled Ponduit Street. What most of those who are supersensitive on the subject seem to mean is that if the name of a street is mispronounced by the inhabitants that name shall always be so mispronounced in every possible context. Let me remind them that Conduit Street is not the only street in London. There is in the City an ancient thoroughfare labelled Ave Maria Lane. The more cultivated of its denizens call it Aivmeryer Lane, the less fastidious Hivemerawyer Line. Are we of the B.B.C. Committee expected to instruct the announcers to say: "Miss Jenny Lind will now sing a group of songs beginning with Schubert's Aivmeryer"? Are we to beg the songstress to adapt that pronunciation as best she can to Schubert's notes?

These are the questions that go over such bumptious novices as my friend Mr. Edward Marsh[4] like a steam-roller. They have long since left me as I remain at present,

In extreme humility,
G. Bernard Shaw

[4]Poet, biographer, and editor, and also a member of the Advisory Committee.

THE CORONATION

[*Time and Tide,* 22 May 1937.]

Sir,—Now that the rejoicings are over,[1] and I cannot be a spoilsport, I may be allowed to recur to a proposal of mine that has never met with any public support: that is, to institute a Society for the Prevention of Cruelty to Royal Personages.

Of all the instruments of torture employed the Coronation would be the worst if it were not so seldom employed. Besides, as its physical discomforts are voluntarily shared with every possible aggravation by so many of the monarch's subjects, who could see it all painlessly in the cinema for a few pence, there must be some fun in it which does not appeal to me. I therefore leave it to others to deal with the doctor's bill, which must be considerable, and with the sanitary problems involved, which seem to me insoluble. I will confine myself to those features of the Coronation of which the postulant for the monarchy is the sole victim.

I cannot blame that sturdy Protestant, Henri Quatre, for deciding that *"Paris valait bien une Messe."*[2] He was at war; and Paris was a key position. That many sceptics, from Voltaire to James Connolly,[3] have had to do likewise to avoid consequences which the priests were able and bound to enforce, is excusable. Professions made under duress do not count.

But the Coronation ritual has no such justification. On the contrary it is either offensive or ridiculous to an enormous majority of the inhabitants of the Empire. *The Times,* which is expected to say something polite about it, calls it "Tradition consecrated by a thousand years." Now the lapse of time does not consecrate a tradition: it makes an anachronism of it. If the British Army were to attack the Waziris and the Mohmands[4] with bows and arrows it would be carrying on a thousand-year-old tradition. That is just why it does not do it. The thing has become so absurd that from every quarter we are urgently reminded that the proceedings are symbolic, and that the King himself is a symbol.

Now all rituals are symbolic; but their value and impressiveness depend on whether the symbols symbolize present realities. If

[1]The coronation of George VI took place on 12 May 1937.

[2]Henri IV, who reigned in France from 1589 to 1610, is often cited as the originator of this *mot*: "Paris is well worth a mass."

[3]Irish republican leader and socialist.

[4]Tribes of Pakistan and Afghanistan, respectively.

they symbolize the realities of a thousand years ago they are nothing but superstitions which we have neither brains nor energy enough to bring up-to-date. In the Coronation the symbols are not merely obsolete: they symbolize conditions which have been reversed. They represent the king's investment with powers that he no longer wields and of which it has cost us two revolutions and several regicides to deprive him. They make him high priest as well as king, and commit him to the 39 articles of a little sect called the Church of England,[5] the subscribers to which are described by our greatest Churchman as necessarily either fools, bigots, or liars. The clothes used are the clothes of William the Conqueror and Queen Matilda,[6] transmogrified by generations of costumiers into fancy dresses symbolic of nothing but the Russian ballet.

Now there is no objection to pageantry in a pageant or fancy dress in a ballet. And there is no objection to symbolism in a religious service if the things symbolized really exist and can be sincerely celebrated by the parties officiating. A certain degree of idolatry is not indefensible, as the brainless will not obey anything but an idol, and the final object of the ceremony is to give authority to the throne. But the effect of a mixture of pageantry, religious ritual, and idolatry is not pleasant unless the ritual part is very sincere and the symbolism alive and contemporary. And in these days, when the realm extends to the ends of the earth over a hundred religions, it should be carefully purified of the sectarianism that offended nobody in the days when England was a right little tight little island and when Queen Elizabeth could not only concoct a ritual and send everyone who did not attend it to prison, but hang anyone who officiated at any other ritual.

The Communion service has no business in a Coronation ritual at all; and if the sword and the orb and the sceptre are to symbolize actual or historical truth they should be violently snatched by the Prime Minister from the hands of the monarch, who should thereupon swear never to make any attempt to take them back from that living symbol of an entirely imaginary democracy and liberty who lives at 10, Downing Street.

If I were in the royal succession, I would renounce fifty limit-

[5]The thirty-nine articles are the official creed of the Church of England.

[6]Queen Matilda of Flanders, wife of William I ("the Conqueror"), was crowned on arrival in England after serving as regent in Normandy during her husband's absence.

ed monarchies sooner than go through such a ritual. I should not be at all surprised to learn that Edward VIII had flatly refused to endure its thousand-year-old tomfooleries, and that this and not his diplomatic masterstroke of marrying an American lady[7] was the real cause of his abdication.

Yours, &c.,
G. Bernard Shaw

PUNISHMENT BY FLOGGING

I

[*Daily Telegraph,* 21 February 1938.]

Sir,—May I be allowed to express my disgust at the sentences of flogging[1] that have just been passed. What is the use of this relapse from civilised law into savage retaliation?

The effect on the criminals will be negligible: they will spend a week in a fury of hatred of society and of the law; but at the end of years of imprisonment this will have faded out. It will have no deterrent effect; for nothing is better established than the fact that it is certainty of detection and not brutality of punishment that deters. These criminals, for instance, were not deterred by the sentence of flogging added to no less than ten years' imprisonment passed by the Lord Chief Justice some time ago which was made specially sensational by the prisoner committing suicide[2] before it could be executed.

The transient pain to the flogged men is now worth considering in comparison to the gratification and encouragement given to

[7]Wallis Warfield Simpson, for whom Edward VIII, later Duke of Windsor, abdicated on 11 December 1936.

[1]Flogging was not outlawed as a punishment in England until 1948. The sentences of flogging had in the present instance been imposed by the Lord Chief Justice, Lord Hewart, on two convicted criminals, David Wilmer (fifteen strokes) and Robert Paul Harley (twenty strokes), in addition to respective prison sentences of five and seven years (two at hard labor), for their complicity in a £16,000 robbery in the course of which they had brutally assaulted a representative of Cartier's jewelry firm in a Mayfair hotel.

[2]James Spiers, 37, an habitual criminal, sentenced to ten years' penal servitude and fifteen strokes with the "cat" for assault with intent to rob, committed suicide in Wandsworth Prison on 3 February 1930. At the inquest, however, his wife testified he had told her "I don't mind the flogging, it is the ten years I object to."

all our Sadists and flagellomaniacs, who would be only too delighted to have the sentence carried out at the cart's tail in the old fashion so that they might have the pleasure of actually witnessing it.

The whole business appears to me as a national shame and disgrace.

Yours, &c.,
G. Bernard Shaw

II

[*Daily Telegraph*, 2 March 1938.]

Sir,—It is unfortunately impossible to hammer into the heads of children and savages that the objection to flogging and cognate tortures is not that they hurt the criminal but that they demoralise the nation and lower its standard of civilisation.

The Puritan who objected to bear baiting not because it gave pain to the bear but because it gave pleasure to the spectators[3] hit the nail on the head exactly.

Your pro-fustigation correspondents are evidently in the mental condition of children and savages; for they are unable to reason on the facts. They ask me how the Mayfair criminals are to be punished if they are not flogged, forgetting in their fear of losing the promised treat that a man who has to suffer eight years' penal servitude can hardly be said to go unpunished. They repeat the old plea that flogging is the only effective deterrent with the Mayfair crime staring them in the face as a proof that it is not a deterrent at all.

The morning after they are promised the flogging they read in the papers of a labourer who shares their notions of "larning" wrongdoers. This man, having to bring up his child, aged four, in the way it should go, knocks it down four times with his fists and explains to the magistrate that he was doing his duty as a father. The magistrate thought he was overdoing it, and sentenced him to three months' imprisonment.

Some of your correspondents will no doubt present him with a testimonial when he comes out; but for my part I heartily wish

[3]A paraphrase of Macaulay's remark about Puritans in vol. I, chap. 2 of his *History of England* (1849).

he could not plead the example of a British court of justice for his method of educating his naughty child.

I hope Sir Samuel Hoare,[4] the most humane Home Secretary within my recollection, will have cut out the cat from the sentences before this letter appears in your columns.

Yours, &c.,
G. Bernard Shaw

III

[*Daily Telegraph,* 3 March 1938.]

Sir,—I am loath to trespass on your space again; but I now have a grievance as a taxpayer.

The convict, David Wilmer, has been flogged, and is now, according to law, an absolutely reformed and safe member of society, deterred by his punishment from any attempt to repeat his crime. Why, in that case, should I have to share the expense of maintaining him in prison for five years? His reformation has already cost me my share of the five shillings paid to the warders for the operation.

If the operation has been unsuccessful there is no excuse for repeating it on Harley. If it has been successful there is no excuse for keeping Wilmer in prison at the public expense for the next five years. His release would no doubt be followed by a lively competition for his services by the believers in flogging as a preventive deterrent. If we are to adopt flagellomaniac logic we may as well pursue it to its conclusion.

The obligations of the Lord Chief Justice and the Home Secretary can, I think, be got round. It is the law that violent robbers should be flogged; and the Lord Chief Justice is therefore obliged to pass a sentence of flogging just as he is obliged to pass a sentence of death when a distracted girl kills her illegitimate infant.

The Home Secretary, as minister of the King's clemency, must not use his powers to nullify the law and by implication rebuke the judge unless some doubt or extenuating circumstance or obvious obsolescence of the law calls for his interference. In the

[4]Longtime Conservative MP for Chelsea, home secretary under Neville Chamberlain since 1937, who devoted much of his attention to the preparation of a penal reform bill which would have abolished flogging had not World War II intervened.

present case there is no doubt, no extenuating circumstance, no obsolescence. Nothing can be more modern and deliberate than the flogging law.

But the Lord Chief Justice evidently does not believe in the efficacy of flogging, as he has taken care to add severe sentences of penal servitude to the lash. May we not, therefore, surmise that he was relying on the Home Secretary to eliminate the flogging exactly as he relies on him to eliminate the hanging in the cases of infanticide? I suggest that it is up to Sir Samuel Hoare to save us from another day spent in the streets with contents bills inscribed "Mayfair Man Flogged" making us shiver with disgust at every corner.

Finally, however, the responsibility lies with our flogging Parliaments, busy as usual keeping us a couple of thousand years behind the times when Moses thought 40 lashes enough for the worst criminal.[5] Our "20 strokes" means 180 lashes, as the cat, rather unfairly, has nine tails.

Yours, &c.,
G. Bernard Shaw

A NATIONAL THEATRE

[*Daily Telegraph,* 13 June 1938.]

Sir,—People ask me, "Do the English people want a National Theatre?" Of course they do not. They never want anything.

They have a British Museum; but they never wanted it. They have Westminster Abbey. They never wanted that either; but now that it stands there, a mysterious phenomenon that came to them they don't know how, and don't care, they quite approve of it, and feel the place would be incomplete without it. What we have to do is to produce the phenomenon of a National Theatre on the site that has been acquired at South Kensington, London.

We have not only got the site, but we have paid for it; and we are not yet at the end of our resources. The first thing we have to do, in order to fill this site worthily, is to find an architect, and we have found one in the person of Sir Edwin Lutyens.[1]

[5] *Deuteronomy,* 25:3.

[1] Architect and president of the Royal Academy; his work included the British embassies in Washington, D.C., and New Delhi, and, in Rome, the British School of Art and the British Art Exhibition Building.

He will find this site a very appropriate field for his efforts, because most of what the 19th century was able to do for London in the way of public buildings was done in South Kensington.

You have the Natural History Museum, Waterhouse's[2] masterpiece; but it is really 13th century architecture. You have the Albert Hall. What sort of architecture that is no human being has been able to say; but at any rate there it is. You also have the building which replaces what used to be called the Brompton Boilers.[3] And you have the church of the Oratorians. Now I think we may depend on Sir Edwin Lutyens not to go back to the 13th century, but to give us something original, and something belonging to our own time.

Although, as I have said, the site is paid for, we cannot really afford it; but we can go ahead for some distance, far enough to oblige the Government who will have to come and help to keep on foot an indispensable national institution when we have solidly founded it.

The way the National Gallery, the British Museum, and all these places begin is always by a small group of people who understand their national cultural importance. They make a beginning, and after a time the beginning becomes an institution. Then the Government comes along, or rather the Government does not come along, but the created institution confronts the Government; and the Government, which never wanted it, says, "Here is something which for some reason or other we have got to keep going."

Now we here have to carry this institution to the point at which the Cabinet will be up against it. I remember [in] the year 1922, which was when we were on very good terms with our neighbours the French, the third centenary of the birth of Molière, the great French dramatist, who stands in France as Shakespeare does here. For the sake of the Entente Cordiale we were expected to celebrate it. The business fell, in due course, into the hands of the Foreign Office.

[2]Alfred Waterhouse, who died in 1905, is best remembered for his Manchester Town Hall, 1869.

[3]The "Brompton Boilers," one of the outlying buildings of the South Kensington Museum, was a monstrosity constructed of corrugated sheet iron painted in green and white stripes. The South Kensington Museum was razed to make way for the Victoria and Albert Museum.

When the heads of the Foreign Office heard that we had to celebrate Molière, they naturally said, "What or who is Molière?" and nobody could answer the question until a young attaché—perhaps it was Sir Robert Vansittart[4]—said, "My governor has a library of which he is very proud, and there is a row of books in it called 'The Works of Molière.' " The Foreign Office said, "Ah! Works. Good! This is a job for the First Commissioner of Works."

Accordingly, the First Commissioner of Works took the thing in hand. By an extraordinary piece of good luck the Commissioner at that time was Lord Crawford,[5] who with some three or four other peers—Lord Lytton and Lord Howard de Walden[6] among them—represented culture in the House of Lords.

Yours, &c.,
G. Bernard Shaw

NEWS AT TEN

[*The Times,* 7 July 1938.]

Sir,—This island is inhabited by 46 millions of people. Its breadwinners rise at 6 or earlier to begin their daily share of the nation's work. Therefore they have to be in bed at 10 to make room for their eight hours' sleep. The present rulers of the B.B.C., presumably belonging to the insignificant fraction of the population which gets up at 11 and goes to bed at half-past 3 or thereabouts, have altered the hour of broadcasting the third news from 9 o'clock to 10.

Would it not be well, now that Sir John Reith[1] has gone, to replace him by someone who knows at least a little about the lives

[4]British diplomat, permanent under-secretary of state for foreign affairs (1930–38) and foreign affairs adviser to the foreign secretary (1938–41).
[5]David Alexander Edward Lindsay Crawford, twenty-seventh Earl of Crawford, was first commissioner of works in 1921–22 and later a trustee of the National Gallery, the National Portrait Gallery, and the British Museum.
[6]Victor Alexander George Robert Lytton, second Earl of Lytton, had been under-secretary of state for India (1920) and governor of Bengal (1922); Thomas Evelyn Scott-Ellis, eighth Baron Howard de Walden, was the first president of the British Music Society, a trustee of the Tate Gallery, and a composer, dramatist, and antiquary.
[1]First director general of the BBC, 1927–38.

of the common people whose 10 shillingses[2] keep the B.B.C. going?

Yours, &c.,
G. Bernard Shaw

THEATRES IN TIME OF WAR

[*The Times*, 5 September 1939.]

Sir,—May I be allowed to protest vehemently against the order to close all theatres and picture-houses during the war?[1] It seems to me a masterstroke of unimaginative stupidity.

During the last War we had 80,000 soldiers on leave to amuse every night. There were not enough theatres for them; and theatre rents rose to fabulous figures. Are there to be no theatres for them this time? We have hundreds of thousands of evacuated children to be kept out of mischief and traffic dangers. Are there to be no pictures for them?

The authorities, now all-powerful, should at once set to work to provide new theatres and picture-houses where these are lacking.

All actors, variety artists, musicians, and entertainers of all sorts should be exempted from every form of service except their own all-important professional one.

What agent of Chancellor Hitler is it who has suggested that we should all cower in darkness and terror "for the duration"?

"Why, brother soldiers, why
Should we be melancholy, boys?"[2]

Yours, &c.,
G. Bernard Shaw

[2]The BBC was sustained by a licensing fee on receiving sets.

[1]*The Times* reported on 4 September: "The Home Secretary has decided to close all places of amusement during the initial stages of hostilities. Their reopening will be in accordance with the experience gained of the nature and extent of air attack. . . ." World War II began on 1 September.

[2]"Why, soldiers, why" (the "brother" is Shaw's addition) is a traditional military song, featured in Thomas Odell's ballad opera *The Patron* (1729).

POLAND AND RUSSIA

[*The Times*, 20 September 1939.]

Sir,—May I again point out that the news from Russia is good news for us, as far as any war news can be called good?

The question for us is not whether Mr. Molotoff's[1] speech resembles certain utterances of Herr Hitler's or not. What concerns us is whether Mr. Molotoff's statements are true or not. They are obviously true to the last syllable. We have encouraged Poland to fight by our pledge to support her; and we have encouraged ourselves by silly reports that the Polish army was unbroken and that the Poles were performing prodigies of valour. The truth, as we now have to admit, and as Mr. Molotoff notes, is that our support has so entirely failed that the Polish resistance has been wiped out, and with it the Polish army and the Polish Government, leaving Poland derelict to be picked up and put on by Herr Hitler as a shepherd putteth on his garment.[2]

At this point, we being helpless, Mr. Stalin steps in and says: "Not quite. If the Ukraine and White Russia are going begging, Russia will occupy them, Hitler or no Hitler." No sooner said than done. The Red Army is in occupation. Mr. Stalin, who was very explicit as to his objection to be made a catspaw to take our chestnuts off the fire, has no objection whatever to using Herr Hitler as a catspaw. The unfortunate Führer is compelled to disgorge half his booty and to face yet another army saying "Thus far and no farther."

And instead of giving three cheers for Stalin we are shrieking that all is lost.

Mr. Stalin lately sent us a photograph of himself laughing at us. When will we learn to laugh at ourselves?

Yours, &c.,
G. Bernard Shaw

[1]V. M. Molotov, veteran Politburo member, was presently commissar for foreign affairs and one of the negotiators of the Soviet-German Nonaggression Pact, signed on 23 August 1939. It cleared the way for the German invasion of Poland on 1 September. After Molotov's speech to which Shaw alludes, the two countries amended the agreement in a treaty signed on 29 September, which in effect traded much of eastern Poland for Lithuania in terms of "spheres of influence." All agreements collapsed with the invasion of the Soviet Union by Germany on 22 June 1941.

[2]*Jeremiah*, 43:12.

NEVILLE CHAMBERLAIN'S REPLY TO HITLER

[*Manchester Guardian,* 11 October 1939.]

Sir,—We are promised a speech from the Prime Minister in reply to Herr Hitler's last.[1] It will have to be a good one; for Herr Hitler's speech was a very good one; and the farrago of schoolboy heroics and vulgar abuse which our mouthpieces have been debiting so far (always excepting the Archbishop of York)[2] is sickening after the frankness and realism of the other side. Herr Hitler changes his mind pretty quickly and boldly as the circumstances change. He has a perfect right to do so; and it is waste of time calling him a liar for the hundredth time. Especially in his change of attitude towards Russia, on whom for twenty years we have heaped as much insult and calumny as he, he has simply done what we ought to have done and in fact half-heartedly tried to do. And now we are ridiculously attributing to Stalin the mentality of Mr. Eden and Mr. Duff Cooper,[3] and still more ridiculously reviling him for it, whilst our Bitter-enders demand the inclusion of these two gentlemen in the War Cabinet and the extrusion of Mr. [Prime Minister Neville] Chamberlain to make room for them. The time has come to drop all that childish nonsense. The Budget, mercilessly realistic, has knocked it on the head and brought us down to tin tacks that have suddenly grown to tenpenny nails.

What I want from Mr. Chamberlain—and I am not unique in this respect—is complete frankness as to a quite unforeseen and very hopeful breakdown of the plans of all the combatants. They are not so wicked as they thought they were. Mr. Chamberlain, an

[1]Hitler's Reichstag speech of 6 October was reported in *The Times* the following day. The speech both celebrated and justified the victory in Poland—as a "revision" of the despised Treaty of Versailles—and denied expansionist aims despite such reports due to "the enmity on the part of British statesmen and journalists which has profoundly shocked me."

[2]William Temple, Archbishop of York (1929–42) and Canterbury (1942–44), was a popular and enlightened church figure who for many years broadcast commentaries on religious and social matters on the BBC.

[3]Anthony Eden, presently dominions minister, and three times foregn secretary, later prime minister; Alfred Duff Cooper, first Viscount Norwich, biographer and holder of various ministerial offices, and Unionist (later Conservative) MP, 1924–45.

honest Liberal, anything but bellicose, was bullied by our Imperialists into threatening Herr Hitler with war if he attempted to retrieve the Polish Corridor. Our Premier's pledge to Poland was explicit: we were to come to her aid "with all our resources," which meant that when the first German soldier crossed the Polish frontier the R.A.F. would bomb Berlin; for in no other way could we help Poland, being unable to put a British solider into Poland or a British ship into the Baltic before Poland was conquered.

On the strength of that pledge Poland put up a desperate resistance and slew ten thousand young Germans, besides damaging thirty thousand more. Now bombing Berlin meant beginning a series of retaliations in which our cities and the German cities would be changed into rubbish heaps. And when it came to this point Mr. Chamberlain found simply that he could not bring himself to do it. Now this was only one instance of what was happening all round. The Berlin-Rome Axis was to have annihilated us, but when Signor Mussolini realised what he was letting Italy in for at the hands of the French and British aces and the Mediterranean Fleet he backed out. The Anti-Comintern Pact was to have rallied all capitalist Europe against the U.S.S.R., with the Leader and the Duce as the saviours of the world from Communism; but what actually happened was that when all capitalist Europe, with Japan into the bargain, realised that the Red Army held the military balance they all sought an alliance with Russia. Stalin just pushed them out of his way and took what he wanted of Poland. An eminent English Church dignitary [Dr. W. R. Matthews, Dean of St. Paul's] called him Judas; but Herr Hitler, seeing that the Anti-Comintern Pact had gone phut, quickly decided to claim Stalin as an ally and share the spoils with him. When we and the French attacked him on his Western Front in the old-fashioned way on the old-fashioned Balance of Power lines and it was his business to raid London with his famous Air Force, he, too, recoiled from starting that ruinous game. In his speech he urges that if we go on Saarbrücken will be avenged on Mulhouse, but not a word of Paris or London.

What Mr. Chamberlain has to declare now is whether he is going to bomb Berlin or not. If he does, the consequences will go far beyond our maddest intentions and be quite different from anything either we or Herr Hitler contemplate. If not, the sooner we stop the war and arrange for a tabling our respective grievances and those of the little States we have destroyed the better.

Among the grievances, by the way, is the fact that an idolised One Man autocracy is never a reality, because the Idolised One cannot be everywhere, and must therefore delegate his autocracy to a host of nobodies whom he is obliged to support no matter what atrocities the worst of them may commit. Another is that the One Man may, as in the special case of Herr Hitler, suffer from the well-known Jewish complex of belonging to a Chosen Race which must hew all other races to pieces before the Lord in Gilgal;[4] and this, as Mr. H. G. Wells contends, disqualifies him on the ground of lunacy.

Yours, &c.,
G. Bernard Shaw

BALLET FOR THE TROOPS ON LEAVE

[*Daily Telegraph,* 6 February 1940.]

Sir,—We have just been told by Mr. Churchill[1] that we have a million and three quarter men in the field. He added many encouraging assurances as to the efficiency with which these men are being equipped and provisioned. So far so good. But men "in the field" are not always in the field. I wonder how many of those who cheered Mr. Churchill thought of asking him what provision has been made for their recreation when they are at home on leave.

During the last war, when we had 2,000,000 men in the field, we had 80,000 of them to entertain every night, with the result that theatre rents rose enormously. House full was the rule.

Unfortunately the quality of the entertainment did not rise: it fell to ridiculous depths. The pre-wireless soldier of 1914–18 was incredibly primitive in his tastes. No joke was too old for him (ask Mr. Robey) and no farcical comedy too stale provided there were four beds on the stage and the characters got often enough into the wrong ones.

The laughter of the Tommies and the squeals of the equally

[4]Where Saul "hewed Agag in pieces" in *I Samuel,* 15:33.
[1]Winston Churchill was first lord of the Admiralty, 1939–40; he became prime minister on 10 May 1940.

unaccustomed young women who took them to the theatre made a sort of noise that our actors had never heard before. The artistic level sank to such a point that *The Bing Boys*[2] became relatively a classic. And in *The Bing Boys* Mr. Robey convulsed the house by calling his legs his understandings.

One night at the Coliseum I sat beside a soldier who did not know what a theatre was, and stared in utter bewilderment at the proceedings until we had a turn in which the performer imitated farmyard noises, whereupon my neighbor became ecstatic, and was buoyed up through the rest of the programme by the vain hope that the farmyard man would come again.

Yet this was an enormous improvement on the days when soldiers were supposed to be sufficiently provided for if there were plenty of places to get drunk in and plenty of prostitutes to get drunk with. Soldiers were not admitted and not served in decenter places. The Duke of Wellington avowedly won his battles with "common soldiers" assumed to be blackguards and drunkards. He was by no means always mistaken in that assumption.

The Kitchener volunteers and conscripts of the last war were decent lads, but nine out of ten of them had no artistic culture and had never heard a scientific lecture in their lives.

The wireless has changed all that. The B.E.F. [British Expeditionary Force] comes this time from a world in which the concerts of the B.B.C. Symphony Orchestra, leader Paul Beard, conducted by Sir Adrian Boult (to say nothing of Toscanini), and lectures and sermons by eminent scientists and bishops are everyday incidents. Meanwhile the cinema has raised their standards of drama to such a point that I no longer count as a highbrow.

My present purpose is to call attention to the danger of this change being lost on our official and theatrical stick-in-the-muds, who have already shown the gravest signs of believing that now we are at war we must have *The Bing Boys* and the bedrooms with four beds and all the old sillinesses over again. They should all be shot instantly.

Let me give a howling example. One of the most astonishing

[2]*The Bing Boys Are Here,* a revue billed as "A Picture of London Life in seven panels," adapted from the French by George Grossmith and Fred Thompson, with music by Nat D. Ayer, and starring George Robey, opened at the Alhambra in April 1916 for a year's run. Robey later returned to the Alhambra (1918) for another extended engagement in *The Bing Boys on Broadway.*

artistic developments in the theatre of our time has been the rebirth of the high art of ballet at Sadler's Wells. We thought it had died with Diaghileff.[3] That it could revive in its fullest excellence as an English institution in London, in an outlying theatre in a neighbourhood making no pretence to West End fashionableness, would have seemed 20 years ago the dream of a madman. Well, it has happened, and our British male dancers are as good as any in the world. Necessarily they are young; their 10 years' technical training has to begin when they are children, and they are superannuated from leading parts when they are 35. Consequently they are all of military age.

What I want to know is whether these irreplaceably rare and highly skilled artists, providing a most delectable entertainment of the highest class for our 50,000 soldiers on leave every night, are to be sent into the trenches to fill 30 places which could be better filled by 30 unskilled labourers?

If they were key men in any of the mechanical trades they would be exempted as a matter of course. Being artistic key men their importance may not be appreciated by our often Philistine authorities.

In the last war the composer of England's most famous serious modern opera, *The Immortal Hour,*[4] was treated as a vagabond and sent into the ranks, where they could do nothing with him but make him their bandmaster, while a young gentleman in another district was exempted with the greatest respect on his proving that he had once composed a waltz.

Now a dancer is in worse case than a composer, because he can compose melodies and form threes in a barrack square at the same time; but the dancer can keep himself up to the mark only by arduous daily practice. A year of soldiering would ruin him.

Besides, if the Sadler's Wells leading dancers go, bang goes the whole concern. Three hundred people of all grades are turned into the street, not to reinforce the Army, but to join the unemployed. There will be an end of our supremacy in one of the finest of the theatrical and musical arts. The theatre will become a military warehouse. And the soldier on leave will find nothing to re-

[3]Serge Diaghilev, noted Russian impresario, first brought his Ballets Russes to London in 1911.

[4]The one immensely popular opera by Rutland Boughton, first produced in 1914.

create him after the miseries of the trenches except rubbish that the wireless has taught him to despise.

Yours, &c.,
G. Bernard Shaw

GUILTY OR NOT GUILTY

I

[In an anonymous review ("Wilde in Life and Letters") of Lord Alfred Douglas's recently published *Oscar Wilde: A Summing Up,* in the *Times Literary Supplement* on 3 February 1940, the reviewer commented on the 1895 trial of Oscar Wilde and the guilty verdict: Wilde's "sin of the flesh was one forbidden by the law; and a man who was on the right side of the law but a cruel and immoral character [the Marquess of Queensberry, Douglas's father] was the means of bringing him under its notice. This is the least judicious and pondered part of Lord Alfred's book. Misled by Mr. Bernard Shaw"—Douglas had quoted Shaw's preface to Frank Harris's biography of Wilde (London, 1938)—"he has confused crime with vice." To argue, the reviewer continued, "that Wilde ought to have pleaded 'Not Guilty' because he himself did not think his offences were a vice is to miss the point. He was not asked for his opinion on the morality of his practice, but simply whether or no he had done certain deeds which were punishable by the law of England. When it was proved that he had, the law had no choice but to condemn him." Shaw responded in a letter published on 10 February, citing the 1688 trial of the Seven Bishops for seditious libel during the reign of James II as evidence of his point, that "no fact or act can be guilty in itself."]

Sir,—Your reviewer, in the course of his notice of Lord Alfred Douglas's book on Oscar Wilde, says that Lord Alfred is wrong in his law, and adds that I have misled him. This is interesting as an example of the extent to which an English writer on the staff of our foremost literary journal can be in the mental condition of the simplest agricultural labourer as regards the most vital and famous clause in Magna Carta. He has not even considered his words sufficiently to remember that no fact or act can be guilty in itself, though its agent can be guilty or not guilty in respect of it, and that consequently a juror giving a verdict, or an accused person pleading to an indictment, would be talking nonsense if they applied the word guilty either positively or negatively to mere facts. The leading case in British history is the acquittal of the seven bishops in 1688, where there was no dispute about the facts. After that, the judges tried, as they still do, to sidetrack the jurors and get the law into their own hands by putting questions of fact to the jury and interpreting the replies as verdicts. This abuse became so intolerable in cases of political libel that it was finally outlawed by Fox's Act.[1]

Can it be that your reviewer is a judge? Or is he, on this point, only an innocent ignoramus? If the latter, he had better apologize to Lord Alfred. He need not worry about me: I forgive him.

Yours, &c.,
G. Bernard Shaw

Our reviewer writes:

I did not say that "a fact or act can be guilty in itself," which is obviously nonsense. I quoted from the O. E. D. that "a crime is an act punishable by law, as being forbidden by statute or injurious to the public welfare," which is a very different thing. Mr. Shaw should read, and write, less hastily. For his responsibility for Lord Alfred Douglas's confusion between crime and vice I refer your readers to pp. 28–9 of Lord Alfred's book. [Ed., *Times Literary Supplement.*]

[1]Charles James Fox, the great eighteenth-century liberal reformer and leader of the opposition in Parliament, was the author of the Libel Act of 1792, which restored to juries the right to decide the question of guilt or innocence.

II

[The next issue of the *Times Literary Supplement* (17 February 1940) carried a letter from Lord Alfred Douglas, in which he said in part: "So far from confusing vice and crime, I insisted strongly on the distinction between them. My argument was that the law should not properly be concerned with sin as distinct from crime, and I gave instances of sins which are not crimes. I fail to see how this can fairly be described as 'confusing vice and crime.' " Douglas added that he had quoted Shaw only because "he had made the very point I wished to make with his usual skill and acumen."

A leading article on 24 February took issue only with Shaw's letter, however: "Writing with the accent of a man stirred to almost uncontrollable rage, Mr. Shaw began by a personal attack upon our reviewer. . . ." The leader concluded with the strong view that Shaw's intemperate argument "is the very technique whereby the friends of Hitler in Germany besiege the world . . . and the friends of Stalin in England deafen us. . . ." Shaw's reply appeared in the next issue, 2 March.]

Sir,—The case of the Seven Bishops is not irrelevant. It is, I repeat, a leading case on the subject. Ask any lawyer. The Seven Bishops were commanded by King James the Second to read from their pulpits his Declaration of Indulgence to Roman Catholics. They deliberately disobeyed the royal command. When they were brought to trial for their disobedience they pleaded Not Guilty. The Crown established the facts of the command and their disobedience. They did not deny the facts nor conceal their intention of persisting in their disobedience. According to your reviewer they should have pleaded Guilty; and the jury should have returned a verdict of Guilty. If that were so, there might as well have been no jury at all; and the particular clause of Magna Carta that established trial by jury might as well be torn up. What actually happened was that the bishops returned a verdict of Not Guilty. This was perfectly correct. It did not mean, as your reviewer would infer, that the bishops had read the Declaration (like the Vicar of Bray)[2] or that the King had not commanded them to read it. It meant exactly what it said: namely, that the bishops had acted commendably and not guiltily in disobeying the command, and that the King was in the wrong. (He was, in fact, presently dethroned for it.) That is not our opinion, but it was theirs.

[2]Shaw is alluding to an anonymous eighteenth-century song, the boast of a vicar that he will survive the differing religious views of several monarchs and keep his post; the song reveals pride in being expedient.

Oscar Wilde, being a convinced pederast, was entirely correct in his plea of Not Guilty; but he was lying when he denied the facts; and the jury, regarding pederasty as abominable, quite correctly found him Guilty.

The first thing a jury has to do is to ascertain the facts, as it can arrive at no judgment in ignorance of them. The police may fail to establish the facts against the accused; but it does not follow that the verdict must be one of Not Guilty. I can recall a murder at Clapham and one at Oxford in which the police failed to connect the accused with the murders. What they established to the entire satisfaction of the jury was that the two men were respectively a dangerous villain, quite capable of a savage murder, and a worthless fellow who was a public nuisance. Accordingly, they were both found Guilty. The worthless fellow was hanged; but the Home Secretary jibbed at the obvious hiatus in the case against the villain, and sent him to prison, where he died fifteen years later. In his case the jury was right, and the Home Secretary, who should have jumped at the chance of liquidating a bad citizen, wrong.

In a third case, though the facts were clear and undisputed, they were of such a nature as to make it impossible to prove that the case was one of murder; but the police proved beyond a doubt that the accused man was a polygamist. The jury, as good monogamists, found him Guilty; and he was duly removed from the sphere of British domestic morality. A Moslem or Mormon jury would have seen no evidence of general depravity in his keeping two homes instead of one, and would have preferred the Scottish verdict of Not Proven.

I hope the matter is now clear. Its enormous constitutional importance is the explanation of what you call my "uncontrollable rage," which, I assure you, does me credit.

Yours, &c.,
G. Bernard Shaw

INTELLECTUALS AND RUSSO-FINNISH DISASTER

[On 6 March 1940, the *Yorkshire Evening Post,* Leeds, in a leading article "The Intellectuals Intervene," reflected on the Russian invasion of Finland and observed that "Mr. Shaw has intervened in the Russo-Finnish war, not alone but with other intellectuals, including Professor J. B. S. Haldane, Dean Hewlett Johnson, the Webbs, Sir Charles Trevelyan and Lord Listowel." The leader alluded to a public letter signed by all those mentioned, which urged a more conciliatory policy toward the Soviet Union, if only because "a very large section of the people of this country . . . would interpret the action of our rulers as an attack upon Socialism." "We cannot," the leader-writer commented, "admire the Olympian aloofness which enables intellectuals to regard social experiments with no thought of the tragedies of human experience involved in them." Shaw responded in a letter published on 14 March.]

Sir,—It would be discourteous of me to leave your article of the 6th unacknowledged. Let me remind you of one or two things that were not in your mind when you wrote it.

I am English only by acquired habit of 70 years standing. By birth I am an Irishman. Now, Ireland is the British Finland. Rather than allow Ireland to be occupied or invaded or even threatened by a foreign Power, or to use her present measure of independence and neutrality to place her nationality under the protection of a foreign Power, England would be strategically obliged to reoccupy Ireland, and if necessary to exterminate her inhabitants, by sheer force of arms with crushing odds in the Empire's favour.

That is exactly the Russo-Finnish situation;[1] and I do not see how England can decently reproach the U.S.S.R. for doing what she has done in Ireland since the days of Strongbow[2] and would undoubtedly do again, and may indeed have to do again, if the attention of her enemies should turn from the south-east of Europe and the Baltic to the west coast of Ireland.

The Soviet Government has had to deal pretty drastically for the 23 years of its existence with the modern crime of political

[1]On 1 March 1940, the invading Red Army captured the Finnish city of Vyborg on the Karelian isthmus; on 12 March, the Finns signed a peace treaty that ceded to the Soviets the territories they had earlier demanded.

[2]Richard Strongbow (Richard De Clare, second Earl of Pembroke and Strigul) was employed by Henry II in the late twelfth century to regain lost territory in Ireland's Kingdom of Leinster.

sabotage. It is not yet a crime with us when it is committed by ourselves: our industrialists and financiers ruthlessly destroy vast quantities of food to keep up prices. They put scientific inventions in the ice box to save scrapping their obsolete machinery with the full approval and complicity of our governments, because it is a necessary feature of our capitalist system. The Soviet Government, having to operate a Communist system, makes sabotage a very serious crime, involving liquidation in bad cases.

You are shocked at this, and think that it must have been carefully concealed from me when I visited Russia. Why should the Bolsheviks have concealed from me an advance in civilisation of which they were not ashamed, and which I should like to see introduced everywhere?

But how do we ourselves treat sabotage when it is not a matter of business? The Russians read our newspapers and know. The Irish Republican Army has adopted sabotage as a method of waging war on England. Liquidation or imprisonment for life are ruthlessly used to suppress it.

When next you feel inclined to denounce Stalin and his colleagues as bloodthirsty monsters for dealing sternly with saboteurs, ask yourself how you yourself would deal with saboteurs if they were members of the I.R.A. at work in Birmingham, Coventry or London. Will you then call the Russian law "a system of tyranny which we would certainly not tolerate for ourselves in our own country"?

Compared to Russia we are politically and morally behindhand. And our comment on that cast iron fact is that God is on our side in War and that we are therefore sure to win. For 20 years we have been lying ourselves into that selfrighteous infatuation. Is it any wonder that the Intellectuals feel uneasy about it?

Yours, &c.,
G. Bernard Shaw

DEFENCE OF AUTHORS

[A review of *Edith Sitwell's Anthology* appeared in *Reynolds News* on 18 February 1940. Among its observations were the following: "It would be a delightful bedbook if it were not so heavy to hold. The 160 pages of 'critical introduction' might well be omitted from future editions." But the range of the review expanded to take in all three Sitwells, Edith and her brothers Osbert and Sacheverell: "Among the literary curiosities of the nineteen-twenties will be the vogue of the Sitwells, sister and two brothers, whose energy and self-assurance pushed them into a position which their merits could not have won. One brother wrote amusing political verse. The sister produced a life of Alexander Pope. Now oblivion has claimed them, and they are remembered with a kindly, if slightly cynical, smile." The Sitwells promptly sued Co-operative Press, Ltd., the printers and publishers, and on 10 February 1941 were awarded damages of £350 each. *The Times,* commenting on the decision in a leader the next day, called the judgment "Another notable victory . . . in the long struggle of the persecuted race of poets to emancipate themselves from the oppression of the critics, 'those cut-throat bandits of the path of fame.' " The leader also referred to Whistler's libel suit against Ruskin in which he was awarded one farthing damages and to Edith Sitwell's comparison of the poetry of Alfred Noyes to "cheap linoleum" and that of the poet laureate's work to a steam-roller. Shaw joined the fun with a letter published in the *Daily Telegraph* on 26 February 1941.]

Sir,—The action of the Sitwells was entirely correct professionally. It raises no question of the freedom of criticism.

The written law of libel forbids critics to hold up authors to hatred, ridicule, or contempt. This law is a dead letter, because the unwritten law actually in force forbids them to do anything else when their criticism is disparaging. Otherwise criticism would be impossible, as every disparagement holds up its victim to hatred, ridicule or contempt. During the quarter-century of a highly distinguished career in literature the Sitwells have endured every extremity of such holding up, and have never resorted for redress to the written law. They have not needed to; for they have always been able to give their vituperators as good as they gave and a bit over. But they have never incurred the slightest suspicion of being litigious and not playing the game.

Why, then, their recent victorious action? Simply because the defendant paper forgot itself for a moment and did not play the game. It is part of that game that though the critic may indulge in vulgar abuse to the utmost that is printable, and ridicule the writer's artistic pretensions, the writer's commercial credit and personal honour must not be questioned directly or indirectly.

Macaulay, in a review of the works of a fashionable poet named Robert Montgomery, tore him to pieces as a poet.[1] Montgomery took no proceedings, though the review must have damaged his reputation seriously. But if Macaulay had hinted that Montgomery's bank account was overdrawn, or that he kept two domestic establishments instead of one, Montgomery would have been bound to sue his detractor under the written law.

Whistler took an action against Ruskin, and won his case with a farthing damages, because Ruskin had said that his pictures were not worth the £200 he asked for them. He should have said that they were not worth a tuppeny damn, which would have been privileged abuse. Whistler could easily have got £1,000 damages if he had behaved sensibly in the witness-box in the character of "a man done out of his job."

Miss Sitwell herself said that So and So's poetry reminded her of cheap linoleum. She was within her customary rights in this; but had she said anything that would have made So and So's tailor send in his bill with a pressing request for immediate settlement and an intimation that future dealings must be on a cash basis, the fat would have been in the fire.

It was because the defendant paper said something that might have produced this effect on Miss Sitwell's dressmaker and the tailors of her brothers that it became their professional duty to resort to the written law.

There is no danger of a general legal crusade against the newspapers, because the newspapers can retaliate with a weapon so deadly that they must not come to an explicit understanding about it among themselves lest they should be prosecuted for conspiracy. If any public person breaks the unwritten law and refuses to play the game, no editor will risk mentioning him or her again. The late Mrs. Georgiana Weldon[2] had once a publicity comparable to that of Gladstone. She acquired a taste for litigation, and

[1]Montgomery, widely praised for pious poems like "The Omnipresence of the Deity" and "Satan," was vigorously derided as a serious poet by Macaulay in the *Edinburgh Review* in 1830.

[2]A popular soprano in the nineteenth century, who became the plaintiff in various lawsuits (25 in 1883 alone) concerning divorce, lunacy, copyright, and libel matters. She was also the defendant in a number of suits, one of which, brought by the conductor Jules Rivière, led to a jail term of six months. The damages she won in her various actions amounted to £20,000.

was never mentioned in the papers until she died totally forgotten 20 years later.

The case should be a lesson to young critics and journalists as to what they may and may not write; and this must be my excuse for asking for so much of your space for the explanation of it.

Yours, &c.,
G. Bernard Shaw

BOMBING OF CITIES

[*The Times,* 28 April 1941; drafted entirely by Shaw.]

Sir,—First, may we make clear that though we are about to propose an arrangement with the Axis, it is not in the nature of an armistice or a statement of war aims or anything else that could be interpreted as a symptom of weakening on the part of the Allies. Nor is it a new departure. As a precedent we cite the dealings between our postal authorities and those of the enemy by which at last prisoners of war on both sides are receiving letters from home with certainty and regularity in three weeks after their date. This enormous improvement on the pre-existing state of things could not have been effected without negotiations which, if not precisely cordial, were governed by a reciprocal disposition to listen to reason and make a bargain benefiting the belligerents equally.

There are methods of warfare which not only cannot produce a decision but are positively beneficial to the side against which they are directed. The bombardment of cities from the air may be one of them. Its conditions are quite unprecedented. Both victory and defeat are impossible, because the vanquished cannot surrender, and the victor must run for home at 300 miles an hour, pursued by fighters at 400 miles an hour. The recent bombardments of Berlin and London, though quite successful as such, have not produced any military result beyond infuriating the unfortunate inhabitants. Some of them have been killed. If raids could be maintained nightly and each raid killed 1,000 persons, half of them women, it would take over a century to exterminate us and a century and a half to exterminate the Germans. Meanwhile, as both sides are depending for victory on famine by blockade, the reduction in the number of civilian mouths to be fed would be a relief to us.

As to one specific course which the War Cabinet has been provoked into taking: to wit, the threat to demolish Rome if Athens or Cairo be attacked from the air, it forces us to ask whether Rome does not belong to the culture of the whole world far more than to the little Italian-speaking group of Benitos and Beppos who at present are its loyal custodians. By destroying it we should be spiting the noses to vex the faces of every educated person in the British Commonwealth and in America, to say nothing of the European mainland. We may smash it for the Italians; but who is to give it back to us? In Rome no one is a stranger and a foreigner: we all feel when we first go there that we are revisiting the scene of a former existence. As to the effect of the threat, surely the way to save Athens and Cairo is not to defy Herr Hitler to bombard them and thus make it a point of honour for him to reply by a shower of bombs on them. He, far from the seven hills, may even echo the late Lord Clanricarde's reply to his Irish tenants, "If you think you can intimidate me by shooting my agent you are very much mistaken."

That we should in the same breath indignantly deny that our last raid on Berlin was a reprisal, and announce a major reprisal which must have staggered the historical conscience of the world, shows that our heads are not as clear as they might be on this subject. The more we endeavor to think it out the more we find ourselves driven to the conclusion that whatever may be said from the military point of view of our treatment of Bremen, Hamburg, and Kiel, there is nothing to be said for the demolition of metropolitan cities as such, and that the Bishop of Chichester's[1] plea for a reconsideration of that policy is entirely justified.

Yours, &c.,
Gilbert Murray
G. Bernard Shaw[2]

SHAW'S MISTAKE

[*New Statesman,* 5 July 1941.]

Sir,—For the second time, I have blundered badly about Führer Hitler and must apologise to your readers. The laugh, I must own, is against me.

[1]George Kennedy Allen Bell, Bishop of Chichester since 1929, had publicly condemned the indiscriminate bombing of German cities by the Allies as well as parallel acts by the Germans.

[2]H. G. Wells, invited to be a co-signator, had declined.

The first time was when the late Neville Chamberlain[1] was negotiating with him at Munich. Making the best of him, I took him to be a politician clever enough to calculate accurately just how far he could go in tearing up the Versailles Treaty clause by clause without provoking us to begin the Four Years War all over again. He had seen Mussolini firing on Corfu and getting away with it, though if we and the other Powers had been in earnest about the League of Nations we should have brought him to book sternly. He had seen the creation of Manchukuo by Japan, and how, in spite of the report of our commission headed by Lord Lytton, Japan got away with it as completely as if neither the League nor its constituents had ever existed. When Italy annexed Abyssinia, we got so far into a huff over it that we refused to call the King of Italy by his new title of Emperor; but we did nothing positive.

The Führer concluded that if we would stand all this without firing a shot or even rattling a sabre we would stand almost anything. So he armed Germany to the teeth in defiance of the Versailles Treaty, and marched his troops up and down the Rhineland, not only tearing up the Treaty but throwing the fragments in our faces. He got away with it easily. Feeling how much farther he dare go, he demanded the city of Danzig and a right of way across the Polish Corridor. He complained that in Czechoslovakia Germans were maltreated and enslaved. It was evident that he would not be satisfied until he had recovered the Kaiser's colonies and regained his frontiers.

We were not in the least frightened into appeasing him. Simply we were having a good time and did not want to be bothered. To rouse the British Lion to fighting pitch over the Rhineland, or the Polish Corridor, or indeed any place farther off than Marylebone Lane, was impossible. Besides, by that time the Treaty was so thoroughly discredited, and the policy of kicking Germany when she was down had brought her so much British sympathy, that we had no moral case against the Führer. He could go so far without having to fight for it that I did not believe he would venture beyond that point; and I said there would be no war.

I was wrong. I am always making mistakes by imagining that other people are as clever as I am myself. The Führer was not the first statesman to take me in, and will probably not be the last. When we let him alter the Czech frontier to Germany's entire ad-

[1]Former prime minister, who died on 9 November 1940.

vantage it seemed to him that he could do what he liked with us. He snapped his fingers at our guarantee to Poland, and took it by force. Stalin immediately seized half his booty, making his new conquest only the old Partition; and this time it was Stalin who got away with it.

The moment the guns went off, the British Lion woke up. The smell of powder was enough for him; and without stopping to consider that we were utterly unprepared for so big a job, we declared war on Germany. Führer Hitler had made the same mistake about Neville Chamberlain as I had made about himself. We, who had put up with so much from Italy and Japan on vital issues, now suddenly charged at him as Don Quixote charged at the windmills. It was pure knight errantry and quite out of order. Just like us! Poland was not our business: she was the business of the League of Nations. We should have called a meeting of the League as in the case of Finland (arming hard meanwhile) before breaking the peace. But that is not our way. We just went for the Führer with horse, foot and artillery, calling him every name we could lay tongue or pen to, without a thought of the League or of anything else that stood between us. If Adolf Hitler had been Julius Caesar, wise enough to make his conquests blessings instead of detestable subjugations, we should not have had a leg to stand on.

Incidentally, the House of Commons was informed that we were at war, but not until the fat was in the fire. That, also, is our way.

As usual, we had put ourselves technically in the wrong; but the Führer did not notice this, the point not being in his line. He told the world that we were the dupes and slaves of a parcel of rascally Jews, and that his Germans, as the superior race, would wipe the floor with us. And he certainly did wipe the floor of Europe with us so promptly that even the sleepiest of our Isolationists and the mildest of our Pacifists could not deny that we had to turn the tables on him or never hold up our heads again as a nation. Mr. Churchill told him that we would never parley with him again; that we would fight him wherever we could catch him on sea or land without regard to anyone's neutrality; and—this was a hot novelty—that he personally was fighting with a rope round his neck.

In spite of all this I blundered again when the news came of his massing troops on the Russian frontier. Knowing the strength and resources of Russia, I could not believe that any man with intelligence enough to lace his own shoes could in the middle of a very tough war deliberately complete his own dreaded encirclement and make war on six fronts under no ascertainable compulsion to commit military suicide. Can it be that he is as blind as all our own Tories and Clericals who persist in believing what they have been telling themselves for twenty years: that Stalin is a vulgar brigand and assassin whose rabble of tatterdemalions must scatter before the Nazi legions like autumn leaves before October winds? If so, he is lost; for if he is as far behind the times and as obsolete politically as our Old School Ties, we shall not be able to put the rope round his neck when Churchill, Roosevelt and Stalin have him finally by the collar. We shall have to send him to Broadmoor. But he is not as mad as that. The only sane explanation possible is that when Russia refused to join the Axis he concluded that Stalin was waiting to attack him in the rear when he was fully engaged on the west with Britain and America, and that his only chance was to smash the Red army first. The gambler's last throw: double or quits.

Though the Führer has let me down so heavily, my estimate of Russia's power remains unchanged. I have not forgotten that when Russia was half-starved (because Lenin had not sufficiently studied my works and those of the Fabian Society), and at her last gasp militarily, with the White army in Kazan and Mr. Churchill planking down a hundred millions voted for the Four Years War to equip the B.E.F. for the stamping out of Communism, all Europe seemed in at the death of Unholy Russia; and yet, having no arms, uniforms, or even boots to her feet, Russia easily appropriated those of our B.E.F.; raised an army out of the red earth of her villages; and cleared her soil miraculously of every enemy. Mr. Churchill was the first English statesman to call Lenin great. Japan's practised and disciplined army, the terror of the Far East, tried a couple of falls with the Red Army in Mongolia, and took care not to try a third. The Finns, led by Mannerheim,[2] put up a brave fight against Stalin, with our press declaring every day that the Red Army was disgracing itself; but Major Hooper's pamphlet on that campaign[3] seems to establish the fact that Mannerheim

[2]Carl Gustaf Emil, Baron von Mannerheim, supervised construction of the Mannerheim Line in defense against Russia and defended Finland during the Soviet invasion. He became president of Finland in 1944.

[3]Major A. S. Hooper, *The Soviet-Finnish Campaign* (1941).

was "out-generalled" all through and, with our journalists, kept barking up the wrong tree. If Russia could do this with the rest of the world against her, I see no reason for expecting her defeat as a matter of course with the British Commonwealth and the U.S.A. at her back, however unwillingly.

Mr. Eden, not too tactfully, has seized the opportunity to declare that there are fewer Communists here than in any other country. Mr. Churchill, not to be outdone, expresses his lifelong horror of Communism. Fortunately, Mr. Maisky[4] has been here long enough to be able to assure Stalin that in the mouths of British Ministers the word Communism is a purely vituperative expression, of the meaning of which neither Mr. Churchill nor Mr. Eden have the faintest notion. For all the vital services that cannot be exploited commercially we are absolutely dependent on our Communism. If Russia is up to the neck in it, we are up to the waist; and neither Mr. Churchill nor Mr. Eden refuse their salaries as public servants, nor protest when most of the money is taken back again from them by a taxation which makes our amateur Communism predatory without making it also productive. This half-and-half Capitalist Communism will be the undoing of us if we cannot find a few statesmen who know what they are talking about.

And now, what next? Well, Stalin, for a wonder, did not abuse his victory over Finland as America abused the victory of the North over the South, and as Clémenceau and Poincaré and British Democracy abused the victory of 1918. Suppose Stalin objects to our abusing the next victory when he has beaten Hitler for us!

Yours, &c.,
G. Bernard Shaw

[4]Ivan M. Maisky was the Soviet ambassador to England, 1932–43; he later took part in the Yalta and Potsdam conferences.

FROM THE FÜHRER'S MOUTH

[*New Statesman,* 11 October 1941.]

Sir,—Surely Hitler's last speech[1] is worth more attention than the explosion of vulgar abuse with which it has been received. When he attacked Russia it was pointed out in your columns that the only explanation of this apparently insane step that fitted all the facts was that he was convinced that Russia was only waiting to attack him until he was fully engaged with Britain and the U.S.A., and that it was a matter of life or death for him to vanquish Russia before we were ready to take him on.

He has now told us that this explanation was precisely true. He makes no secret of it; for he still believes that he was right about Russia's intentions, and therefore had no alternative but to dash at her and finish with her before the winter.

This suggests that National Socialism in the Reich is a plutocratic sham, and that Hitler is a figurehead who has no experience of what governing a really Socialist state means. If he had he would have known that Stalin would have gone to the utmost prudent lengths to avoid war and pursue his prodigious work of internal development without interruption or diversion of the Russian national capital from construction to destruction. Hitler clearly believed that Stalin would do exactly what he, Hitler, would have done in Stalin's place: in other words, that Stalin was his other self. No two living men could be less alike, and no two political and economic tactics more different.

But even from Hitler's own point of view it was clearly Russia's interest to make a trade agreement with both belligerents, and maintain strict neutrality while they battered one another to pieces.

I do not think Hitler's figures justify us in calling him a liar. They are not plausible enough for that. Liars always take the greatest pains to be plausible. The reasonable and civil conclusion is that the Führer is kept as carefully misinformed as to his mili-

[1]On 3 October, Hitler spoke in Berlin at the opening of the Winter Relief Fund, using the occasion to justify the invasion of the U.S.S.R. on 22 June. He called the British "lunatics" and Churchill a "war-monger" and defended the invasion: "In May there was no doubt that Russia would attack as soon as she got a chance. It was clear by the end of May that a conflict of life and death could not be prevented."

tary position as Napoleon III was in 1870. He has evidently no suspicion of his danger in the East. It is not my business to enlighten him; but I will ask our Old School Ties to remember that, like Hitler, they made a howling mistake about Russia, and must be careful not to make the same mistake about India.

From all this I cannot infer that the Führer is quite so longheaded as the people who fear him most imagine. I must point out to them that instead of making the peoples he has subjected glad he came, as Julius Caesar did, he has made the enormous mistake of making no better use of his victories than to raise up implacable enemies behind him as well as before him. Fighting on two fronts, or on half a dozen, is all in the day's work nowadays; but fighting on half a dozen backs is another matter.

Yours, &c.,
G. Bernard Shaw

MUSICAL INSTRUMENTS

[*The Times* reported on 15 April 1942 that "Musical instruments, including gramophones, player pianos, and other similar instruments and accessories to, and parts of, musical instruments" were among the items on which purchase tax was proposed by the government to be doubled during the budget year 1942–43, from the current rate of 33⅓ percent of their wholesale value to 66⅔ percent, the increase to take effect immediately. Shaw's response was published in *The Times* on 25 April.]

Sir,—May I beg *The Times* to remind the Chancellor of the Exchequer that musical instruments are among the first necessities of civilized life, and not luxuries to be made unobtainable by a purchase tax of 66⅔ per cent.? To exempt wireless receiving sets, and by the same stroke cut off the supply of instruments and skilled players by which the masterpieces of music are broadcast, suggests that the Government is still in the hands of gentlemen from our public schools left to believe that anyone who can read the satires of Juvenal in their original tongue, but is unaware of the existence of the symphonies of the great masters, from Haydn and Mozart to Elgar and Sibelius, is an educated man.

The simplest orchestra which can give us the eighteenth-century symphonies needs at least 32 instruments. For a full range of nineteenth-century music the minimum must be put at 80. And each instrument is dumb without a skilled professional player, each of whom must have been provided with it by his parents in his or her teens. Now the parents of orchestral players are not luxurious millionaires. Many of them come from families living so closely within modest incomes that a sudden demand for £20, or even £10, is a very difficult matter. In my boyhood I had a chance of being qualified as an oboist; and I should have jumped at it if I could have obtained the £14 which was the price of a second-hand oboe 70 years ago. For want of that sum I was lost to the wood wind for ever, and had to adopt a profession in which the equipment was sixpennorth of stationery.

The notion that not only the players in the B.B.C. and London Philharmonic orchestras, but in the brass bands of the Salvation Army and in the factory and colliery bands which competed every year at the Crystal Palace, the best of them being of first-rate artistic quality, are extravagant voluptuaries whose instruments may be classed with blue diamond rings and dispensed with on the smallest provocation, betrays a breath-bereaving cultural and social ignorance. I hope all the bands in London will hasten to Westminster Hall and do to the House of Commons what Joshua's trumpeters did to the walls of Jericho rather than let the Appropriation Bill pass as it stands without a protest.

Yours, &c.,
G. Bernard Shaw

VANSITTARTITIS

I

[H. G. Wells instigated a discussion of "German Militarism" with a letter, published in *Tribune* on 4 September 1942, in which he cited the recently published *Black Record: Germans Past and Present,* a full text of broadcasts delivered on the BBC overseas program by Robert Gilbert Vansittart, retired British diplomat who had been created a baronet in 1941. Shaw's rejoinder was published on 11 September.]

Sir,—I number Lord Vansittart and Mr. H. G. Wells among the most eminent of my acquaintances, to put it no more warmly. Vansittart is not only an experienced diplomatist, inoculated against vulgar insularity by his profession, but a poet of peculiar distinction. Wells is not only our most famous author but a sage and prophet of wide influence. Nobody can justly accuse me of taking them too lightly. But they being both very English and I an

Irishman, they amuse me sometimes. I fancy my amusement is shared by Mahatma Gandhi, Mr. Wellington Koo and President de Valera[1]—if Mr. de Valera is ever amused by anything.

Vansittart provoked a scandalised "Hush! For shame!" lately; and so did Lady Astor at Southport.[2] They both said something that was undeniably true: a feat not easily tolerated in England at any time, and quite inadmissible when we are at war. Vansittart's indiscretion was a *Black Record* of what Germans are capable of at their worst. It was all as true as any history can be: he could have documented every sentence of it. It has just been confirmed by Emil Ludwig, a German of the Germans, in his masterly book entitled *The Germans,*[3] which we should all read because it is a mirror in which we all can see ourselves. And Wells, instead of joining in the hush hush, comes to Vansittart's rescue and holds the bridge with him valiantly.

What is there amusing in this? Why do I not make three on the bridge instead of contemplating the scene with a broadening smile?

Simply because every word that is true of the Germans is equally true of the English, and of every militant nation on earth. Any Irishman, any Indian, any Chinaman, can cap the indictment of Germany with an indictment of Britain fully as inky. If when the war ends as it must in a negotiated settlement we or any other of the Powers start recriminating, we shall get as good as we give. We no less than the others have been a bold bad people, bunkfed and braggart, "deceitful above all things and desperately wicked";[4] and if we give ourselves moral airs at the next Peace Conference, or Holy Alliance, or Supernational Congress, or whatever it may call itself, we shall only confirm an impression largely prevalent on the Continent that the last enemy to be overcome is the old British Empire.

Why are Vansittart and Wells so naïvely unconscious of this? Well, why are they unconscious of the taste of water? Because it is always in their mouths. The Germans have to write elaborate trea-

[1]The best known statesmen of, respectively, India, China, and Ireland.
[2]Nancy Lady Astor's recent utterances had led to a parliamentary question of the propaganda value of her speeches to the Germans.
[3]Just published in England, in a translation by Heinz and Ruth Norden.
[4]*Jeremiah,* 17:9.

tises to persuade themselves that they are a Chosen Race, a *Herrenvolk,* appointed by God to rule the world and the waves; but the same delusion is so natural to Englishmen that they are unconscious of it: they believe it automatically. And the Irish, the Indians, the Chinese, the Welsh Dissenters, the Jacobite Scots and a good many Americans cannot help laughing at them, though they all have the same good opinion of themselves.

Unfortunately the conclusions drawn from this universal delusion are no laughing matter. The notion that we must knock down the German Reich, and spend the rest of the century sitting on its head to prevent its getting up, is applicable to a horse fallen in harness, but not by any sane person to the future of Europe. We can neither exterminate the Germans nor "re-educate" them by outbombing them, out-tanking them, and serving their cities worse than they have served ours. The Germans must cure themselves of their own folly in their own way. The inevitable reaction must come; and we must wait until it does. Meanwhile we must fight to keep our fate in our own hands; for we also must cure ourselves of our own follies in our own way and not in Adolf Hitler's way. We declared war on him in our own way without consulting any foreign Power; and we must go through with it for all we are worth.

When the devilment is over our business will be to insist on all the Black Records being thrown into the waste paper basket, and the future Commonwealth established on the sites of the demolished empires. The Life to Come is our concern, not the Past that is past praying for.

Which of us dare say "Vengeance is mine"?

Yours, &c.,
G. Bernard Shaw

II

[*Tribune,* 18 September 1942.]

Sir,—One word more about this Vansittart business. I contemplate the dispute with the utmost impartiality, because my mother land of Kent was swallowed up by the English long ago and my blood is Kentish with a slight infusion of genuine Irish by way of the Ulster Neals. But G. B. S. (a scion of the English garrison in Ireland) must really watch his words. I agree there is a black record against every colonising and aggressive people; nevertheless it is not true that "every word that is true of the Germans is equally true of the English, and of every militant nation on earth." The whole Vansittart case is against that. Vansittart asserts and shows that an ancient tradition of fury and systematic ruthlessness has been cultivated and developed with a modern efficiency and thoroughness by the Germans beyond all precedent. And who are the "we" who are going to do this, that, and the other foolish thing at the end of the war and widen the grin of the lookers-on? Who asks for Vengeance? Neither Vansittart nor myself. But this earth will be ruled entirely by pampered old lags, and that future World Commonwealth will remain a dream, unless the practice of the due execution upon open criminals is sustained, and until one single Declaration of equal Human Rights has been made the fundamental law of a federated world. So far G. B. S. has not lifted a finger to help in this obvious but complex and difficult task. (Yet on second thoughts I qualify that. He has done some very valuable work upon the production of a universal alphabet, saner and better than any other project of that type I have ever encountered.) But he must drop that "equally true." It is utterly false.

Yours, &c.,
H. G. Wells

ENGLISH USAGE

[On 22 December 1942, *The Times* published a letter from Sir John Squire, poet and parodist, literary critic for *The Observer,* and journalist. Squire complained about recent usages in *The Times*—especially "loaned" for "lent" and "chided" for "chidden"—in a general lament for the state of the language: "We seem to be reaching a point at which an Englishman won't be able to call his language his own." Shaw's response appeared in *The Times* on 28 December.]

Sir,—Sir John Squire, like all poets, loves the euphonious past participles of our irregular verbs. So do I. But we must not shut our minds against the hard fact that irregular verbs are the worst enemies of any language. *The Times* does a great national service every time it regularizes one of them. I hope to see in its columns some day such regular participles as thinked and buyed, though I shall still sing "Joshua fit the battle of Jericho" rather than spoil the line.

English usage is just what we need to get rid of: it is overloaded with unnecessary grammar; and our mad persistence in trying to spell the sounds of our speech with an ancient Phoenician alphabet costs us the price of a fleet of battleships every year in writing and printing superfluous letters. As it happens, the most civilized nation in the world, the Chinese, have taken our language in hand for business purposes, and produced an English with a minimum of grammar which has immense advantages over our academic English. It may yet become the language of *The Times.*

Meanwhile we might use an entirely new English monosyllabic pidgin. The only one I know of needs only a seventeen-letter alphabet. Current English cannot be spelt recognizably and economically with less than 42 letters.

Yours, &c.,
G. Bernard Shaw

ON WAR AND CONSCIENTIOUS OBJECTORS

[*The Tribunal: Independent War-Resisters' Forum,* March 1944.]

Sir,—No act of war is "justifiable," because war as an institution is not justifiable. But neither is the existence of the human race (or any other living species) justifiable. That men and women are pugnacious is a fact that has to be faced, not argued about.

The bombing of cities is perhaps the worst atrocity yet practised; but if I were of military age I might do it, just as I might poison rabbits in Australia, which is also an atrocity.

Future historians will rank Conscientious Objection as one of the greatest inventions of the English people. It may have enormous developments. It and not the General Strike (which is folly) will stop war. But it is neither reasonable nor "justifiable."

Yours, &c.,
G. Bernard Shaw

BRINGING UP THE CHILD

[*The Times,* 21 July 1944.]

Sir,—It is now many years since Judge Henry Neil, the American philanthropist who successfully agitated for mothers' pensions, convinced me of the importance of what he called "maternal massarzh" in the nurture of infants.[1]

At that time the most famous institution for infants in the world was the Kaiserin Augusta's House in Berlin. Within its green marble walls, children in beautifully tidy brass beds were tended by trained nurses under the best medical advice, the service being so perfectly regulated that every nurse knew exactly how many minutes an hour she could devote to each child in her care. At the same time infants in Connemara were tumbling about half naked on the mud floors of cabins little better than cowhouses under the eyes of mothers who knew rather less about the scientific nurture of children than about electronic physics. Out of doors the children combined sport with business by driving the family pig under the wheels of the motor-cars of British tourists, who paid on the nail more than the slain animal would have fetched alive in the nearest market.

And under the ideal Berlin conditions the infants died like flies, while in Connemara there was no mortality rate because children never died there. At least so I said. I will not pretend that the statement was capable of statistical verification; but it dramatized the facts effectively enough to drive them home. Judge Neil held that the difference was due to the fact that in Berlin the nurses tidied up the children's beds, and fed, and took their temperatures, and weighed and measured them very efficiently for carefully calculated divisions of their time, whereas in Connemara the mothers hugged them, mammocked them, kissed them, smacked them, talked baby talk to them or scolded them; in short, maternally massaged them to their heart's content.

Now neither of these methods can be accepted as civically satisfactory. The Berlin child either did not grow up at all, or grew up a nervous wreck or a disciplinarian terrorist. The Connemara child grew up humane and healthy, but at best a noble savage. The problem is how to produce adults who are both humane and cultivated. Clearly they must have not only the Berlin discipline but the Connemara massage.

The trained nurse with no time to spare for cuddling must be supplemented by affectionate masseuses. Have we not enough

[1]Judge Henry Neil of Chicago was obsessed with a scheme called Pensions for Mothers, for which an ever-indulgent Shaw in and after 1917 provided propagandizing press releases.

motherly and grandmotherly women, married or unmarried, maids or widows, to volunteer for this service before and after they have reared their own children? What have Lady Allen of Hurtwood and all the institution champions to say to this? It is no use their hitting and countering as if there were only one end in view, and that an extreme one.

Yours, &c.,
G. Bernard Shaw

SENTENCE OF DEATH

[*The Times,* 5 March 1945.]

Sir,—From a well-known passage in the Book of Genesis we learn that our method of executing criminals is the same as that in use at least 2,000 years ago. Is it not time to reconsider it?

We have before us the case of a girl[1] whose mental condition unfits her to live in a civilized community. She has been guilty of theft and murder; and apparently her highest ambition is to be what she calls a gun moll, meaning a woman who thinks that robbery and murder are romantically delightful professions. She has earned her living as a strip tease girl, which I, never having seen a strip tease act, take to be a performance as near to indecent exposure as the police will allow, though after 20 years' observation of sun-bathing I find it difficult to imagine anyone being entertained by the undress that would have shocked Queen Victoria.

Clearly we have either to put such a character to death or to re-educate her. Having no technique of re-education immediately available, we have decided to put her to death. The decision is a very sensible one, as the alternative is to waste useful lives in caging and watching her as a tigress in the Zoo has to be caged and watched.

Unfortunately our method of putting such people to death is so primitive that when it has to be practised on a girl in her teens

[1]Elizabeth Marina Jones, eighteen, occupation listed as a "dancer," was charged with the murder of George Edward Heath ("the man with the cleft chin," as the newspapers sensationalized him) on 7 October 1944. She and her accomplice, an American paratrooper, Karl Gustav Holten, twenty-two, were found guilty. Holten was executed on 8 March 1945; Miss Jones received a reprieve in early March from the home secretary.

every one, including the Sovereign who has to sign the death warrant and the Home Secretary who has to decide whether it shall be carried out or not, is revolted by it. They agree that the thing should be done, but not in this unnecessarily unpleasant way. The jury, moved by the girl's age and sex, recommend her to mercy, leaving her adult male accomplice pitilessly to his fate. As this "mercy" takes the form of a dozen years of the daily torture, demoralization, disablement, and cutting-off from all the news of the world which we call penal servitude, and is far crueller and wickeder than burning at the stake, the only people who are satisfied with it are our anti-Christians who lust after vindictive punishment, and would welcome the spectacle of a burning or flogging, and the capital punishment abolitionists, who, shrinking from killing as such, but having no conception of State responsibilities, sign every petition for reprieve, and drop the case the moment the condemned person is left alive, no matter under what conditions.

Surely it is possible nowadays to devise some form of euthanasia more civilized than the rope, the drop, and the prison chaplain assuring the condemned that she has only to believe something she obviously does not believe, and she will go straight to eternal bliss in heaven. The fact that the horror of such a business will oblige the prison authorities to drug her to endure it only adds to the disgust it creates.

The matter has long been pressing. The savage superstitions of vengeance and expiation, the exhibition of executions as public entertainments, and the theory of deterrence, which depends on an impossible certainty of detection in which no criminal believes, and also makes it a matter of complete indifference whether the person we hang is guilty or not provided we hang somebody, are discredited; and as the necessary work of "weeding the garden" becomes better understood, the present restriction of liquidation to murder cases, and the exemption of dangerous lunatics (who should be liquidated as such, crime or no crime), will cease, and must be replaced by State-contrived euthanasia for all idiots and intolerable nuisances, not punitively, but as a necessary stroke of social economy.

If the strip tease girl had been told simply that her case was under consideration, and she were presently to be found dead in her bed some morning in a quite comfortable lethal chamber not known to her to be such, the relief to the public conscience would be enormous. And the survivors would acquire a wholesome sense of public obligation to make the preservation of their lives by civilization worth while.

Yours, &c.,
G. Bernard Shaw

THE ATOMIC BOMB

[*The Times,* 20 August 1945.]

Sir,—Now that we, the human race, have begun monkeying with the atom,[1] may I point out one possible consequence that would end all our difficulties?

For some years past our too few professional astronomers have been reinforced by a body of amateurs whose main activity is the watching and studying of the variable stars. They have been excited several times by the sudden flaming up of what they call a new star, though it is in fact an old star, too small and cool to be visible, which has suddenly burst and blown up, leaving nothing but a cloud of star dust called a nebula. The heat energy liberated in the explosion is beyond human apprehension.

Apparently what has happened to these stars, and may happen to this earth of ours, is that the protons with their planetary electrons, and the heavier planetless neutrons of which their matter is composed, have combined, and produced a temperature at which the whole star has pulverized and evaporated, and its inhabitants, if any, have been cremated with an instantaneous thoroughness impossible at Golders Green.[2]

What we have just succeeded in doing at enormous expense is making an ounce of uranium explode like the star. The process, no longer experimental, will certainly be cheapened; and at any moment heavier elements than uranium, as much more explosive than uranium as uranium than gunpowder, may be discovered.

Finally, like the sorcerer's apprentice, we may practise our magic without knowing how to stop it, thus fulfilling the prophecy of Prospero. In view of our behaviour recently, I cannot pretend to deprecate such a possibility; but I think it is worth mentioning.

Yours, &c.,
G. Bernard Shaw

[1]The first atomic bomb was dropped on Hiroshima and a second on Nagasaki by the United States on 6 and 9 August 1945.
[2]North London site of a crematorium, in which Shaw was a stockholder.

THE GOD OF BERNARD SHAW

[In *The Freethinker* of 16 June 1946, in the continuing department called "Other People's Gods," C. G. L. Du Cann wrote on "The God of Bernard Shaw." Du Cann, a popular writer and journalist as well as a barrister, observed that Shaw's conversion from "a convinced and aggressive Atheist to a vitalist" came from his "horror of a mindless, purposeless universe engaged in a meaningless struggle for hogwash," and asserted that in the preface and play *Back to Methuselah,* "you may find his God." Shaw responded in a letter published on 30 June.]

Sir,—I have to thank Mr. Du Cann and your good self for an astonishingly accurate account of my philosophy, such as it is.

When I described the heart of the despairing pessimist as sinking into a heap of sand I was not thinking of any experience of my own nor of any of the atheists, secularists, freethinkers, and other godless persons of my acquaintance. I never suffered the least inconvenience from my desertion of my old Nobodaddy,[1] nor as far as I know did they. But the others did and do; and I had to take them into account in a rhetorical passage written for platform delivery.

My biology starts with the fact that there is no discovered chemical difference between a live body and a dead one. The same creature has ceased to breathe and pump its blood; and it presently disintegrates and rots, nobody knows why. Until we do know, the Life Force, as I call it, though visibly at work everywhere, is a miracle and a mystery; but we can say of it that it has evident purposes which transcend those of self-preservation and reproduction by visible physical operations. It has an evolutionary appetite for power and knowledge, in pursuit of which it will risk martyrdom and face the extremity of hardship and danger. The man who might be the prosperous village churchwarden prefers to be the persecuted village freethinker. The squire abandons his comfortable country house, and undertakes "the worst journey in the world"[2] to gather an egg or two of the Emperor Penguin because it is a missing link in genetic theory.

Rationalism, Materialism, Hedonism cannot account for

[1]William Blake's "Father of Jealousy," defined by S. Foster Damon in his *A Blake Dictionary* (1965) as "Blake's name for the false God of this World."
[2]A reference to Apsley Cherry-Garrard, whose book of this title (1922) chronicled the ill-fated second Antarctic expedition of Robert Falcon Scott.

this—it is just a hard fact of incalculable importance and promise. Freethinkers and Fundamentalists alike must face it, whatever arguments or legends they may decorate it with.

I am no more a Christian than I am a Confucian, a Moslem, or a Jain. The sentimental "Love one another" and "Our Father" of Jesus do not fit into a world of thinly veneered unlovable savages. To love them would be unnatural vice. The counsel of perfection is to be just and humane to those whom we rightly detest. Jesus was deeply right in urging us to discard revenge and punishment. Two blacks do not make a white. We must weed the garden, but not unkindly.

As a crude political agitator Jesus must be classed with Essex, Emmet,[3] and the many other novices who have attempted an insurrection without an army, and have been at once taken by the police and executed. And his advice to the rich young man will not hold water.

In short, "the god of Bernard Shaw" is very obviously not a god at all as the word goes. The Life Force is a metaphysical hypothesis deduced from undeniable facts, not the imaginary sitter painted by Michael Angelo, Raphael, and Blake. Mankind is an experiment in godhead, so far not a successful one. But the Life Force will no doubt try again.

Yours, &c.,
G. Bernard Shaw

BROADCASTING A BULLFIGHT

[*Daily Telegraph,* 22 July 1947.]

Sir,—May I, through your influential columns, call for a public inquiry into the mental condition of the B.B.C.? It has just treated its high-brow third-liners, of whom I am one, to a description of a bullfight.

In defence it will probably plead that we have set the example in broadcasting descriptions of boxing matches. But these events are placed in the light (low-brow) programmes, and do not in-

[3]Robert Devereux, second Earl of Essex, attempted a coup of the enemy party for the favor of Queen Elizabeth I with a small band of supporters on 8 February 1601, for which he was tried and executed. Robert Emmet, Irish nationalist, led an aborted rising in Dublin on 23 July 1803 in an effort to capture the English viceroy, for which he was eventually tried and executed on 20 September.

volve any cruelty to animals, nor more hurt to the boxers beyond what they voluntarily face, and are more liberally paid for than a parson for a church service.

In a bullfight an innocent animal is driven into an arena, where it is goaded, tormented, and infuriated until it is exhausted, in which pitiable condition it is murdered by a swordsman splendidly attired, giving himself the airs of triumphing in a fair fight with a dangerous bull.

In my early days England was proud of having abolished bear baiting and all such savageries, and made bullfighting a national reproach to Spain. But now!!!

Yours, &c.,
G. Bernard Shaw

"MARXISM REVIEWED"

[*New Statesman*, 16 August 1947.]

Sir,—Mr. Kingsley Martin's[1] article under the above title in the *Political Quarterly*, much needed as it is, will be an arrow shot in the air unless and until it is possible to view Marx before reviewing him. Some sixty-five years ago my complete conversion to Socialism was effected by the first volume of *Das Kapital;* but I read it not in English but in the French translation of Deville. I have never read it since; but I had occasion to refer to it last month, and bought the English translation in three volumes now on the market. It cost me £3 15s. This means that *Das Kapital* is unobtainable in English for at least 95 per cent of our population.

But, what is worse, for the 5 per cent who can afford to buy it (and don't) much of it is obsolete and unreadable. In the nineteenth century, authors disputed and quarrelled endlessly about what they called their originality. To read the second and third volumes edited (I forbear to say faked) by Engels[2] one would sup-

[1]Editor of the *New Statesman*. Martin's article "Marxism Re-viewed," in the *Political Quarterly* for July 1947, was almost wholly concerned with economic determinism, the fallacies of which had been exposed by the events of World War II. Thus, Marxism is too theoretically rigid to take into account elements of human feeling.

[2]Friedrich Engels, German social philosopher and businessman, had begun his collaboration with Marx in Manchester (site of Engels's father's textile firm), the first fruit of which was the *Communist Manifesto* (1848).

pose that the whole question of Capitalism *versus* Socialism turned on whether Marx or Rodbertus originated the labor theory of value. Now that Rodbertus is forgotten, and all the labor theories of value, from Penny's version to Ricardo's and Marx's, swept into the dustbin in 1871 by Jevons, Walras, and Edgeworth,[3] their mathematical theory being more favourable to Socialism, all this stuff has become quite unbearable and its discussion waste of time.

Engels was a very able author. His reputation relatively to Marx's has been steadily growing; but he was virtually mad on one subject: the infallibility and prophetic omniscience of Marx, and the erroneousness, not to say the rascality, of all who questioned them. I was afflicted in that way myself for a few weeks.

Now Marx, with an 1848 mentality, spent the succeeding years in the reading room of the British Museum without any administrative experience. In nineteenth-century fashion he was so jealous of rival Socialist authors that his contacts with British movements and personalities were limited, and his quarrels with them endless.

Old Matilda, Hyndman's first wife, told me that Marx's quarrel with Hyndman did not begin with the omission of his name from Hyndman's book *England For All* [1881], but from a certain day when, visiting the Marxes, her husband put on Marx's hat by mistake and found that it fitted him exactly instead of being much too large for him. Without attaching too much importance to this reminiscence, I mention it as an example of the enormous gap between the vast outlook of the Communist Manifesto and the littleness of its authors' disparagements of Lassalle, Bakunin, Hyndman, the Fabians, the Trade Union leaders: in short, whoever was not an idolatrously doctrinaire disciple of Marx.

Such Marxism is pre-Fabian, and as hopelessly and boringly out of date as the pre-Marxism of our most reactionary Diehards and military Glory Merchants. It was the first and only quite authentic volume of *Das Kapital* that changed the mind of Europe

[3]Léon Walras, French economist, whose *Éléments d'économie politique pure* (1874–77) was influential long before being translated by William Jaffé in 1954 as *Elements of Pure Economics;* Francis Ysidro Edgeworth, British economist and statistician, whose *Papers Relating to Political Economy* (1925) offered serious revisions to Marxist theory.

by, as I have so often put it, lifting the lid off hell and substituting an apologetic compunction for the optimistic complacency of the great Exhibition of 1851. It can keep that work going if only it is corrected and made readable in a single cheap volume.

Marx's tedious preliminary attempt to deduce Surplus Value from an analysis of the circulation of commodities must be jettisoned ruthlessly: Morris's definition of the process as "robbing the poor" is enough for British proletarians. As to Historic Materialism, it may be left to longheaded Scots like J. B. S. Haldane: the Englishman in the street has no use for it.

Here, then, is a job for some young world-betterer at a loss for something important to do. Who speaks first?

Yours, &c.,
G. Bernard Shaw

WESTMINSTER ABBEY

[Sidney Webb, first Baron Passfield, died on 13 October 1947. On 16 October Shaw requested interment at Westminster Abbey for Webb in a letter to *The Times,* and in a second letter on 25 October observed that the Abbey "owes its peculiar sanctity not to its stones but to the mighty dead it enshrines." The Reverend Wilfrid Clayton responded in a letter on 28 October which attempted to emend Shaw, insisting that the sanctity of the Abbey "is due to the fact that it has been a place for the worship of God since the seventh century." Shaw replied in a letter published on 30 October.]

Sir,—May I remind your reverend correspondent that the sanctity of the Abbey as a place of Christian worship is not peculiar to it? It is shared by every other parish church in the kingdom, whether 13 centuries old or 13 days.

Its peculiar sanctity is conferred on it solely by the valour of our illustrious dead commemorated there.

They were not all churchgoers.

Yours, &c.,
G. Bernard Shaw

CAPITAL PUNISHMENT

[*The Times,* 5 December 1947.]

Sir,—Had not the ambiguous and confusing terms capital punishment and death penalty better be dropped?[1] The public right and power of civilized States to kill the unprofitable or incorrigibly mischievous in self-defence can never be abrogated. Were it abolished verbally it would be restored or evaded by martial law in the next emergency. Punishment is a different matter. It should be got rid of altogether on the simple ground that two blacks do not make a white, to say nothing of the fact that criminals cannot help their nature and that retaliation is flatly un-Christian. Why not call the subject judicial homicide, or, to avoid unpleasant associations, judicial liquidation? It would clear our minds, now so confused that discussion seems hopeless.

As to deterrence, there are insuperable objections to it. It must be cruel or it will not deter. It is effective only when detection is certain. This could be secured only by providing a police officer to watch every citizen, which is impossible. And it involves the very undesirable consequence that when a crime is committed it does not matter who is punished provided somebody is punished. The police are not impartial. They must do everything in their power to obtain a conviction. As one of Dickens's characters put it, "Much better hang the wrong fellow than no fellow."[2]

Criminals should be liquidated humanely, not because they are wicked, but because they are mischievous or dangerous. A vitriol thrower should be got rid of as ruthlessly as a cobra or a mad dog. A man who lives by promising to marry women and deserting them as soon as he has spent all their money is a social weed to be uprooted no less than if he drowned them in their baths. Dangerous insanity, instead of exempting from liquidation, should be one of the strongest grounds for it.

To simply ostracize liquidation as something that is "not done" is not humane when the alternative is long deterrent imprisonment, involving the waste of man and woman power by staffs of tormentors and maintenance of prisons. At present our death

[1]A penal reform bill was under discussion in Parliament; among the possible provisions was a proposed suspension of the death penalty for five years.

[2]"The debilitated cousin" of the Dedlocks, with the affected speech, offers this opinion ("far better hang wrong fler than no fler") in chap. 53 of *Bleak House.*

dreaders are quite satisfied when a murderer is reprieved. If they were really humane it would horrify them.

What is greatly needed is an institution to deal with people who, under tutelage, discipline, and support (like soldiers and "good" prisoners) are well behaved and useful citizens, but when left to their own resources are presently in the dock or helpless on the street as beggars.

Criminals who can be reformed raise no problem and should be left out of the discussion. If they are reformable, reform them: that is all.

Most of what is being said in your columns at present has been said over and over again for thousands of years in vain. My excuse for cumbering your columns with more of it is that it may still be possible to clear our muddled heads about it.

Yours, &c.,
G. Bernard Shaw

CHEAP JACK

[*Boston Sunday Post,* 21 March 1948.]

Sir,—In your issue of the 8th February there is a very generous and friendly notice of myself. I am obliged, however, to correct it on one point. It declared that whenever a play of mine is performed I exact a royalty of "15% of whatever comes in at the box office from the first dollar," and that these are the highest fees ever paid to a playwright.

The truth is, I am, and always have been, the cheapest playwright in the market. I have not raised my terms for fifty years, though my living costs me so much more. My fifteen per cent operates only when the gross receipts exceed fifteen hundred dollars. When a few devoted amateurs pawn their shirts to give a performance in a village schoolhouse, and take three dollars from a crowded audience (front row twenty cents: back rows four), my competitors think it beneath their dignity to charge less than twentyfive dollars. I charge eighteen cents, and touch my hat, expressing a hope for future patronage. When the receipts anywhere do not exceed $250 my royalty is five per cent. I ask for no advances: if there are no receipts I get nothing. The leading playwrights of my prime would not have condescended to such popular terms.

Big fifteen per cent successes, such as Mr. Maurice Evans[1] is now enjoying in Man and Superman, are windfalls that occur once in a blue moon.

I am the Cheap Jack[2] among playwrights, and, as such, your very humble servant.

Yours, &c.,
G. Bernard Shaw

REBUILDING BABEL

I

[*The Times,* 19 August 1948]

Sir,—May I, as a man of letters, appeal to the Government to appoint a Select Committee to settle our political nomenclature? The matter is extremely urgent; for the present confusion of tongues is heading straight for a war which none of the Powers can afford and nobody desires.

Until we clear up our political nomenclature, our political oratory and journalism can come to nothing but the pot calling the kettle black without either of them knowing what they are talking about. We all lack a common and exact dictionary, and are at dangerous cross purposes over imaginary differences and delusive agreements that are only verbal. I myself find it impossible to make myself understood, though when I describe myself by this or that adjective I know precisely what I mean. As a citizen and one of the founders of British Fabian policy I am basically a Marxist Communist; but I cannot say so without being set down as an infantile advocate of catastrophic insurrection, with capitalism in full swing on Monday, revolution on Tuesday, and Socialism in full swing on Wednesday. I do not wish to see private enterprise made a felony: on the contrary, I look to private enterprise for experiment and invention in industry, art, and science as the proper sphere of individual talent and genius in the leisure which Socialism alone can gain for everybody. There is the alternative of State-aided enterprise, largely practised here in public utility

[1]Popular British actor, resident in America, whose John Tanner was one of his greatest successes in New York.

[2]A peddler who usually can be prevailed upon to cheapen (that is, reduce) the price of his wares.

schemes and friendly societies and the like. As these are so well spoken of here, why in the name of common sense should they under their Italian name of Fascism be denounced as murderous anti-Semitic tyrannies?

Communism and private enterprise are only methods of civilization, each with its proper sphere. Communism, like private enterprise, has to have many methods, one being distinguished as Socialism. Bread and milk could be communized like street-lighting and sewerage, and suburban travelling by rail or air made free of fares, because everybody needs them; but it would be silly to provide trombones, microscopes, cyclotrons, ounces of radium, atomic bombs, and hundred-inch astronomical telescopes for everybody. Everybody does not use them, nor could afford them if they did. They must be provided by various and mixed social methods. They cannot be sold to the public over the counter like postage stamps.

Compensation for confiscated private property is nonsense; but to nationalize or municipalize any acre or share of private property at the expense of its particular proprietor is manifestly unjust: he should be paid its market price at the expense of the whole body of proprietors, including himself, by taxation of income. But the process should be called adjustment, not compensation. The Liberal Party delayed temperance legislation for 20 years by mistaking this adjustment for compensation.

Pressingly important just now is the difference between diplomatic arrangements and human rights. Mr. Bevin,[1] speaking colloquially, declared that we have a right to be in Berlin, and mean to stay there, following this by a flourish of implacable detestation of Communism. As this implied war on Russia, the four military commanders governing the four zones into which the military occupation of Berlin had been divided began skirmishing to the extent of every annoyance they could inflict on one another short of actual shooting. Yet if Mr. Bevin is not fundamentally a Communist he is not a civilized man.

Now, we have no divine right to be in Berlin, nor has the Soviet, the State Department in Washington, nor the French Re-

[1]Ernest Bevin, labor leader and Labour MP for Central Wandsworth (later East Woolwich) from 1940, minister of labor and national service, 1940–45, was presently the secretary of state for foreign affairs.

public. We are there as invaders and conquerors, as Mahomet and Joshua were in Palestine and William the Conqueror in England. There is nothing to prevent all or any of us from withdrawing from Berlin if such a rearrangement should seem expedient. Such withdrawals can be ranked as defeats only if they are fought for instead of negotiated.

There are several alternatives to play for. There is the unity of Germany. There is the division of Germany into two federations, western and eastern, with the western capital in Frankfurt and the eastern in Berlin. There is Germany disarmed or not. There is Germany disabled industrially by reparations, formerly called plunder, or not. England and America care not a snap of their fingers whether Germany is disarmed or not; France is mortally afraid of her anyhow; Russia is out for precautions. The three European Powers would have to borrow the cost of another war from the United States, and bilk their creditor as in 1914–18: a transaction which America could not afford.

I am stating the obvious facts, not advocating the various views one way or the other. I am insisting that negotiation is impossible unless the parties use the same words for the same things, and understand what the words mean. The present Babel threatens a war that nobody wants, countered by a flood of Conscientious Objection from those who think that their rulers are backing the wrong horse, as we did in the American civil war until Karl Marx protested, in South Africa until Ibsen protested, and in Russia after 1917 until our Proletariat began setting up little imitation Soviets all over the place.

I repeat that I am not here advocating this or that policy, party, or personality. I am asking all the politicians, all the partisans, all the eminent personalities to support my demand for a Select Committee on political nomenclature, charged with the production of a political dictionary before the next General Election, on the common ground that logomachy is the very devil. Even liars need a language that will enable them to lie unambiguously. To the truthful the present impossibility of wording their messages without being misunderstood is an agony.

A dictionary will not cure our habit of mistaking association of ideas for logic; but it will do all that can be done at short notice to clear our heads.

Yours, &c.,
G. Bernard Shaw

II

[*The Times,* 30 August 1948.]

Sir,—Under the heading "Rebuilding Babel" I did not intend to start several new hares to be hunted round the world for the next hundred years and never overtaken. I agree with Sir Ernest Barker, of whose authority and experience I stand in awe, that a universal language in which British supercargoes, Turkish porters, and Chinese coolies can converse intelligibly would be a convenience. I admit that glossary is more accurate etymologically than dictionary. I defer to a more leisurely occasion that question whether French should be the language of diplomacy.

But there is no time to go into these matters now. Any attempt to moot them would defeat my object and add to our habitual discoveries of How Not To Do It.

Let me give one leading example of what I am driving at. Sixty years ago the Fabian Society established the word "permeation" in our political nomenclature at a time when to define revolutionary Socialism there was no verbal alternative to (*a*) instantaneous metamorphosis of Capitalism into Communism by class war, or (*b*) military world conquest. Through its disuse today it is being assumed that as Stalin holds that Marxism will finally become the standard policy of civilization his tactics must be those of Alexander and Napoleon. But in fact he, like Lenin, was converted by bitter experience of Military Communism in 1921 to the N.E.P. (New Economic Policy) which is in effect a Fabian policy beginning with Socialism in a single country and spreading to the rest of the world by permeation, example, and success.

In short, England has converted Russia, and does not know it. If Stalin could say unambiguously that he is a Permeatist in foreign affairs, and in domestic policy bound by a constitution as much as American and English statesmen are, the air would be clearer. He is a twentieth-century responsible Cabinet Minister and not a sixteenth-century Münster Anabaptist [John of Leiden]; and nothing is to be gained by treating him as one.

I repeat my point. The Berlin crisis is facing us with the alternatives of negotiation or war. Negotiation is impossible unless the parties know what their words mean and express it consistently in the same words. That is all.

Yours, &c.,
G. Bernard Shaw

THE AUTHOR'S GAMBLE

[*The Times,* 18 January 1949.]

Sir,—May I call attention to certain gambling industries that are neither understood nor distinguished from sport? I am myself engaged in such an industry, and dependent on it for my livelihood. All professional authors, playwrights, composers, painters, publishers, theatre managers, music sellers, and picture dealers live by gambling in values more desperately uncertain than the chances of any starter in a horse or dog race.

No turf book-maker would budget for such odds. But the few occasional winnings are so great, and the prestige and eminence they confer so ardently desired, that punters are never lacking. Let me illustrate. The late William Archer, foremost as a theatre critic, wrote several plays, but without success until he was an elderly man, meanwhile being too poor to travel otherwise than in the steerage, or, when he went to the theatre at his own expense, to sit elsewhere than in the pit. When at last an actor, the late George Arliss, made a huge box-office success of a play by Archer called *The Green Goddess* [1920], Archer ended his days in comparative affluence. But he was taxed on this windfall at the same rate as if he had been equally affluent all his life.

I am an author and playwright of some note; but my first book [*Immaturity*] had to await publication for 50 years during which it lay unproductive on my shelves. No publisher would gamble on its chances of being bought by the public in remunerative quantities; and I, having no capital, could not afford to plunge until I was too old to desire the publication of a juvenile effort. Meanwhile I had earned or acquired enough spare money to gamble on my own account after one English publisher and two American ones[1] had been bankrupted at the game. The odds against me are still astronomical: of the fifty-odd plays I have written, a few have proved "gold mines," a few more silver mines, the rest tin and pewter. A play called *Pygmalion* is performed again and again: others, in my mature Third Manner, are not performed at all. The film rights of the gold mines are worth in cash from £25,000 to £50,000: others hardly worth a hundred.

No human power can foresee whether a work of art will be commercially successful, nor ever will. A first-rate theatre produc-

[1]The English publisher was Grant Richards. The American firms were Herbert S. Stone and Brentano's, although the latter did not go into bankruptcy until 1932, long after Shaw had become his own publisher in England.

tion of a play costs at most a couple of thousand pounds. The filming of a first-rate film costs at least £50,000, sometimes more than half a million. If either "flops," the loss may be a dead loss. I could cite instances in which box-office receipts, even with famous actors in the cast, have amounted to 16s. If this is not gambling, I do not know what gambling is.

Time was when some sense of this was shown by taxing authors not on their actual year's income but on its average for three years. It should have been 20 years; but still it was better than nothing. Unfortunately John Galsworthy, a great humanitarian author but no economist, was so moved by the plight of the authors who failed to average their expenditure, and left themselves destitute in the second two years, that he demanded the abolition of the average, which was thoughtlessly done, leaving my unhappy tribe where they were before it was instituted. Still, I can thank Providence that I am not an inventor. My copyright costs me nothing, and lasts 50 years after my death. An inventor can at considerable expense obtain a patent for at most about half that period, and may die before his invention comes into lucrative use. He often, to pay for models and fees, has to sell his rights to Luddite[2] firms which acquire them to suppress, not to exploit, them.

How we authors and inventors envy the gamblers on the turf and the Stock Exchange, the insurance companies, the pawnbrokers, the casino exploiters who, without running a tithe of our risks, are not taxed on their winnings! Why should we suffer what is virtually a tax on our capital which other gamblers incur only in the form of estate duties against which they can afford to insure? Why is property in our creations communized after less than two lifetimes, and that of simple distributors made perpetual? Why is property in turnips made eternal and absolute when property in ideas is temporary and conditional?

I do not know. WHY? is the fundamental question that nobody can answer. As well ask why the British people dread and hate intellect. But could not the Exchequer ease matters a little either by restoring and extending the old average, or making the privileged gamblers pay their fair share?

Yours, &c.,
G. Bernard Shaw

[2]The term originally was applied to English textile workers (including Ned Lud), c. 1811–16, who destroyed labor-saving machines as a protest against depressed wages and unemployment.

"GUEST CITIZENS" OF BRITAIN

[*The Times,* 26 April 1949.]

Sir,—I am now a political nobody, subject to nameless penalties if I attend the meetings of the parish council of the village where I have resided and paid taxes for 40 years. Of my 93 years 70 have been spent in England. My many political activities have been occupied with English questions, never with specifically Irish ones. I am a Freeman of the City of London. But I am also an Irishman, honorary Freeman of the City of Dublin, and registered as a citizen of the former Irish Free State. Net result as aforesaid, I am a political nobody.

May I suggest that aliens residing permanently within the Commonwealth shall, under a new category of Guest Citizens, enjoy all the rights and privileges, and bear all the responsibilities, of natives? This could be extended to any international combination; but its application to Ireland (and perhaps India) is urgent.

Yours, &c.,
G. Bernard Shaw

THE LEISURE INCENTIVE

[*The Economist,* 29 October 1949.]

Sir,—Among the many who never read what I write, and could not understand it if they did, I have a hearsay reputation as a paradoxmonger. One of my so-called paradoxes is classing *The Economist* as foremost among the few advanced press organs that know with any precision what they are writing about. I read it religiously.

But I miss from its articles one prime factor in the national economy. That factor is not labour, not product, not ability, but leisure. Yet to be a sweated proletariat, overworked and underpaid for centuries past, more leisure is a stronger incentive than more money. It is the only reality of freedom, and is made possible by division of labour, invention, mass production and scientific management of which last only 5 per cent of the human race are born capable. Its distribution is as fundamental as the distribution of income.

At present, when labour becomes, say, for instance, twice as productive as before, the skilled piece-worker takes his share of the gain not in earning twice as much, but in working from Monday to Wednesday, and from Thursday to Saturday lying late in bed in the morning and loafing for the rest of the day. And when the piece-work rate is reduced by half to compel him to put in a full week's work or starve, he strikes and stops production instead of doubling it.

To correct this, continuous industrial service should be made as compulsory as military service, and employers who now pay for holidays on full wages in days of casual leisure, compelled to pay it in weeks, fortnights or months, duly staggered (in short, banking it on deposit), thus abolishing absenteeism.

Yours, &c.,
G. Bernard Shaw

ATOMIC WELFARE

[*The Times,* 24 December 1949.]

Sir,—Much of your space and time is being wasted on the subject of atomic warfare. The disuse of poison gas in the 1939–45 war, because it was as dangerous to its users as to their targets, makes it very unlikely that atomic bombs will be used again. If they are, they will promptly make an end of all our discussions by making an end of ourselves. Meanwhile, they are distracting attention from the far more vital and pressing subject of atomic welfare. Our present concern is with the threatened water shortage, which may leave us crying, like Coleridge's Ancient Mariner: "Water, water, everywhere; and not a drop to drink." This could be averted by distilling sea water, were it not that the cost of the necessary heat is greater than we can afford. Atom disintegration will some day make heat cheaper than can coal-burning. We shall carry in our pockets tiny pips, one of which, dropped into a cup of water, will instantly make it boil. Such pips would be worth incalculably more than atomic bombs, which nobody would dare to use. I have no hope of any notice being taken of these potentialities any more than my old urgings that our monster tides change the old lay to "Power, power, everywhere; and voltage minus one." Still, give me space for another cry in the wilderness, that my unquiet spirit, wandering among the ruins of empires, may have at least the mean and melancholy satisfaction of saying: "I told you so."

Yours, &c.,
G. Bernard Shaw

SHAW ON PRAYERS

[On 6 October 1949, the Australian newspaper the *Daily Visitor* reported that at the end of July "some Irish newspapers" had quoted Shaw as saying "that he wants no more ceremonies in his honour, but would like the Irish people to pray for him." When one of the Irish papers, *Indiu (To-day),* asked Shaw for verification, he replied that his preference was for "prayers rather than for gifts that can be bought for money." *The Freethinker,* picking up the story from the *Daily Visitor,* then asked Shaw if he required people to pray for him. Shaw's reply was published by *The Freethinker* on 5 February 1950.]

Sir,—I never "required" anyone's prayers. But when friends began sending me from all over the world parcels of food and clothing that they could ill afford imagining that here in England we are all starving and in rags, I had to stop them somehow. I told them to pray for me, as I wanted and needed nothing that money could buy.

Modern psycho-analysis has taught us that prayer is a first-rate prescription for despairing pessimism, and that the therapeutic value of confession is enormous.

Whoever does not know this much science is not an up-to-date Freethinker, only an outmoded anti-clerical, as full of Secularist superstitions as Jehovah's Witnesses and Plymouth Brothers are of Bible superstitions.

Yours, &c.,
G. Bernard Shaw

THE WATCH STORY

[*The Freethinker,* 26 March 1950.]

Sir,—Scratch an Atheist, and you find a Plymouth Brother. When the Watch Story revives, the laugh is always against the Atheists; for when they indignantly deny that Bradlaugh ever took out his watch and challenged God to strike him dead within five minutes for denying His existence, they mean that so great a man could not do such a horribly wicked thing, which is just how a Jehovah's Witness would put it.

If Bradlaugh did not do it he ought to have done it, as it is the short and entirely proper and practical way of determining, not whether God exists or not, but whether, if He does, He is a savagely violent and vindictive tribal idol like Blake's Nobodaddy.

Years ago I told in print[1] how I was present at a doctor's [J. Kingston Barton's] bachelor party when the watch story cropped up and started the old protests that it is a wicked and shocking falsehood. I said it was, on the contrary, a legitimate experiment, and that if Bradlaugh had omitted to try it, I would do so myself. And I took out my watch.

An amazing ballyhoo ensued. The whole company, Freethinkers, Evangelists and all, were so terrified lest the threatened thunderbolt should consume them as well as me, that our host begged me to withdraw my awful challenge, or at least put up my watch and change the subject. This of course I did; but, none the less, apprehension reigned until five minutes had expired.

Such challenges are quite common. In England a lie is emphasized by "Lord strike me dead if I am not telling the truth." In Ireland the formula is "Hell to my soul, but I etc."

Genuine Freethinkers do not trouble about such nonsense.

Yours, &c.,
G. Bernard Shaw

75 YEARS AFTER

[*Public Opinion*, 19 May 1950.]

Sir,—My first appearance in print was in a boys' paper: two lines in the correspondence column.[1] But it was in *Public Opinion* that I made my *debut* as a critic and controversialist. The only

[1] "Defying the Lightning: A Frustrated Experiment," in the preface to *Back to Methuselah* (1921).

[1] In the shortlived *Vaudeville Magazine* (which was *not* a boys' paper), September 1871, under "Editorial Replies," a response to G. B. Shaw of Torca Cottage, Torca Hill, Dalkey, Co. Dublin, reads: "You should have registered your letter; such a combination of wit and satire ought not to have been conveyed at the ordinary rate of postage. As it was, your arguments were so weighty we had to pay *two pence* extra for them."

result was an emergency meeting of my uncles to discuss the horrifying news that the Shaw family had produced an Atheist. I still hold that thinkers who are not militant atheists in their teens will have no religion at all when they are 40. I was already a Creative Evolutionist in the bud. I have ever since had a warm corner in my heart for *Public Opinion*.

Yours, &c.,
G. Bernard Shaw

Index